Cathy

Nancy

Harold

Barbara

Ken

Lorene

Steve

Rose and Nello

A Mastery of Motherhood
Life Story

16 x MOM

I hope you enjoy reading this
as much as I enjoyed writing it.
My best wishes always!
Barbara "Bobbie"

A Mastery of Motherhood

16 x MOM

Sixteen Children

Inspiring and Compelling Life Story
Mom, Rose

Barbara Olivo Cagle
Rose's 13th of 16

Publisher: Bobbie

A Mastery of Motherhood
Life Story

16 x MOM

Published by Bobbie

4575 Wanakiwin Dr.

Loon Lake, WA 99148

Orders @ http//www.barbaracagle.com

Produced by Walsworth Publishing Company

Library of Congress Pre-assigned Control Number: 2007900384

ISBN 978-0-9792360-0-6 (printed edition, soft cover)

978-0-9792360-1-3 (printed edition, hard cover)

Printed in the United States of America

First Printing 2008
Limited Edition 1,000 Copies

Acclaim…

"A remarkably told story about one woman's plight through a both difficult but ultimately rewarding life. Jacqueline Rose Olivo's biography by Barbara Cagle endears the reader to her life by blending intimate narrative, timeless photos, and a well researched family history into a book that is hard to put down."—John Bob

"Barbara Cagle has crafted a compelling story. The reader will immediately become engrossed in the humor, tragedy, and everyday experiences of the remarkable family."—Fran Bennett Wicht, author of *Fifty Years Ago in Letters*, a family memoir published in 2005

"Well researched and enriched with dozens of photographs, *16 x MOM* provides an enjoyable tribute to one mother's triumph over a lifetime of hardship and family challenges."—Michael Hinz, author of *Satan's Gold* and *How to Argue With an Atheist*

"Anyone interested in California history will enjoy the unfolding of this saga, embedded with charming details and rich with colorful characters, chronicling the author's family heritage from Sierra mining lands to the southern San Francisco Bay Area."—Rita Beamish, author of *Perils of Paradise: Amazing True Survivor Stories from Hawaii*

"I couldn't put the book down; it started as an interesting story with a lot of interesting history tidbits. As the characters grew on me, they became family. I laughed, I cried, and I couldn't put the book down because I wanted to know what happened next! By the end of *16 x MOM* I felt a part of this incredible family!"—Joni Adkins

"Barbara Cagle's book is an entertaining biography of a unique American family. The story of Jacqueline Rose Olivo and her sixteen children is enriched by Rose's wise, insightful words of poetry and philosophy, and an album of photographs. The veritable treasure chest of intriguing, poignant, and sometimes funny vignettes, may warmly remind readers of their own youth."—J. Douglas and Connie Causey

"You will find that this story of an extraordinary mom sends you from laughter to tears and back. Imagine—this all happened in one life time. A great story!"—Lona Dyer.

“An emotionally touching love-story, *16 x MOM* is a candid insight into the fabric of family.”— Louise A. Raimundo

“I’ve known Barbara Cagle for many years and hearing of the ups and downs of her large family has been most interesting. The in-depth story of her mother’s challenges and triumphs raising sixteen wonderfully successful children should be inspiring to many young families.”—Myra Hilton

“An extraordinary story about an extraordinary family, carefully researched. I truly enjoyed it.”—Ron Robie

“Your book was like reading an epoch novel, memoir, and biography. Most of all—what a great tribute to your mom. She was the ultimate matriarch. After reading about Rose, I wanted to get up, clean my house and quit complaining about how stressed I am.”—Cynthia D’Anna

“After reading Rose’s story, I sat back and thought; this woman was pregnant 4,500 + days. What a fantastic story Barbara wrote filled with humor and compassion. It is a great read.”— Lee Anne Reber

“This book is filled with Rose’s philosophy. She seems to have handled every situation, good or bad, trivial or not, with aplomb and dignity (a classy commodity) and never ever damaged anyone’s little id. There were places that brought me to tears. I loved the photographs and the histories. What a great tribute to your mom and a priceless heirloom.”—Bobbee Hepworth (Retired Librarian)

“I finished your book with tears. I was very touched with the stories you have woven so beautifully. All families should be so blessed.”— Barbara Deuel

Rose’s biography in *16 x MOM* is a refreshing example of how our country is strengthened through the enduring struggles of the family. I am impressed with the detail of documentation that Barbara has incorporated in this book. This was fun to read. I am convinced that Rose has made a significant contribution to this great country and to our society.”—Steven L. Bates

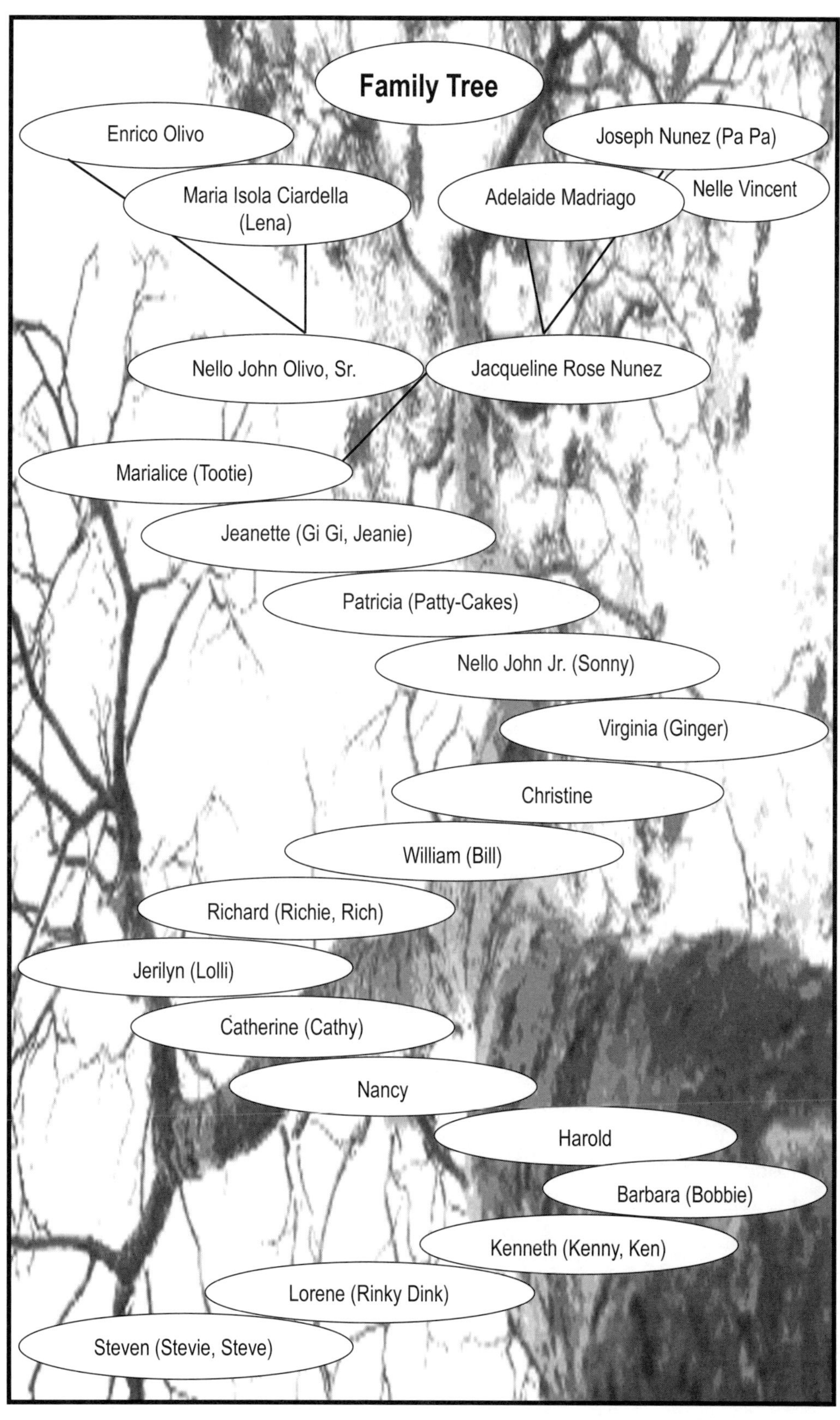
Family Tree
Enrico Olivo
Joseph Nunez (Pa Pa)
Maria Isola Ciardella
(Lena)
Adelaide Madriago
Nelle Vincent
Nello John Olivo, Sr.
Jacqueline Rose Nunez
Marialice (Tootie)
Jeanette (Gi Gi, Jeanie)
Patricia (Patty-Cakes)
Nello John Jr. (Sonny)
Virginia (Ginger)
Christine
William (Bill)
Richard (Richie, Rich)
Jerilyn (Lolli)
Catherine (Cathy)
Nancy
Harold
Barbara (Bobbie)
Kenneth (Kenny, Ken)
Lorene (Rinky Dink)
Steven (Stevie, Steve)

Acknowledgements

I acknowledge the loving support
of my husband, Donald John Cagle, my children,
Jocilyn Roselle Stevens and Jason John Cagle,
Mom and Dad,
Fifteen brothers and sisters,
Uncle Rodger Nunez, Aunt Helene Nunez,
Aunt Marie Bueno, cousins, and nieces and nephews,
Special thanks to Dan Poynter, Leigh Poitinger, Sauro Bertolozzi,
Anne Richardson, John and Virginia Smothers, Jan Moellering,
Louise Raimundo, Bobbee Hepworth, Fran Wicht, Mike Hinz,
Doug and Connie Causey, Tony Bamonte,
Suzanne Schaeffer Bamonte, Deborah Faye Molina,
Steven L. Bates, Robert Pillsbury,
Bert and Vivian Heyworth, Patt Periera,
John Bob, Rita Beamish, Joni Adkins, Lee Ann Reber,
Connie Williams, Lona Dyer, Myra Hilton, Karri Samson,
Ray McCasland, Cynthia D'Anna, Barbara Deuel,
Kent Goodman-San Jose High School,
Calaveras Historical Society, San Benito Historical Society,
Martin Luther King Library, San Jose Mercury News,
San Jose City Hall Vital Records,
Spokane Authors & Self-Publishers,
www.ancestry.com, www.4crests.com,
St. Joseph's Catholic Church,
Special thanks to all my extended relatives who so graciously
shared with me their treasure chest of photos and old family stories.
Uni Walker, Shirley Capps, Nadine Eck, Darrell Eck, Thelma Ralston,
Sherry Clanton, Humbert and Mary Ciardella,
Pasquale Greco, Allen Greco, Betty and Mel Facey,
Harold and Louise Saluan, Harley Doughty, Loretta Olivo, Evelyn Simon,
Violet Davis, Carol Hodges, Robert and Marge Madriago,
Robert and Darlene Grey, Fortunato Valeroni, Ronald and Edith Robie,
Francis Knablock, Merrie MacDonald, Rose Geerts, Didier Nunez, and
Amparo Lopez Vazquez

Mostly thank you, Lord, for your inspiration
God Bless You All!

Contents

Introduction

Mother's Day
Spokane, Washington
1987

Morning activities at the hospital awoke me and I stared at the bouquets of flowers sitting on the windowsill. My hysterectomy went well. I trusted and put my life in God's hands. It was "Mother's Day" 1987. Reflections from the pine trees danced against the beautiful clear sky. Memories tapped my mind. Unanswered questions and dreams remained a mystery in the two beige file boxes sitting on the floor that I brought along to read. The files contained secrets to writing a book about my mother and her family. Secrets that took years to research, secrets that needed to be brought to life. What better day than "Mother's Day" to commemorate a book about my mother—Jacqueline Rose Olivo, "Rose," "Mom," "16 x MOM."

A full stay at the hospital for the serenity of peacefulness—something rather unattainable during Motherhood, sounded good to me. The stay proved to be just what I needed to get me started on writing my Mom's incredible life story.

Winter of 2003

Sixteen years have passed since "Mother's Day" 1987. Research was a long journey with several paths taken in obtaining material. The original two beige file boxes grew in volume. Discussions with relatives, visits to Santa Clara County Vital Records, and numerous hours spent in the California Room, Martin Luther King Library, San Jose, California created more research as research begot research. I found myself scouting cemetery records and grounds for long lost relatives, I then challenged myself to find any living relative through Internet ancestry resources. A vast listing of people with a possible ancestral links surfaced. When a connection was made, I traveled to meet with those relatives in the United States and corresponded with those outside the United States. We exchanged family histories and photographs, many of the photographs neither party knew existed. The appendix contains the fruits of my efforts—family trees, additional photographs, and ancestral histories.

Disclaimer: foreign quotes are in rough translation, and opinions are expressed as experienced, remembered, or related to me. Prayerfully, you will enjoy Mom's story.

Dedicated to:

Jacqueline Rose Olivo
and Family

Chapter One

Fried Eggs

"As the children grew up and embarked upon their careers, established their homes, married and had children, I found myself with more time to do the things that I had always dreamed of doing, that is, a little traveling. I have been an armchair traveler all of my life. I have learned about, seen and experienced many places of interest in this world through narratives, books, pictures, and magazines," said Rose one April morning in 1980. She was preparing an audio recording to give to her daughter, Barbara. Rose continued with her thoughts:

> Menopause came and went with very little effect on my home life. There were many happy times in my life, all involving my children, in their activities, their accomplishments, and in the pride that I felt toward each one of them. Unhappy times did occur, and it seems that they happened when I wasn't in control of the situation.
>
> A very happy and fulfilling time for me was when I joined the Mother's Guild at my children's respective schools. Being involved in the activities of the guild, and later when the mothers elected me president of the St. Joseph's Mother's Guild, was rewarding. I thoroughly enjoyed that time in my life, and it gave me a good feeling to know that my children were proud of me and proud of what I was doing. I felt there was something that I could do outside my home, something that my family and friends would acknowledge.
>
> When I was growing up, there weren't as many doors open to women. When I look back on the wonderful strides that women have made in the service professions, I can place my fullest confidence and trust in the women who endeavor to succeed in the occupations and lifestyles offered to them now, and in the future. Some of the highly-regarded judges are women. Some of the greatest teachers in the world are women. Yet, for all of this, would I trade my God-given right to bring new life into the world? No, women can do both today.
>
> Oh my, I have many philosophies, so many in fact that I couldn't get them all on paper. There is one philosophy that I have given much thought to: that is the question of success in one's life. Whether they are striving to attain success in whatever they do, what they attempt to do, or what they think they can do. The people who have found true success are those who have lived well, laughed often, and loved much. They have earned the respect of intelligent people. They found their niche, accomplished their task, and they left our world a better place, whether by a perfect poem, a song, or a rescued soul.
>
> To live well is to fulfill one's duties with a happy heart; to enjoy the pleasures of life and to sow no seeds of dissension. To live well is to fill the lives of others with

love; to be able to laugh at oneself and not at others, in the midst of any adversity. Laugh often with those around you, and they in turn will laugh with you. Laugh aloud when your child responds with a witty off-the-wall remark to a severe reprimand. Let them know that you appreciate witticism, a smart response, and quick thinking in the attempt to divert your attention from their transgression, and then get on with your reprimanding. Why suppress laughter? If a child's action upsets and annoys you so much, a good laugh would be just what you need to calm yourself so that you can go on and explain to the child intelligently why their action was wrong and why they were a disappointment to you.

If you suppress the laughter, your anger will intensify. You would not only be angry because of the offending act, you would also be angry that the child had the audacity to speak out with something that lessened your anger for the moment. You just can not stand to have that happen before the offending act completely spent you with ranting and raving. This is when too-severe punishment becomes unfair. A child's ability to come up with a witty remark in the face of strong opposition is a God-given talent and armor against over-powering giants. What else could they possibly use—their fists?

Yes, it's true that a true success is that person who has loved much. Who has grasped at every opportunity to allow loved ones to experience that person's love for them; to be able to say to them, 'If I didn't love you so much I probably could dislike you at this moment for what you just said or what you just did.'

There are many successes in life other than being a business person making lots of money. I have been asked, 'If you had it to do all over again, would you do the same thing? Would you have changed anything?' The only thing that I might have done differently, if I knew then what I know now, is that I would have stood up for my rights a little stronger than I did. I would surely have reached out and tried to do more with the talent that God gave me, and maybe I would have realized the dream that I had of becoming a commercial artist. Then I think for all of that, would I not have had one, just one, of my many wonderful children? Ah, I do not think so, not for all the art in Egypt.

I will tell you a secret. I have had a strong desire to sing. I love to listen to someone singing. Before I began giving lectures and speeches in front of large groups of people, I doubted that I could ever get up and sing before an audience.

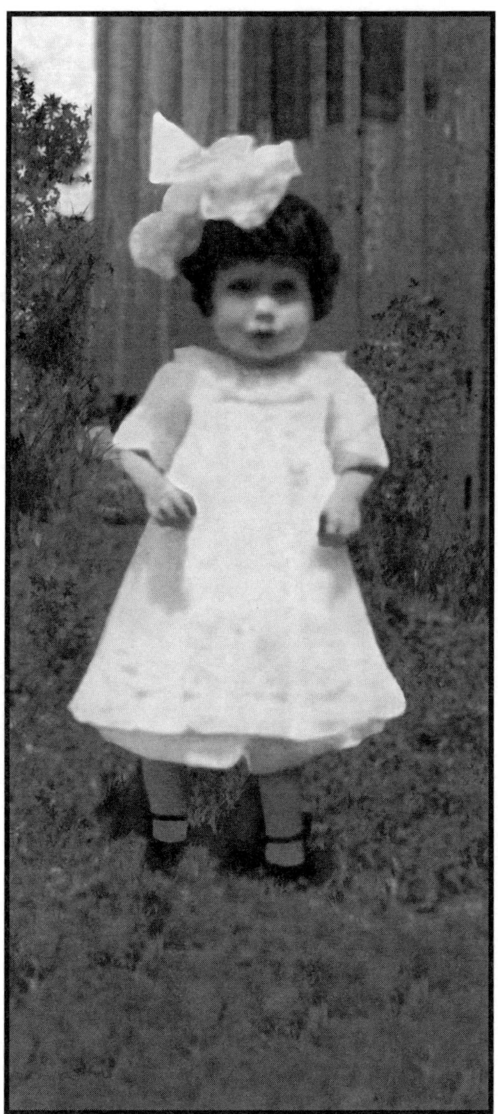

Jacqueline Rose Nunez at two-and-a half
(Courtesy Rose Olivo)

Jacqueline Rose Nunez "Rose"

"Pa Pa" she cried. What little in life she knew. Her mother was gone.

Mrs. Sommers of Children's Aid grabbed her and placed her in the car. She pressed her face against the window and again she yelled, "Pa Pa, Pa Pa."

She sensed the same trepidation she felt the day of her mother's funeral. Her sobs were uncontrollable.

Adelaide Madriago Nunez passed too young. She was twenty two when Joseph Nunez buried her in the Santa Clara Mission Cemetery, Santa Clara, California. The grave site was modest with a wooden cross, no monument, and no engravings.

Those in attendance were dressed in traditional black mourning clothes. Jacqueline Rose stood next to her father and he held her hand. Joseph did not like the name Jacqueline, it was too long and hard to pronounce. He called her by her middle name, "Rose" (Ros-a.)

Rose was four years old. What she remembers of that day is being lifted up by her Aunt Josephine to kiss a cross on her mother's coffin. The casket was lowered and she delicately tossed a red rose down along with it. She watched as her mother's grave was covered by a mound of dirt and rocks.

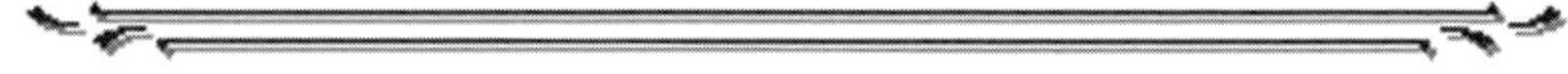

Life is what happens
For it could have occurred
No other way
Than how it happened

—Jacqueline Rose Olivo

Rose's mother and father, "Lydia" and Joseph Nunez *(Courtesy Rodger and Helene Nunez)*

Adelaide Madriago Nunez was born June 20, 1900, in Campo Seco, California. Family and friends called her "Lydia." At age fourteen she stood five-feet-five inches, and weighed approximately one hundred ten pounds.

A traveling photographer would come through the town on a covered wagon and make door-to-door rounds. The Townspeople would open storage trunks to find the family's finest shirts, hats, and dresses. There was little time for pressing the creases out of the clothes. After the photographs were taken, the clothes would be carefully folded and put back in the trunks, which served as closets. In the early 1900's, cost was a factor and few family photographs were taken.

Joseph Nunez, was born February 2, 1883, in Ruitelan, Leon Province, Spain. At age thirteen his father sent him to Galdames, in the Basque Country to work the mines, learn a trade, and provide financial support for the family. The family expected this of the eldest son. He learned how to mine, operate a hoist, and assay. In April of 1900, the entire family also moved to Galdames.

At age twenty-four, Joseph was a very handsome man. He stood five-feet-six inches and weighed approximately one hundred thirty-eight pounds. He was the eldest of five children.

Joseph was the first in the family to go to America. On May 23, 1903, his parents boarded him on a steam-powered ship heading for the Pacific coast of

Nicaragua, with several other young men his age. He left taking sweet memories of his father, mother and siblings. Although his parents were proud to have a son start a new life in America, his departure was sorrowful. During the ten-day voyage to Cuba, the memories of the town of Galdames and his mother's singing and dancing comforted him.

Joseph's family nick-named him "Pepe." When he left Spain, he used Joseph or "Joe." He was determined to wend his way to America, doing whatever it took to make it to the land of milk and honey. Arriving in Cuba, he wrote to his parents about his new friends, experiences, and the exciting sights he saw on the coast. After a couple of weeks in Cuba, the ship proceeded to the Pacific Coast of Nicaragua, via the long and often-stormy journey around Cape Horn. With several stops along the way, the ship took port at Corinto in the fall of 1903.

Joseph and many of the other young men signed a contract with an American company to work on the construction of the Panama Canal—a bypass that would shorten, by up to 9,000 nautical miles, the marine route between the Atlantic and Pacific Oceans. Actual construction on the canal did not begin until 1904 because of the virulent diseases in the Panamanian jungles. Once started, it became the largest civil engineering project in United States history.

In the meantime, Joseph found work paving roads, installing sewer and water systems, and repairing buildings. Once work began on the canal, Joseph befriended the double-named Jackson Jackson, captain of the Steamship *City of Sydney*. Captain Jackson captivated him with tales of the mines in California. With thoughts of the mines in America, he gave up work on the canal and sailed with Captain Jackson for San Francisco. Arriving in October of 1907, he bought three new suits and was ready to explore the world and claim his "fame and fortune." From San Francisco, he headed out to the gold, silver, and copper mines in the Mother Lode Country. In 1914, he settled in the gritty little mining town of Campo Seco, California, and found work at the Penn Copper Mine Company. He rented a house in Campo Seco while he worked the mines there and throughout Northern California.

Campo Seco is a small country town, one mile from the south bank of the Mokelumne River, between Camanche and Paloma in central California west of the Sierras. The historic Calaveras County community was originally called Oregon City. Campo Seco, meaning "Dry Camp," in Spanish received the name do to the severe scarcity of water needed to wash gold from the rocks during the "Gold Rush" days. Though placer diggings were rich and plentiful in the early days of the "Gold Rush," Campo Seco's greatest wealth came from copper with enough gold veins in its lodes to pay working expenses for mining the copper.

A fire in 1854 razed all the camp's wooden buildings; however, with

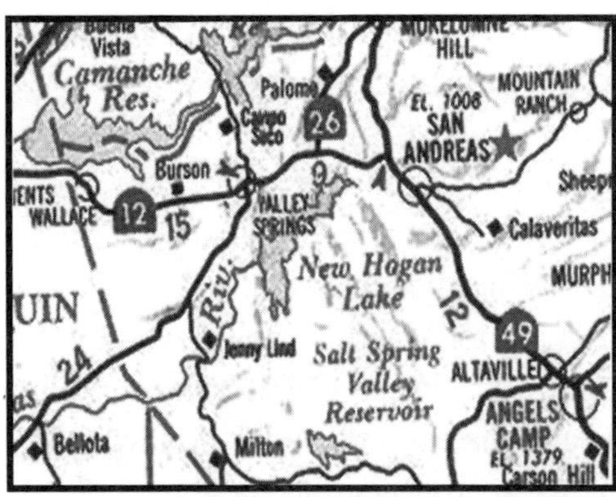

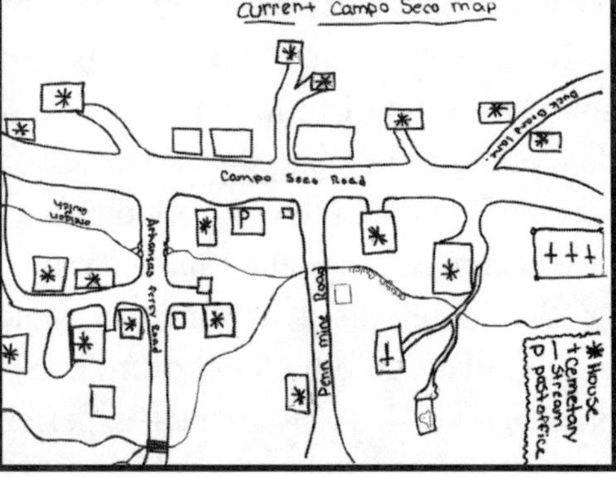

Map to Campo Seco and current plat of Campo Seco *(Courtesy Rose Olivo and Patt Pereira)*

Original plat of Campo Seco *(Courtesy Rodger and Helene Nunez)*

Merchant Store

Bakery

General Store

Remodeled Post Office with original security boxes *(Photos courtesy Barbara Olivo)*

placer gold still flowing, the town structures were re-built. In 1859, Campo Seco experienced a disaster and a discovery. Another fire, reportedly started in a Chinese store, destroyed the business district within thirty minutes. That, coupled with exhausted placer gold claims and quartz veins pinching out, had the camp headed for extinction. A variety of international camps existed in the Campo Seco area and later that year two Mexicans and a Chilano discovered The Great Copper Lode.

The discovery saved Campo Seco and it became one of the most cosmopolitan of all the mining camps in Northern California. At one time it had a Catholic and Methodist church, a post office, express office, two hotels, a restaurant, four stores, livery stables, blacksmith shop, bakery, saloons, a brewery, and quite a number of private residences with several large orange groves and orchards. The population was over 3,000. It was a thriving and brawling early gold rush camp that became a prosperous copper mining town. Mule trains laden with ore traveled over Campo Seco road, the town's main street, to the railroad platforms in Valley Springs. Bandits and murderers coexisted in town, with nightly knife fights. The last big fire in 1928 leveled most of the business district, except for the general store, post office and a couple of saloons. Many homes, orange groves and orchards were destroyed. Today the sleepy settlement of approximately fifty still stirs to life with the daily opening and closing of the original post office.

Joseph knew all the townspeople, including the children in Campo Seco. When he went to the General Store, owned by Angelo and Mabel Perreira, he would see Lydia shopping. Lydia was thirteen at the time, her womanly figure belied her age, and the men around town were beginning to notice. She enjoyed the attention and would often wear her hair in a long and lovely French braid that she could swing in her sassy walk. Lydia had a quick intellect. She was good at remembering faces and names. She noticed Joseph's sharp clothes, good looks and did not overlook the fact that he was the first one on Penn Mine Road to own a car. He would proudly ask, "How do you like-a my 'prinny' car?"

Joseph and Angelo were best friends, except when they were arguing over something. Whenever Lydia heard them in a heated debate at the General Store or "Cool Café," she would peek into the entrance and giggle. Joseph would be hollering in Basque, *"Zer? Zer? Hau ez zait gustazen! Nire diru, nire diru! Non dago?"* ("What? What? I don't like this! My money, my money! Where is it?") When he became angry and spoke in Basque, it was impossible to understand him, except to know he was fighting mad. Angelo was his best friend, until Angelo won at poker!

Matt Busi, a young man from Italy and an accomplished carpenter, helped Joseph build his first home on the lot next to Lydia's grandmother, Jessie.

Lydia's parents had separated, and she was living with her mother, Annie, on the property owned by Jessie. Her father, John G. Madriago, Jr., "John Jr.," at times assisted Matt and Joseph with the house, which allowed Lydia to spend time with her father. This gave her a reason to hang around Joseph. She would hide behind the boulders in the back of the property and watch Joseph work. It did not take long for her to catch his attention and, eventually, he asked her mother, for permission to date. She was fourteen and he was thirty-two.

Joseph's property overlooked a valley that had outcrops of many different size boulders and a babbling brook. The brook was a wonderful place for children to keep busy catching pollywogs, French frogs, turtles, and small perch. The frogs would burrow themselves deep into the mud to stay clear of the raccoons that came out at night. The brook had a pond-fed stream, run-off from the West Portal Pond situated just outside of town. During the rainy season, water from the nearby Pardee Dam would drain through the pond.

Boulders and Babbling Brook *(Courtesy Barbara Olivo Cagle)*

Joseph and Lydia Nunez *(Courtesy Rodger and Helene Nunez)*

Joseph was spellbound by Lydia's Mona Lisa smile. He was proud of her and her desire to pursue a career in nursing. After a few months of courtship, Joseph asked Annie for written consent to marry. The legal system at that time required it for those who wished to marry underage. Joseph proposed to Lydia in the secluded surrounding of boulders on the hillside behind his home; the same place where her father had proposed to her mother. Being happily married to a good man and starting a family was what she wanted. On January 1, 1915, Justice of the Peace C.F. Walter formally married Joseph and Lydia at the Calaveras County Court House. Witnesses were her maternal Great Aunt Victoriana and Uncle Antonio Gomez.

Lydia's parents, John Jr. and Annie Madriago remained separated without divorcing. In 1915, Annie became involved with Manuel Lasada. Together they had her last child, Jessie, named after her mother. So as not to mistake the two Jessies, the family referred to Annie's mother as "Nana."

John Jr. worked at the Penn Copper Mine Company and stayed in Campo Seco. In 1918, Annie and Manuel moved to San Jose following Nana and her brother Cooney.

In Campo Seco, Joseph had established himself as an experienced hoist operator. His knowledge and expertise gained him recognition to the point where he was sought by other mining companies as a troubleshooter. He would travel up and down the Mother Lode for weeks at a time. When Lydia chose to accompany him, they would close-up the house and re-open it upon returning.

During one of these "road" trips Lydia gave birth to their first child. Rodger Joseph Nunez was born on October 6, 1915, in Stockton, California. Teaching Rodger to say "Pa Pa" and "Ma Ma" became a playful race to see which word Rodger would learn first. Marriage and motherhood was more than Lydia ever dreamt it would be. Except—life was not perfect.

Pa Pa began to cough incessantly. His time in the mines took the toll it did on most men who worked the mines. In 1917, he temporarily moved the family to Arizona. A warmer climate was needed to clear his "Miners' Consumption." The doctors at that time referred to it as the "Black Lung Disease," a condition caused by habitual inhalation of coal dust, or, in this case, ore dust.

Joseph at Penn Copper Mine *(Courtesy Patt Pereira)*

In Arizona, Lydia became pregnant with Rose, her second child; christened Jacqueline Rose Nunez. She was named after her Great Aunt Rose Robie. Rose was born March 1, 1918, at 3:00 a.m. on Hercules Hill, Ray, Arizona. Dr. W.G. Carson was the attending physician. Ray, in Penal County, Arizona was a small mining town being worked to death. Today it is a ghost town, not even appearing on a map.

St. Joseph's Church *(Courtesy Barbara Olivo Cagle)*

A few months later, Pa Pa and the family moved to New Almaden, California, near San Jose. This allowed Lydia and the children to visit Annie and Nana. Joseph was feeling better, as the "Black Lung Disease" was clearing up, and went to work in the Quicksilver Mine. Lydia made a good friendship with a young woman named Adelaida Artnour and asked her to be Rose's godmother. There was no godfather. Reverend I. Lopez baptized Rose at St. Joseph's Church in San Jose, on July 15, 1918.

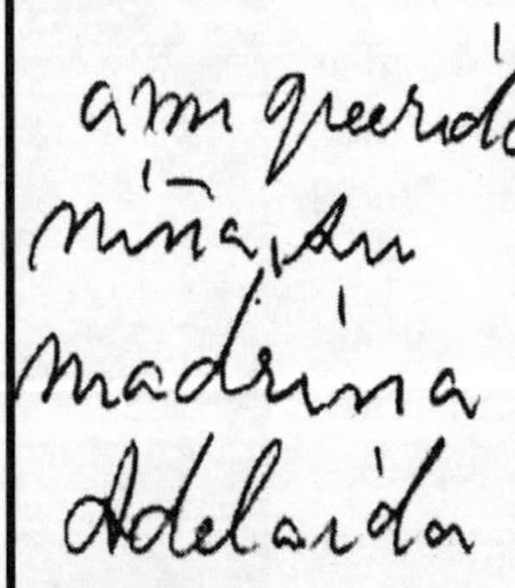

a mi querida
niña, su
madrina
Adelaida

Adelaida Artnour, To my dearest godchild–your godmother. *(Courtesy Marie Bueno)*

Later that year, a call from the Penn Copper Mine Company urged Pa Pa to return to Campo Seco. Lydia and Adelaida remained good friends and wrote each other. Adelaida gave Rose a Christmas card with a note and a photograph of herself. Rose did not see the card and photograph again until eighty-six years later when found amongst old family papers.

Lydia with Rose, and Rodger *(Courtesy Marie Bueno, Rodger and Helenez)*

Frank, Lawrence, Josephine, James, and Annie Madriago "Mater" (left to right)
(Courtesy Evelyn Simon)

Two years went by and Lydia was expecting a third child. During the pregnancy, she wanted to be close to her family in San Jose and Pa Pa again found work at the Quicksilver Mine in New Almaden. In the fall of 1920, they closed-up their home in Campo Seco and went to San Jose. Before leaving, Pa Pa took a picture of Lydia with "one on the way" and Rose at age two-and-a-half. They had just finished a meal and Rose was still wearing her red smocked bib over her white eyelet dress.

Upon arriving in San Jose, Cooney, "Uncle Cooney," was of great assistance. He arranged for Pa Pa and Lydia to move into a rental home next door to him and Nana. Annie lived a few blocks away and Lydia could not have been happier.

She had three brothers and two sisters who were still living with Annie: Frank, Lawrence, Josephine, James, and Jessie. They were pleased to be together. Now that Lydia was back in town, Adelaida came to visit. She took her position as Rose's godmother seriously and with good intentions of being a role model.

All was well until the influenza swept through Annie's house in late 1920. Her son Lawrence, at age sixteen, spent nine grueling months in the hospital suffering from Tuberculosis (TB), and the family worried he might not survive. When Lydia was younger, she had watched her eight year old sister Gertie die of the influenza.

On June 24, 1921, Grace Marie Nunez was born in Nana's house on Fourth Street, across from San Jose State College. Pa Pa called her "Marie."

Influenza leading to TB continued to plague the community. In 1922, Lydia became very ill. It started with the flu, got worse, and the doctor admitted her into Santa Clara County Hospital.

Quarantine access was in effect at the hospital with viewing through a glass windowed door. On one occasion, Adelaida took Rodger. They could see Lydia through the glass—she was at the other end of the room. Rodger pressed his hands and left cheek against the window and their eyes locked. He sensed her thoughts, "We will see each other again someday, my dear son. I love you with all my heart." He saw her eyes well up with tears of love, anguished by the pain of separation from her children.

The nurses would not let Pa Pa in to see Lydia. They were worried that the infectious disease could spread. All he could do was look at her through the windowed door. He yearned to hold her once again, so when the nurses went on break, he sneaked into the room. Lydia reached for his hand and caught the sleeve of his shirt.

"Joe, I need to see Rose—and my baby, just one more time. Just one more time. Please, Joe, please. I need to tell them I love them."

" Go! Take Marie. Please have her baptized," quivered Lydia. She gasped for air; her lungs were failing. She knew the hospital would not allow her to realize her final wish to see the children. It broke Pa Pa's heart. He promised he would do what he could do.

Pa Pa was alone when he took Marie to St. Joseph's Church to be baptized. He did not have a godparent for Marie, an assistant at the church, Sara Quevedo, stood as witness.

After a month and ten days in the hospital, Lydia died of pulmonary TB. She was twenty, Rodger was six-and-a-half, Rose was four years two months, and Marie was nine-and-a-half months. It was hard for Pa Pa to accept her death. "Too young-a, too young-a she died. She was-a prinny. She was-a so prinny, she was-a, ooh," he would hang his head, slowly shaking it, deep in thought.

There were many details for Pa Pa to take care of following the funeral. A few months later he left Marie with Nana and Uncle Cooney, and took Rose and Rodger with him to Campo Seco. He needed to tie up loose ends there. At the house he left Rose and Rodger upstairs and went to the basement. He opened the storage trunk and took out Lydia's jewelry and the few photographs he had of her. He sat down sadly at the table and poured himself a glass of wine.

Nothing seemed to ease the hollow pain felt deep in his heart. He was tired, and his eyes were sore from salty tears. When Rose became hungry and started crying seven-year-old Rodger picked her up, set her on the table, stepped onto a stool, and started frying eggs. Pa Pa could smell something cooking and came back upstairs.

"Whadda you doin?"

"Making fried eggs. Rose said she was hungry," replied Rodger. Choked up with grief, all Pa Pa did was hug them and then helped Rodger finish cooking.

When Pa Pa returned to San Jose he gave Lydia's belongings to her mother Annie. Rose, Rodger, and Marie called their grandmother "Mater" (May-ter). Pa Pa thought the logical place for his family was with her; she had a large house with plenty of bedrooms. Yet, she was quick to declare no part in caring for the children. Mater and Manuel had their own children and did not want to take on three more. Pa Pa was bitter, he did not have much time for her to begin with and this only added fuel to the fire. Alas, Mater said she would take Rodger. That set Pa Pa off, and when she asked why she could not have him, Pa Pa let her have it.

"Cuz I don't like-a you cuz you won't take-a all three my kidzes." Pa Pa always referred to his children as "my kidzes."

Nana and Uncle Cooney were the two family members he could count on most. They helped watch his children for about a year after Lydia's death. As a widowed father, they knew Pa Pa needed all the help he could get. Nana and

Uncle Cooney would take over during the day. It was a convenient arrangement with them living next door with a common driveway between the two homes. They spent time together as a family, telling stories and sharing meals. When Pa Pa went hunting he would bring home venison to barbecue. He did the best he could to care for them. At night, he would warm a baby bottle to take to bed for Marie. He laid it under his arm to keep it warm until she awoke. In the morning he got up early to change Marie's diaper, dress Rose, and fix breakfast before leaving for a hard days work.

Mater's house on St. James Street *(Courtesy Marie Bueno)*

Mater's house on the corner of St. James and San Pedro Streets in San Jose has been remodeled, and is used as a lawyer's office.

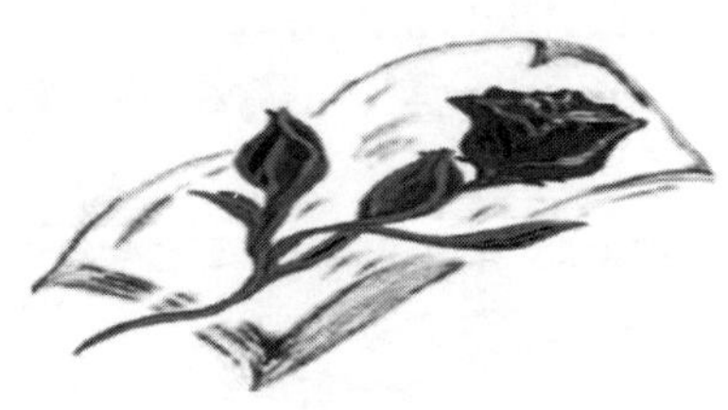

Chapter Two

She Lied!

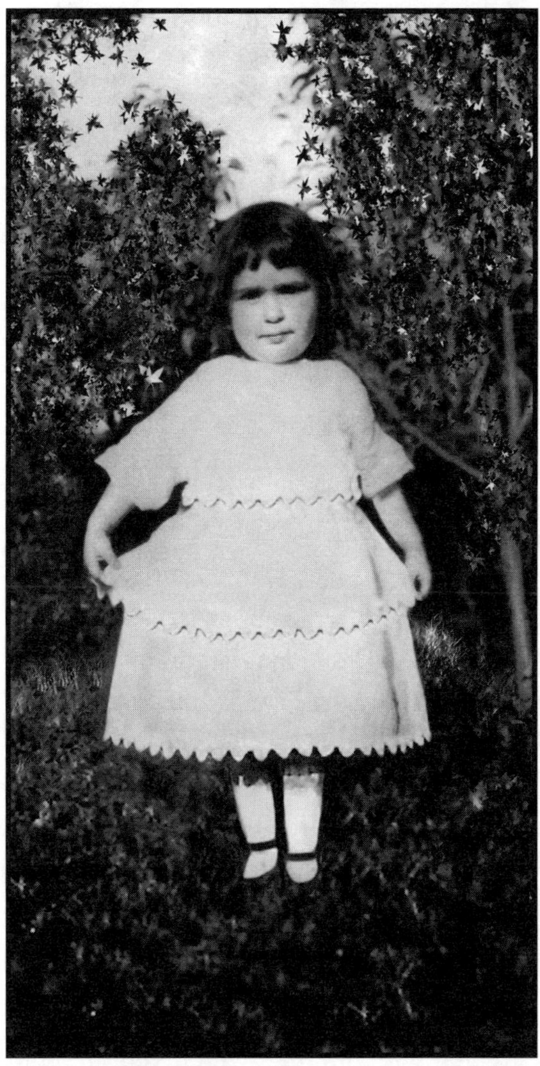

Rose at five *(Courtesy Rose Olivo)*

Pa Pa knew he would have to make care arrangements for the kidzes. It had been a year since their mother had passed and he was traveling more. The kidzes became comfortable staying with Nana and Uncle Cooney. They also liked visiting with Mater, their aunts, uncles, and especially for Rose, her Aunt Jessie. They were two years apart and often played together.

The epidemic of TB continued with health officials mandating that the counties quarantine those people who did not have a vaccine and tested positive.

Pa Pa had a terrible cough and had coughed up blood. Health officials suspected he might have TB. The county wanted him to go to a sanitarium, or return to Arizona. When he learned that the suspected TB was a bad case of emphysema, he returned to the mines in Campo Seco where there was plenty of mine work. The warmer climate would be good for him, he still had a home there, and he needed the money. The mining industry thought of him as one of the top mining assayers in the Mother Lode Country. Some even said he was able to smell gold! It was a difficult and involved process locating new mines. Dynamiting required the technical expertise only a few men possessed. He speculated whether a particular location was worth mining, or continuing to mine, and what type of ore it may hold. That was his job—they called it Ore Assaying. Today there are more up-to-date methods of determining the feasibility of locating or continuing to work a mine. Then, speculation was the primary method utilized.

Cool Café at the General Store owned by Angelo Pereira Ryno and The Dirty Dog Saloon owned by George and Eliza Ryno *(Courtesy Patt Pereira)*

Pa Pa was still a relatively young man and, over time, he became a "Man About Town." For a while, he was involved with one of Lydia's shirt-tale cousins, Jessie Ryno. He always said he loved her long red hair. Perhaps the philandering was his way of mending a broken heart.

He did like his wine--a lot of red wine and beer. He also loved playing cards, "Pedro" or "Whist," and singing. He hung out at the "Cool Café," and "Dirty Dog Saloon." He sang La Paloma in the Basque language. It was a long song. Other songs were De la Bolina, Cielito Lindo, and Las Corazones. One of his favorites did not have a title. It went something like, "The pal that I loved, stole the gal that I loved; he took all my sunshine and joy. He was my pal when we were young and played with our toys on the floor. I just can't believe my pal would deceive me. Oh, Gee! I'm sick and I'm sore. The pal that I loved stole the gal that I loved; that's why we're not pals anymore." He liked to sing because his mother was a singer and dancer. She knew many songs and, at family gatherings, people would dance while she sang.

On trips to San Jose, Pa Pa reported to the Santa Clara County Clinic to be tested for TB. He continued to be treated with quinine, which kept him out of quarantine. The children were tested for TB annually and one time Rose tested positive for TB. She was four-and-a-half. There were so many deadly diseases at the time that it was common for the county to quarantine exposed children. She was placed for five days in a sanatorium in San Jose that allowed her visitation.

Pa Pa visited her daily. On one occasion, they met in a walnut grove on the grounds. It was autumn and walnuts were falling from the trees. Rose was wearing a full-skirt dress and, by the time Pa Pa arrived, she had filled up her skirt with nuts. They were sitting on a bench shelling the nuts when one of the "Head Wardens" marched up full of fury. Signs had been posted to not pick or pick-up the nuts. The warden confiscated the "haul" and rushed off. Rose was confused as to why her father did not stand up to the lady. Later she learned that he knew the walnuts were not for picking. He just did not have the heart to tell her and since his visits were short he wanted them to be as special as possible.

Pa Pa could not rely on the good graces of Nana and Uncle Cooney forever. He would have to find a home for the kidzes. He still wondered why Lydia's family had not offered to take all three; Mater's home was certainly large enough and had plenty of rooms.

Did Mater's refusal to help, let Pa Pa's stubbornness get in the way of having them raised by other family members? He could have considered her great aunts, Rose Robie and Eliza Ryno. Except they lived in Campo Seco, and after losing Lydia, he had decided that he did not want his children growing up in a mining town. There were better opportunities for them in San Jose than in Campo Seco.

Marie would be easy to place in a foster home. Couples wanted to rear a baby. Rodger was older, and families were more apt to take on another pair of hands. Raising a young girl took money, which most people did not have.

Nana and Uncle Cooney offered to continue to raise Marie. Pa Pa knew they would take good care of her and would love her like their own. It was difficult for Nana to pronounce Marie. She spoke in a strong Spanish accent and it came out sounding like "Mol-lie." Uncle Cooney and the rest of the family mimicked her and called Marie, "Mollie." As for Pa Pa, Rodger, and Rose, they used Marie.

Pa Pa had to find a home for Rose and Rodger, and he was adamant not to separate them. He was still bitter toward Mater, and his sharp tongue let others know how he felt. He told them, "I didn't like-a Mater, and she didn't like-a me. She no wanna take care of my kidzes. She ain't got no two kidzes from the same father. She's-a had too many kidzes; some died. She's-a had thirteen children or more."

In 1923, Pa Pa went to the Children's Aid at the Hall of Justice in San Jose to fill out the legal documents necessary to place his kidzes in foster care. Although, he found Nana and Uncle Cooney to care for Marie, the three siblings became wards of the state. The Children's Aid, governed by the Child Welfare League of America, assigned a guardian, "Mrs. Sommers," to act as liaison between the children and their families. The organization stressed temporary rather than permanent institutional care of dependent children for the preservation of family.

Rose was five years old, and Rodger seven-and-a-half, when Mrs. Sommers reviewed Teresa Espinosa's application for foster care. She was Portuguese, her maiden name was Romero. She stood five-feet-five inches, with dark hair, dark

Rose's foster mother Theresa Espinosa "Ma"

Rose's foster father Gabe Espinosa

Rose at five *(Photos courtesy Rose Olivo)*

eyes, thick eyebrows, and a full figure. She dressed plainly, to the point of drab. Her previously attractive figure had vanished.

There was talk that Teresa had been one of the most famous "Ladies of the Night" in the red light district of San Francisco. After the 1906 earthquake, she reportedly walked from San Francisco to San Jose to start a life with Gabe Espinosa. A man whose last name she would use as though they were married.

Gabe was a tall, dark, thin man. He wore a Fedora hat most of the time and all you could see was a bushy, black mustache. He and Teresa lived in a small home in San Jose, on East Santa Clara Street. It was close to the corner of Twentieth Street and a Chinese grocery store. She kept their home very dark and gloomy, seldom drawing open the curtains or shades. She had heavy green drapes, patterned with petunias, that divided the living room into another bedroom.

Teresa was reformed and remained with Gabe for years. As they grew older, she became lonely and ill with a heart condition called myocarditis, an inflammation of the inner and outer membranes of the heart muscle. Gabe said little; he was preoccupied with gallivanting around town. Teresa, at fifty-two years of age, wanted children to keep her company. She heard of the Children's Aid and filled out the paperwork, noting she had room for two children.

Mrs. Sommers was not aware of Teresa's past, or that she was not being truthful. She looked somewhat younger, lied about her age and her promiscuous life. All Mrs. Sommers knew was that Teresa wanted companionship and had agreed to take both Rose and Rodger. Most importantly, she was Catholic and promised Pa Pa the children would be raised in the Catholic religion and go to church every Sunday.

Pa Pa explained to Rose and Rodger that Mrs. Sommers was there to take them to live at another home. He would see them once-a-year on their annual visit to the Health Clinic. Leaving his kidzes with non-family was one of the hardest decisions he made. Rose cried uncontrollably and her fears escalated as she continued to cry on the way to a strange home.

Rodger held her hand securely as they met Teresa and Gabe. Teresa showed them around and settled each in separate bedrooms. Rose sat for a long time staring at the four walls. She wanted her father and mother and cried until there were no more tears. The new environment confused her. She reverted back to bed-wetting and would sneak out of her room to crawl into bed with Rodger.

Even though his kidzes were now wards of the state, Pa Pa felt he had done what he was capable of doing and relieved in knowing the children could get on with their lives. Albeit, without him on a regular basis. He returned to Campo Seco, worked hard, and sent money to the Children's Aid for his children.

Adapting to life with Teresa and Gabe took time. Rose's hair was cut short. A bob just under her ears kept it trim and easy to manage. Teresa insisted that Rose and Rodger call her "Ma," and Gabe, remained Gabe. When spoken to, they were to respond with "Yes ma'am, No ma'am, Yes sir, No sir."

The one thing Ma did well was make enchiladas and tamales. That is how they made a living. Her recipe was special and she would not reveal it to anyone. She and Gabe took orders from customers living within walking distance and prepared the enchiladas and tamales daily. The back porch was the primary preparation area and Gabe would jump right in helping. When Rodger came home from school, he and Rose would make deliveries in the neighborhood. They learned the routes, met the customers, and collected the money together.

Once a month, Ma's sister, Juanita Higuera, would bring her children: Teresa, Evelyn, and Tony, over to visit. Juanita's girls looked like twins, with the prettiest copper-colored curly hair, and freckles. The children would play together in Ma's backyard, taking turns on their pull-wagon scooter. The get-togethers were special, Gabe would barbecue, Ma and her sister would visit, and the children played.

When Pa Pa came back to visit his kidzes, Rose was in kindergarten and Rodger attended a full day of school. He stopped to pick up Marie, then Rose and Rodger. He led most of their conversations. The kidzes had not seen each other and Pa Pa often enough to strike up their own conversation. Marie was a baby when Mrs. Sommers uprooted Rose and Rodger. They were like strangers.

Pa Pa figured out what his kidzes needed to get them talking; that was cake and ice cream. From then on The Crystal Creamery became an expected stop when he came to town. Next would come the shopping trip. Pa Pa liked to look good and he wanted his kidzes to look good, too. He had a saying he believed in and said to them, "You look-a sharp! You feel-a sharp! You are-a sharp!"

After the cake, ice cream, and shopping, Pa Pa would take his kidzes to the Health Clinic for their annual check up. Rodger showed some signs of TB on one of these visits and the clinic sent him to a sanatorium for boys in San Mateo. He was eight and Rose was nearing her sixth birthday. Rose watched as Mrs. Sommers took him away. Once more the tears welled in her eyes. Ma assured her Rodger would come back. The truth was Ma and Gabe did not want him back. They feared he might expose them to TB. Little did Rose know that she and Rodger's childhoods would rarely touch again.

She missed having her brother's companionship. Gabe as the male figure in the house remained distant. Ma wore the pants. The relationship between the two became purely one of companionship, with Rose obligated to care for Ma.

Ma rarely showed affection toward Rose and did not want her to visit Rodger or Marie. Lydia's family tried to keep in touch, to no avail. There was no form of communication between Rose and any of her relatives. Ma would not allow it. She wanted to keep her all to herself. Maybe there was jealousness on Ma's part, or maybe she was afraid of becoming too involved with Lydia's family. The family may have disapproved of the way she was caring for Rose.

Ma tried to replace Lydia. She told Rose that they had adopted her and were her real parents. Since they were raising her, not her father, she was to go by the name of Rose Espinosa.

Rose's sixth birthday *(Courtesy Rose Olivo)*

On her sixth birthday, Ma and Gabe arranged for a goat carriage ride and took a photograph of Rose wearing a blue vest that her mother, Lydia, had knitted. It was her secret security, to this day, the memory is clear and real. "I would like to have had little things like a hand-knit vest that my mother made. I wonder what happened to it?"

When the sanatorium in San Mateo became over-crowded, Rodger was moved to a facility in Menlo Park. After a couple of months, he was cleared and

Pa Pa, with the help of Mrs. Sommers was able to place him in the Sunnyholme Preventorium for boys in San Jose. The "home" was a pink brick building on Park Avenue, next to a market, across the street from O'Connor Hospital. Rodger was not at Sunnyholme Preventorium for long. Mrs. Sommers was contacted through Catholic Charities that a family was interested in foster care.

A German couple, Fred and Antoinette Wirz, had wanted a large family. They lost twin boys at birth when it was determined they were wrapped in their umbilical cords. After trying again, they had a daughter, Rita. She was also born with the umbilical cord around her neck and at the age of six-months was diagnosed with cerebral palsy. The Wirz' then learned they could not have more children. Through Catholic Charities in San Jose, they were referred to Mrs. Sommers and applied for foster care. Mrs. Sommers showed the Wirz' around the Sunnyholme Preventorium and informed them that foster care would include a nominal monthly stipend per child.

The Wirz' wanted boys for manual help around the house, and later for financial help when the boys got jobs. At Sunnyholme Preventorium they chose Rodger. He was sitting atop of a black traveling trunk, which was loaded with his collection of comic books. Arrangements were made quickly, and soon he was in a nice home on Montgomery Street, San Jose. At first, he was not too happy. The Wirz' disposed of his comic book collection and they were sorely disappointed when the trunk did not contain clothes and valuables.

Mr. and Mrs. Wirz, Rita, Rodger, and the Ferreira boys *(Courtesy Rodger and Helene Nunez)*

Lydias family did not visit the children and Ma did not take Rose to visit them. On occasion, the Wirz' would take Rodger to visit his father in Campo Seco. On Pa Pa's visits to San Jose, now only Rose and Marie would go on the shopping sprees and the Crystal Creamery runs. If the Wirz' had Pa Pa for dinner, all the kidzes were included.

A couple of months after taking Rodger into their home the Wirz' returned to Sunnyholme Preventorium. This time they arranged to take three of the five Ferreira boys. Although they were born in the Azores they were eligible for foster care. Mrs. Sommers placed Fred, Frank, and John Ferreira with the Wirz'. Their older brother, Joseph, remained at the home and the eldest, Manuel, stayed with his father. Mrs. Ferreira had died giving birth to a girl, who also died. Mr. Ferreira could not take care of all the boys alone and had elected foster care. Later, the

Wirz' took in yet another young boy, Frank Ramos. He was also born in the Azores. They provided these boys with a good home and a good education. The boys were expected home right after school and homework took precedence. Each boy had his own chore. Rodger's was to vacuum the house.

With Rodger gone, Ma guided Rose on the enchilada and tamale deliveries. That lasted until Rose was seven and took over the route. She and Rodger met up once when he was on his way home from school and spotted her. He was concerned, and thought her too young to be out by herself, so he walked her home. At first he was pleased to see Ma. Then she began babbling about Rose wetting the bed and the need for a good stick to whip her. He got the message; Ma did not want him around. Before leaving, he hugged Rose, ran his hand over her head, and pulled her close.

"Everything will be okay. I am here," whispered Rodger.

Rose did not have many friends. School work and reading became her priorities. If she did not have to be home, she could be found at the San Jose Library on Twenty-Fourth and Santa Clara Streets. Next to roses, her second love was reading.

She got lonely for family. She adored her Pa Pa and not once blamed him for having been placed with Ma. He continued working the mines up and down the Mother Lode Country and kept his promise of visiting his kidzes once-a-year. As wonderful as they were, the once a year visits were not enough. Many a night Rose would go to bed cherishing the special moments she had with her father and thought of her mother's family. They lived close, within blocks, yet, Ma would not take her to see them and they did not come to visit. Ma did ensure she went to church every Sunday and received her First Communion. Maybe Ma was trying to make retribution for her rowdy background. As for education, her attitude was "take it or leave it; get it or not get it." Rose chose to get it, and she got it. Later in life she would discover why she needed this great wealth of knowledge—sixteen times over.

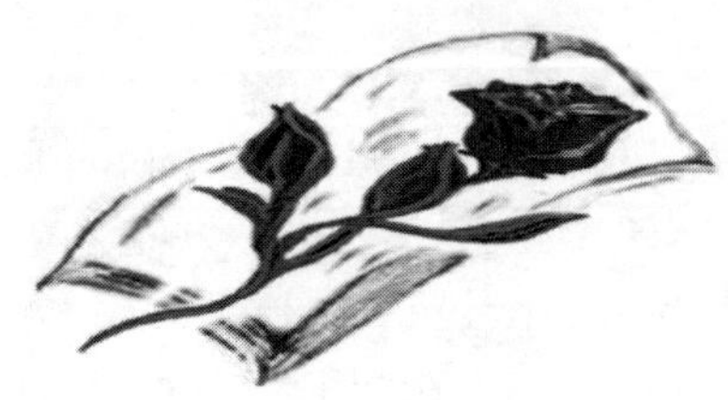

Chapter Three

Enchiladas and Tamales

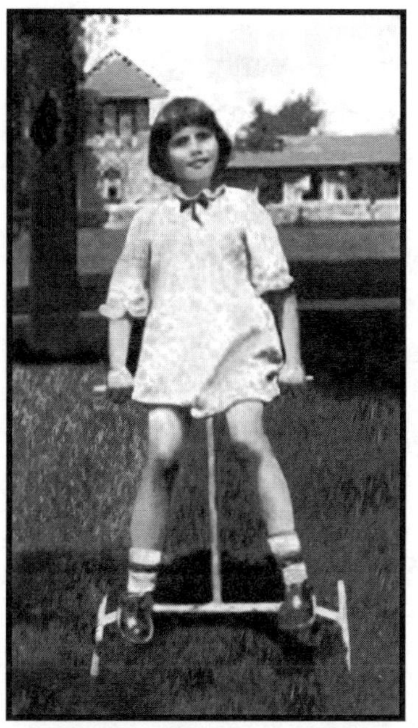

Marie twirling on a sprinkler head *(Courtesy Marie Bueno)*

Rose's Great Grandmother Jessie Maria Lopez Carabajal "Nana" *(Courtesy Marie Bueno)*

Marie was a curious little daredevil, preferred most tomboy activities and was "growing like a weed." She did play occasionally with paper dolls that her Aunt Josephine bought for her at the Kress Five & Ten Cent Store.

Life with Nana and Uncle Cooney was good. Nana enjoyed telling Marie her story of how a handsome young Portuguese vaquero kidnapped her when she was seventeen. The cowboy took her up into the San Benito hills of California, kept her there for three months, and got her pregnant with her son Cooney.

Uncle Cooney told stories of his childhood in Campo Seco. As a blue-eyed tow-headed youth, he would join the neighboring children on hot summer days and race down Penn Mine Road to the swimming hole at West Portal Pond, about a half-mile outside of the town. Sometimes the children would strip off clothes along the way to the pond until they were naked. One day, Uncle Cooney seriously injured his foot jumping in the pond. He hit underwater rocks and broke his foot, leaving him with a noticeable limp for the rest of his life.

Uncle Cooney's foot injury kept him out of military service. He did work for the Army, both in Campo Seco and later in San Jose, knitting men's sleeveless sweaters for soldiers. The government sent the yarn, and he sent them the sweaters.

He also worked as a barber/bartender. The barbershop, with a barroom in the back, was in east San Jose across the street from the Five Wounds Church in a Portuguese Community. Uncle Cooney would cut hair by day and tend bar at night. He was well liked, handsome, charming, and unmarried. He dressed neatly, with every button on his jacket closed to the top of his collar.

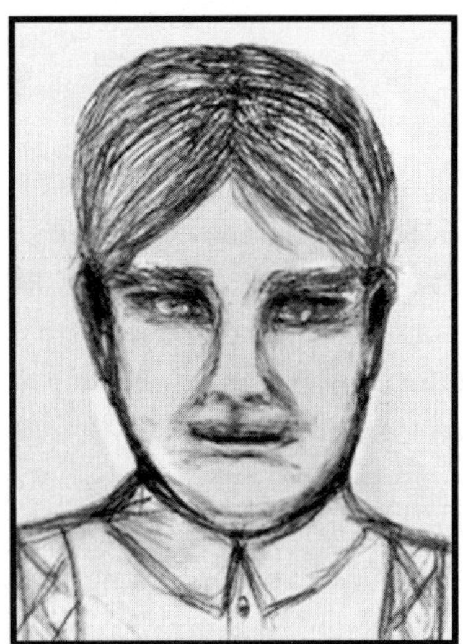
Fecundo A. Carabajal "Cooney"
(Courtesy Marie Bueno)

West Portal Pond, Campo Seco
(Courtesy Barbara Hunter)

Whenever the Five Wounds Church held functions and fiestas, Uncle Cooney would take Marie. They usually hired him as a bartender and Marie loved the kiddy carnival. He would use his tips to keep her supplied with riding money and would reach down into his pockets for all of his nickels, dimes, and quarters. When she was out of money, she would run back to him, and he would dig deeper into his pockets for more coins. When the functions wrapped up, the church would send them home with pots full of leftovers.

The effects of the Great Depression touched everyone. Known as the longest and most severe economic depression in American History, it began with the New York Stock Market Crash of 1929 (Black Tuesday) and lasted through the 1930's. However devastating, it did provide Uncle Cooney an opportunity for additional income. The county gave pensions to men who were jobless and he rented out rooms. The house was long and narrow with rooms in the front and a central bathroom equipped with a big basin, claw-foot bathtub, and toilet. A spacious porch separated the rented rooms from Uncle Cooney, Nana and Marie. They had their own bathroom, kitchen, and bedrooms. Uncle Cooney was good at carpentry and had converted the large front rooms into studios. He provided a small table and gas-fired cook top in each room. Everyone entered through the front door, where there was a covered porch extending across the width of the house. A row of chairs lined the porch for the men, who had nothing to do all day than to watch the trains go by and talk.

When Uncle Cooney sat on the front porch with the renters, he would send Marie across the street to play in the park where he could keep an eye on her. She loved playing on the tall sprinkler heads, twirling herself around in circles. One of the renters was an out-of-work vaudeville musician who sometimes would provide entertainment for them.

Marie had a good time with her uncle. They were "buddies." He took her everywhere. She loved to go to Alum Rock Park and would beg him to take her there. "Next week, maybe next week," he would say. Then, come Sunday, he would surprise her with a visit to the park and concert at the round bandstand. They would take the train that ran from Alum Rock Avenue to the middle of the park. They were great Sundays.

Uncle Cooney's main form of transportation was his motorcycle and, when Marie was old enough, he attached a sidecar for her and her dog, "Jiggs." Jiggs was a big, fat, black and white terrier mutt that wanted to be with Marie constantly. This proved to be a problem when she tried to avoid her uncle's leather belt discipline. She would run off and hide under the bed and Jiggs would follow. It was no mystery when he spotted Jiggs' tail wagging back and forth from underneath the bed. Her hideout was a dead give-away.

Rose and Rodger did not have the kind of freedom that Marie enjoyed and were interested in hearing of her adventures.

Pa Pa's black Model "A" Ford

Rita Wirz *(Photos courtesy Rodger and Helene Nunez)*

On Pa Pa's annual visits he drove a black roofless Model "A" Ford. He would stop by and pick up Marie first; always Marie first before Rose. Then they would stop to see Rodger. Sometimes he was not there. Pa Pa was not one to give his kidzes advance notice that he would be in town. He would spend the first day shopping with his girls, and afterwards they went out to eat. The Wirz' would invite them over for dinner the following night. Pa Pa would arrive wearing a dress shirt and tie. That was something he, his father, and brothers did at meals out of respect for his mother, and he carried on that tradition throughout his life. If the lady of the house went to the trouble of fixing the meal, the least he could do was dress for the occasion.

Rita, the Wirz' daughter would greet them at the door. She sat crippled in her wheel chair waving her arms in excitement over seeing them. She loved hearing about the shopping day and seeing the girls in their new outfits. She knew they would give her the golden treatment. Rose and Marie would take turns brushing her long blonde hair and telling her how beautiful she looked.

The girls looked forward to Pa Pa taking them to Hart's Department Store. They would get new matching dresses and black patent leather Mary Jane shoes with ankle-strap buttons. One year they could not find matching dresses. Rose was jealous when Marie got the prettier dress with ruffles.

Rodger fourteen, Rose eleven, Pa Pa forty-six, and Marie eight, 1929

Rose with Marie (left) and Rose, Rodger, and Marie *(Photos courtesy Rose Olivo)*

Pa Pa was feeling a bit melancholy on this visit. He had received word that his father had passed away on February 15, 1929. His parents both died in the month of February, his birth month. He regretted not having a family picture with them and made a point of taking a picture with his kidzes.

Rose was eleven and began to take notice of the clothes and other niceties girls her age had. Ma could afford little more than the bare necessities. Her support from the state and the sale of enchiladas and tamales were the means of income. A new store in the neighborhood advertised for help in the delivery of a "Grand Opening" handbill door-to-door. Rose went up to the owner and asked if she could do it. He responded with a laugh, "You know, I was looking for a boy." Opportunities were not available to both girls and boys alike, as they are now, and she did not get the job. Undampened, she vowed to emphasize her efforts in delivering enchiladas and tamales, more determined than ever to do her best. She enjoyed the deliveries and conversations with the people. It gave her something to do after school besides take care of Ma.

The next few years she expanded her enchiladas and tamales route in the neighborhood and did well until she was spotted by two of her uncles, Lydia's brother Lawrence and Aunt Josephine's husband Tony. They were upset! Rose did not recognize them. She was little when she last saw them. When Uncle Tony came home, he told Aunt Josephine he had seen Rose. Marie was baby-sitting at the house and stood outside the kitchen door, listening to the conversation. She was trying to be inconspicuous when she heard him saying, "We saw Rose again delivering enchiladas and tamales. That is no such thing for her to be doing!" They had a discussion with Pa Pa before contacting Mrs. Sommers about taking her from Ma. Pa Pa was livid:

"Why you want her now? Why you not take her when she was little?

Perhaps their efforts were sincere after all these years, however, he and Rose wondered about their sudden interest. She was fourteen and knew, through Marie, that Aunt Josephine was a young mother with plans on having more children. She suspected her aunt's motivation was to get a built-in baby-sitter. The truth was, of Lydia's siblings, she was the first sister to finally be of an age and position to care for Rose.

Mrs. Sommers and Pa Pa went to see Ma. The visit was unpleasant and disturbing. This was when they learned that Rose was using the last name of Espinosa. Rose made a scene, ran into her father's arms and begged him to let her stay.

She could not leave Ma—not now! Gabe and Ma had separated. Besides, she had been delivering enchiladas and tamales for several years, why all the concern? Everyone was upset. In the end Pa Pa let her continue to stay with Ma. The after affects of these events caused Rose to mention little about Lydia's family in her later life, as she swore her feelings and thoughts to secrecy.

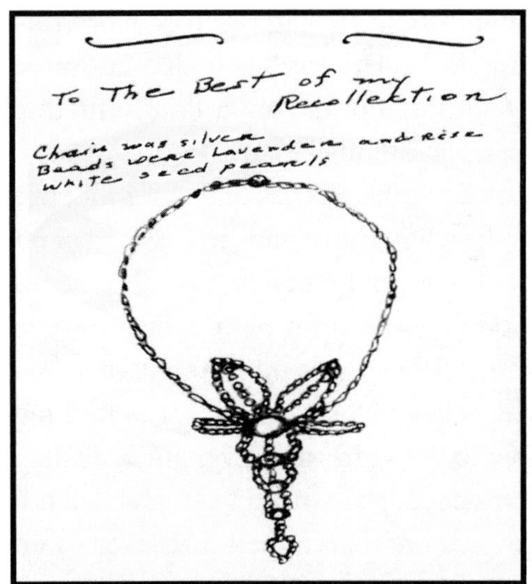

Rose's Lavaliere *(Courtesy Rose Olivo)*

Marie's Bracelet *(Courtesy Marie Bueno)*

That evening Pa Pa returned to Ma's. He had a special memento of Lydia's for Rose. Her memories of her mother were the blue knitted vest she made for her as a child, and laying a red rose on her casket. He handed her a beautiful lavaliere. She was speechless. She held it next to her heart and expressed tears of joy. This piece of jewelry from her mother was one possession she wanted to hold onto forever. The golden lavaliere hung on a silver chain with a beautiful amethyst stone that accentuated the pearl drops and seeded pearls. Oh, how Ma's eyebrows raised with special interest when she saw that lavaliere!

Rose asked Pa Pa, "Do you have any photographs of our mother? What did she look like?" He took a deep breath and with pride in his voice, he answered, "She was-a Spanish. She was-a-beau-ti-ful woman." Long ago, he had forgotten where his few photographs of Lydia were and had none to give her.

The next day, Pa Pa also gave a memento to Marie. It was a thick gold bracelet engraved with Lydia's, Mater's, and Nana's initials intertwined. Both pieces of jewelry were family heirlooms. Nana handed them down to Mater; Mater handed them down to Lydia; and now Pa Pa handed them down to Rose and Marie. He told them he knew this is what their mother would have wanted him to do.

Ma insisted that the lavaliere was too nice, and suggested that she put it in a special jewelry box until Rose was old enough to wear it. She assured her that she could look at it whenever she wanted—Ma did not keep her promise. Rose asked many times to see it, and Ma said, "No!"

Ma and Rose were alone now. Gabe had been gone for months and money was tight. Ma gathered all their expensive jewelry and anything else they could sell. When she reached for the box with the lavaliere in it, Rose's heart stopped and she asked her, "How can you? How can you sell the only possession I have from my mother?" She recalls making a scene and bitterness welled up inside her. After suppressing her feelings, she could no longer shed any tears. Through God, she learned to be strong in every situation, swallowed her pride and allowed forgiveness.

East San Jose Public Library—historical site *(Courtesy Jeanie Olivo)*

Rose's first school was Hawthorne Elementary located on Twenty-Fourth Street. Originally East San Jose School, the school dated back to the early 1890's. In those days the school employed corporal punishment for errant pupils and separate recesses for boys and girls. Selma Olinder, the first woman principal in San Jose, served at the school. She also was the founder of the first Parent Teachers Association (PTA) in Northern California. Rose looked at Mrs. Olinder as a great inspiration in her determination to excel and she went on to become a straight "A" student, with honors. The East San Jose library next to the school entrusted Rose with many loaned books at one time. They knew she would return them within a week.

Upon graduation from Hawthorne Elementary, Rose gave the "Address of Welcome" speech at the graduation ceremony. School officials knew she had a keen memory, and they could depend on her to give a good presentation. There were several salutations given by other students that day. The "Address of Welcome" speech came first. It was the most important and the longest. The night before, Rose caught the flu; fever, chills, vomiting, diarrhea. She wanted to give the speech badly and did not let on to anyone that she was sick; not Ma, her classmates, or her teachers. At the graduation, she gave the speech perfectly. Her teachers thought she did a wonderful job and were exceedingly proud of her. None of her family, including Ma, attended the ceremony, so the recognition was important to her. As was the custom, graduation from grammar school meant a huge plate of ice cream and cake for the graduates. Still feeling the effects of the flu, she could not eat a bite of it. She had looked forward to the treat all through her sixth-grade year and now had to set and watch the others.

For Rose, The Great Depression and junior high school began in the same year. She was beginning to get around more in school, as most teenagers seem to do. She attended Theodore Roosevelt Junior High for one year, made good grades and the honor roll. When the city remodeled the school for expansion in 1930, Ma moved to the north side of San Jose. Peter Burnett Junior High School turned out to be a wonderful place for her. She soon had three close girl friends, and they did the usual things big city depression era teenagers enjoyed like noticing boys, going to sporting events, and even watching some of the game. They would spend their time doing what was free, such as, swimming. Rose took a course in Junior Red Cross Lifesaving, and received a certificate of completion. Today she says, "I do not think I could save myself, let alone anyone else."

Rose's art project entered into Brussels World's Fair *(Courtesy Rose Olivo)*

All forms of art enthralled her. It became evident in her early years of school when teachers often praised her drawings and frequently exhibited them. Her ability to learn quickly impressed art instructors in junior high and one of her instructors entered a block stamping art project in the 1932 World's Fair in Brussels, Belgium. It was a square of linoleum with a dove carved print. When brushed with black paint, the image of the dove could be transferred onto a piece of cloth or paper.

Ma brought Rose up in an old-fashioned atmosphere with antiquated values and standards. Dating during her junior high school years was forbidden. Going out on dates was not as big an issue for her as it was for some of her friends. It did not really bother her. There was no sex education in school at all in those days. Sex was discussed by a parent at home, if at all. Sex was a dirty word.

She learned that the principal of Peter Burnett Junior High School was assigning speeches for the graduation ceremony. Since she had maintained an "A" average through her years there, she approached the principal, mentioned the "Address of Welcome" speech she had given at Hawthorne Elementary, and asked to be considered for an assignment. The principal selected a boy for the Valedictorian speech and she was awarded the "Address of Welcome."

On graduation evening, she gave her speech with no family in attendance—not her father, her brother or her sister. Important events worthy of recognition Ma kept from them. Rose begged Ma to attend. She sat in the audience with little expression or emotion to the point that Rose could not tell if she was proud of her or not.

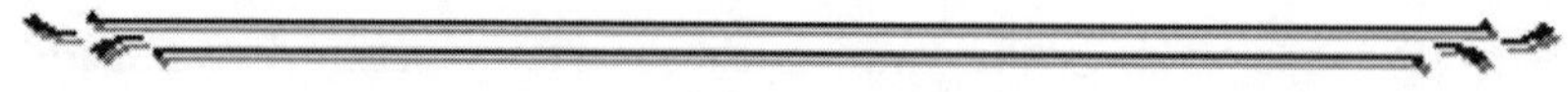

Rose's father Joseph, and uncles Antonio, and Balbino Nunez (left to right), Jackson, California *(Courtesy Rodger and Helene Nunez)*

That summer, Pa Pa took Rose and Marie to San Francisco to meet his younger brother, Balbino. He had not seen Balbino, or his other younger brother, Antonio, since they had arrived in the states. After their mother passed away on February 27, 1920, the two brothers decided to leave Spain. They sent news of their mother's death and, just as Pa Pa had, booked passage on a steam powered ship to Corinto, Nicaragua. Once in Nicaragua, they had to establish residency and citizenship. Antonio's birth records were lost in a huge fire at the old church in Ruitelan, Spain and the legal documents and affidavits took years. Finally, in 1924, permission was granted and Pa Pa sent money for his brothers, and their friend Pete Monsalo, to come to America. They sailed on the ship *Venezuela* to San Francisco, where he met them. He took them on a tour of the Mother Lode Country, with visits to Sutter Creek, Plymouth, Amador and Jackson. In Jackson, they dressed up for this photograph. It was customary to have photographs taken holding a cigar, a sign of wealth and prosperity. Pa Pa proudly sent the photograph to his father reflecting how well his sons were doing in America. After a couple of days in Campo Seco, Balbino and Antonio returned to San Francisco. During Pa Pa's visit with the kidzes, Balbino was working as a laborer in a machine factory. Antonio was a watchman on a barge.

This was the only time that Rose and Marie were to meet their uncle. Rodger had met him once before. Balbino lived in a hotel for men on Stockton Street. Rose still remembers all the steps that they had to climb to reach the second floor. They entered a large dining room where the men gathered for their meals. The girls' eyes grew wide when they saw a big platter of boned pork chops and baskets of bread. There were two other women having lunch with them. One was Balbino's girlfriend who owned the beauty shop downstairs. It was a short memorable visit with their uncle. After they said their good-byes, Pa Pa took the girls sightseeing in San Francisco.

They returned to San Jose for dinner at the Wirz'. The three kidzes could not stop talking! They were older and had stories to share of their lives. At that point the Wirz' realized they would not be able to keep these three apart.

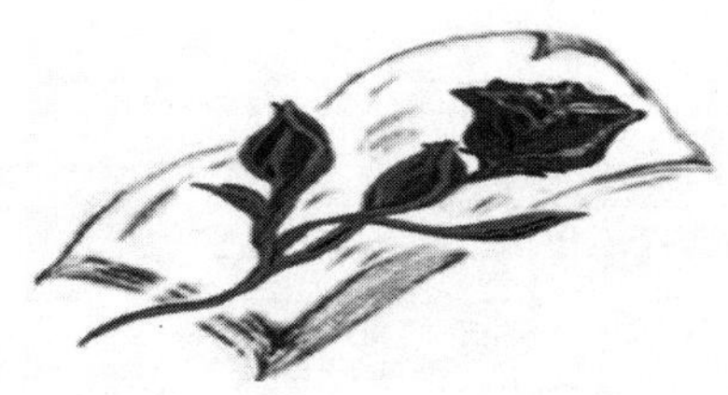

Chapter Four

"Oh, Throw Me a Towel"

Rose at fifteen *(Courtesy Rose Olivo)*

Rose was fifteen, Rodger eighteen, and Marie twelve. Pa Pa made an unexpected trip to San Jose with exciting news. He announced to his kidzes and the rest of the family that he had been granted American Citizenship. He was proud to show them the certificate dated September 14, 1933.

Rodger was a senior at St. Joseph's High School and recently received his driver's license. On his sisters' next visit to the Wirz', he excitedly asked if he could take them for a ride. They agreed, and he felt proud as a peacock driving them in the maroon-colored 1933 Chrysler DeSota four-door sedan.

The usual dinner at the Wirz' ended with the three kidzes sitting on the front porch and exchanging stories. Marie gave updates on the latest news about their relatives. The doctor had diagnosed Nana with diabetes and she was giving herself insulin shots. Rose squirmed and Rodger rolled his eyes.

Marie sometimes spent the weekend with Uncle Jim or Aunt Josephine and Uncle Tony. Once they took her to visit Pa Pa in Campo Seco, and stopped in Gilroy to visit Aunt Michaela, Nana's sister. She had not changed a bit, wearing the same-feathered hat, black blouse, and black full-length flared skirt. The aunt and uncles were good to Marie. They would take her to the movies and to the Moose Lodge for dancing. She had recently been to a Shirley Temple movie and told her sister and brother every detail. Rose had not yet been to a movie theatre and enjoyed the story.

Rose and Rodger listened intently when Marie gave them a detailed account of the time Uncle Cooney took her to watch the lynchings of John M. "Jack" Holmes and Thomas H. "Harold" Thurmond. The county had imprisoned the two men for the murder of Brooke L. Hart, the twenty-two-year-old son of Alex

J. Hart, the owner of San Jose's second largest department store. The lynchings took place at the corner of First and St. John Streets in St. James Park, near the county jail. The outrage in Santa Clara County over the Hart murder had brewed to a boiling point. Uncle Cooney and Marie stood and watched as the mob grew to over five thousand. They saw many of their neighbors and friends. Attempts to control the mob were fruitless. Rodger had arrived late and had to watch from the back of the crowd. Rose listened to it on the radio at home.

The murder occurred over Thanksgiving Holiday weekend and arraignment was scheduled for Monday. On Sunday, the townspeople stormed the jailhouse, broke down the doors, and dragged the prisoners out into the street. Those within reach beat on the prisoners, leaving them a bloody mess. Uncle Cooney and Marie watched as the mob tore off the prisoners' clothing and spat at them. Newspaper reporters from the San Jose Mercury Herald snapped photographs. The vigilantism went on all day, November 26, 1933.

San Jose Mercury Herald

MOB LYNCHES HART KIDNAPERS

Citizens Storm Jail Overpower Officers

San Jose Mercury Herald, November 27, 1933 *(Courtesy San Jose Mercury)*

EXTRA

THE POST ENQUIRER EXTRA

SAN JOSE VIGILANTES LYNCH 2 HART KILLERS

The Oakland Post Enquirer *(Copyrighted © 1933)*

The next morning, the San Jose Police Department in their Black Moriah arrest vehicles tried to collect all the newspapers before they hit the stands, still a good portion got distributed. The New York Times declared: "It was an outburst characterized by hysteria and ribaldry, with a frenzied rush for souvenirs after the naked bodies of the slayers were cut down." Newspapers across the nation reported on the lynchings in San Jose, as a "crazy," "bloodthirsty," and "savage" act. Many reflected on how such a thing could happen in a quiet, civilized town like San Jose. No one was ever prosecuted for the lynchings, and the Governor James Rolph, praised the mob's actions. He said, "If anyone is arrested for this good job, I'll pardon them all."

Hart's Department Store opened in San Jose in 1866. It was located at the intersection of Market and Santa Clara Streets, just two blocks from City Hall, and two blocks from the County Jail. When he was in town, Hart's was one of Pa Pa's favorite places to take the girls shopping.

Pa Pa and the kidzes met again a year later. They did the typical shopping at Hart's and dining at the Wirz'. They had plenty to talk about, and had established a closer relationship. Rodger remained with the Wirz' while he worked and paid his own way through college. Tuition was thirty-five dollars a semester. Rose wanted to date, and Marie had more stories to tell.

Marie's big story this year was how she spent Uncle Cooney's rent money. During the Depression, he had allowed a tenant to live rent-free. The tenant subsequently left, a year passed, and the tenant showed up to pay the back rent. Uncle Cooney was not home, and the renter handed the money to her. He said, "Make sure you give this to your Uncle Cooney." Well, the temptation was too great and she spent the money. Rose and Rodger laughed in disbelief, all wide-eyed and dropped-jaw as she told them of her mischievous deed. Uncle Cooney had taught Marie to drive his Model "A" Ford when she was thirteen. She primed it, cranked it up, quickly ran back, jumped in and took off for the National Dollar Store. With the rent money, she bought a new coat, high-heel shoes, and a dress. Wow, was she excited! The dress was pretty, and this was the first time she ever wore high heels. When she returned home, she told Uncle Cooney what had happened and gave him what was left of the money. He was angry and stayed that way for a couple of months!

Hearing about the rent story piqued Rose's curiosity. She envied Marie's adventurous spirit, and wanted to get out more; Ma could not hold her back any longer. She shared with Rodger and Marie that all these years she thought Ma and Gabe had adopted her. The two of them were shocked to hear that and knew not to broach any further on the subject.

Rodger learned that Rose and Marie tried calling him many times—Mrs. Wirz did not pass on the messages. When his sisters would ask to speak to him, Mrs. Wirz answered, "I'm sorry, he's studying, and can't talk on the phone."

Rodger at sixteen and in 1944 *(Courtesy Rodger and Helene Nunez)*

Rodger was enjoying life at San Jose State College, a teachers college with a limited pre-med curriculum. He was pursuing his interest in medicine. During the summers he worked full-time, and during the school year he worked weekends, as a wholesale buyer for the Garden City Produce Company in San Jose. He drove a semi-trailer hauling produce for the company from southern California distributors. He bought melons in San Joaquin Valley, potatoes in Bakersfield, bell peppers in Coachella Valley, and citrus in Riverside. After two years in pre-med, he decided to change his major and pursue a career in sales. A year later he left college to work full-time for City Produce. Later he moved into a wholesales food job with the Bonfante Brothers in Watsonville, California. The Bonfante Brothers owned the Knob Hill Grocery chain. He worked for them until 1941, when he received a draft notice and joined the United States Army.

San Jose High School, 1930's *(Courtesy San Jose High School Year Book Advisor)*

Rose's new-style dress *(Courtesy Rose Olivo)*

The first day at San Jose High School was no different for Rose than any other young teenage girl. There was a definite hint of romance in the air. Her beautiful shapely figure and her mother's Mona Lisa smile intrigued many of the opposite sex. Over the years, her deep auburn hair had darkened to a rich silky black, complementing her attractive brown eyes, delicate fair skin and rosy cheeks. She was a natural beauty.

Friends considered her as conservative and studious. Her secret ambition was to become a commercial artist and to work for a big-name newspaper. She could sketch an illustration within minutes. One of her assignments was to sketch a new-style dress for a clothing store advertisement. The art instructor was in awe of her work.

With encouragement from Pa Pa, she took art courses that would further her goal of becoming a commercial artist. He had told her that her artistic ability ran in the family and she believed it. "I knew I could do it. It was what I wanted to do, and I was determined. I knew I could accomplish something as a commercial artist." In her junior year of high school she learned what she was up against. She attended a two-hour seminar at a career faire held in the school's auditorium. The faire included presentations on careers in commercial art. To her dismay, all the presenters were male and the majority of students were boys. The girls were directed toward opportunities as secretaries and receptionists. The day was a huge disappointment and she left disillusioned and doubtful about her ambitions.

A frightening thought occurred to her. The field of commercial art was a man's world and she felt intimidated. She wondered what the future would hold. She knew Ma could not, and would not, send her to college. Hopes and aspirations had gone by the wayside. She did not try to pursue commercial art any further. It was time for concessions and to make the best of things.

She excelled in food preparation and sewing. She was frugal, coaxing nutritious meals from a shoestring budget, making them attractive and delicious. She could take fabric remnants and expertly sew garments in the latest styles.

While reading books, she would pause to write some poetry. She was an avid reader and often finished an entire book in a day. She found comfort in the Lord and in the Bible. Singing was her other secret ambition. She had a beautiful soprano voice with a great appreciation of music.

Pa Pa came to town again and picked up Marie and then Rose. They went shopping for the day at Kress and Hart's Department Stores. Due to their age, it became difficult for him to please the girls when it came to shopping. He had to start a new tradition of giving them money, and they would go off on their own. He and the girls would still make their stop at the Crystal Creamery and go out for lunch. Then they would end up at the Wirz' for dinner.

She had two special friends through high school: the Torreto twins, Rose and Mary. Her other high school friends were Leona Gori, Leona Chimenti, Olga Gileo, Angie La Fano, Liz Desino, Marietta Companio, and Elaine Gustason who lived across the street and walked with her to and from school. Like most teenagers, they spent their spare time talking on the phone, exchanging teenage secrets. The girls wore Oxford shoes, sweaters, and long skirts, innocently showing off their girlish figures. They enjoyed going to football games. After the games, they would meet boys around the school building to sneak a kiss. If the boys were lousy kissers, the girls would say, "Oh, throw me a towel."

Mid-day dances at school were a big hit, as was an occasional movie on the weekend; mainly Shirley Temple movies. That was about the extent of her outside socializing. Ma was sixty-three and weak from age-related ailments. With Ma, school, and the hardships of the Depression, she felt emotionally torn apart, pulled in all directions.

Rose met Rodger occasionally, in passing, on their way to school; it was a welcomed surprise and joy. The two tried to walk the same route to school at the same time. When they did meet up, it was usually prior to eight o'clock in the morning somewhere along San Fernando Street, between Third and Fourth Streets. They kept each other up-to-date on what was happening in their lives. Sometimes it gave her and her friends an opportunity to meet college boys. They would whisper and giggle in their girlish way whenever they saw some handsome boy with Rodger. Rose would give him a gentle nudge or roll of her eyes which meant an introduction was in order.

Chapter Five

"Hiya Rose"

Rose noticed Rodger talking with one of his friends on the corner of Third and San Fernando Streets. The friend was Nello, whom she had seen around quite often. The boys and girls called him "James Cagney," because he looked so much like him. They could have been twins.

Nello John Olivo *(Courtesy Rose Olivo)*

Nello was asking Rodger about getting into San Jose State College. He was taking a high school postgraduate course in The Mechanical and Vocational Arts Department at San Jose Technical High School, located next to San Jose High School. The instructor was A.R. Nichols. Nello's childhood dream was to become a scientist. His friends had chosen the Technical High School and influenced him to consider the plumbing trade instead of college.

The two chatted while many people walked by. Nello did not know Rose, and when she walked up to them he did not ask Rodger to introduce him. Instead it was Rose who gave Rodger a nudge and asked for an introduction. He turned and said, "Hiya, Rose, you on your way to school? Here, I want you to meet Nello." That is all he said. It was an unexpected yet delightful introduction. Rose was sixteen at the time and Nello nineteen. Once she got Nello's attention, he could not take his eyes off her. He asked to walk with her toward the school and then they parted at Fourth Street. He walked in one direction and she the other. When the two learned they lived in the same general area, they began walking to and from school together and became more acquainted.

Nello did not have a phone at home and relied on meeting Rose on their way to school. It was love at first sight. They became an item, and he called her "Honey." She spent most of her study time at the East San Jose Library and Nello would meet up with her there after his school to walk her home. Eventually he was introduced to Ma, who reluctantly accepted the courtship.

George, Wayne, and Nello on three-seater bike (left to right) *(Courtesy Rose Olivo)*

Rose found Nello quite handsome, well-dressed, clean cut, and polite. They spent the next year-and-a-half courting. They loved walking through the town square and stopping for ice cream at the Crystal Creamery. It was a hot spot where the high school kids went after school. In fact it was the same Crystal Creamery Pa Pa took her to when he came to town. Vanilla, strawberry, and chocolate were the choices, Rose and Nello stuck with vanilla. After they were served they would sit on a park bench and talk. For group get-togethers they would cook a pot of beans at Ma's to take to Alum Rock Park for a picnic.

The two occasionally rode bikes. Nello even built a three-seater by matching parts from three old broken-down bikes. He, his brother George and their friend Wayne, rode that bike to and from San Francisco on a stretch of dirt road that later became the Bayshore Highway. "All in a days ride," he would say.

She admired his musical talent. He played a twelve-finger Nick Hale Accordion his father bought for him from Anderson's Music Store when he was ten years old. He received private lessons and learned to play *Peg O' My Heart*, *Roll out the Barrel* and many polkas. He had permanently injured the fourth finger on his left hand and had no feeling in that finger. He told her the oft'-repeated story of how it happened.

He was with his younger twin brothers, Georgie and Jimmy, walking along Santa Clara Street. They stopped and were staring at some candy on display in the window of a restaurant. Nello spotted his favorite candy and the twins dared him to shove his hand through the window to get it. They started wrestling and accidentally knocked Nello into the window. He shattered the glass, cutting his hand and finger. From then on, he was unable to bend his finger. He was injured for life and when he returned home, got a beating from his father.

Nello had a rough time at Longfellow Elementary. He started to skip classes and the school notified his father. The "ole man," gave him the belt, as he did many times. Sometimes, he would break loose and run for it. When he did, his father would run after him, cussing and throwing rocks. Finally the school put Nello on probation, with a truant officer to keep track of him. It was rough in those days—the truant officers knew where to find you and what to do with you when they did. Nello said, "Yeah, then I had a school teacher by the name of Michael. My mother had invited him over to the house to teach me math and give me private tutoring, because I wasn't getting all my lessons done in school. I was skipping school and playing hooky. I got a beating for something I didn't do, and I got mad, so I didn't want to go to school. Well, I'd go to school, and I played hooky a lot. They beat me up for a reason, not my mother, my father did anyhow, and I deserved the licking I got. After a while, I buckled down with my studies, became a good student, and joined school activities."

When Rose read on the front page of the San Jose Mercury Herald that her Aunt Jessie Lasada had died in a tragic car accident, she insisted that Ma let her attend the funeral. Nello too, read the paper and stopped by to see her. She learned that he knew her Aunt Jessie and they comforted each other.

Nello was a year older than Aunt Jessie. They attended Longfellow Elementary together and were in the same class. They would meet at the Majestic Dance Hall on Third and Santa Clara Streets for dances.

At Longfellow Elementary, Rodger knew of Nello before they became friends through Aunt Jessie. Rose felt a connection to her aunt from the time they used to play together as young girls, before she and her siblings were separated. Throughout the years Rose stayed apprised of her aunt during her annual visits with Rodger and Marie.

Aunt Jessie was adventuresome, on the wild side. She loved to take Marie shopping. In the stores, she particularly liked the lacy undergarments and nylons. She would try them on and then stuff them in her purse. When the two of them returned home, Nana would grab her purse and look through it. No doubt she knew what Aunt Jessie was up to, she had caught her with sticky fingers before, and she did not want Marie picking up bad habits. Nana would reach for the 'leather strap,' and Aunt Jessie would run upstairs to jump into the laundry chute. She would hide halfway down the chute, balancing on a narrow ledge, far enough from either end that Nana could not reach her. She waited until she heard Nana leave, and then she would climb out and escape from the house.

Nello in back row with traffic star pin, Jessie seated in front row second from right, and Alice A. Treat Principal of Longfellow School *(Courtesy Rose Olivo)*

Other times, Aunt Jessie would walk past the avocado farm near her home and helped herself to the ripe avocados. She would eat them along the way, without any thought of paying for them.

When she was nineteen, she was in a serious motorcycle accident. She and her boyfriend were riding on the eucalyptus-tree-lined El Camino Real when he lost control and crashed into one of the trees. Her boyfriend broke an arm and banged up his leg; Aunt Jessie fell backwards onto the street, fractured her skull and was unconscious for four weeks.

She loved the "Roaring Twenties" and fit right in as a fashionable flapper, wearing shapeless shift dresses and high heels without stockings. She styled her hair in a wind-blown fashion, short and sleek. Her fiancé, Bill Yeomans, was a twenty-one-year-old Stanford University student from Coxsackie, New York. The two planned to marry after spring semester. They went to a dance party in San Francisco and on their way back were involved in a terrible auto accident. They crashed head-on into a car driven by Dr. C. Bruce George, age twenty-six, and his companion Miss Corabelle Tillson, age twenty-three, a nurse at the San Jose Hospital. Bruce and Corabelle were returning from a dance at the Los Altos Country Club for the San Jose Hospital Nurses Alumnae Association. The crash occurred between Mountain View and Sunnyvale in the middle lane of the Bayshore Highway, known today as Highway 101.

Like her sister Lydia, she died at a young age. The county considered the crash as one of the most disastrous collisions in highway history. Negligence

Jessie Lasada *(Courtesy Evelyn Simon)*

on the part of both drivers was the verdict of the coroner's jury. Coroner C.C. Spaulding and his Chief Deputy, Louis Provenzano, conducted the inquest held at Spangler Mortuary in Mountain View. They heard from twelve witnesses. It happened at 3:00 a.m. Sunday morning, May 12, 1935. The four young people involved all suffered severe head injuries and were unconscious upon impact. All except Aunt Jessie died on the way to Milo Hospital. Aunt Jessie had a basal fracture of the skull, a brain concussion, bruises, lacerations, and was unconscious. The doctors thought for a while that she had a chance to survive, instead she died two days later. Marie was present at Aunt Josephine's home when the police delivered the personal effects and bloody clothes. She was horrified at the sight and burst out crying.

The memories of Aunt Jessie were vivid for Rose and Nello. They held hands in prayer as they sat on Ma's front porch. Nello was unable to attend the funeral, Rose went alone.

Marie was sitting in the front pew of the church as she looked over her shoulder and watched people enter. She noticed Rose standing shyly and alone in the back. None of the family members saw her or greeted her. Freddie and his sister Frieda Hinman, good friends of the family, spoke with her. Freddie was tall with dark brown hair and a secret admirer of Aunt Jessie. He left the funeral with Rose, and as he walked her part-way home, he fell to the ground and cried. She helped him back up and they consoled each other.

The family returned to Aunt Josephine's home on Anita Street for a reception. The buffet table was decorated with orange geraniums. They were Aunt Jessie's favorite color and flower. People kept arriving, bringing platters of food. Marie wondered—what happened to Rose?

That evening, when Nello visited with Rose, he proceeded to tell her more about the Majestic Dance Hall. She had heard it was the hangout for the young group. Nello would sneak out of the house around nine o'clock at night after everyone went to bed. It was a little tricky keeping his pet dog, "Boots," quiet. He would get dressed and leave. After a couple of hours at the Majestic, he would head home, crawl through the window, and go to bed. He said, "I didn't dance with anyone in particular, I just went to dance. I love to dance." Sometimes he took his accordion with him and played.

Nello in scout uniform with his pet dog, Boots *(Courtesy Rose Olivo)*

In his first year at San Jose Technical High School, he played with one of the Figone brothers in a five-piece band at the "Poppy Cabin" nightclub, on Highway 101 in Palo Alto. The band consisted of an accordionist, bugler, drummer, clarinetist, and pianist, as well as a singer. In retrospect, he wished he had stayed on with Figone who did quite well for himself, and later on opened his own music store.

Nello was talented, good looking, and popular in high school. He had a number of girls interested in him. He said, "Some would follow me home, and I'd run into my back yard, jump the fence, and beat it down the street to my friend's house. I'd leave them there talking to my father."

Pa Pa was surprised when Nello greeted him at Ma's home on his next visit to town. He immediately was not impressed and played the fatherly role, questioning him. He was not pleasant. He was troubled, and seemed ready to lash out at anyone.

"I no like–a him, he's–a trouble," said Pa Pa.

Rose tried to convince him that Nello was a good man and a good catch. "Rodger introduced us." She told him, "Nello is an over-achiever. He was student body president at Longfellow Elementary, captain of the baseball team, captain of the traffic department, a community chess player, and a Boy Scout Trooper until the age eighteen. I love to listen to him play his accordion. He is attending San Jose Technical High School, with a promised five-year apprenticeship in plumbing with the H.J. Pasco Plumbing Company. What more would you like to know?"

The fact that she had obviously done her homework when it came to presenting Nello to Pa Pa did not faze him. He had made up his mind—he did not like him! No man would be good enough for his daughter. He stood there, stroking his cheek and chin with his right hand, half-frowning with a raised eyebrow and piercing look.

The visit with Pa Pa was short, yet special. He gave Rose spending money and a few gold nuggets for safekeeping. He said nothing of the sadness that seemed to overshadow him. He had received news that his brother Antonio, was missing. Antonio was employed as a watchman and fell overboard from a barge at Pier 40, in the San Francisco Bay. The crew reported the incident to authorities as an accident. On May 24, 1935, a rescue diving team found Antonio's body, too badly decomposed for an autopsy. Pa Pa and Balbino believed the incident was not accidental, and filed for an inquest. None of the children had met their Uncle Antonio and Pa Pa spared them the news of the sad loss of his brother.

Rose and Nello enjoyed each other. They went out to eat at "The Five Spot" hamburger joint, and to Shirley Temple, James Cagney, and cowboy movies at "The Victory Theatre" on First Street. They would go to her school dances every Friday at noon and visited with his friends on the weekend.

Ma was renting a home at East Santa Clara Street when, without notice, the property owner told her, "You have to leave right away. The house is sold." Ma and Rose had spent years in the home and were shocked. The new owner tore it down after they left to make a parking lot for the corner Chinese Grocery and Furniture Store. Ma took Rose and moved to Oakland to stay with relatives for the summer. Nello could not stand being apart from her and went there to see her.

Ma shared Pa Pa's apprehension toward Nello and did not want Rose to be with him. She was jealous. He said, "She did not want me around. I think she heard us talking about wanting to get married." They had been dating for six months when they started talking about marriage. They even talked about having four children, two boys and two girls.

East Santa Clara Street *(Courtesy Barbara Olivo Cagle)*

Rose and Ma returned to San Jose in the fall and found a rent-to-own house on East Santa Clara Street, a few blocks from the last house. Rose resumed her studies at San Jose High School and dated Nello. He got his first job at the Bell Foundry, working after school on bells for fire trucks and ambulances. He earned fifteen cents an hour grinding and polishing bells.

Chapter Six

Baby Doll

Nello's parents, Enrico John Olivo and Maria Isola "Lena" Ciardella *(Courtesy Rose Olivo)*

Enrico John Olivo was born July 17, 1874, in the small town of Todi and grew up in Massa Martana, Province of Perugia, Italy. He was fifty-seven years old when Rose met him; a short, stocky man standing five-feet-two inches and weighing one hundred and eighty-two pounds. His dark brown eyes and balding grey hair gave him a distinguished appearance, as did the noticeable scar on the right side of his mouth. He often wore dark glasses and a cap.

Maria Isola Ciardella, "Lena," was born June 28, 1887, in Capannori and grew up in Lammari, a small town in the Province of Lucca, Italy. She was forty-one years old when Rose met her; a short woman, standing four-feet-eight inches, with brown eyes and long brown hair that she kept coiled and pinned on the top of her head. As the years passed, Lena also became stocky, weighing two hundred and twelve pounds. She noticeably wore a few different housedresses at the same time, one over the other.

Nello took Rose to his house to introduce her to his parents. He lived with them in a seven-room one-story home on Bush Street, across from the Western Pacific Railroad Station. It had a barn and a garden lined with a long row of

Bush Street *(Courtesy Rose Olivo)*

grapes and various fruit trees inside of a large fenced yard. As he walked her up the front steps, his parents were waiting at the door. Before he could say anything, his mother, Lena, came out, grabbed her hand and greeted her, pulling her into the house and offering her a seat in their living room.

"Ciao! Ciao! Come Va? Molto bella!" ("Hello! Hello! How are you? Very pretty!") Lena nodded her head in approval and waved her hands to Nello, "Neela, what a 'Baby-Doll.' Where your manners are? Go, go get us all something to drink." From that point on, she called Rose, Baby Doll.

Rose glanced at Nello and quietly giggled at how she pronounced his name "Neela." He whispered to her, "My mother called me that every since I can remember, it's her accent."

Lena sat down next to Rose, holding her hand. She sincerely tried to communicate in broken English. As Nello returned with some iced tea, Lena looked at her and then up to Nello for reassurance in translation, and with raised eyebrows, said *"La capisco benissimo,"* ("I understand you very well.")

Absorbing the family history and realizing some of their common background had Rose intrigued. Both of their parents had immigrated to the United States to start a new life, leaving their families behind. Enrico and Lena met in San Jose, and that is where they married on July 25, 1913.

She enjoyed the visit and delighted in meeting his parents. When it was getting late and time to go Enrico and Lena said their good-byes, *"E stato un piacere conoscerla. Arrivederci!"* ("It was nice meeting you. See you later.") Now that his parents met her, they expected him to bring her often. On the next visit, Lena greeted her, *"Vieni, entra Baby Doll. Voglio farti incontrare Zia Asunta, Zio Peter e suo Zio Giuseppe."* ("Baby Doll, come on in. I want you to meet Aunt Asunta, Uncle Peter and Uncle Joseph.")

Asunta Ciardella and Peter Masini
(Courtesy Pasquale Greco)

Aunt Asunta was the oldest of the Ciardella family. She was sweet and quiet, and spoke little English. She and Peter were friendly and invited Nello and Rose to their ranch in Gilroy for a barbecue. They had four grown children, Mary, Frances "Fanny," Dominic and Joseph, and three grandchildren, Harry, Doris, and Mary, belonging to Fanny. Aunt Asunta looked like her sister Lena, short in height and stocky. At the barbecue, Nello brought Rose up-to-date on the rest of his family.

Uncle Joseph "Zio Beppe" enjoyed the women too much to be interested in marriage. He loved music and took his turntable and microphone to the family get-togethers; it provided an opportunity for everyone to listen to music and dance. Later during World War II, he took over the Novelty Cleaners and Laundry on East Empire Street in San Jose. The government interned the Japanese owners during the war and after the war they could not return to claim the ownership of the business.

Joseph Ciardella *(Courtesy Rose Olivo)*

Many times Uncle Joe would take Nello with him to pick-up and deliver the laundry. He would sit on the front seat, and they would talk, laugh, and have a good time together.

The business had famous customers. Once in 1929, he took Nello with him on a delivery to President Herbert Hoover's home at Stanford University, in Palo Alto. As it happened, President Hoover was in Washington, D.C.; none-the-less it was an exciting experience to be at the home.

Humbert Joseph Ciardella, Sr.
(Courtesy Humbert Joseph Ciardella, Jr.)

Uncle Humberto dropped the "o" from his name when he arrived in America. He went by "Johnny." Uncle Johnny became a successful businessman, owning rentals and several cafés: the Capitol Café, Roma Club, L.A. Club, and the Shamrock which burned down during his ownership. He used his clubs for gambling, meeting halls, band performances, and dances.

Rose enjoyed hearing Nello's stories and did not realize how late it was getting. "I need to get back home soon," she told him. After she said her good-byes, Aunt Asunta interjected, *"Hei voi due! Per favore venite presto al nostro ranch in Gilroy, va bene? Avremo un barbecue e potrete incontrare il resto della famiglia."* ("Oh, you both! Please come to our ranch in Gilroy soon, yes? We will have a barbecue and you can meet the rest of the family.") Uncle Peter said, *"Ricorda, chi va piano va sano e va lontano. Chiao!"* ("Remember, if you go slow—you go strong for a long time. Bye!")

Ma was annoyed when the two got home late. Rose could not stop talking about Nello's family, and Ma feared that she was beginning to lose control of their relationship.

On Rose's next visit with Lena, she said, "I'd like to hear more about Nello and his brothers. I want to know everything about your family!" She knew the adage: "Give any mother a cue to talk about her children, and you'll sit for a long time." This is what she learned:

Nello was born on December 12, 1914, at 11:16 a.m. in the family home on Balz Aley Street, in San Jose, with the assistance of Mrs. M. Belssani, a midwife. He was the oldest of four boys. When he was one year old, the family moved to South Montgomery Street, the third house from the south corner, near Santa Clara Street, where the Chase Lumber Mill, Greyhound Bus Depot, and Holy Family Catholic Church were located. As he grew up, he would hang around the lumber mill. Harold Chase, the mill's owner, was a first baseman for the New York Yankees. He took a liking to Nello, and they became good ole "buddies." He spent time teaching him how to play baseball and pitch.

Nello was a pitcher and captain of his school's baseball team. He told of the day when he was peeking through the fence of the Sodality Ballpark, on the future site of the Orchard Supply Hardware store on White Street. It was where the Major League Baseball teams came to San Jose to play their games. He had removed one of the fence boards to get a better look; he was right behind the batter's cage. The day was October 26, 1927. Babe Ruth, Lou Gehrig, Lefty O'Doul and other pros were there for an exhibition baseball game. San Jose had 60,000 inhabitants then. Babe Ruth called San Jose "that little burg in the prune trees." The Yankees were playing, and he was at bat. He saw Nello and said, "I'm going to knock a home run for you and give you the ball with both our names on it." Babe Ruth hit an inside-the-park home run and did as he promised. Nello ran home with the ball in excitement, showed it to his family and friends, and then hid it in a safe place.

He dug out the baseball and showed it to Rose that day. He had the ball for years before it was lost in the shuffle of moving.

Lena, Georgie, Jimmy (left), and Georgie, Gino, Jimmy, and Lena *(Courtesy Pasquale Greco)*

Nello told of the birth of his twin brothers, Georgie and Jimmy, on May 11, 1916. He vividly recalled his mother holding the twins in her arms. He said that was his earliest recollection of them.

Rose enjoyed hearing the stories, yet it was time to go home and check on Ma. Lena hugged her, looking forward to seeing her again, she said, *"Ci sentiamo domani sera."* ("I will talk to you tomorrow evening.") On the way home, Nello told a story about his mother and his youngest brother Gino who was born on August 24, 1920. His family was living on Bush Street, Nello was fourteen and Gino eight. Gino regularly hung around the nearby icehouse. He loved sucking on ice chips and swallowing them whole. The family thought the constant cold environment ultimately resulted in his fatally contracting scarlet fever and diphtheria. It was devastating to Lena when she found him dead in his bed. Enrico purchased the family's cemetery plot. Gino's casket was visible through the glass door of his above ground monument. It set on a slab of cement, not far from Lydia's grave site, at the Santa Clara Mission Cemetery.

Gino and his grave site *(Courtesy Rose Olivo)*

Lena could not get over Gino's death. What mother does? She took the sorrowful loss to a higher dimension when Nello accompanied her to the cemetery. He watched as his mother literally got down on her hands and knees to break through the glass door of Gino's monument. Moaning she scratched and pried open the casket with her cane. She gasped and screamed as she managed to clutch onto the bones of her son's feet. Bellowing out with grief, and uncontrollable tears, she cried, "Gino, mi bambino! Oh, Gino mi bambino!" Rocking back and forth on her knees, she stuffed both of his foot bones into her purse. She took them home and kept them by her bedside. The story was shocking and took Rose by surprise.

Following Gino's death, Lena needed someone to look after her. Nello's father hired a French woman to help her with the boys and housework. She was a nice woman, and the two got along great. The adults had difficulty speaking English and understood little of it; at home they preferred to speak the Italian Tuscany dialect and French. Lena had been a nurse in France, and could speak French fluently. The French woman helped Lena teach the boys Italian and French. Despite the fact that the boys understood all three languages, they would only speak English.

Nello on deliveries *(Courtesy Rose Olivo)*

Rose, and sometimes Nello, helped Ma with tamale and enchilada orders. It was becoming evident that her health was declining and she needed extra help. Her myocarditis was now chronic. Nello visited more often and Ma was beginning to warm up to him. He kept the two entertained while they prepared the tamales and enchiladas, and packed them in boxes.

He even offered to help deliver the orders, which allowed Rose to stay at home with Ma. He rode his bike to the stores, homes, and business locations, and collected the money.

He found himself juggling his time carefully after his father, Enrico, broke a leg at work. A railroad tie fell on him and he could no longer drive the car. Enrico had no choice other than to retire after the accident. He gave Nello use of the car, a 1930 Dodge sedan.

Chapter Seven

Giant Dipper

Nello and Rose Olivo December 5, 1935 *(Courtesy Rose Olivo)*

Rose's academic standing allowed her to graduate in early June 1935, the end of her junior year at San Jose High School. She, like many of her friends, had completed the required high school courses. Her busy schedule, shuffling time between Ma, Nello, and school, had not affected her grades, and she graduated with honors. It was a huge disappointment to join the many students whose families could not afford to pay for the graduation ceremony. Yet, she took pride in her grades and accomplishments.

At the Five Spot, she and her friends chatted about going out into the world. Some of them were going on to college, others into the work force; most of them had marriage plans.

The following week was busy making plans for Nello's graduation from San Jose Technical High School. Rose and his mother proudly attended the ceremony. The Technical High School did not have an assembly hall and the event took place in the San Jose High School's auditorium. His mother left after the ceremony and Rose stayed. There was a big party for the graduates. Nello brought his accordion; he had promised the Student Body President, Lawrence Herrera he would play the accordion to kick off the celebration party. Many people were in attendance and he was nervous.

When Nello opened the accordion case he realized that he had misplaced his music sheets. He knew the music; however, he normally played from the sheets. He started playing "Peg O' My Heart," by Fred Fisher, and played the whole piece off-key. He knew it was off-key and hoped no one else knew, except Rose. She knew the song well—he had played it for her and Ma many times. It did not seem to faze anyone and his classmates danced in celebration. He cringed; he wanted to play his best. After the performance, he introduced Rose to his friends and some of their wives. They laughed when he mentioned his off-key performance and then left to go out to dinner at the Oyster Loaf on East Santa Clara Street.

A few days after graduation, the H.J. Pascoe Plumbing Company of San Jose contacted Nello to begin his five-year plumber's apprenticeship. He now had a secure job with H.J. Pascoe Plumbing and joined the Plumbers' Union Local 393. Within a month, in his spare time, his father purchased the supplies and he installed all new plumbing in the house on Bush Street.

Rose and Nello had been dating for more than a year-and-a-half and he had not yet popped the question. On a Tuesday, December 3, 1935, he rushed home after work. He had thought about it all night the night before and all that day at work. After taking a shower and getting dressed, he stood combing his hair and staring in the mirror. He was particular about the way he parted his hair, wanting to look like James Cagney. He was practicing how he was going to ask Rose to marry him. He rushed over to her home and told her he wanted to speak to her privately. She turned her head and called out to Ma, "Ma, I will be right back. I am sitting out on the front steps with Nello."

Nello was not a flower and gift type of man. He did not have a ring to give to her. What he did have was magnetic charm. With his humor and music, he swept her off her feet and stared into her beautiful brown eyes, as she did his. He clasped her hands in his and bent his head close toward her. She could feel the warmth of his breath.

"Honey, I love you. I want to marry you now. Let's run away. Let's just do it. Let's elope. We can tell our parents after the fact. 'Anyhows', you know they will not approve otherwise," he said softly with conviction.

The Christmas season was well on its way with a chill in the air. She lived on a busy street with the light posts decorated in Christmas lights, garlands, and wreaths. The Christmas lights reflected in her eyes, making them glisten with excitement and emotion.

"Yes, I want to marry you, too. I love you, Nello. I don't want to wait any longer either. Our other friends are married or getting married, so why don't we?" she answered.

As young people in love do, they started to plot their plan of action. They had to use their imaginations. There were obstacles to get pass. She was not yet eighteen, and though Ma warmed up to him, she still did not like the Italian people. His parents would certainly not approve. With his new job they looked forward to any additional income he could provide. Pa Pa who was out of town should be consulted. Coupled with all these situations, Nello had little money to bring into a marriage.

Uncle Joe and Dorothy *(Courtesy Jeanette Olivo)*

Lena's brother, Uncle Joe and his friend Dorothy Leighton were in on the master plan from the beginning. Both were aware that the two loved each other and wanted to be together. They knew Nello was going to ask Rose to elope and came up with the perfect plan.

The plan was to take the scenic winding road through the rolling hills of the prominent resort community, Santa Cruz, which means 'holy cross.' Going to Santa Cruz, thirty miles west of San Jose, was a regular Saturday outing for the two. Whenever Ma's sister came in for a day's visit to relieve Rose, Nello would take her to Santa Cruz in his father's car. They loved going for a stroll on the boardwalk, sunbathing, and walking along the beach. Swimming was out of the question, all Nello would do was get his feet a little wet; he had not learned to swim and would not have anything to do with it even though Rose tried to teach him.

Santa Cruz *(Courtesy Diane Zuniga)*

December 5, 1935, was a cool day on the coast. Nello took the day off from work and looked handsome in his light gray pin striped suit. Rose arranged with Ma's sister to come and help her for the day. She looked radiant in her silky orchid-colored dress. Peeking between the curtains of the living room window, she anxiously awaited for Uncle Joe, Dorothy, and Nello to pull up in the laundry truck. When they arrived she quickly grabbed her sweater, went to Ma, and with a secretive smile, kissed her on the cheek. It was still early in the morning. He was a few days from his twenty-first birthday and she three months to her eighteenth.

Santa Cruz Court House, 1935 and Miramar Fish Grotto in Santa Cruz *(Courtesy YoungHea Olivo and Diane Zuniga)*

Giant Dipper *(Courtesy Diane Zuniga)*

The drive to the courthouse and filling out the proper papers took most of the day. There were so many discrepancies on their marriage certificate: they fudged their ages a little and said they were twenty-one and eighteen; the witnesses and parents' names were misspelled; Rose gave Espinosa as her last name. It was not until after the county clerk recorded the marriage certificate that she found out that Espinosa was not her legal name. Yet, Ma had always told her that she had adopted her. The one thing they knew for sure was that they were getting married at the Santa Cruz Court House, by Donald Younger, Judge of the Police Court. Uncle Joe and Dorothy were there as witnesses. When it was all over, the four of them were starving. They went their separate ways and agreed to meet up around dusk.

Nello surprised Rose by taking her to dinner at the Miramar Fish Grotto, an Italian restaurant that had opened earlier that year on the Santa Cruz Wharf. He had saved up his money for a crab dinner, her favorite. The restaurant's cuisine and ambiance were exquisite. It was the best. A band played *You May Not Be An Angel*, a song written for the movie musical, *Twenty Million Sweethearts.*

The two turned to each other and said with emotion and grins, "There's our song!"

After dinner, they walked hand-in-hand along the boardwalk, breathing in the fresh sea air, living in the moment of love, wishing the moment would last forever, and then BOOM! Reality set in. Now what were they going to tell their parents when they got back? Except for Uncle Joe and Dorothy, no one knew of their elopement, soon the whole world would know.

They decided to top off the celebration with a big finish and what could be bigger than the Giant Dipper roller coaster, a four-minute ride on one mile of wooden track on the boardwalk. It was one of the big attractions at Santa Cruz and they had yet to ride it. The seaside view of the ocean from the roller coaster was spectacular. They sat in the front and braced for an exciting and thrilling ride. Rose snuggled up tightly into Nello's side, holding onto the steel hand bar in front of her for the take-off. Its dark tunnel entrance, with sweeping fans and the solid, steep drop brought laughter and delight. Little did they know that their life together would be much like the roller coaster ride.

Uncle Joe and Dorothy spotted them as they exited the Giant Dipper. They met up and decided it was time to head for home. Uncle Joe and Dorothy had spiffed up the van with "Just Married" written on it and cans stringing from the bumper. It was a fun ride all the way home, with cars honking at them, waving, and cheering.

They went to Ma's home first. Nello went in with Rose to announce the good news. She stood shyly, turning her head aside while raising her right shoulder into her cheek, worrying what Ma's reaction would be. An old woman now and weaker from her illness, Ma mustered enough strength and authority to say, after a long sigh, "The deed is already done. Nello, I cannot allow Rose to leave. I need her. You can come here and live with us. Besides, you know I can certainly use your help. My only request is that you do not sleep together until Rose turns eighteen." The two of them hugged Ma, and then Nello left.

Uncle Joe and Dorothy drove him home. His parents and brothers were in the front room. "Boots," their dog greeted him first, and then he came right out with the news.

"Mom, Dad, I have something to tell you. Rose and I got married today."

"Scusa, che cosa hai detto? Cos'é successo?" ("Excuse me, what did you say? What happened?") asked Enrico unbelievingly.

Nello's parents began releasing a great deal of their hot Italian feelings. Lena stood up with her hands on her hips, shaking her head back and forth, "No! No! No! No! Neela!" she exclaimed in disbelief. She put her hands on her head, as if she was pulling her hair out, and cried, *"EEEE-I-YI-YI! Che cosa ti é saltato in testa di fare una cosa del genere, Dio mio! Che cosa farai adesso, Neela?"* ("EEEE-I-YI-YI! What were you thinking, running off and doing such a thing like that? Oh my God! Oh my God! What are you going to do now, Nello?") Enrico was so infuriated, that his face turned beet red, and he shook his finger at him and yelled, *"Stronzo, che cazzo hai fatto! Che cazzo hai fatto!"* ("God-damn you, you bull-shit! You bull-shit!")

Nello told them, "It's done! I'm packing my things and moving in with Rose and Ma. I'm going to lay low for awhile until both of you cool off." He did not waste any time, packed up as much as he could into his father's car, and took off back to Rose's house. Within three days, he was completely moved into Ma's.

Even though there were no wedding showers or receptions, the news of elopement spread like wildfire. Uncle Cooney wrote to Pa Pa and let him know. A couple of days later on their way to the library, they met up with Rodger who greeted them with a hug.

"Oh, you guys got married! Have you told Pa Pa yet?" he asked. He knew Pa Pa did not like Nello, and he would be hot!

"I sent him a letter right away. In fact, he should have it by now. I imagine we will be seeing him soon. Nello will talk to him." Rose answered nervously.

No sooner had the letter reached Campo Seco and Pa Pa was on his way to San Jose. Arriving at Marie's house he anxiously pounded on the door, yelling for Marie.

"Marie, let'sa go, I wanna go see Ros-a. I heard she married. I gotta go see her. Come on, we gotta go see Ros-a," he demanded.

Rodger was working at the time, so Pa Pa and Marie drove up to Ma's home unannounced. Nello rushed to the living room window, when he heard brakes screeching and a car door slamming. He watched Pa Pa get out of the car with a stern look on his face and obviously in a huff. He straightened out his trousers and headed for the front door. Nello knew he could speak piercingly mean, and did not want to face him. Rose opened the door. It was dark in the living room; there were no lights on. A flower-print curtain hung from a cord stretched across the center of the living room to separate the sleeping area. Marie stood behind Pa Pa, covering her mouth with her hand and chuckling when she saw Nello dart behind the curtain, leaving Rose to stand alone with Ma in defense of the marriage.

Pa Pa quickly swept a view of the living room, looking for Nello, his first words were, "Where'd that fella go? I gonna grab him by the throat and squeeze the livin' lif-e outta him!" Rose froze in embarrassment; everyone stood silently staring at him. He was so upset and over-heated that he grabbed for a handkerchief to wipe his sweaty brow.

Ma came through with words of wisdom and calmed Pa Pa down. She reassured him that they would have a place to stay as long as she was alive, and that they would not be sleeping together until Rose turned eighteen.

Pa Pa was a very proud and old-fashioned man. He said, "I'm-ma disappointed! Where'd I come from, the man ask-a ta take-a hand of another man's dahtar to marriage. That-a all I'm gonna say." He said his good-byes and gave Rose a tight hug. Then he held his hands firmly on her shoulders, looked her in the eyes and whispered, "You-a write me. You-a needs me you-a writes!" Moving away from Rose, Pa Pa said to Marie, "Marie, get your things, lets-a go."

Living under the same roof with Ma was difficult. They agreed that the rental house was too small; especially for later when they would be starting a family. Ma was practically an invalid and could not be left alone. She received a small monthly pension, about thirty dollars, and with Nello working, they managed. Rose did not look for outside work; she stayed at home taking care of Ma, it had become a full-time nursing job. Sometimes she and Nello went house hunting, most of the time he went alone, searching for the right-sized home for the three of them. He finally found the perfect place on North Montgomery Street.

The house on Montgomery Street was ideal. It was one block away from Rodger's home and would allow them to see each other more often. It also would make it easier for Pa Pa when he came to town. The family could go over to Rose and Nello's for get-togethers. Ma was not thrilled with the idea of more family, everyone else looked forward to time together.

The move worked out well. Rodger visited often, Marie not as much.

Rose read in her spare time. She liked reading Shakespeare, Chaucer's *Canterbury Tales,* and an anthology of poetry, especially Robert Frost, Walt Whitman's, *Leaves of Grass* and the *Holy Bible.* She drew closer to the church and would discuss her personal problems with a priest, rather than her friends. She had lost touch with them, their priorities and activities were so different now that she was married.

Whenever Nello had time to take her, she would visit with Marie. However, Marie would not stop by to see her, she did not like Ma.

"I don't want to see Ma! What do I want to see that OLD LADY for?" Ma had not softened her feelings with regard to Rose's family stopping by to visit, and she had no problem making the family feel unwelcome.

At the age of fourteen, Marie was well-endowed and looked like a woman. Rose was concerned about her. In the summer of 1935, Marie applied for her first job and got a job with the Greco Cannery on Julian Street. She lied about her age, passing herself off as eighteen. They hired her to work upstairs on the conveyors, packing string beans, peaches and other fruits and vegetables into cans. When the personnel office learned unofficially that she was not eighteen, and had not yet confirmed her real age, they assigned her downstairs to work alongside the younger help. She trimmed rejected fruit for gallon containers that the company would send to prisons and institutions. Even then, she continued lying about her age. The job required her to be at least fifteen. Rose realized she needed to be closer to Marie, and made it clear that the two could talk about anything, anytime.

Soprani Inc. Accordion, made in Italy *(Courtesy Nancy Castenholz)*

Summer and fall breezed by, and December 5th was around the corner. For their first wedding anniversary gift, Rose wanted to surprise Nello with an accordion. He had been admiring one for quite some time at Allen Young's Piano Store. It had the brilliance of ivory black with pearl inlay mosaic designs and rhinestones that shined like diamonds. Allen Young, the proprietor, attractively displayed the accordion in the window. Every time they strolled around the town square, Nello had to stop to look at it. On one particular stroll, she pulled his arm, and with little effort, coaxed him into the entrance of the store. He took a closer look at the accordion and gave it a trial play. Its quality-built bellows created the most amazing sound.

Rose looked into his eyes and said, "Nello, I've decided you deserve this accordion. I want you to have it, so I am buying it for you. I already spoke with Allen. He mentioned your friendship from your high school days and agreed to let us take it home today with just five dollars down and five dollars a month until paid in full. He is willing to sell it to us for one hundred and twenty-five dollars. We must not pass up such a good deal. I plan to make the monthly payments out of my allowance. Come on, Honey, let me buy this for you." With no hesitation, he kissed her, and with the biggest smiles, they purchased the accordion on contract. He was excited and could hardly wait to get home to play it. When they arrived home, he carefully unpacked his new accordion and played for hours. Rose knew that indeed, it was the best decision. Nello played it practically everyday for her and Ma.

One day Ma announced she could no longer make enchiladas and tamales. She was unable to get out of bed and required around-the-clock care.

Nello soon found it easier to conveniently sneak into Rose's arms for a kiss and to make love. The two took advantage of every opportunity to be together and were anxious to start a family. It was not an easy beginning with two miscarriages. Dr. Edward Amaral, Rose's family physician, assured her that it was common for women to miscarry in their first and second pregnancies. The next time she became pregnant in the early part of May 1936, she decided not to mention anything until her fourth month. Still slender, it was hard to tell that she was even pregnant.

Marie was not with Pa Pa on his next visit to town. She was fifteen now and had a new summer job sorting fruit for the California Packing Corporation, commonly referred to as CPC.

Pa Pa stopped to see Rose and Nello and they announced the good news. Rose was pregnant! The three of them drove to Enrico and Lena's home, and the celebration began. How funny it is that even the thought of becoming a grandparent can clear the air between families. Nello's parents brought out the "vino," he played the accordion and Pa Pa sang. Pa Pa said to Rose, "Ah, you gotta pretty nice fella." The merriment continued for hours. She took it easy, sitting back on the couch with that glow women get when they are expecting.

Lena had news of her own. For a long time, she and the French women that lived with them had been preparing her for citizenship. Her lack of English was a problem, so she was determined to memorize and recite the Constitution of the United States forward and backwards. The French woman translated every word for her and helped her with the pronunciation. Her citizenship date was June 9, 1936, at the Superior Court, Santa Clara County. Enrico and Lena's sister were there to witness. When her name was called, she became fearful the judge would ask her a question exposing her inability to speak English fluently and started reciting the Constitution, the whole Constitution! Fascinated that she knew it so well, probably better than he did, the judge leaned forward to listen intently as he rested his elbow on the bench—chin in hand. Needless-to-say, Lena became a United Stated Citizen. Later that year Lena shared her knowledge of the Constitution with Enrico and, on December 14, 1936, he became a United States Citizen.

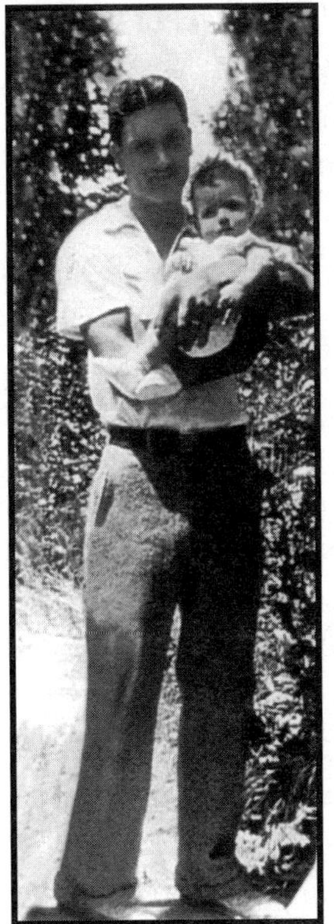

Nello and Marialice
(Courtesy Rose Olivo)

They discussed naming children and wanted to name their first son after Nello. It took awhile before they decided on a girl's name. Rose was reading a story in a high-society magazine about a ballerina whose name was Marialice Veronica. She knew right then, that is what she wanted to name their daughter.

Rose made time to prepare for the baby; gathering baby clothes, bottles, diapers, and decorating a bassinet. She wanted everything for her baby that she dreamt of at one time or another. She did not drive, so Nello would take her to shop in the evening and weekends.

On January 31, 1937, Nello contacted Dr. Amaral and excitedly drove Rose to O'Connor Hospital. She gave birth at 1:36 p.m. to their first child, a beautiful baby girl, named Marialice Veronica. Nello, a non-smoker, proudly handed out cigars.

Rose was a natural at motherhood and attentive to her baby's every need. Ma's heart condition progressively worsened, and yet, as weak as she was, the joy she felt around their first child was profound.

Enrico and Lena made visits more frequently. They could hardly pronounce the name Marialice and nicknamed her "Tootie." She was a good baby, perfect and beautiful.

Pa Pa began visiting more often, every three months. He wanted to see his first grandchild and Marie wanted to see her first niece. The two would come and spend the day. When the grandparents got together, there was plenty of eating, wine, and good times.

The timing was not appropriate so Marie did not mention their relatives. Aunt Josephine's twin son Jamesie, their youngest cousin, died from cancer at fourteen months old. She had helped care for him before he died. Aunt Josephine and Uncle Tony were taking the loss hard.

The squeeze of the Depression was felt and Ma moved in with her sister on South Autumn Street. Rose and Nello moved into his parents' house on Bush Street. His twin brothers, Georgie and Jimmy, still lived at home, along with their beloved dog, "Boots."

On February 4, 1938, Ma died of chronic myocarditis. It was a relief to know that she was no longer suffering. Grieving and feeling a little lost without her, Rose sat alone at Lena's kitchen table late one night going through important papers. She tried to choke back her tears as they rolled down her cheeks. Ma was not an Espinosa; she was Manuel Bettencourt's widow.

Rose thought for a moment, "What about Gabe?" Gabe had filled in as the head-of-household when Ma applied to be a foster parent. When she no longer needed Gabe, she booted him out, falsely used his last name, and allowed Rose to believe she had the same right. Ma had been married before to a Manuel Joseph Farquet. There was no further information about him. Among the papers, were personal memoirs of Ma's rowdy and risqué activities in the red-light district of San Francisco. She put the papers down shocked and confused…she thought she knew her?

The planning of the funeral was simple. She made all the arrangements at the Calvary Catholic Cemetery in San Jose. There was enough money to bury Ma, nothing for a headstone or for a reception after the funeral. Her sister, nieces and nephews attended. Nello took Tootie and left Rose alone at the grave site to say her good-byes.

Bittersweet memories of her life flashed through her mind, she recalled the first funeral she ever attended—that of her real mother. She wondered how life would have been had her mother not died, and what it would have been like to feel her real mother's love. She thought of the separations from her family she once knew, her upbringing, her brief visits with Pa Pa, the loss of her Auntie Jessie, and now Ma.

At the grave, she slowly lowered herself to the ground on one knee, and then the other. She sat back on her heels and covered her face with both hands. Cries came from deep within her. She grabbed the dirt in her hands, made fists, and raised them skyward. "Ma, did you ever really love me?" Her mind raced as she thought…Was your love real or was I a possession you needed to care for you? If Pa Pa had known the truth, would he still have left me with you? She promised herself that her own children would come to know their mother's love and know that it was real and everlasting. She stood up, left that part of her life there and walked away. She did not look back. From that day on, she did not return to the grave and lost contact with Ma's sister and family.

Living with Nello's family was fun for a while, even though it lacked privacy. Rose received first-hand cooking experience from Lena, and she learned to cook Nello's favorite Italian dishes.

Masini's home site in Gilroy *(Courtesy Barbara Olivo Cagle)*

As more of the Ciardella family left Italy to settle in California, she found it difficult to remember their names. Aunt Asunta's daughter, Fannie, took a particular liking to Rose and Nello, visiting them regularly. Although Fannie had children of her own, Sonny, Doris and Mary, she could not see enough of Tootie. The whole clan would go to Gilroy every other weekend to have a picnic with Aunt Asunta at the family ranch, or sometimes at Uvas Creek. Rose would make enchiladas to take as a main-dish. Nello's family was delighted over the enchiladas and looked forward to her making them for the family gatherings.

Rose and Nello began inviting Marie to ride along whenever they went to Gilroy, and Marie stopped by their house after school or work to visit. One Easter weekend they went to Gilroy for Aunt Asunta's family picnic. Rose and Marie were inside the house with Tootie and the other women, helping to prepare the food. The men gathered at the back of the ranch house to practice rifle shooting. With their 22 Springfield bolt-action rifles they aimed at bottles and cans that were placed along the fence-top. Marie heard the shooting and went to investigate. She quickly joined in with the men and soon proved her worthiness as a shooter. Nello rushed in, amazed and excited, to tell Rose and then offered to watch Tootie while she went out to see Marie's display of marksmanship.

Learning to walk for Tootie was an adventure. Nello was holding Tootie's hand on a tour of the house when she slipped and hit her head against a door jamb. She had been getting braver on her legs for over a month. A big 'goose egg' started protruding just as Rose returned to the house and she became concerned and annoyed with Nello for not being more careful. Crying and putting her little hands to her head, Tootie became the center of attention with Aunt Asunta and the other family members. She took in all the sympathy she could get. This was the second accident she had in two weeks. The week before, at Lena's house, Tootie had followed Nello outside to the backyard and leaned over to look into an old wash bucket full of water. She fell headfirst into the bucket with her little legs dangling in the air. From the screen door Rose saw it happen and yelled for Nello. He quickly lifted her out probably saving her life.

Tootie was their pride and joy. A few of the first years of memories include…Other than "Ma Ma" and "Da Da" she spoke the word "Ca-ta-ba." No one could figure out—what that meant. Also, the family showered her with dolls and pretty doll clothes. However, for some reason, she did not like dolls. Before long, off came the clothes, arms, legs, and heads from every doll she was given.

For Pa Pa's birthday, Nello surprised Rose by taking her, Tootie, and Marie to visit him in Campo Seco. Rodger was working out of town or would have joined them. It was a long drive, so they planned to spend the night. The last time Rose had been there was when she was four.

As she entered the front door, a feeling of dé-ja vu swept over her like a strong wind. It was a good feeling, a loving feeling, one that made her think of her mother. There were still a few items there which had some familiarity. She brushed by the rocking chair and looked out the living room window. Then she followed Pa Pa into his bedroom and watched as he opened the trap door in the floor that led to the basement. She had been down there a few times before, when she was little, with her mother.

Pa Pa, Tootie, and Rose *(Courtesy Rose Olivo)*

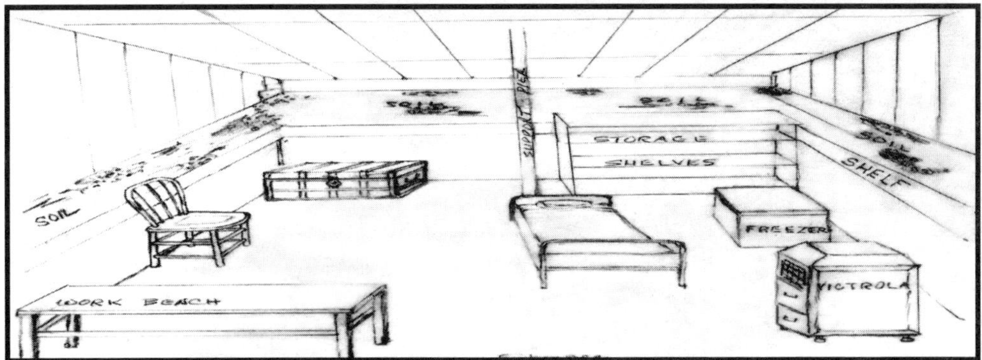

Pa Pa's house and basement *(Photos courtesy Rodger Nunez)*

Pa Pa had Nello go with him downstairs to bring wine up for dinner. He was telling him about the card parties held in the basement, and how he furnished the wine. He called the basement "Joe's Bar," and "Joe's Bucket of Blood." Nello saw a table and lots of wine. During Prohibition, Pa Pa and others would go to Stockton to buy a big barrel of wine and whisky and then sell it from the basement. He bragged to Nello about his shot glasses that had very thick bottoms short of a full shot. He was the first in the area to own a Victrola, and he put it in the basement, where he danced with and courted the "ladies." Nello was very interested in the Victrola. He decided that he wanted one, too, and became obsessed with the idea.

That day it was sunny and they planned a picnic for the birthday celebration. Pa Pa cranked the pump to get fresh water from the well and filled up the wooden bucket for everyone to drink from a long old-fashioned ladle. Rose bought a new camera, and Nello snapped a photo of her and Pa Pa holding Tootie. In the evening they had a chicken and rice fricassee that Dolly Villegas, his "lady friend" prepared for dinner.

After dinner, Pa Pa brought in another bucket of water for the kitchen necessities and everyone relaxed for the evening.

Chinese stone houses *(Courtesy Jeanie Olivo)*

Rose and Marie went to sit on the front porch and take in the fresh air. Dolly watched Tootie inside to give the girls time alone. The night was cool, with a full moon. Across the street from Pa Pa's house, the remains of two old crumbling stone houses cast eerie shadows in the moonlight. Long ago, a Chinese family owned these two houses. They sold candy in one and had a gambling hall in the other. The walls were two feet thick, made from the rocks of the terrain. Now with the wooden slat roofs caved in, and the iron doors gone, the stone shells exuded creepiness. Sitting on the porch and looking across the street, Rose and Marie made up ghost stories about these old stone houses, agreeing that they had to be haunted. They thought they saw ghosts, the way the moonlight would shine through the openings, and they would "see things." They wondered what might have happened there. Pa Pa had told them that at one time, the gambling hall was a lively place where the Chinese men gathered to gamble. The cigar and cigarette smoke-filled room was noisy and crowded, with men squatting down, huddled in tight circles, throwing their money in and ready to grab up big bets. The haunting sounds of winning and losing still lingered in the cool night breeze.

That evening, Marie also brought Rose up-to-date on the latest family events. San Jose State College bought Nana's property on Fourth Street and tore the house down for college expansion. Nana, Uncle Cooney, and Marie moved to a larger house on Fox Street, with enough space to rent out the extra rooms, as they did before with the house on Fourth Street. When she mentioned their past, Rose did not want to remember the not-so-pleasant times. The one common thought they both did share was—what would their life have been like if their mother had lived?

Not sure of Pa Pa's reaction, and a little afraid to say anything too soon, Rose waited until she and Nello were ready to leave before announcing, "Pa Pa, I am expecting. I am due in early August. Nello and I are looking for a place of our own now." Rose learned right then and there that he was not so happy to hear what most fathers might think is good news. He responded with an unexpected, "Humph!" He was good at blowing off steam when told things he did not like to hear. He would reach into his coat pocket, bring out his pouch of Bull Durham tobacco and the tobacco papers, take his time rolling a cigarette, and then light it up to smoke. He looked amusing as he puffed at his cigarette with one hand and pointed his finger at Rose with the other. *"Listo? Arinegi berriro ere, arinegi!"* ("Already? Too soon again, too soon.") Pa Pa did not wish for his daughter to get pregnant. He did not want to hear it, especially so soon again. Rose gave him a goodbye hug, while Nello extended his hand for a handshake. Pa Pa chose not to return the handshake. "Humph!" he responded frowning like a grumpy old man, and looked piercingly into Nello's eyes. Disturbed by the news, he just stood on the road and waved as they drove off.

This was the beginning of many visits to see Pa Pa, and usually included a couple nights stay. He was excited and proud whenever his kidzes came to visit. He would have Dolly come over ahead of time to clean his house and prepare food. She would be there early in the morning to cook breakfast, and then come back to prepare lunch and dinner. He had a liking for her for some time and bought her children new bikes and toys. The thought of how Rose would have loved to have a new bike when she was younger crossed her mind. Those kinds of thoughts would come and go, as she wondered what it would have been like to live there with her mother and father.

Word got around the town whenever Rose and Marie visited. Their Grandpa John Madriago, Jr. and his brother Great Uncle Emmet hung around outside their house down to catch a glimpse of them when they walked up the road. Grandpa John and Uncle Emmet did not dare say anything to the girls. They and Pa Pa did not get along and fought over one thing or another constantly. Pa Pa would pass them off or say mean things about them. From his home you could see the two brothers sitting on their front porch, drinking from their jugs of wine. Rose and Marie did not know what to believe, so they kept their distance. One day as the girls walked by the two men, their eyes met. They all knew who the other was, yet not one word was spoken. They stared at each other as if to say, "A penny for your thoughts?"

You alone, make yourselves happy or unhappy
No one else can do it to you or for you

—Jacqueline Rose Olivo

Chapter Eight

"It's a Little Rough"

Miller Street *(Courtesy Rose Olivo)*

Nello was doing odd jobs on the side fixing up homes for a real estate agent, Gladys McCormack, who worked at Cypress Realty. She hired him to do plumbing, electrical, and paint work. She knew that he and Rose were looking to buy a home that did not require a down payment—they were cash poor. She showed him one of her listings. It was a five-room house on a large lot with a garage and a second house in the back that was more like a barn/shop. It needed a lot of work, which was why the estate had not closed. Nello could work fixing it up in his spare time. The estate was selling "As Is" condition with a sale price of twenty-five hundred dollars. Wow! With zero down, a contract, and monthly payments of fifteen dollars until paid in full, it was a sound deal that he could handle. He went to pick up Rose.

"Hey-a, Honey, let's go take a look at a home I heard about from Gladys…. you know, the real estate agent I've been working for. Hurry! Grab Tootie. I'll tell you about it on our way there."

She hopped in the truck with Tootie on her lap and talked with Nello about the details while they drove to Miller Street.

"Honey, look! There it is. The yard is perfect. See, Honey, we can have a big garden over there. Get a load of all the fruit trees. Holy mackerel! Look at the garage and barn. There will be plenty of room for all my stuff."

Nello had accumulated all sorts of plumbing material, and as long as she did not have to look at his stuff, it did not bother her. He jumped out of his truck, took Tootie and reached for Rose's hand.

"Honey, let's walk around the house. Gladys said the back door is unlocked so we can go right in and take a look."

Once inside, she walked ahead of Nello, carefully studying the floor plan and noticing the condition.

"It's a little rough—mmmmm—I think it will do. I can make it a real home for us. I like the front porch and the two orange trees in the front yard. Is that a bay tree out there by the street?" she asked.

"Oh yeah, look at the size of it. Gladys told me that tree is over one hundred years old," responded Nello.

Holding Tootie in one arm, he swung Rose around with the other, pulling her in close to him, bringing her lips to his while dancing them into each room.

The two drove straight to Gladys' office. They made their offer of twenty-five hundred dollars and all parties agreed on the terms later that evening. Since there was no formal financing involved, the estate's agent agreed to give them the keys for immediate occupancy. Overwhelmed with the thrill of purchasing a home, they excitedly shared the news with his parents. They moved a little at a time each day after Nello came home from work. It took two weeks to clean the house, complete the necessary repairs, and move in their belongings.

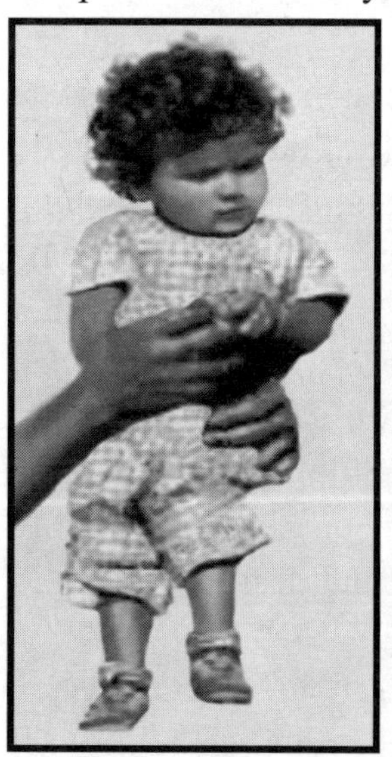

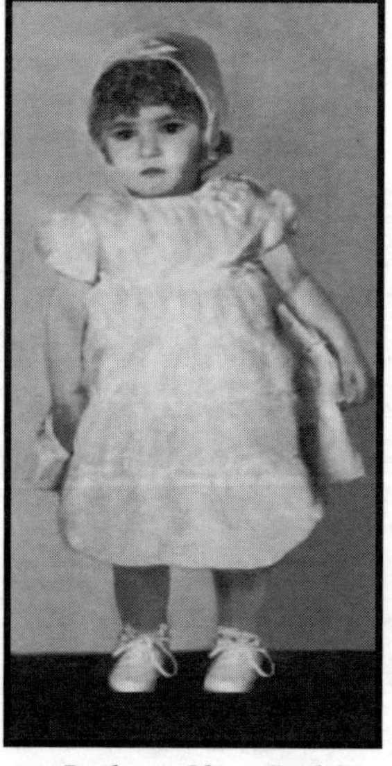

Jeanette, "Gi Gi" *(Courtesy Barbara Olivo Cagle)*

They had looked forward to the first real night alone in their own home since the day they were married. Both of them were exhausted from the move. Then, WHAM! Labor pains began. The night turned out to be a hectic one. Nello took Tootie back over to his parents and drove Rose to O'Connor Hospital. Dr. Edward Amaral, the same doctor who delivered Tootie, was on duty. The following morning Rose delivered her second baby on August 1, 1938, at 8 a.m. They decided to name their daughter Jeanette Elaine, "Jeanie," from the MGM blockbuster musical, *Rose Marie,* starring Jeanette MacDonald and Nelson Eddy, "America's Singing Sweethearts" of the 1930's.

Other than saying, "Ma Ma, Da Da or Ca-ta-ba," Tootie did learn to call Jeanie, "Gi Gi." As a mother for a second time, Rose was amazed at her instant love for more than one child. Her love was neither greater nor less. It just was!

Pa Pa did not have a telephone so Rose wrote a letter informing him of Gi Gi's arrival. Marie stopped by when she could after school or work. Rodger was working out of town most of the time. Rose and Marie saw him once that year.

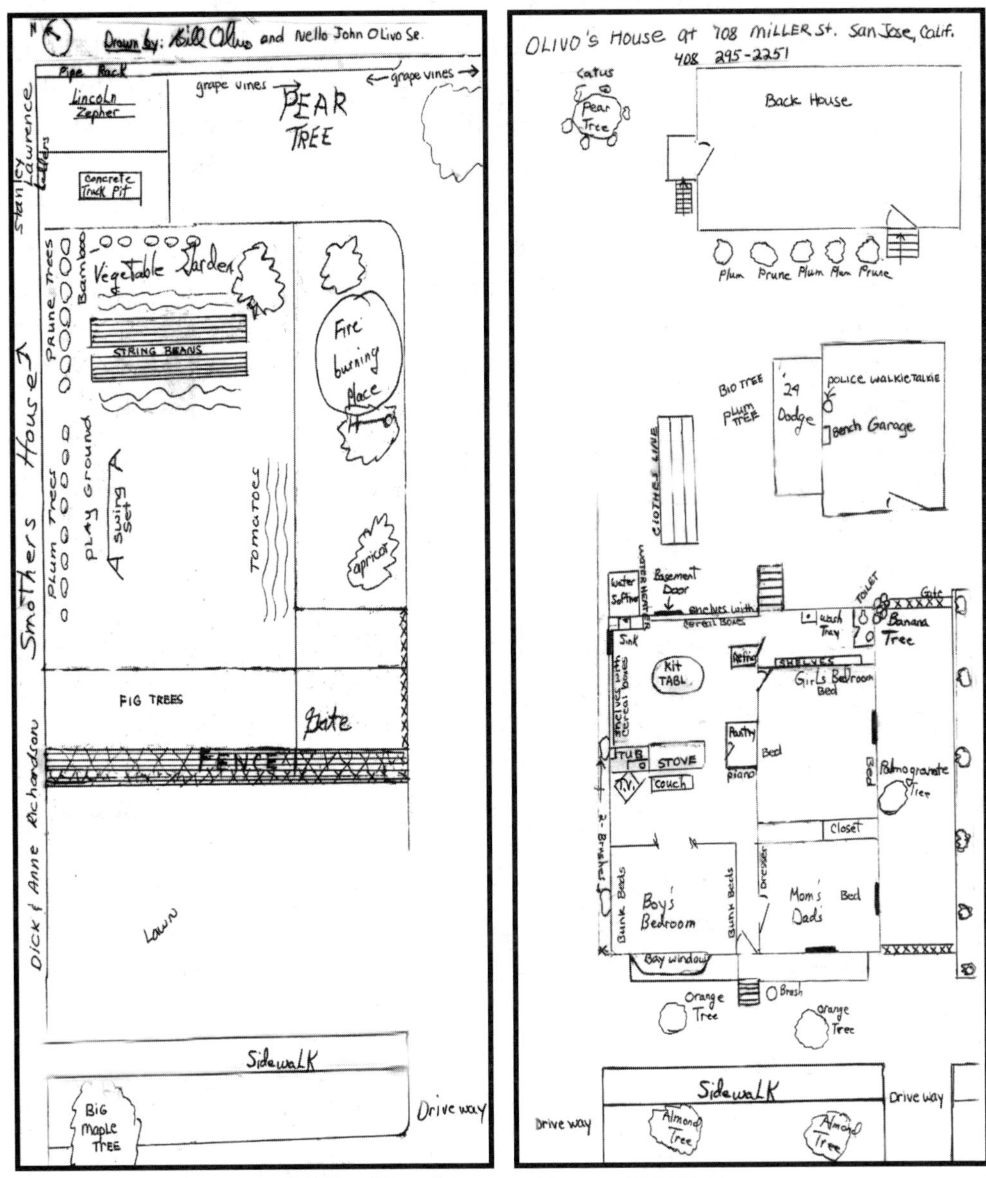

Miller Street house *(Courtesy Bill Olivo)*

They were a busy little family. The home needed work and, of course, planting a garden was a priority—they both loved gardening. Nello's family paid regular visits and brought grafts from their grape vines and various fruit trees for them to plant.

The home on Miller Street was close to the county jail. When the hoboes and bums the county threw in jail for the night sobered up and were released, it became a concern. They would roam by the house and beg for food. After a closer look at them, Rose's concern was eased. She realized they were harmless and mostly hungry. If one of them showed up, she would bring out a sandwich and send him on his way.

Rose's Uncle Frank was a U.S. Navy Seabee, a member of a "Construction Battalion." The battalions were charged with building bases, airfields, landing facilities, and miles of roadways, in combat areas. When on leave, he lived in San Francisco and spent most of his time drinking, often to the point of a stupor. He did not drive and took taxis wherever he went. When he came to San Jose, he would stop at Aunt Josephine's house first with a sack of live chickens. He learned from her that Rose and Nello bought a house and one day he decided to stop by and see her and the children. Rose had not seen her Uncle Frank since he joined the Navy. A taxi brought him to the house. She opened the door to find a sailor standing there, swaying from side to side, obviously inebriated. She thought he was one of the drunks released from the city jail.

"Hello, I want to talk to you." Uncle Frank said.

Rose was busy with her babies, and did not recognize him. She slammed the door in his face. He would not go away and knocked on her door again. She opened the door once more, a little annoyed—Uncle Frank was insistent.

"I come to see my niece, Rose."

He handed her a sack of chickens and they both had a good laugh. Uncle Frank did not stay long. He wanted to make the rounds visiting his brothers and sister. He often checked in at the Montgomery Hotel and returned to San Francisco the following day. The next time Rose heard from him, he had married a wonderful woman named Gil, a godsend to him. They did a great deal of fishing together and shared their catches with the rest of the family.

On occasion, Uncle Joe and Dorothy would come by the house to take Rose, Nello and the babies for a barbecue at Alum Rock Park. Marie would meet them at the park with some of her friends, and Uncle Joe would bring his music for dancing.

On days when Marie could not come over, she would call Rose. Marie looked to her for advice. She was vacillating whether or not to attend Edison Vocational High School to learn sewing, rather than graduating from San Jose High School, where she had six months to go until graduation. She opted for the vocational school; Rose was not necessarily the deciding factor, Marie was anxious to get out into the world. When Uncle Jimmy and Uncle Lawrence heard about it, they were devil mad at her for not finishing high school. Their anger did not seem to faze her. She enjoyed the sewing projects and kept Rose informed of the latest sewing notions and such.

Rose and Nello wanted two more children to complete their family, hoping to have at least one boy. Four months after Jeanie was born, Rose realized that she was pregnant again. Oh, how she wished for a little more sleep, Jeanie was colicky and cried at the drop of a pin. Recalling how Pa Pa had reacted about the news the last time, she and Nello decided to keep silent about her pregnancy. It was easy to do, she did not look pregnant, even up to the day she had the baby. In the last months of pregnancy, she would wear an apron and a loose sweater over her housedress. She kept her slender figure and no one was any the wiser. She packed a suitcase and placed it underneath the bed, available at a moment's notice. There were a couple of baby-sitters she used and could call upon. Also, Nello's family would assist if necessary.

Nello drove Rose to O'Connor Hospital where Dr. Amaral again assisted her in delivering. On August 10, 1939, at 8:03 a.m., Patricia Clarese "Patty" was her third bundle of joy. She was a good baby, and very quiet. Tootie and Gi Gi adored their new baby sister. Bottle-feeding was the fashion. Then there were the cloth diapers—there seemed to be no end to them and no way of getting around them. They became a fixed décor hanging from the clothesline in the backyard.

Although Tootie was older, it did not take long for Gi Gi to start talking, and when she did, she spoke a mile-a-minute and did all the talking for her and Tootie. Tootie did not have to talk and did not for some time.

Nello at work *(Courtesy Rose Olivo)*

Gi Gi preferred crawling, even after she learned to walk. She liked to crawl under the kitchen table to play with people's feet. Once, Stanley Lawrence, their next-door-neighbor and Nello's good friend, accidentally stepped on her hand. Upsetting her was not the thing to do, she would cry for hours. The only remedy that worked to calm her down was a concoction of whisky and honey that Nello mixed up for Rose to rub on her gums.

Nello stayed busy during the war years, often traveling far distances for work. There were few plumbing jobs for him in San Jose. He worked at the

United States Navy Hospital in Oakland, and for big contractors in Richmond, Rodeo, Pleasant Hill, Menlo Park and Chico. There were days he had to spend the night.

"I did all the plumbing: kitchens, baths, showers, toilets, dental chairs and stuff like that."

Sometimes he would play "poker pool" with his coworkers using the draft number on their checks as poker hands in order to win cash.

"We'd get our checks on Friday night. I'd look at the check number, and I'd get three aces and win maybe one-hundred dollars, and I'd come home with it" he boasted.

One of his lengthier jobs was at the United States Army Fort Ord Base. It required him to stay in Monterey for some time. The military base set up quarters for the workers to stay on the job throughout the week with weekends off. Rose had no means of transportation and rarely left the house. Peers Dairy delivered bottled milk twice a week. Kelly Brothers' Grocery Store and Butcher Shop, fondly called "Kelly's," took orders over the phone and delivered groceries as needed. A good book kept her company in the late evenings and the two wrote letters to each other every day they were apart. As for the letters Nello said, "Oh yeah, I don't know what happened to them all."

Rose and Marie in 1940 *(Courtesy Rose Olivo)*

Marie visited Rose during the days when Nello was away on jobs. She was eighteen now, and they became the best of friends. They would sometimes take the bus and go shopping together at Hart's, where Pa Pa used to take them when they were younger. After shopping, they would go to Mel's, the diner on the corner of Twelfth and Santa Clara Streets. The teenaged waitresses there wore roller skates to deliver food orders to the customers waiting in their cars in the parking lot.

Marie told Rose about a man she had met at a dance. He swept her off her feet with his sweet talk, and in no time they married. Pa Pa now had two men he did not like, and both of his daughters were expecting at the same time.

When Pa Pa came to visit, all he could say was "Humph!" while pacing and stomping around, filling up the home with his cigarette smoke. Rose, Nello, and Marie were sitting at the kitchen table. Marie's husband was not with her. He spent more time away in the Marines than he did at home.

"We were hoping to have a boy to carry on our name," said Nello.

Pa Pa, directing his comments as though Marie's husband was present, and spewed like spark lights afire, "To hell with names, you killin' my dahtars!" Marie was like Pa Pa. She would go right back at him with her "Humphs!" facing him stomping like he did.

"Well, you robbed the cradle!" Marie spitefully said to her father.

"You too smart!" he responded.

Rose's Grandmother Annie Madriago, "Mater"
(Courtesy Marie Bueno)

On the other hand, more than anything else Rose wanted to have her father's approval and respect. She sat frozen, with a tear trickling down her cheek. Truth was, Pa Pa worried about them and was scared of losing them in childbirth. He spent time with the little ones and then left, angry. He went to visit Rodger at the Wirz' home and stayed there for dinner.

In life's cycle, there are those coming into the world, and those leaving the world. Marie had sad news concerning Mater. She had become seriously ill with diabetes and passed on February 6, 1939. From the times before Rose went to live with Ma, she had noticed the little things in Mater's habits with snack foods; like the way she would cut up lettuce, wet it and dip it in a sugar bowl, before eating it. She also dipped French bread in milk with sugar and dipped cracked nuts into honey. Rose recalled Mater's hot gravy and hamburger over rice and her hot tuna over toast. These memories of Mater always remained with Rose, and now they were a bit more vivid. The same memories made Marie smile, thinking of the times Mater baby-sat her and made her the same snacks and meals.

A couple of months passed and Pa Pa returned to town on his way to San Francisco. He was more somber this time when he visited Rose and Marie. Word was that his brother, Balbino, had died. He had been aware that his brother was ill. He did not realize that it was TB. Balbino had the chronic lung disease and the pain was so great, that on April 7, 1939, he took his life with a razor incision to his left brachial artery. Pa Pa went alone to pick up the personal affects of his brother, which were: forty cents, a safety razor, a W.M. Ingersoll watch, a small scissors, a penknife, an address book, a Declaration of Intention, a driver's license and a social security card. Balbino's girlfriend, who ran the beauty shop downstairs in the same building as the men's home, took all of his money and belongings while he was in the hospital. The men's home ended up paying for his funeral expenses.

A year later, Uncle Jimmy and Uncle Lawrence saw Rose, Marie and Rodger, and informed them that their Great Uncle Emmet had died on March 20, 1940. Knowing about family members and when they died, gives reason to pause and think of them in a moment of silence.

On September 17, 1940, at 3:15 a.m. Dr. Amaral was again with Rose as he delivered her first son, Nello John Jr. On September 20, Marie had her first child, a son, Manuel Jr., "Junior." They were in the hospital together. In those days, postpartum patients remained in the hospital for at least ten days. Rodger stopped by to visit Rose and Marie. It was important. He needed to keep in touch with his sisters, and more so now that he was an uncle.

Nello's cousin, Fannie and her children came by the house to help take care of the little ones when Nello was at the hospital visiting Rose. He was excited, finally a son. When he told his parents the good news, Lena kept trying to pronounce Nello Junior, and it just would not come out right, so she called him "Sonny." From then on, that was his nickname, "Sonny." He was a good baby, and being the first-born son, spoiled. Nello took him everywhere, every chance he had, and anything Sonny wanted, he got.

Later that year Fannie moved to Medford, Oregon. Her children, Mary, Doris, and Sonny stayed behind with Rose and Nello. They wanted to finish their high school years in San Jose. Not to confuse the two Sonny's, Rose and Nello called their son Little Sonny and Fannie's son Big Sonny.

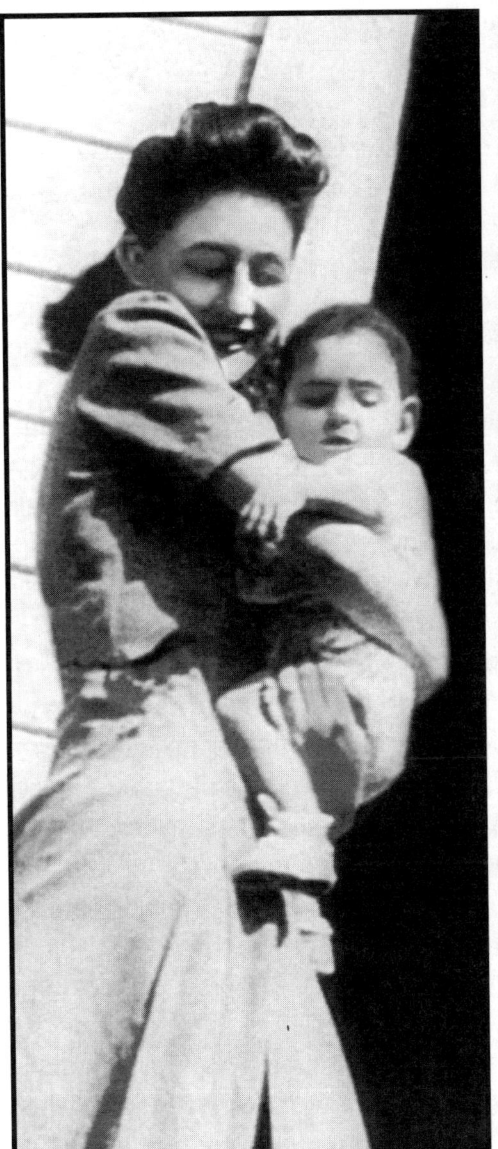

Doris, Fanny's daughter, with Little Sonny (left) and Fanny with Virginia *(Courtesy Rose Olivo)*

In January 1941, Rodger received a draft notice from the United States Army instructing him to report to The Presidio in San Francisco. There was little time for family visits. He took the train from San Jose. At The Presidio, draftees received physical examinations. The Army sent those who passed by train to Fort Ord, in Monterey, for I.Q. tests. Three days later, the Army sent Rodger to a new Basic Training base at Camp Roberts in Paso Robles, California. He was assigned to the Field Artillery School. In August 1941, he applied for and was accepted for transfer to the United States Army Air Force (USAAF) and reassigned to Moffett Field, California. Moffett Field was between San Jose and Oakland, allowing him to visit his family on weekends. When he earned a set of wings to pin on the collar of his uniform, he proudly showed them off to the family.

The excitement of a baby boy and the idea of having four children, sort of "run-amok." Rose was expecting again. Neither of them let on to anyone that she was pregnant. No one knew except for Rose, Nello and Dr. Amaral. Marie did not even know.

Virginia Anne arrived on November 24, 1941, at 4:00 a.m., peacefully, with the biggest baby smile.

Marie had telephoned Nello to speak with Rose.

"Rose is in the hospital. She had another baby," Nello told her.

"Oh yeah? I just saw her last week. I didn't know she was expecting," replied Marie.

Once Marie knew, everyone knew! Except for Pa Pa, he found out the next time he was in town. Virginia was three months old.

Pa Pa was looking forward to getting to know his grandson, when he noticed Rose holding a new baby. He said with surprise, "How many kidzes now?" He stood there, learning the names of the children, while counting on his fingers. It was a good visit and it appeared he had accepted the fact that he had no control over Rose's life. In front of her, he would suppress his opinions and concern for her health. When she was out of earshot, he had no qualms letting Nello know that he still did not like him getting her pregnant. In spite of his concern for her, he loved his grandchildren and the grandchildren loved their grandpa.

Pa Pa went on to visit Rodger that weekend. Rodger's assignment to Moffett Field was short-lived. His new assignment effective in February 1942 was at a new air base training center in Lemoore, California. It would be sometime before he would see family again.

Cousin Fannie did not like living in Medford, Oregon. She returned to San Jose, picked up her children, and settled into a place of her own. She visited Rose often and loved spending time with the children. It was cousin Fannie that nicknamed Virginia "Ginger."

Rose was organized and mealtimes with the five little ones went well as long as the refrigerator was full of milk bottles. Tootie and Gi Gi graduated to the kitchen table, Patty and Sonny graduated to the girls' highchairs, and Ginger lay sleeping in the beautiful bassinet adorned with woven pink ribbons. Rose displayed her artistic flair by decorating the bassinet differently for each of her babies. Her latest baby apparel fascinated all of the family members.

No one knew how she did it. They were a little envious in the way she kept her slender figure right after having a baby, the way she could sew fashionable baby clothes, and the way she kept a spotless home. One thing she could not control were diapers. They kept coming, rotating out to the clothesline and back to the diaper shelf.

Nello worked hard and was making good money which allowed Tootie to take ballet, tap, and acrobatics lessons at the Andreuccetti Dance School. It was within walking distance of home, conveniently located on North First Street. Rose would get a baby-sitter for the little ones and walk Tootie to her lessons once a week. Dancing was something she always dreamed of doing when she was little and wanted Tootie to have this opportunity.

Marie was busy caring for Junior when she received a call from Uncle Cooney that Great Grandmother Nana, who brought her up, died. She had been very ill with a weak heart and diabetes. She was in the hospital, comatose for the past three months. Uncle Cooney was with her every day. Nana, at seventy-five years of age, died on June 12, 1942. The family got together to discuss burial arrangements. They decided to bury Nana in Aunt Josephine's plot at Calvary Cemetery in San Jose. There was no money for a funeral service. It was a simple burial with Aunt Michaela, Uncle Cooney, and Lydia's brothers and sister present. Rose and Marie wished to attend; however, were unable to get baby-sitters for the children. They spoke to each other on the phone.

Rose wrote to Rodger with the news of Nana, saddened that she had so few memories of her. Whenever they saw each other, which was seldom, Ma would rush her away. Their eyes would meet for a long moment, as they thought of all the "what-ifs and only-ifs." Rose knew her as a little old lady. Marie though, had many memories, especially the feel of her hands as she combed Marie's hair, and the soft sound of her voice calling out, "Mollie." She also remembered her as a little old lady, sitting in her rocking chair, watching Uncle Cooney carefully measuring food for each meal. Marie would help Uncle Cooney dress Nana, and was there when he and Uncle Lawrence carried her into the car to take her to the hospital. She was already in a coma, stiffened in the fetal position. They could not straighten her out.

Soon after Nana passed, Rose received news from Uncle Jimmy that on July 1, 1942, Grandpa John Madriago, Jr. had died. She did not know him personally, only of him, and that he was her grandfather. She bowed her head in a moment of silence, recalling the time that their eyes met when she visited Pa Pa in Campo Seco.

All the children ever learned from Pa Pa was that their grandfather's family was from Chili. When Pa Pa settled in Campo Seco, the Madriago family was already well established. The Penn Copper Mine Company was the best job in town, and as young adults, that's where their grandfather and the Madriago brothers found work. Grandpa John was in charge of the rock crusher at the mine. He also worked as a blacksmith. He lost sight in his left eye when a drop of molten metal flew into it while he was blacksmithing, and wore a black patch over the eye. From then on, everyone called him "One-Eyed Jack," or the "One-Eyed Chilean," until he got a false eye and wore glasses. After the accident, he worked as a carpenter and land surveyor.

Marie was renting a duplex on Delmas Avenue, when Aunt Michaela knocked at her door in need of help. She had been staying with her missing husband's brother, Jacinto when he died, and his family wanted the house and everything in it. They had asked her to move out. Jacinto had told her that he had a bag of money and wanted her to have it if anything happened to him. Marie told Aunt Michaela, "Don't worry about the furniture, it's worthless and only made out of the wood from an old fence."

The two went to Gilroy to get Aunt Michaela's personal items. The bag of money and the few clothes she had are all she took. Marie drove back to San Jose and settled her into one of the small rooms that her godmother had for rent on Grant Street. Marie was glad that she was able to help. Aunt Michaela was now within walking distance to her, and Uncle Cooney was close enough to visit. There were two other old ladies who lived in the house with Aunt Michaela, which made good company for all of them.

Marie's godmother had kept in touch with her every year at Christmas, bringing her a big bag of green oranges. It was thoughtful, yet strange why she brought them green.

Rose and Marie decided that it was about time they got a break from the children. Whenever Marie suggested that they go out together, Rose's usual answer was, "Maybe, if I can arrange it."

Nello did not stay home to baby-sit the group. He would take a couple of the children with him, usually rotating them, not all of them.

Marie brought Junior over to Rose's and helped her look for a baby-sitter. She wanted to go out. The two usual sisters were unavailable and it took some time to find a baby-sitter. They decided to go to the Victory Theatre and see the Academy Award's Best Picture of the year, *Mrs. Miniver,* starring Greer Garson and Walter Pidgeon. Marie did all the driving whenever they went out; Rose still did not drive.

After the movie, they pulled in to the Five Spot, a drive-in hamburger restaurant where the waitress came out to the car, attached a tray on the driver's side door, and took the food order.

"Could you please move your car?" The waitress asked Marie.

"Where to?" Marie asked. "Over there," pointed the waitress.

Marie moved the car as directed. The waitress came back to the car and said, "You are not where I told you to go!" Again, the waitress walked back to the restaurant, and Marie moved the car once more.

"I told you—over there! You still are not where I want you to park! You are not supposed to park here!" the waitress angrily exclaimed while she once more approached the car window.

"Look, I moved twice already. I'm not moving again!" steamed Marie.

She opened the car door and stepped out. She looked taller in high-heels, and stared down the waitress. The waitress took one look at her and ran back to the restaurant. Marie's eyes were bulging in anger, and her fighting spirit was in high gear from adrenalin, when she turned around to look at Rose. Rose had squeezed down underneath the dashboard, as far as she could.

"I don't fight" quivered Rose.

"What if I would have taken a poke at that girl? What a big help you'd have been—Chicken!" Marie could not keep from laughing.

The management sent out a new waitress and she did not have to move the car another time.

Marie told Rose that her schedule was going to be hectic. She decided to go to night school after her day job and enrolled in a government trade school to be an electrician. Her mother-in-law was going to take care of Junior. After eighteen weeks of night school, she got a job with the Moore Dry Dock Company in Oakland, working with a crew of electricians, keeping the ships well lit for the welders. It was especially exciting for her when touring the navy ships at the outfitting dock. It gave her an opportunity to hear of the many voyages the ships and sailors had taken all over the world.

Wartime required gas rationing and one of Marie's coworkers was more than happy to pick her and others up to ride along with him to work. He would get more gas tokens if he had more riders. Marie stayed with the Moore Dry Dock Company for six months. Then she went to work for the Food Machinery Corporation. They had a government contract to build amphibious army tanks. She connected the cables to meters on the dashboards of the tanks. Her coworkers were Marie, Mary, and Mary. Talk about confusing. The weekends were more fun as the four of them became close friends.

One weekend, Marie took Marie, Mary, and Mary for a ride in her old Chevy to Campo Seco for a visit with Pa Pa. He worked the weekend swing shift, 4:00 p.m. to midnight, and was not home when they arrived. She did not know he was at work and went looking for him. The girls went downstairs at the General Store to the *Cool Café,* where Marie knew Pa Pa played cards. She decided to wait there and the four of them amused themselves with a slot machine. In a small town, it did not take long for word to get to him that the girls were at the *Cool Café*. When he stormed in, Marie and her friends were at the slot machine which sat in the corner of the room. Ohh, he was mad!

"Why you putta money in there? There no money in it to win! Angelo, he come and take money every night," blurted Pa Pa.

He got them out of there and offered to show the girls around Penn Mine. He took them down the hoist he operated. Marie was afraid of heights, yet going underground did not seem to bother her. She found it exhilarating riding down nine-hundred feet into the earth. It was dark, cold, and mining tunnels ran in every direction. The large wooden conveyor bucket was big enough to hold three people at once. Pa Pa took Marie and one of her friends down first, and then went back and got the other two. The tour was educational and amazing. The girls found the experience unforgettable and talked of it for days.

When Rose heard of Marie's adventure, she got creepy, crawly, goose bumps. The thought of descending deep into the ground was inconceivable to her. There were many stories of miners who had died falling down shafts. She was not afraid of heights though and would have loved to climb to the top of Mount Everest.

Chapter Nine

More to Come

July 13, 1943 was one of the hottest days that summer; Christine Ann was born at 4:16 a.m. Rose and Nello, "Mom" and "Dad," had left the children with the nuns at the Mission San Jose Elementary School. The nuns would baby-sit children during the summers and after-school hours for extra income. It was costly and Mom begged Dr. Amaral to release her early from the hospital. Her doctor suggested the opposite and kept her in the hospital for a full recovery. He knew she would not get the proper rest at home, and even suggested that she consider not having any more children.

Tootie and Gi Gi

Patty

(Courtesy Rose Olivo)

Sonny and Ginger

The children were away from home a long time. They did not like the nuns confining them within the school's fenced perimeter and they thought the nuns were mean to them. The five little Olivos laced their fingers together and pressed their faces into the chain-link fence, wondering how long they were going to be imprisoned. They feared something serious was wrong and kept asking the nuns for their mother. Their imaginations ran wild and their thoughts grew worse day by day, thinking Mom was dying.

After a long two weeks, Mom and Dad arrived at the school to take the children home. The five little Olivos were overwhelmed with joy at seeing their parents and new baby sister. They were jumping up and down and running to gather up belongings.

The remainder of the summer flew by, and it was time to register Tootie for kindergarten at Jefferson Elementary School. Mom took her on the first day of school and showed her around. Breathing deeply, and with a little hesitance, she let go of Tootie's hand and walked home.

Mom tended to the little ones during the days. She had Ma's sewing machine and stayed up nights sewing outfits for school, play, and dance. She made dance costumes for one or two other girls in Tootie's class.

School expenses were a major concern to Mom until the day she spoke to Father Grisziegh, the pastor of St. Joseph's Church and the supervisor of the principal at St. Joseph's School. He made all the final decisions for the registrants' contracts and the academic curriculum for the school. Mom asked him if Tootie could start school there, and he said yes.

"It will cost you ten dollars a year if you want her to come here."

"There will be more to follow. I have six children."

"Then it will still cost you ten dollars a year for the whole family, and that will include all their books," shrugged Father Grisziegh not knowing how many more children would ultimately attend the school.

Mom was thrilled to know that she could afford to send her children to a Catholic school. She made an appointment to register Tootie in first grade and Gi Gi in kindergarten. Tootie was Marialice and Gi Gi was Jeanie while in school; after hours it was Tootie and Gi Gi. A few weeks before school began, she took her girls to the Merry Mart Department Store and opened an account to purchase school uniforms; white blouses, green-plaid skirts, forest-green sweaters and white Oxford shoes. The school uniforms were a blessing and saved money in the long run.

Mom was on the phone talking to Marie about her school plans for the children when Marie informed her that Aunt Michaela was at her door. She appeared to be very weak from heart trouble and had been making frequent visits to the Santa Clara County Hospital. Marie had her lay down on the couch. She ended up staying for a week before going to the hospital. Marie knew then that she was not coming out, and got scared when Aunt Michaela gave her an insurance policy.

"Go to my room, and in my trunk I have a bag of money. That bag, it's for you. That's all I have" instructed Aunt Michaela.

Marie did as she asked and went to the house where she had lived. One of the old ladies answered the door.

"I need to get something for my Aunt Michaela," stated Marie.

She went into the room, the trunk was opened. She searched through the trunk and found the bag, grabbing it, she started to leave.

"I see you got what you came for," snickered the old lady.

Marie called Uncle Jimmy and told him what had happened with the old lady, and that she knew about the money. After three weeks in the hospital on February 24, 1944, Aunt Michaela died of hypertensive cardiovascular disease. Marie had no idea what to do.

"Give me the policy, I will take care of it," Uncle Jimmy assured her.

Rose's Great-great Aunt Michaela Tehada Carabajal *(Courtesy Marie Bueno)*

With the insurance policy and money, there was enough to bury Aunt Michael, without a headstone, at the Calvary Catholic Cemetery. Uncle Jimmy and Marie were in attendance. Uncle Cooney did not drive, and he could hardly walk. As for Mom, she did not know her aunt, except for what Marie had told her, and with the children, there was no way she could get out of the house.

Aunt Michaela married Christopher Tehada at the age of fourteen. She was in Hollister expecting her first child when she asked Nana for help. Nana took Mater and Uncle Cooney to Hollister and delivered a beautiful baby boy. Aunt Michaela named him Louis. She would pronounce it "Lou-weez," with a slight Spanish accent and upturned lips. One night, her husband took Louis away. No one in his family knew where they went, and no one ever saw them again. Her heart was grief-stricken and her sadness inconsolable. For all she knew, her husband could have fled to the next town. She had no means of transportation or way of locating him. Christopher had a brother named Jacinto who lived in a shanty and he gave Aunt Michaela a room. She remained with Jacinto until the day he died, and continued to hope that her husband would contact her.

When Aunt Michaela walked around town, she was easy to spot from a distance. She dressed in black, with a funny feather hat, and high buttoned-up shoes. Her full, gathered skirt flared in the back, fishtailed as she walked. She was serious and rarely smiled. Others thought she was in constant mourning over the loss of her baby boy. Hearing her story, Mom reminded herself of the preciousness of children and hugged her children, one by one.

Uvas Creek Dam today *(Courtesy Barbara Olivo Cagle)*

Mom made a practice of having her babies baptized at St. Joseph's Church within a year after their births, with the exception of Christine. Time seemed to fly by quickly after she was born. Fannie's sister, Mary, had a baby boy, Allen Ronald Greco, born on April 6, 1944. Mom and Mary decided to have a double baptism at St. Mary's Church in Gilroy, with a barbecue at Uvas Creek Dam, following the baptism. They planned the event for Labor Day weekend, September 3, 1944, a day before the beginning of the school year. Mom and Dad brought Marie. Junior was at home with his grandmother. It was a big family gathering. Most of the Olivo and Ciardella families were in attendance.

Mom arranged the picnic tables while Dad and Marie brought the ice chests, bags of food, and watermelons from the parking lot. They were on their way back to the car when Mom noticed Tootie, Gi Gi, and Patty following them.

"Take the long way around to the car. The girls are following you" Mom yelled out to Dad.

In opposition to Mom's request, Dad and Marie decided to take the short-cut on the rock and gravel bar that went across the dam from the picnic area to the parking lot. The water was shallow on one side and very deep on the other, where people were swimming. It was a public place. There were people all around. With the three girls behind them, Dad and Marie walked on the rock path, reminding the girls to walk carefully and to stay close to the shallow side. Just as they were telling the girls to be careful, Gi Gi and Patty were watching the swimmers and giggling. They slipped on the wet stones and fell into the deep side. Tootie kept her balance and stayed on the path. Neither of the girls knew how to swim, and their little heads began to bob up and down, causing them to swallow water. It happened so quickly that Dad acted on impulse and reached for Patty. He pulled her out, then fell in while trying to get Gi Gi. All Marie could see at that moment was Gi Gi's long hair, spread out, floating on the surface.

"Oh dear God, let her be okay," Marie prayed covering her mouth in fright.

She then sent Tootie to go and get Mom. In the meantime, Dad was able to grab Gi Gi and push her above the water, where a Good Samaritan reached in and pulled her out. There were no lifeguards. It was a swim at your own risk area. Gi Gi was coughing up water and slowly began to recover. Dad, in a state of exhaustion, began to sink in the deep water. He was struggling to stay afloat, and gasping for air. He did not know how to swim!

Mom, from afar, saw Tootie running toward her. When she heard that Gi Gi and Patty had fallen into the water, she looked up and saw they had been pulled out. She told the other children to stay behind, and she ran for the girls. Shaking with fear, she put her arms around the two and softly reprimanded them. Then she closed her eyes and prayed, "Thank you, Lord, for keeping my girls safe from harm's way."

Relieved that her daughters were okay, another wave of fear overtook Mom. She knew that Dad could not swim. Now she became panic-stricken. Standing paralyzed, looking towards the water she saw him kicking and splashing. He was swallowing water. Realizing that he was beginning to drown, Mom, her adrenalin pumping, ran for Dad. By the time she reached him, some nearby swimmers had seen that he could not swim and quickly pulled him from the water. Two men carried him to the picnic area and laid him belly down on a table, his face and arms dangling over the end. He appeared to be unconscious. One of the men began to resuscitate him by pressing his back and pumping his arms until Dad started to cough. Slowly he regained consciousness. Noticing the fear and obvious panic written on Mom's face, Dad began putting on a show, milking it for all the attention he could get.

Aunt Asunta's son-in-law, Joe Greco, helped Dad to his car and drove him to a nearby emergency facility. The doctor on duty listened intensely to Dad's frantic description of his near-drowning experience, while he performed a routine examination.

"You can snap out of it now. The only thing wrong with you is a belly full of water that you will be passing soon enough," the doctor commented.

Determining that Dad was in no further danger, the doctor released him. Dad and Joe had been gone for an hour before returning to the barbecue. It was a hot day, and he joked with the girls that they got to cool off in wet clothes.

Later that day, Aunt Asunta sent Mom home with several fur pelts from the white rabbits she and Peter raised on the ranch.

Once the children had settled down for the evening, Mom read her mail. She received word from Pa Pa that he would like her and Marie to come and visit soon. Marie and her talked everyday on the phone discussing married life, kids, and other family members. Now they were curious as to what was going on in Pa Pa's life. Why the sudden urgency to go visit him? Was he sick? Did he get hurt? Was he moving? Was he getting married? Their imaginations wandered in many directions. They planned to go see him the following weekend. The two rode in the front seat with Dad, and Tootie and Gi Gi rode in the back. Doris, Fannie's daughter, watched the rest of the children, and Junior stayed with his grandmother.

Everyone assumed Pa Pa was lonely and wanted visitors. Then he brought out a letter he had received from Rodger. It had been a long time since anyone had heard from him. The last Mom and Marie heard he was transferred to a B-17 Air Base in Casper, Wyoming, in January of 1943. Pa Pa told them that Rodger had become an officer in the Army.

In September 1943, Rodger had applied for and was accepted for Officer's Candidate School (OCS). After graduation, in January of 1944, he was commissioned as a Second Lieutenant and assigned to Anti-Aircraft School at Camp Davis, North Carolina. The war in North Africa was winding down and the USAAF cut back on the need for Anti-Aircraft officers. Given the choice between the Tank Corps or the Infantry, Rodger chose the Infantry. He had been assigned to Infantry School at Fort Benning, Georgia, and then the Infantry Recruit Training Center in Spartanburg, South Carolina. After infantry training, he was shipped overseas and was now in the European War Zone. He was with the 8th Infantry Regiment of the Fourth Division in North Belgium. They had maneuvered north to below Cologne, Germany, then south to Luxembourg, then further south to France, and then back up north to Germany. They prayed for Rodger to have a safe return home.

Pa Pa had another surprise. He announced he wanted to take everyone out for dinner at Pete's Café in Valley Springs, just outside of Campo Seco. Pete's had an excellent reputation and attracted many out of town dinners. When they arrived, Mom and Marie noticed a flirtation in Pa Pa's eyes as one particular waitress approached them.

"I wanna you to meet Nelle, a very nice-a lady," said Pa Pa.

Pa Pa exchanged some small talk with Nelle, while they were seated in a comfortable booth. Mom and Marie were a little annoyed. His attention was focused on her. He spent a great deal of time talking to her, and at the same time, tried to be coy. Mom gently kicked Marie's ankle under the table to get her attention, darting eye signals while Nelle took the orders. It was obvious that she was interested in Pa Pa. He was handsome, an available widower, and dressed sharply! Experiencing a little jealous apprehension for his attention, Mom and Marie were not sure this lady was the woman for him.

Nelle M. Vincent *(Courtesy Barbara Olivo Cagle)*

Nelle was born in Jackson, Kansas, December 24, 1885, and of Irish ancestry. There she married, had a son, Eugene Vincent, and divorced. She had raised Eugene as a single mother. She lived with her parents and siblings until their house burned down during a devastating drought and sand storm. Her youngest sister, Kathleen, died trapped in the burning house. The family was horrified and helpless as they listened to her dying screams. They lost everything in the fire. Nelle, Eugene, and her sister, Sadie, uprooted and went to Hughson, California, traveling by both stagecoach and train. Their parents decided not to make the trip, electing to stay in Kansas with family and friends. The catastrophe haunted Nelle throughout her life and gave her nightmares. "My poor mother, no mother should have to suffer losing a child that way," she explained. Nelle established herself in Hughson and worked at a doctor's office as an assistant. Later she moved to Valley Springs and now worked as a waitress at Pete's Restaurant.

Mom went with Tootie and Gi Gi on their first day of school at St. Joseph's to familiarize them with the school grounds and their classrooms. She particularly wanted to make sure that Gi Gi was comfortable starting kindergarten, and knowing that her big sister, Tootie, was there, made it easier.

The school bus stop was kitty-corner from the house. Mr. Leo, an Italian, was the school bus driver. It became a daily event for Mom and the children to watch Tootie and Gi Gi across the street to board the bus, waving to each other, and to Mr. Leo. When the bus dropped Tootie off after school, Mom and the children watched from inside the house. The kindergartners did not take the bus, they were carpooled. The mothers took turns bringing the children home from school. One of the neighboring mothers was happy to give Gi Gi a ride. She knew Mom did not drive and was busy with the younger children.

Mom had the children on a rigid schedule. She had to, with six children and yes, another on the way.

The girls sat at the kitchen table to do their homework after school At night, they lined up by the kitchen sink as Mom dabbed the water to set bobby-pinned curls in the girls' hair. They slept that way. Mom stayed up late starching uniforms and preparing lunches.

In the morning, after an oatmeal breakfast, the girls stood in line again. Tootie first, as Mom removed the bobby pins, and styled their hair into banana curls. She would gently wrap each curl around her left index and middle fingers, smoothing out any tangles with a comb. Sometimes the curls came out so perfectly that all she had to do was straighten them out with her finger. If the girls had disobeyed her at any previous time, this is when she would get her chance to discipline them. She would yank on the curls and say, "And that's for…" When she finished with Tootie's curls, she began again with Gi Gi. When she was finished, the two girls would inspect their hair in the one and only mirror on the kitchen wall and were off to school. After Tootie and Gi Gi were on the bus, Mom would style Patty and Ginger's hair.

Christmas was around the corner, and Mom spent as much time as she could making presents for the children. The rabbit pelts she had received from Aunt Asunta were sent to a local tannery for curing. She then took them to a furrier and told him what design she wanted to use to make new fur coats, hats and hand-warmers for Tootie, Gi Gi, and Patty.

Over the years, Mom had collected a variety of Christmas decorations. The children's favorite tree decorations were the bubbling lights and tinsel. On the piano, she set up a manger scene, using angel hair for an ethereal effect.

Uncle Georgie and Uncle Jimmy often took the children for rides to the park or to see their grandparents. They liked taking the children and the children looked forward to it. This allowed Mom and Dad some free time during the holiday season to make presents.

Uncle Jimmy was careful to keep his weight down by staying clear of the snack foods. He was a chain smoker and drank lots of coffee. Uncle Georgie was on the chubby side. Grandpa and Grandma were pleasantly plump and did a good share of baby-sitting which included doughnuts and bags of popcorn ready for the children whenever they came to visit.

Grandma could not understand the children's apprehension whenever they were around her. Although the children loved her, they tried to dodge having to sit on her lap. She had an overpowering perfumed smell that reeked from the same several layers of dresses that she wore day after day. Sonny especially feared her habit of pinching his cheeks so hard that they would turn beet red, and then gently slapping him silly. She would do anything to keep Sonny from touching things. As the children would pass by she would grab them, tickle them, and punch them gently on the arm, saying, "I pun-cha, pun-cha, pun-cha." Whoa, was she ever a pincher, tickler, and puncher!

An aroma of meat with garlic simmering on the old iron wood stove was recognizable when the children were at their grandparent's house. They used the stove for cooking and for heating the house. It was a large house with three bedrooms. Grandpa, Uncle Georgie, and Uncle Jimmy shared one room, another room was reserved for guests. Grandma had her own room that she kept locked at all times.

The plumbing for the kitchen faucets hung from the wall, over a flat sink. When Dad became a licensed plumber, Grandpa had him tap into the adjacent lumberyard's water system. "Get something for nothing" was their mentality.

As Grandpa sat on a stool in the middle of the kitchen, Uncle Georgie or Uncle Jimmy would lather his face with shaving cream and shave him with a straight-edge razor. With eyes wide open, and curious, the children would stand and stare from the kitchen entrance.

There was a large arbor of grapes in the back yard, and in the fall, the older children would stomp the grapes in the old grape press out back. Sometimes even Dad joined in, rolling up his pant legs just like the children. They all giggled as they felt the grapes squushing between their toes. The Olivo family made wine for themselves at home, and bootlegged.

While the children hung out with their uncles and grandparents, Dad would shop for good deals on used bikes to fix up as gifts for the children. Every Christmas Eve, Uncle Georgie and Uncle Jimmy stopped by with presents from the J.C. Penny Department Store. The children received new pajamas, robes and slippers.

Opening presents on Christmas Eve and going to mass on Christmas Day became an Olivo tradition. The three older girls felt special wearing their new fur coats. They looked like triplets with their banana curls bobbing up and down, as they walked up the long aisle in St. Joseph's Church. It was hard not to notice the Olivo family occupying the front pew, reverently listening to the pastor, Father Ring.

With the size of Mom and Dad's family, it was best to schedule the activities and gatherings at their place. Mom would stay up late preparing a magnificent spread of food and the guests would bring a special dish to try. There was plenty to go around, with leftovers for days. Dad brought out his accordion and played. The girls took turns practicing little tunes they learned on the piano and the boys amused themselves with the pinball machine.

Whenever time allowed, Dad would tune in the radio and everyone could listen to *The Whistler, Inner Sanctum*, *Lights Out*, *The Shadow*, *Roy Rogers*, or the *Jack Benny Show*. The children would cuddle up together on the living room couch, sometimes playing tug-o-war between them with the blankets tucked tightly under their chins, and listen to the radio shows.

Mom, in the meantime, would scoop up individual bowls of ice milk for everyone to enjoy. It was the best ice milk ever! Dad got it fresh, packed in five-gallon tin containers, from a nearby ice cream plant.

There was talk about television becoming a household item. Mom and Dad decided that when it did, and if it was affordable, they would get one. However, with the war going on, television production was at a halt. They relied on radio shows, dancing to the music on Dad's jukebox, and playing their instruments.

After the holidays, Mom took Ginger, along with Tootie, Gi Gi and Patty, in for dance lessons. The dance school was four blocks away and they enjoyed the walk. Ginger was a particularly cute three-year-old who looked like a little Shirley Temple. Her hair took to the banana curls as tightly as Shirley Temple's, bouncing at every movement. She would turn and look up to Mom as they walked, saying, some of the darnedest things.

"Oh Mom, what would you ever do without me?"

"Oh, I just don't know what I would do without you."

Ginger truly believed Mom was the real Blessed Mother. She wanted to do anything that would please her.

Tootie and Ginger were the dancers. Gi Gi and Patty, on the other hand, were not interested in the dance lessons. They thought it was strenuous and hard work, and would rather go outside to play.

Mom was a firm believer in encouraging her children when they showed an interest. Rather than dance, Gi Gi and Patty wanted to try their talents with the violin. It humored Mom to watch the girls practice with the instrument. Patty could not keep the violin under her chin. She would tire easily and say it was too heavy as she let it slowly slide down to her hip. Patty then took piano lessons from a music teacher down the street. When St. Joseph's School offered piano lessons, Patty received instructions from Sister Veronica. Gi Gi liked playing the violin. As soon as she began to master it, the School of Music closed down due to lack of interest. There was no more talk of the violin once Dad put it away for safekeeping.

Chapter Ten

"It's Over, It's Over"

Letters from Rodger were infrequent, yet kept Mom and Marie informed of his involvement in the war in Europe and his social life. In March 1945, he and his company were at rest in the village of Rehainviller, France. During the War, it was customary for the mayors of the French towns and villages to call a town square meeting whenever troops were on stand-down. Requests for temporary living quarters were coordinated between the Army Quartermaster and the mayor. American officers were housed in private homes, with alternative shelter for the troops. Rodger was staying at the home of Celestin and Louise Ferry.

The evening was stormy, with heavy rains and wind, the night Rodger and two other officers arrived at the Ferry home. They had rode in an open jeep and were splattered with mud. After freshening up, they joined Mr. and Mrs. Ferry, and their daughter, Helene, sitting around the stove in the kitchen. Mr. and Mrs. Ferry spoke German, Helene spoke both German and French. Rodger utilized what he remembered of his high school and college German to communicate and translated among them.

After a weeks rest, they returned to their unit in Germany. The next time Rodger had a weekend off, he went to visit the Ferry family, and brought gifts from the Post Exchange. On a visit in September, he gave Helene a watch, a bracelet, and perfumes.

One weekend he arrived with her name written on the jeep. Helene's parents began allowing her to go for walks with him, and once, he took her for a ride in the jeep.

Near the end of the war, Rodger's ability to act as an American German translator got him assigned to Prisoner of War Labor Supervision. He was sent to a Prisoner of War Camp near Rheims, France. Mom and Marie were fascinated and interested to hear of his military experiences. When he mentioned meeting Helene, they were sure he was in love and wanted to hear from him again to learn of any new developments.

Tootie, Gi Gi, and Patty thought they had it figured out. Whenever Mom had a suitcase packed and stashed under her bed, she was going to the hospital to buy another baby. They loved to snoop around her bedroom when she was not looking.

"Hey, look at the suitcase under the bed," Tootie would say to the others. Mom did not talk about it and she looked slender in the housedresses she wore. The suitcase was really the only way they knew.

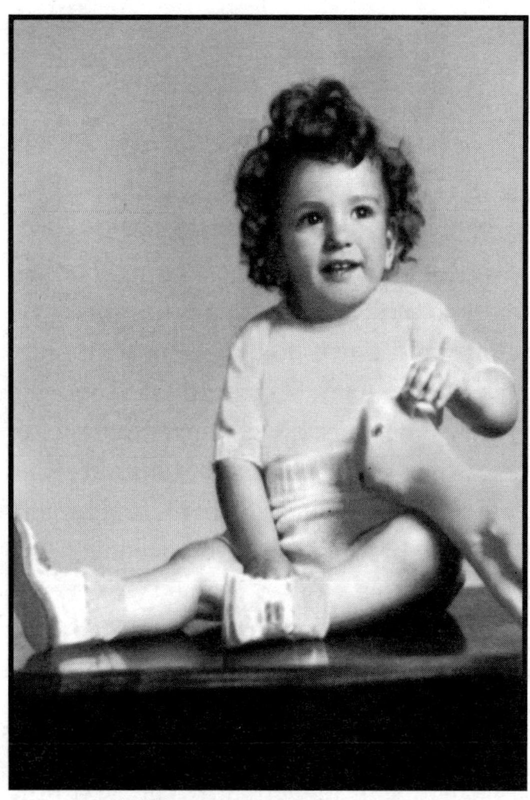

William *(Courtesy Rose Olivo)*

Mom was close to having her seventh child. None of her family or friends knew or suspected and on May 8, 1945, she went into labor. The children preferred to stay at home. They did not want to go back to San Jose Mission Elementary. The memories of the nuns lingered. Making a list out for the baby-sitters was new. Dad rushing her to the hospital was as exciting as the first trip. O'Connor Hospital was full with injured soldiers and Mom was sent to the Santa Clara County Hospital. William Rodger was born on May 8, 1945, at 6:14 a.m., the day the hospital received news of victory in Europe, the defeat of Nazi Germany and the end of Adolf Hitler's Third Reich. The excitement of the news prompted the hospital doctors and nurses to encourage Mom to name her son Victor, in honor of the victory. However, she had already decided on a boy's name, and Dad agreed with her decision.

Marie visited Mom and could tell immediately that she had a rough time with the delivery. Her eyelids were heavy from lack of sleep, and the sweat still on her brow reflected the total exhaustion that she felt. Her palms and fingers were swollen with edema, from tightly gripping the metal bars of the bed frame behind her head. There is no pain as severe as that of childbearing, and Mom already had her share.

William's curly golden locks and sparkling hazel eyes, won over others easily and Marie made visits regularly to see him.

The baby outfits Mom sewed for William interested Marie, especially now that Mom had a fancy new sewing machine. It was the Singer model 401A, with a redwood cabinet. It produced every straight and zigzag stitch imaginable.

The children loved to play with their new baby brother. Even though Tootie and Gi Gi were now old enough to help Mom, she was adamant not to impose the changing of diapers on the girls.

"I don't want to spoil any dreams of you having your own babies some day" she said. Mom wanted all her children to enjoy the innocence of childhood, and not rob them of it the way Ma had done with her.

Pa Pa and Nelle *(Courtesy Rodger and Helene Nunez)*

Pa Pa and Nelle were married early in the summer morning of June 24, 1945, by the Justice of the Peace in the little town of Wallace, Calaveras County, California. Cail Hamrick and Helen Fowler witnessed their nuptials vows at 9:05 a.m. They drove home, packed suitcases, and went to San Jose to surprise Mom and Marie with news of the wedding.

They were not happy that Pa Pa married, afraid that Nelle regarded him as a handsome, dapper bachelor who lived alone and made lots of money. Mom, Rodger, Marie, and Pa Pa had become the close-knit family they had hoped for since Lydia died. A wife would occupy his time, and perhaps lessen the time he spent with them. As it turned out, Nelle loved Pa Pa. She had a big heart, big enough to welcome into her life his children and grandchildren. Mom and Marie agreed the children adored her. She was their grandma in every way that counted. Tootie, Gi Gi and Patty returned to Campo Seco with Pa Pa and Grandma Nelle and spent a week with them. It turned out to be a "win-win" situation for everyone.

The Second World War ended on August 14, 1945, with the surrender of Japan and the streets of San Jose filled with celebration and confetti. Mom had the radio on and listened with excitement, wanting to be part of the celebration. Marie was at work at the Food Machinery Corporation, when she heard the news. She and her coworkers threw their tools into the air and ran out into the street. People were coming out of their homes, running wildly up and down First Street, while others raced for downtown. It was crazy! Clear into the night people chanted, "It's all over! The war's all over!" The streets were a mess with papers thrown from upstairs apartments and work places.

The following morning, Marie went back to work to pick up her tools. With the war over, there was no need to make any more tanks. She was actually relieved to be out of work, and decided to pick up Junior to go visit Mom. After finding a baby-sitter, they went downtown to see the aftermath of the street celebrations and had lunch together. They talked about Rodger, wondering what he was going to do after the war. Mom discussed making clothes on her new sewing machine. She excitedly told Marie of the stitches she had mastered and they decided to go shopping for fabrics and notions.

Tootie in back, Sonny, Ginger, and Patty in front-left to right *(Courtesy Rose Olivo)*

All seemed to be in order at the time Mom and Marie arrived home. The baby-sitter was playing with the children, trying to keep Sonny in line with his sisters.

Sonny liked to box around, wearing the boxing gloves Dad bought him for Christmas. He was Dad's right-hand man, and loved tinkering about in the garage next to him. They had fun wrestling; however, Dad had a rule and told Sonny, "Don't ever hit your sisters." That did not seem to stop him from throwing a punch or two, and poking at Gi Gi, making her cry.

They found Junior inside, by himself; they were shocked! He had Mom's sewing machine disassembled and strewn all over the floor. At first, they just stared, and then anger began to set in.

"Don't worry Auntie Rose. I can put it back together for you. You'll see," Junior said looking up at her. Sure enough, he had put the nuts, bolts, and screws, except for one, back in place. He was bothered that he could not account for the lost screw. He got the sewing machine running and Mom was happy again. Although he was five years old, it was apparent that Junior was mechanically and electronically inclined. Everyone who met him considered him to have the intelligence of a little genius. He was not interested in playing; he would rather find something to take apart and put back together. When he was left alone, Mom and Marie feared what he might find next to take apart. Junior and Sonny were quite a handful in opposite directions.

September meant the start of a new school year. This year the three older girls were in school, and the four young ones were at home. Mom was doing her fall cleaning and took inventory of the children's clothes and shoes, deciding which ones to keep and which ones to throw away. While Gi Gi and Patty's wardrobes looked well-worn, Tootie managed to keep her clothes looking new. Ginger's wardrobe was set and she would receive Tootie's hand-me-downs.

She was especially thrilled when given Tootie's rabbit coat, hat and hand muffs. With a little mending and darning the inventory looked good. Everyone's darned socks got mixed up in the laundry. None of the children liked wearing the darned socks. They were uncomfortable and sometimes required a second pair of socks to cover the holes in the first pair.

Despite the workload required to run her household, Mom made time for herself to read, even if it meant getting fewer hours of rest. She could not resist reading a good book. She would multi-task, holding a best-seller such as *Glory for Me*, written by MacKinlay Kantor, in one hand, and tending to the children or doing housework with the other. Dad felt, that she read too much!

"I wish I could have a nickel for every book she's read. I'd be rich," he said of her.

Every kid in the neighborhood loved to come over and play with the Olivo children. Mom and Dad purchased playground equipment to keep their youngsters active and it allowed them to keep a better watch on them.

One day, while the girls were playing ball, Tootie fell into a prickly pear cactus that grew wild along the backyard fence. Mom had to remove every thorn from her behind as she lay on the kitchen table, screaming in pain. The mishap was unusual for Tootie. She seldom got dirty, and her clothes looked neat and clean, no matter what she did.

Unlike Tootie, Gi Gi was a tomboy. She was athletic and sweaty, with her collars wrinkled and her shirttails loose. Gi Gi loved to help Dad work in the yard, and she even helped him whenever he took her on a job with him. He would hand her a shovel and say, "Dig." "You can dig for China if you want." She would dig and dig, once, actually hitting water. Gi Gi believed that if she dug deep enough, she would eventually get to China. She was a terror! When she got started, there were holes everywhere.

Dad taught the children how to garden, and each child had a row to plant whatever he or she wished. Patty especially loved to garden. She planted tulips and buttercups in her row. During the summer the youngsters would be outside working in the garden or playing.

When Marie came over, the only way to spend time with Mom was to offer to help her cook. She was always cooking something, clad in an apron over her sweater and dress. Marie could not tell that she was pregnant again with her u-um, eighth child.

Marie recalled the first time she had asked, "Rose, can I help?"

"Sure, you can peel some potatoes."

"How many?"

"Here, peel them all and use the large wash bowl to put them in."

Mom handed her a ten-pound sack of potatoes. Marie was dumbfounded, when she realized that was for just one meal of mashed potatoes.

Rather than serve the children inside, Mom served them outside; it kept the house cleaner. She had two picnic tables set up in the backyard and covered them with a pretty tablecloth.

Mom knew she needed to be a disciplinarian and gave the children incentives for behaving. She hung a chalkboard on the wall next to the refrigerator, and she would write two weeks' worth of duties at a time. Sonny bought into it and behaved for a while. He liked earning the most stars and truly did want to please Mom. He would even plant flowers in the yard for her. What Mom did not know is that he dug them up from other homes on the block.

In the evenings, whoever had the most stars got served first when the time came for ice milk dessert. The children played with their dessert to see who could out-last the other, making it appear as if Mom had served one child more than she did the others. Everything became a contest with the children: Who had the most? Who had the best? Who was the smartest? Who won? Who got the attention? If the children got a whiff that Mom had bought some cookies or other treats for their lunches, they would hunt high and low through the house and when found would be gone. There was no way to find a perfect hiding place for all the goodies.

Patty especially loved bananas, and she could not resist having more than her share. When it came time for Mom to pack the lunches, there were not enough bananas to go around. The banana phantom had struck again.

Daily life in the Olivo household was competitively fun, with never a dull moment! There was a camaraderie that made the Olivo children a tight-knit group that watched out for each other.

When Mom and Marie made plans to visit Pa Pa and Grandma for his birthday, Dad drove. They took Tootie, Gi Gi and Junior along with them. They started out early and arrived in Campo Seco at 10:00 a.m. Grandma Nelle was outside fetching a live chicken from their chicken-coop to prepare for an early dinner. Pa Pa's work shift was 4:00 p.m. to midnight. She twisted the chicken's neck, plucked it clean, and prepared it to deep-fry.

Pa Pa let Mom and Marie take his car to the store in Valley Springs. Grandma Nelle needed a few items and some ice milk to go along with his birthday cake. It was about a four-mile drive. This was the first time ever that he allowed anyone to drive his car. Of course, Marie drove, and they brought along Tootie and Junior. Gi Gi wanted to stay behind.

On the way back, as they approached the junction to Campo Seco, Marie noticed the sign to Pardee Dam.

"Oh, look! Pardee Dam is only four miles away. Have you ever been there?"

"No, I don't believe I have."

"Oh, that's not far; shall we go see what it is?"

"All right," replied Mom and off they went.

The two looked at Pardee Dam, then saw another sign that read, Michigan Bar Ghost Town. Since it was not like Dad to stop and do a lot of sightseeing whenever they were out driving, Mom glanced at Marie.

"I wonder what that's like?"

They figured they would take a quick jaunt to the ghost town, turn around, and drive back to Pa Pa's. There was still plenty of time before dinner, and Mom and Marie were not comfortable enough with Grandma Nelle yet, to hang out with her. They headed north on Gwen Mine Road, a very narrow, winding, washboard road that was carved into a steep hillside. As they were going along, Marie noticed the car would lurch to the right when she applied the brakes. She knew something was wrong and stopped the car.

"I don't think we can go back the way we came. I'm afraid we will go off the cliff if I have to brake," uttered Marie.

Tootie and Junior began to fuss and wanted something to eat and drink. Mom found Pa Pa's lunch box in the car with some silverware in it, and she used it for everyone to eat the ice milk before it completely melted. Of course, now they were thirsty, sticky from the ice milk, and wished they had some water. Marie looked down the cliff side of the road.

"Hey look, there are a bunch of houses down there. Maybe they will have some water,"

Mom stayed in the car with the children and Marie went down a path to one of the houses. A group of beautiful dark people, with long dark hair and sky blue eyes, greeted her. They gave her a pitcher of water and said to leave the pitcher on the side of the road and they would pick it up later. When Marie got back to the car, she told Mom what happened and the two of them realized they were on the Miwuk Indian Reservation. The American Federal Government considered the Miwuk's as "Peaceful People." After they were through with the water, they left the pitcher on the roadside and drove on. By now they realized they were not going to find the ghost town. Marie continued to drive for hours and finally ended up in a ditch. She said she could hardly see driving into the setting sun and ran off the road.

"It was so bright; it was like a big ball of fire."

They sat in the ditch and watched the sunset. When it became dark, they saw some lights from a nearby town. The pair of them freed the car from the ditch and continued on to the town of Jackson. After stopping for gasoline and a bite to eat, Mom asked for directions. She got directions to Lodi and from there, they knew the way back to Campo Seco.

Back at the house, initially Dad, Pa Pa, and Grandma Nelle were angry! Then when it neared four o'clock, they began to worry. Pa Pa usually drove to work. Without his car, he had to arrange for a coworker to pick him up. Before he left for work, he called the county sheriff and reported Mom and Marie missing. In those days, there was only one sheriff in each county. It was not likely that he would find them. At the mine, the work bus that shuttled men who lived in the outlying areas to work, had arrived. Pa Pa asked if anyone saw two women and two kidzes in his car. They described his car with Mom, Marie, and the children.

"Yeah, that's them. They-a probably lost."

Pa Pa got home that night shortly after midnight. Mom, Marie, and the children arrived a half hour later. They were glad to be back and ready to face a confrontation. Pa Pa was relieved to see them, even though he was angrier than a rabid bat grumbling and stomping.

"I knew you gotta lost on the reservation! Some workmen from the bus, they see you on the wrong road!"

Grandma Nelle did not want to interfere with Pa Pa's children, she tended to the little ones, who were extremely tired. She put them down for the night. Dad, on the other hand, had trouble showing his true feelings of concern. Instead he blew up with unmentionable accusations, and questioned Tootie before she went to bed for the details, not willing to believe Mom or Marie. He believed Marie was a bad influence. She got mad and snapped at him.

"You don't even want to know what really happened."

It was a stressful night. By morning, after a good nights rest, yesterday was a closed chapter and everyone was happy to be together. Grandma Nelle fixed eggs and biscuits for breakfast before the group drove back to San Jose.

Helene in France, 1945
(Courtesy Rodger and Helene Nunez)

When Pa Pa drove into town Grandma Nelle went to see her son, Eugene, in Catheys Valley, California. The two rarely traveled together to San Jose, they had their separate families to visit.

Pa Pa had heard from Rodger and sat at Mom's kitchen table reading the letter telling of Rodger's engagement to Helene.

After the war, Rodger had gone to visit Helene, and while they were together on the balcony of her home, he proposed to her. "Rodger asked me to marry him!" Helene exclaimed to her parents. The two married on January 21, 1946. It was a modest wedding, with Helene's family and Rodger's friends present. Mr. and Mrs. Ferry used every material and commodity they had to make a perfect wedding day for their daughter.

After the wedding Helene remained at her parents' home while Rodger continued with his military duties. He transferred to the U.S. State Department in Paris and joined the Foreign Liquidation Commission (FLC). The FLC sent him to Erding, Army Air Base in Munich, Germany. In his letter, he wrote that he had a months leave in July to visit family in the states.

Mom decided to have William baptized when Rodger was home and could stand in as William's godfather, with Marie as his godmother.

The planning of the homecoming and William's baptismal would be a challenge for Mom. She had a due date to consider and no one had a clue—until the children noticed her packed suitcase and her putting notes on the refrigerator door. They knew this meant she was going to the hospital to buy another baby. They played the guessing game of whether she would bring home a baby boy or baby girl.

The children piled into the back of Dad's truck when it was time to leave. Mom had William up front and she instructed Tootie, Gi Gi, and Patty to keep the other children seated. Dad dropped the children off at Aunt Josephine's before going to the hospital. Richard Wayne was born June 30, 1946, at 4:35 a.m.

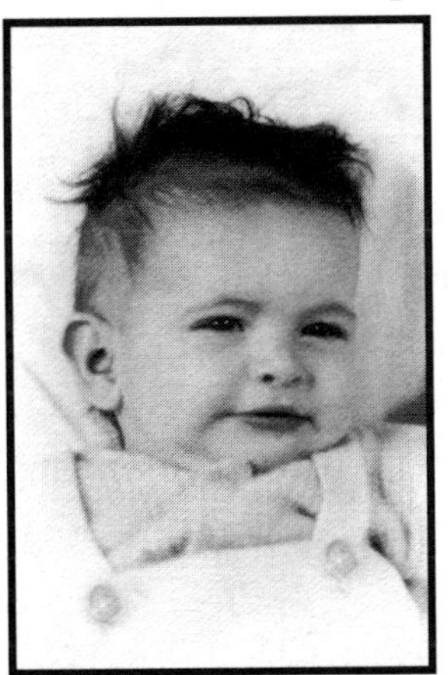

Richard "Richie" *(Courtesy Rich Olivo)*

By coincidence, Marie visited Aunt Josephine that day, not knowing Mom was pregnant, and asked why she was baby-sitting.

"Nello left them here to take Rose to the hospital to have a baby," Aunt Josephine told her.

Marie went to visit Mom whenever she knew she was in the hospital. Richard, "Richie" was a quiet, docile baby. God could not have blessed Mom with a better angel. With so many brothers and sisters doting over him, he seldom cried.

Rodger, Tootie, and Pa Pa *(Courtesy Rose Olivo)*

After Richie was born, Rodger arrived home, and of course, stayed with the Wirz'. It was a merry event having him home. He loved seeing the children, and was excited to go and visit Pa Pa and meet Grandma Nelle. The following weekend he took Tootie and headed for Campo Seco.

On July 21, 1946, The Reverend P.J. Carrol baptized William at St. Joseph's Church. The baptismal celebration continued at Mom and Dad's home. It was amazing how Mom managed to display a beautiful spread of food for such a large family gathering. She delivered Richie three weeks earlier and had spent much of the night with preparations. Not once did she complain that her legs were hurting. She was thrilled to have her family together and her excitement radiated.

Pa Pa was there for William's baptismal and was surprised to see another baby. He started counting on his fingers how many grandchildren he had, when Rodger interposed.

"Our mother died at twenty-two. Who knows how many more you would have if she had lived."

Rodger had a way of keeping Pa Pa's sharp tongue under control. Pa Pa was on his best behavior whenever around him. It was then that Rodger shared his good news. Helene was expecting in October, about the same time that Marie was expecting her second child. He also announced that he planned to leave the United States Army after his tour was up in Germany. He was ready to return to the states permanently with his new family.

When the celebration was over, Pa Pa went with Rodger to stay at the Wirz' and left for Campo Seco the following day. Rodger's furlough was up a few days later and he returned to France.

Mom was pleased that Father Grisziegh had kept his agreement to charge ten dollars for the entire Olivo family to attend St. Joseph's School. At the Merry Mart, she was buying more uniforms for her three growing girls. She saved the ones they outgrew for when the others would enter school. This time she purchased a boy's uniform for Sonny: white shirt, brown-corduroy pants, forest-green sweater, and brown shoes. She took Sonny to his first day of school. He had to learn to answer to "Nello" while in school.

Sister Lucity was a Swedish nun who taught the third grade at St. Joseph's. The children looked up into her big, blue eyes with the fear of God. She had no problem giving the children a spanking when needed. Mom had given her permission to do so to keep them in line and school rules allowed spanking.

Tootie was popular among her classmates and she was considered one of the "Big Wheels" in school. Gi Gi became intensely competitive and wanted to win at everything. She would cry when she got an "A-minus" on her schoolwork. Her classmates called her "The Walking Encyclopedia." She was involved in school activities and the Campfire Girls.

Patty found her niche playing the piano and continued taking lessons from Sister Veronica at school. She often would let Virginia practice with her at home, believing and hoping that if they kept playing, someday they would get to meet Liberace.

Marie's second child, David Allen, was born on October 11, 1946. He was perfect, and the new baby kept her too busy to visit Mom. For a while, they talked on the phone more often than they saw each other, usually when the children were doing their homework. With the children's activities it was difficult for her to talk with Marie for long periods of time.

"Oh, I wish I didn't stay on the phone so long."

Their conversations would turn to any knowledge of news from Rodger. It was late November when Mom finally received word that he and Helene's first child, Louise Antoinette, was born on October 19, 1946. All three of Pa Pa's children now had their own families.

Thanksgiving, Christmas and New Year's Day brought on challenges for Mom and Dad. The family kept growing, needing more food, clothes, and gifts. Thank goodness for J.C. Penney Department Store and the free items that they used to give away on Christmas Eve. Dad and his brothers would go there and take some of the free Christmas items to give to the children as gifts.

They would give the children bicycles they found abandoned along country roads. They looked good after the brothers had repaired and painted them. Tootie and Sonny were the exception. They received brand new bicycles from J.C. Penney's. They got everything brand new, and when they outgrew their clothes and toys, those items would become hand-me-downs from one child to the next. The children were jealous of Tootie and Sonny, yet understood that was how it had to be. The very little ones did not know the difference.

Dad saved some toys to re-wrap for another child for a following Christmas. Mom would have nothing to do with his shenanigans. She would stay up late at night sewing clothes. The clothes usually turned out to be the best gift of all. The hand-me-downs and Dad's repaired toys were not such a bad deal. They made the children appreciate receiving brand new gifts.

Tootie had the honor of playing Santa Claus. She would put on a Santa Claus hat and beard, and starting with the youngest, hand out the presents. Everyone waited as each gift was opened.

Dad belonged to The Fraternal Order of Eagles, Aerie 8 and took the children yearly to the Eagle's Lodge Christmas party to receive a special gift from Santa Claus. Sometimes Tootie would perform a ballet at the event.

The neighbors, Dick and Anne Richardson, brought over a huge basket of fruit and nuts for the family. Anne was the closest friend Mom had next to Marie. Tootie and Anne's daughter, "Sweetie Pie," took dance together. Anne began taking them to the dance studio which was a big help to Mom.

There was an opening in the white picket fence between the two backyards which allowed the girls to easily go back and forth. Anne made a playhouse out of a three sided shed underneath the walnut tree in her backyard for the girls to play. She attached an old shower curtain across the front, and equipped the playhouse with a play kitchenette and beauty salon, old clothes, old silky nightgowns, and old high-heel shoes. Her daughter Sweetie Pie, Tootie, Jeanie, Patty, and Virginia spent time there playing games, house, dress-up, and holding neighborly tea parties. They made meals out of the fruit they picked from the trees and bushes in the yard. Tootie was the mother and the others were her children. They loved styling each other's hair. Strangely enough, none of them got into cutting hair. When it came to games, such as "Guess the name of a movie star," the bookworms, Jeanie and Sweetie Pie, would usually win.

Neighbors did not see much of Mom unless they caught a glimpse of her tending to the laundry on the clotheslines in the backyard, or spotted her when the children were going to or coming home from school.

Pa Pa and Marie arrived at her house one day after a long absence.

"Getta ready. I come take-a you and Marie to the movies," he said to Mom.

"And you, you watch the kidzes!" said Pa Pa with raised eyebrows and emphatically pointing his finger at Dad.

"Aghhh—I guess so," Dad replied with apprehension.

Fanny had been visiting when Pa Pa arrived with Marie, and said she was willing to stay and help watch the children. Pa Pa took his girls to the movies now and then, just to get them out of the house for some enjoyment and for a break from the children. Every mother needs that from time-to-time. Mom chose the movie and went to freshen up. While Pa Pa, Marie, and Fanny were visiting, Dad sneaked out of the house. When they were ready to leave Fanny went to look for him. She opened the door and stopped short, looking stunned.

"Oh gosh! Joe, you ought to see your car. Your tires are flat!"

Dad had let the air out of all four of Pa Pa's tires. No one saw him do it, yet Pa Pa and the others knew. Dad took it a step too far that day. He craved Mom's attention and had been feeling left out. He was jealous of the time that Mom was spending with the children and got revenge. Oh, was Pa Pa furious!

By the time Pa Pa pumped up the tires, it was too late to go to the movies. He decided it was best for Marie and him to leave. This incident convinced him that he did not like Dad, and made no bones about letting him know it every time he came to visit. Dad could have made it a whole lot easier for Mom, knowing she was with child. Yes, this would be her ninth. They had a pact of keeping news of a new baby exclusively between the two of them.

Chapter Eleven

Five and Five Makes…

In September 1947, five of the Olivo children were in school and three at home. Mom accompanied Ginger on her first day of kindergarten. At school, the children went by their formal names. At home, Jeanie dropped the nickname Gi Gi, and Mom began calling Ginger, Virginia. The little ones used nicknames, they could not pronounce the full names of their siblings.

"Back-to-school" meant Mom would have a tighter schedule to follow. In the morning, there were usually two or three of the children standing in line to use the bathroom. Mom needed it, too, for rinsing diapers. The old pull-chain toilet with the wooden water tank above the seat served its purpose well. Dad kept it working and Mom kept it clean. She cut newspapers into squares for everyone to use, making their little bottoms black. Sonny would go in the bathroom and sit for an hour while the girls suffered. It was his way of getting to his sisters. They would start yelling "Mommm" and that would get him moving. Sonny and Jeanie fought the most, sometimes it sounded like they were going to kill each other. One thing Mom would not tolerate was fighting. She was not a fighter or a yeller. After breakfast, she would style the girls hair, prepare school lunches, and await the school bus.

The children would hear Mr. Leo, the school bus driver approaching down the street and slowly coming to a stop.

"The bus, the bus!" Mr. Leo would scream.

"One minute! One minute!" Mom would shout.

Mom had the children lined up to receive their lunch bags and milk money tickets before sending them out the door. Thankfully, Mr. Leo was patient.

The children normally made their beds first thing in the morning. After they left for school, Mom went back into their rooms to check and remake them. During the day she would cook, clean, and care for the children at home.

After school, the organized confusion began. Each child had a way of keeping Mom on her toes with before, during, and after-school activities. After dinner, the children took turns washing up in the laundry sink next to the bathroom on the back porch where it was cold, and in the one-bathtub room off the kitchen. Three or four of the younger ones would be in the bathtub at the same time. It was a small, dark, and spooky room. The claw-foot bathtub fit snugly up against the old, rotted-out, moldy backboard wall. The children would scare each other, making up stories that a mouse or spider might come crawling out and bite them. There was not enough hot water in the house for all the baths. Mom would have to warm up big pots of water on the stove and pour it over their heads, one after another. Then she would squirt Halo Shampoo on each of their heads and hand them a bar of Ivory Soap. The children had fun scrubbing each others' heads into lather, unless they got soap in their eyes. Meanwhile, she warmed more pots of water to rinse their heads in the same fashion. Halo must have been quite a shampoo, people kept telling the Olivo children how beautiful and shiny their hair looked. Sometimes it was not easy to get the little ones to take a bath; however, once they knew the routine it became easier.

After baths, Mom would towel-dry one child at a time and send them running for the iron-grate floor vent where Dad had installed a gas forced-air heater beneath the house. She placed a chair over the vent for the children to sit on until their behinds got hot. The chair remained there at all times to protect the children from burning themselves.

At night she would help with homework and set the girls' hair. She was up late at night helping them with homework assignments and projects until 11:00 p.m., and sometimes midnight. She would not sit; she would stand, pacing back and forth, looking over each child's shoulder, prepared to answer questions, and help with assignments.

As the children were sent off to bed, she would ensure everyone's school clothes were ready for the next day. She would iron into the wee hours, even using the mangle to press the sheets and pillowcases. She would starch the clothes with Faultless Starch powder, soak the clothes, hang them to dry, then sprinkle water on them for stiffness. The girls had two blouses each and Sonny had two shirts. They were to last them all week. Sometimes there was only one clean blouse or shirt available for the week.

Quite often, just before bed time there was a child at the kitchen sink, at the laundry sink, and bent over the bathtub brushing his or her teeth with Colgate Toothpaste. No one got by Mom without brushing his or her teeth.

The girls' bedroom was off the kitchen, next to the walk-in pantry. A curtain separated the boys' makeshift bedroom from the living room. Bedtime prayers were a must! All the children knelt to pray. There were three beds in the girls' room. Tootie had her own bed next to the exterior window. Jeanie and Patty slept in another bed next to the window by the laundry room. Virginia and Christine slept in the large iron-framed folding bed that was stored up against the wall when not in use. Sonny and William slept in bunk beds, and Richie slept in the crib in Mom and Dad's room.

The children had the normal share of children's sicknesses, mishaps, trials and accidents. Mom spent nights tending to their fevers and colds. It was frightening for her one day when the doctor said Sonny had asthma. Something triggered a reaction that lasted twenty-four hours and then vanished.

A child seemed to be in the hospital every year for a tonsillectomy. Then, it was common to have tonsils removed from young children. Some of the children got jealous when the one having surgery got a Popsicle or ice milk.

A sleeper couch in the living room, close to Mom's bedroom, was used for the children who were ill. She could keep a better eye on them. For the most part, the children were healthy and missed just a few days of school each year.

When the children grew taller and were hungry for a snack, they would use the step stool to reach for one of fifteen-odd boxes of cereals that lined straight across the top of the kitchen cabinets. The cereal boxes were stored there, because the cabinets did not go all the way to the ceiling. Cornflakes, Cheerios, Kix, Shredded Wheat, and Sugar Pops were the usual choices. If the children did not like what was being served or were still hungry, Mom told them to eat a bowl of cereal. That was fine with them, they liked their cereals. She kept the refrigerator filled with a dozen to sixteen bottles of milk at all times.

Jeanie was creative when it came to snacks. Her sandwich of mayonnaise, cornflakes and sugar with cinnamon was a hit. Also, when Mom let her in the kitchen, she would fry walnuts with salt to share them with the family.

On Saturday mornings, Mom would prepare Mother's Quick Oats, which the children labeled, "yucky mush." She would make such a large pot of it that it had lumps throughout. The lumps made the children gag, and they hated it. None of the children could stand eating that mush. She said it was good for them, and they had to finish eating it before going outside to play. The older ones figured out ways to discard their mush without her noticing.

One time, Virginia was sitting at the kitchen table, struggling to finish her mush, she wanted to go out and play so badly. Tootie and Jeanie had not yet finished theirs and said, "Well Virginia, tough to you," and dumped their mush into her bowl. They asked, "Mom, can we go outside to play, please?" and off they went, giggling, leaving Virginia at the table with a huge bowl of mush. She could not eat any more and sat pouting for a while before she got up.

"Mom, can I go outside, too?

"No, you may not!"

Virginia went back to the table to eat a little more, and just could not down it. Still pouting and thinking she could not go outside because she did not finish her mush, asked again, "Mom, can't I go outside and play? Tootie and Jeanie put their food in my bowl."

"No, you may not! You didn't say it right."

Virginia went to her bedroom and into the closet to cry. She came out to the kitchen several times to ask again, "Mom, can I go?"

Marie was there visiting and felt sorry for Virginia. She took her aside and whispered in her ear, "Why don't you try saying, please?"

Virginia then looked up teary-eyed, "Mom, please, can I go?"

Smiling—Mom said, "Yes, you may. That's all I was waiting to hear—the word please."

Mom was firm and gentle in disciplining the children. She seldom raised her voice, and she rarely resorted to using a brush on little bottoms. When she was serious, she would snap her fingers, making the exact same sound of the nuns' clickers at school, it got the children's attention. For the most part, the children sought her approval. She was quick to praise an accomplishment and encourage the smallest good idea.

Dad was not a disciplinarian; he left that up to Mom. He worked most of the time, and when he was home, he wanted to have fun with the children, relax, and play his accordion. On Sundays after church, he would take the older ones to Santa Cruz or Alum Rock Park to play and swim. He especially liked Alum Rock Park where he would relax in the sulfur springs and fill up on the mineral water. It soothed his many aches and pains from the hard labor he did plumbing. Sometimes, he would give the children a sip of his mineral water. They called it the soda fountain, because the water fizzed up. They did not like it, to them it was yucki!

Natural health remedies interested Dad to the point of bizarre. He would read the newspaper and cut out every article on health cures to share with family. Looking strangely at Dad, the children thought him unusually odd when he bought a professional medical machine with switches and wires that he would put over his chest and back, to zap and massage him.

The children received a nickel from him if they walked on his back. They did not know if they were hurting him or not, with his painful expressions and grunts of "ewhs, ow's, and ahh's." The children played a hard bargain with him, and soon a nickel was not enough. Dad got by cheap with Tootie, Jeanie, Patty, and Sonny. By the time he tried to coax Virginia, Christine, and William into walking on his back, they each wanted two nickels.

Mom kept a pot of soup on the stove most nights of the week for anyone who was hungry. The children reluctantly ate the soup, trying instead to hold out for dessert. On Friday nights, she served fish with Swiss Chard fried in egg batter. Their favorite was hot creamed tuna on toast. Also on Friday nights Dad would come home with a steak for her to cook for him. He knew that she and the children would not eat it, not on Friday.

"Why don't you bring the meat home on Saturdays so we all could have some?" She would ask.

Saturday night dinners were mostly chili or spaghetti. On Sundays, the children ate their other favorite meal of hotdogs on buns with pork and beans. Once or twice a month, Mom would have the children try something different, such as liver covered with bacon with sautéed onions. The children needed ketchup to get through that meal!

"Someday you are going to like this."

When the trees were full of ripened fruit and nuts, the children would pick and eat them while playing outside or bring them in for Mom to make pies, or sheets of fruit strudel for dessert. She would have a couple of large pots filled with peach and apricot jams that simmered with an irresistible aroma and wafted throughout the house, yum…those jams were the best! She did not preserve the fruit in jars. The jams did not last that long. At other times when the fresh fruits and nuts were gone, she would make rice and bread puddings.

The "suitcase" was packed, and there were notes on the refrigerator door: "Tootie, help fix the meals and pack the lunches. Jeanie, press the clothes and dress the little ones. Patty, wash and hang the clothes. Sonny, empty the garbage and rake the yard. Virginia, wash the dishes and help watch the little ones. Everyone, no friends in the house!"

Fanny, Doris, Mary, and Big Sonny were there to help. Virginia was seven years old and she tried to do everything around the house to please Mom, especially when the older ones would not do their chores. Mom and Dad left in the middle of the night. Jerilyn Helene was born on September 10, 1947, at 9:49 a.m.

Sweetie Pie was allowed in and out of the house to play with Tootie and Jeanie earlier that day. She noticed Mom was not feeling quite right and asked her, "Mrs. Olivo, are you not feeling well?"

"No, I think I'm getting a cold," she quietly responded.

Later on Sweetie Pie told her mom, Anne, "Mrs. Olivo has a cold."

Anne answered, "Oh my goodness, I believe she's going to have a baby," and spread the news throughout the neighborhood.

The excitement of another baby filled the house with more laughter and joy. When Mom and Dad came home from the hospital with the baby, the younger ones had difficulty pronouncing "Jerilyn," she was nicknamed "Lolli."

The Army discharged Rodger from military service in July of 1947, and he returned to the states in September. Mom was still in the hospital recovering from the delivery with Lolli. This time he brought Helene and Louise to live at the Wirz'. At the end of October, Mom was able to give Rodger a welcome home dinner and meet the new family that she had heard so much about. Marie was invited, and the children were looking forward to meeting their Aunt Helene and cousin Louise.

When they arrived, Louise was wearing a pink sweater and matching bonnet with kitten ears that Helene had knitted and crocheted. Noticing Mom's interest in the little outfit, Helene knew just what to make as gifts for her babies. Mom was good at keeping her children in check. After greeting their uncle and aunt, they went to the living room or to their bedrooms to play, while the adults sat at the kitchen table. Rodger and Helene were asked to be Lolli's future godparents, and they graciously accepted. Having a daughter close in age to one of Mom's children made them feel more comfortable.

Helene was not used to spicy Mexican food and sat quietly at the table as she ate an enchilada. Rodger interpreted when necessary, and she would respond by smiling and nodding, trying to understand the English. As time went on, and with Rodger's help, Helene learned to speak English fluently.

A month later, the whole family group was invited for dinner again. Rodger and Helene had been to Campo Seco to see Pa Pa and Grandma Nelle for the first time and described the experience. Helene remembers that day in Campo Seco. She was standing outside on Pa Pa's back door porch watching a beautiful sunset. She did not notice a rattlesnake that had slithered over her shoes. Rodger was standing behind her and saw the snake.

"Helene, don't move!" he said calmly.

She stood still and looked down at her feet, getting a glimpse of the rattlesnake's tail as it went on its way off the porch and slipped into the grass. She had a keen eye for rattlesnakes after that.

Marie also had something to say and waited until after dinner for the right moment to mention Uncle Cooney. Soon after Aunt Michaela died, he suffered a stroke. The hospital moved him to the County Almshouse, a home for the poor who needed assistance. It was located in Milpitas, a town near San Jose. On November 19, 1947, he died of myocardial failure, ulcers, and arteriosclerosis. There was no burial. Uncle Cooney had signed a will providing that, upon his death, he would donate his organs to the Stanford University Anatomy Department in Palo Alto. It was a noble thing to do. Mom, Marie, and Rodger were proud of him and devoted a moment of silence in his memory.

In addition to preparations for Christmas, the holiday season was filled with dance recitals, piano recitals, and the Christmas school play. Mom was busy. No one understood how she got so much done in a day. Late at night and into the early morning hours she sewed Marialice's and Virginia's dance costumes. During the day and in the evenings she attended the children's plays, dance and piano recitals. Activities would be happening at the same time on the same day.

The children's school and after-school activities were unrelenting. Every year there was a baptism, first communion, and confirmation to plan. Mom would save the outfits from these ceremonies for the next child, just as she did with the school uniforms; pretty, white celebration gowns, and the white, lacy veils attached to white, beaded tiaras.

Virginia *(Courtesy Rose Olivo)*

A busy life does not demean the mind
Human labor is not without dignity
It is not distasteful and burdensome
Rather it is something to be esteemed
Honored and enjoyed

—Jacqueline Rose Olivo

In February, the family gathered in Campo Seco to celebrate Pa Pa's birthday. Babies were the topic of conversation as Marie was carrying her third child and Helene announced she was expecting. Mom as was her custom did not mention she was expecting her tenth. No one had a clue other than her, Dad and the doctor.

Marie was ecstatic to have a beautiful baby girl. Karen Marie Bueno was born on March 30, 1948. Marie was not working and had time to dote over Karen. She bought her the prettiest baby dresses at the Jack and Jill Store, and wanted to spoil her as much as possible.

Easter was as big a deal for the children as the other holidays of the year. They knew Mom would be making outfits and bonnets for the girls, and they would get new shoes. It was a huge event for them to color eggs. After Mass on Easter Sunday, they would return home for the traditional Easter egg hunt. The older children took great pleasure in hiding the eggs for the little ones.

Ryland Park *(Courtesy Barbara Olivo Cagle)*

Summer activities were a fun time for the Olivo children. They spent many afternoons at Ryland Park, a 3.2-acre park, beautifully landscaped, with a free recreation center offered by San Jose City Parks and Recreation. It was a big boon for Mom to send the children there to take swimming lessons and to frolic on the playgrounds. She was comfortable knowing that the park provided lifeguards and organized arts and crafts. There were many barbecues, picnics and ball games to attend. Oftentimes, four or five of the children walked the eight blocks to the park. In those days, you could send your children off to the park without a worry. It did not seem like a long walk to the children and they stuck together. Mom sent them off with lunches, midday snacks, swimsuits and towels, and they would return home by five o'clock.

The children passed a cannery along the way to and from the park, and the workers there would let them watch the conveyor belt that discarded foods that were imperfect. They allowed the children to take as much of the rejected celery, carrots and potato chips as they pleased.

On occasion, Mom instructed the children to stop by Kelly's Grocery Store on their way home to pick up a few items she needed. One day, Jeanie and Patty were on their way home after stopping at the store, and a car hit Jeanie on Taylor Street. It happened that the driver of the car was a German doctor, and he quickly examined her. He concluded she had no broken bones. When he found out the girls lived a block away, the doctor took Jeanie by the hand and walked her home. Patty ran ahead, burst into the house, caught her breath, and blurted out, "Mom, a car hit Jeanie!"

When Mom opened the front door, she saw Jeanie with the doctor approaching. She looked quite bruised and stunned from the accident. The doctor was naturally upset and concerned for her well-being. He left his number and asked to be kept informed on how she was doing, and if there was any change. Mom checked her over and gave her a nice warm bath to ease the soreness. When Dad got home from work, and learned of the accident, he hit the side of his head with his knuckles as he teased Jeanie with one of his common Italian sayings, *"Testa dura!"* ("Hard head!" "Knuckle head!") The doctor stopped by the next day and he, as well as Mom and Dad, was pleased to see that she was going to be fine.

Mrs. Chenoweth, a neighbor who lived across the street, would often invite the girls over to play with her granddaughter, Deone. She had called Mom to express her concern and after hearing that Jeanie was not injured, invited her over to help bake a lemon pie. She was forever baking and would let the girls use their fingers to wipe clean the bowl and mixer blades. It was a real treat, especially for Jeanie.

Lydia's grave site *(Courtesy Barbara Olivo Cagle)*

In midsummer Pa Pa came to town. He still did not care for Dad. On the other hand, Enrico and Lena were "From the 'Old Country'," and he liked drinking wine and talking about their grandchildren together. That night, he went to the Montgomery Hotel for a good night's rest. The next day, he visited Mom and the children while Dad was at work.

At the Wirz', Rodger and Helene talked about how Helene had not met all of the relatives yet.

"I would like to meet your whole family."

"Okay, although you know my mother is dead."

"That's okay. Then we'll go to the cemetery."

Rodger knew Pa Pa and Marie were with Mom when he called her. He requested that they all meet at the Santa Clara Mission Cemetery to pay their respects to Lydia. Mom had apprehensions, uneasy feelings that were deeply rooted from long ago. They inquired at the cemetery office requesting an engraved concrete cover for the entire grave, 27B, to match the neighboring grave sites in Block Ten. The cost for a concrete cover was one-hundred dollars. They agreed to contribute twenty dollars each, and Pa Pa contributed forty. When the cover was placed on the grave, they all, except Mom, returned for a private moment with Lydia.

Rodger and Helene's second baby, Raymond Rodger Nunez, was born on August 5, 1948. The two soon learned what being "busy with babies" was like. They marveled at the thought of Mom managing nine children. Little did they know, that she was about to have a baby.

As the school year began, the older children saw Mom's familiar suitcase packed again. Then one morning, they saw the notes with instructions on the refrigerator door. Catherine Nelle, "Cathy," was born on September 22, 1948, at 6:06 a.m. There were now ten Olivo children: five in school and five at home. Fanny, Big Sonny, Mary, and Doris were at the house to help.

William and Richie stayed with Dad's parents. Grandma Lena treated William more tenderly than she had treated Sonny, and she had called him "My little minio." Then, she would gently slap the boys on the face and affectionately pinch their cheeks. The two prized the chance to go get the eggs from the chicken coop. To them it was like an Easter egg hunt.

The children were excited when Mom returned home with the new baby. She felt blessed to have one that was so quiet and did not require constant attention.

Grandma Lena's grave site along the row of Italian family vaults *(Courtesy Barbara Olivo Cagle)*

Mom had been home with Cathy for a few weeks when Grandma Lena became ill from a coronary occlusion, complicated by her diabetes mellitus and obesity. Grandpa Enrico had her admitted to the hospital, and on October 23, 1948, she died. After Gino's death, Grandma Lena had gone to his grave until she no longer physically could, and she kept his foot bones by her bedside until the day she died. Her bedroom had been off-limits to everyone. When it was opened it, they found a jumble of rubbish and useless items. There was a narrow path from her bedroom door to her bed. Prior to her burial, Uncle Jimmy had gone through her room and retrieved Gino's bones, which he returned to his grave. Mom was by Dad's side at the funeral. Grandma Lena lies at rest next to her son, Gino, in the family plot at the Santa Clara Mission Cemetery.

Grandpa Enrico became very lonely in the weeks that followed. Dad checked in on him daily, sometimes bringing a few of the children with him. He rarely left home, could no longer drive, and became a recluse. He shut himself in with the doors locked and window shades drawn, paranoid at every knock on the door. The house fell into ruin as did the yard. Dad would send Sonny around the house to knock on the bedroom window to get Grandpa Enrico's attention.

"Who is it?" He gruffly spoke out with a hot temper.

"It's me, Nello Jr.—Sonny."

"Gadda-damma-ya, yoo boo-sheet kidda! Whadda you want?"

Then he would go to open the door. No matter how cantankerous he became, Dad made sure he was looked after.

A week before Christmas, Marie woke up feeling terrible. She looked in the mirror and became frightened by the yellow face looking back at her. She noticed her hands were dark brown. A high fever pervaded her body that morning, the same high fever that had occurred intermittently for the past four or five months. Each time the fever became more severe, lasting three to five days. She had lost fifteen pounds with the fever she had in September and refused to see a doctor.

This time was different. Marie was scared. She left Karen and her two boys with her mother-in-law and Aunt Eva, and drove herself to the Santa Clara County Hospital. Without delay the doctor examined her, took blood tests, and told her, "I want you admitted immediately! You are contagious, you have hepatitis B, and I need to test everyone you have been in contact with, family, friends; everyone within the past two weeks." Luckily for Mom, Marie had not been over to see her for three weeks. She thought quickly how she had promised her children she would be back with Christmas gifts, and made up a story to buy time. "Okay, but I have to go home to get my kids straightened up to take them to my mother-in-law's home."

Empathizing with her situation, the doctor let her go. He told her to come right back, or they would have to send someone to get her.

As sick as she was, Marie left to go shopping. It was late in the evening when she finished picking up items the children needed from home. She took the gifts and household items to her mother-in-law's. She did not even have time to wrap the gifts. Karen was eight months old. Marie could hardly hold back the tears when she said goodbye to her children.

At nine o'clock, weakened by exhaustion and high fever, she had a friend drive her back to the hospital. Her doctor had begun to worry, and had prepared to send his assistant out to find her. He put her in isolation, in an old maternity delivery room. She was alone in a big, round, tiled, and sterile room. The doctor literally belted her to the bed, not even allowing her to dangle her feet or get up to go to the bathroom. No visitors allowed!

Marie stared into the large hanging lights above her. There were no phone calls. She was used to speaking with Mom and sharing what was happening in her life. Mom was her lifeline, a good friend, and a good listener. What an irony that she now knew what it was like for her own mom's yearning for her children with the fear that she might not ever see them again.

On Christmas Eve, the loneliness was unbearable and she cried, and cried, and cried, longing to be with her baby and boys. A choir of nuns stood outside the room singing Christmas carols which made her even sadder. Her isolation lasted for two weeks before the doctor saw an improvement. She became non-contagious and was moved to another room with elderly women.

When the doctor finally permitted visitors, Mom came to visit. It was late at night after her children were in bed. She had to sit across the room. The nurses warned her to keep her distance for precautionary health reasons. The two spoke of their mother with compassion. Marie thought about her baby, wanting to see and hold her. Mom's natural warmth, empathy, and keen insight helped to soothe her sister's painful yearning for her baby.

After two month's hospitalization, Marie was allowed to see her children. Her mother-in-law and sister-in-law, Eva, brought the children to visit. She was over-whelmed with happiness, then completely heart-broken when Karen refused to come to her and turned instead to hug her Aunt Eva. Her baby had forgotten she was her mother.

Chapter Twelve

Trouble

Mom could not avoid the rebellious behavior her children occasionally displayed, and no two were the same. She had to be strict and harsh in her method of discipline. There were times when she had to resort to desperate and extreme measures when it became a mind-battle between her, the nuns, and Sonny, as to who was going to get his or her way.

After many telephone calls with the principal's office, Mom reached an agreement with the principal that it would be best to keep Sonny back a year and repeat first grade with Virginia. It was not that he could not learn; it was that he did not want to learn. Perhaps he got some of that from his father—Nello Sr. had his problems in the beginning of his school years.

Sonny would not do his homework, and Mom warned him that he might have to repeat first grade even one more time. Well, he had that covered! He would get up early in the morning to copy Virginia's homework while eating his cereal. He had no regard for her neat homework, as he left a mess of sticky cereal on her papers. He gave Virginia no other choice except to hand in her homework on stained pages; she had no time to redo it.

Mr. Leo, the Italian bus driver, tried to control Sonny's rowdiness on the bus. With intensity in his eyes, and a pointed finger shaking at him, he would say in his Italian accent and stern tone of voice, "You want to get-ta home? Then you shut-ta up!"

Sonny was quite the daredevil, showing off whenever he could. The Olivo home was near a busy railroad crossing on First Street, and the trains would move slowly while changing tracks. When the older children walked to church or Ryland Park, they had to cross the tracks. When a train was stopped and the children could not pass, Sonny would roll under a boxcar. A few times when he did that, the train started up and the children panicked in fright that he might not get out from under the boxcar in time. He would also hop on the side of a boxcar holding on tightly; he would ride down the tracks and jump off when the train picked up speed. It caused his sisters anxiety—they thought his luck might run out some day.

Sonny and Jeanie played together daily. Trying to get in the last word was like a game to them. The game drove Mom crazy, yelling back and forth "LAST WORD!" "LAST WORD!" "LAST WORD!" Jeanie was sure to win, she seemed to get the last word in on just about every conversation or argument. No one could talk as fast as she. She talked so fast, people could not understand what was being said. Sonny was the one who got the brunt when punishment was handed out, and he usually deserved what he got as the instigator.

When swimming at Ryland Park, Sonny and his friends thought it was fun dunking Virginia in the water; once she nearly drowned. Jeanie had finished her life guard class and resuscitated Virginia, saving her life. "That was the straw that broke the camel's back!" Mom experienced a moment of madness and wanted to use the belt on him. The punishment was harsh and too physical for her nature. Instead, she sent him to the pantry room for an hour. He did not like her punishment. It was dark and lonely in there and after a while he started to scream, holler, and kick. He settled down once he found the pull string for the light and sniffed out a bag of cookies. After an hour, Mom let Sonny out and discovered the empty bag of cookies. She decided a teaspoon of pepper might do the trick and Sonny really did not care for that.

Another time, in the pantry, Sonny climbed up the shelves and discovered the attic access. It allowed him to escape through the hatch and crawl through the roof to the front vent that led outside. He removed the vent, climbed down the front of the house to the porch, and ran off to his friend's house in lightning speed. When he got back home, another teaspoon of pepper awaited him.

While other mothers used soap, Mom used pepper. She decided that there would be no more pantry punishment; only the pepper. Pepper would not hurt the children, yet it put the fear of God in them. As they bent over the bathtub, gagging and rinsing their mouths out with cold water, they thought they were going to die.

The children loved to tattle on one another, especially when one of them would stick his or her tongue out, or say, "D A M N!" They would cross their two index fingers in sign language meaning "Shame on you!" They would make snotty expressions, saying to the offender, "Boy, are you in T-R-O-U-B-L-E! YOU ARE GOING TO G-E-T I-T!" The children jumped at the chance to run and tell Mom on someone and then watch and root for the pepper punishment.

Sonny was dragged to dance lessons with the girls. Mom took him there hoping he would learn. He refused to practice and just stood there and glared at the teacher. Mom tried to guide him, except Sonny was not one to accept guidance. She then tried accordion lessons for him. That did not last long after he started carelessly throwing Dad's accordion around. If he made one mistake while practicing, he would end up squashing, banging and hitting it on anything around him.

"If you don't want to play it, don't break it!" Mom told Sonny when she caught him in his temper tantrums. It is a wonder that the accordion did not break. Jeanie and Virginia are the ones who mastered playing it.

The one thing that Sonny did like was boxing with Dad. They would start and work their way into the kitchen, throwing punches around the little ones, and Mom would have to end it. Dad would hug Sonny afterwards, when the two of them were out of breath from the exertion of the match.

Once, when Sonny's bicycle broke, Dad promised to buy him one. Sonny told his friends that he was going to get a brand new bicycle. When Dad came home with a broken-down bicycle that he bought for two dollars, Sonny lost respect for him. It was a long time before they hugged again. As young as he was, Sonny went with Dad on as many jobs as possible. He wanted to earn extra pocket money and buy himself a bike.

Sonny was unpredictable and carried a chip on his shoulder. He thought that anyone who had an inside toilet was rich, and he had one obsession: to make money. Mom and Dad did not know what he was going to do, or what would happen next, from one day to another.

Hanging on the kitchen wall near the pantry was a chalkboard, with a list of chores that Mom assigned to each of the older children. Every week they would switch chores. Teamed up as pairs, two would wash, dry and put away the dishes; two would hang the clothes to dry; two would sweep and mop; and two would rake the front yards, pick up fallen fruit and bag it. It worked out great, with few questions and no complaints. Taking the dry clothes off the lines was the least liked of the chores. Bugs and moths would cling to the clothes and clothespins. Shaking out each piece of clothing, diapers, towels, and sheets was important before folding them in the baskets.

There was no doubt in the devotion and respect the children had for Mom, and they wanted to please her by doing their chores well. That did not mean they would pass up opportunities to stick it to each other. There were sibling spats of anger and jealousness, pulling hair, poke-touching with the index finger, tattling, and subtly borrowing each other's belongings. With the exception of the tattling, Mom did not hear about these sibling rivalries. The children dealt with them among themselves, forgiving each other and having a good laugh about it later.

The Olivo children were busy little workers who minded most of the time—not all of the time. Virginia loved to wash the dishes when it came her turn to do them. One time when it was Patty's week to wash dishes, Virginia beat her to it. Patty stuck her tongue out, and Virginia put her fingers in her ears and stuck her tongue out, too, with a spiteful "Nahhhhhhhhhhhh!" It was not characteristic of her. However, since she did it, Patty could not pass up the perfect situation to tattle, and she turned to Mom to exclaim in a singsong tone, "Look Mom, what Virginia's doinnnnng!" That led to Virginia's first pepper experience. Patty and the others witnessed it and chuckled.

Mom did not find out about every devious, mischievous, shameful or shocking deed. Each child had his or her secrets of appalling deeds left untold. Virginia had more time on her hands when she decided not to continue with dance lessons and was not forced to take them. She thanked her lucky stars when the manager of Kelly's Grocery Store caught her and her older sister stealing candy bars, and he did not call home. It was an embarrassing and discomforting moment for the girls, and would have been worse on Mom. She trusted her girls and they were usually well behaved.

The temptation was too great for Jeanie, Patty, and Virginia when they walked home from Ryland Park and passed by the cherry orchards during peak season. After devouring their fill of tasty cherries, they thought, "Why not pick a whole bunch and bring them home?" Patty was not sure about that, so she stayed, patiently waiting on the roadside, as Jeanie and Virginia ran through the orchard and stuffed their bags without a worry that they were actually stealing. When the owner noticed the two in the orchard, he called the police. The cops waited and watched them until they were finished picking. It was a funny situation when they approached the girls and confiscated the cherries. The cops were intimidating, chewed them out, and when the girls promised not do it again, let them go. The three of them bonded in secrecy to not tell Mom.

No words were exchanged between the Olivos and their other next-door neighbors, Mr. and Mrs. Raviso. Their house was on the corner of Miller Street and Taylor Street. They did not have any children of their own and hated everyone else's. A great many children other than the Olivos lived in the neighborhood. The children played in the streets and went into their yard to retrieve a ball, or to catch the bus that stopped across the street from their house.

Mom kept her house spotless, and liked her yard to look nice, too. She had sent Christine outside to pick up the rotten peaches that fell to the ground along the common fence between the neighbors. There were many to pick up and she used a garbage can to collect them. Just as she finished and was headed into the house, more peaches started to appear on the ground. When Mrs. Raviso noticed Christine picking up the peaches, she started throwing peaches from her side back over the fence. Mom was not convinced that Christine did a good job, saw the peaches, and sent her back outside. Christine began picking up peaches again when a peach fell on her head. She thought to herself, "Golly, one fell down." She looked up and saw these peaches flying over the fence, one after another, bombarding her. Realizing what was going on, she picked up the peaches, threw them back into the neighbor's yard, and started a squishy, squashy, peach swap.

There was an on-going grudge between the Olivo children and the Raviso's over disputes and disagreements about this or that. The children referred to them as "The Grouches." They were just down right fussy, mean, and ornery. For some incidents, they would call the police to complain. One day Christine on her rotational chore duty had the job of sweeping the street gutters in front of the house and "Mrs. Grouch" came out of her house to sweep her gutters, too. Mrs. Raviso aggravated Christine by sweeping her gutter dirt into the Olivo's gutter, and one time their brooms actually touched. Christine thought, "What is it with this lady, fighting with a little girl? There must be something wrong with her."

For the children, studying at home was survival of the smartest. Jeanie studied so loudly, that no one else could think, everyone complained, "Well, she's talking too LOUD, she's studying too LOUD. I can't study."

Patty would block out Jeanie's earsplitting loud studying, by nodding her head in a rocking motion, with her arms crossed, and closing her eyes to concentrate on her own studies and memorizations. Tootie and Virginia centered their attention as best they could and tried to completely ignore her. Of course, this bickering, backbiting, and bad-mouthing went on the moment Mom left the kitchen to tend to the babies. When she returned to the kitchen, the bickering, backbiting, and bad-mouthing stopped, and they were like "Little Angels."

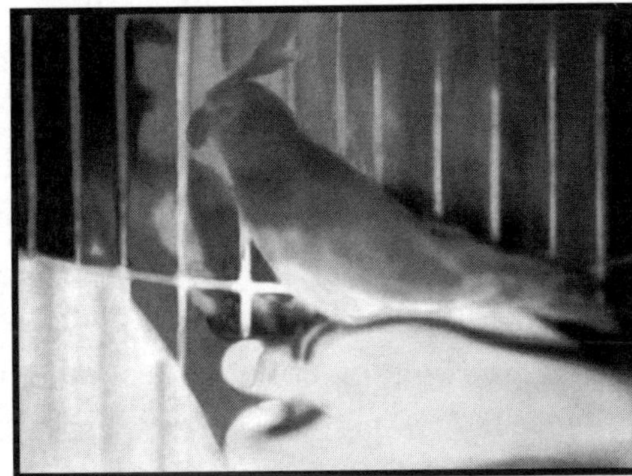

Corky and Tinlizzy *(Courtesy Barbara Olivo Cagle)*

Finishing homework meant that the children could play with the two cockatiels that Dad had brought home, a male and a female. The Cockatiels were as close as the children would ever get to having a pet. The children named the birds, Corky and Tinlizzy, and the whole family had a lot of fun with them, including Mom and Dad. Mom especially liked the birds and did not mind the little effort it took to feed them and keep the cage clean. She loved listening to them sing and talk. Corky learned to say "Pretty Bird," and "Cracker." Dad would whistle a tune and Corky would whistle the tune back. He even tied a long string to the birds' feet and let them fly outside into the fruit trees.

The children kept a daily watch on the eggs that Tinlizzy laid, that did not hatch. While the children were doing homework one night, someone let Corky out of the cage. The kitchen door to the back porch was slightly open and Corky flew through the opening. The family feared that Corky flew to the outside under the eaves where the exterior wall was about two feet short of the roof. The children looked everywhere without success and finally went to bed. Mom had her load of nightly washing and drying to do, the washer and dryer were on the back porch. While doing the laundry she found Corky's lifeless little body when she cleaned the dryer vent.

Mom was involved in the Mother's Guild at the children's school. She invited a few of the mothers over in the evening for coffee and dessert, which was a rare event for her. She told the children to stay in their rooms and be exceptionally quiet. "Children were to be seen and not heard." The children obeyed, and after the ladies left, those who were awake scrambled in a flash out of their rooms to see what was left of the desserts.

On the few occasions when Mom could attend the Mother's Guild meetings at the school, people marveled over how good she looked after having ten children. They would say among themselves that she had to be a "saint."

Mrs. Russo, Mrs. LaSiscero, Mrs. Mateo, and the nuns, would ask the Olivo girls, "How in the world do you do things in your house? How do you buy groceries? Does your mom ever lose her temper and scream?" They were probably thinking that they would if they had that many children. The girls would proudly answer, "My mom has never, ever, yelled at me!"

The girls' bedroom was small to begin with, and now it was getting crowded, with six girls and three beds, they had to share. With the exception of Tootie, who had a bed all to herself, Jeanie and Patty slept in one bed, and Virginia, Christine, and Lolli shared the foldaway bed. Christine and Lolli would sleep alongside each other, with enough room for Virginia's legs as she slept opposite them at the bottom of the bed, with her nose sticking out from under the blanket for air. She was petrified of the dark and feared that some bad man would come to get her. She felt safer and protected at the bottom of the bed.

Sharing beds together was hard for the girls. Someone would ultimately wet the bed. They got used to waking up with warm, wet sheets. If it happened in Virginia's bed, she would crawl into the bottom of Tootie's. It was a real treat for her not to have to sleep together with so many.

One time Virginia cuddled up to Tootie and wet the bed. That was it; she lost her privileges. Evenings ran into mornings, and mornings ran into evenings with no rest for Mom. She would have to get up and take care of the ruckus and rumpus that was going on in the girls' room. She could have used the rest, she was expecting again for the eleventh time!

Summer fun was back. Pa Pa and Grandma Nelle offered to watch two of the children a week at a time, which lessened the frenzied summer months for Mom. Jeanie and Virginia were set to go and packed for a week's adventure in Campo Seco. Mom went along with Dad; she wanted the opportunity to see Pa Pa. Virginia was excited to go. This was the first time for her to spend a whole week with her grandparents. Mom assured Grandma Nelle that she would love having her around. She was such a good little helper, pleasant and always happy. Jeanie had been there several times before with Tootie and Patty. She knew what to expect and what her grandparents expected.

Pa Pa and Grandma Nelle loved and favored Jeanie; she would monopolize their time, making it difficult for them to get to know Virginia's sweet nature. She was first to jump at any of their requests, leaving her sister with nothing to do. She knew that by doing so, it meant a trip to the Crystal Creamery in Valley Springs. When there was something amiss, Grandma Nelle would automatically shake her finger at Virginia, not Jeanie, ever. A bag of lye was used to inhibit the bacteria in the two-seater out-house. The girls went out there together to service the commodes.

"What do I do?" Virginia asked Jeanie.

"I don't know. Just pour the lye down into—you know."

Leaving her alone to her privacy turned out to be a disaster. She did what she thought she was supposed to do and poured the whole bag of lye into the commode, spilling some on the seat. Yep! Grandma Nelle was the next one to use the outhouse and she came back into the house gripping her tush.

"Whoa! That was enough to burn my ass. Virginia, you go sit on the rocking chair for the rest of the day!"

Grandma Nelle went to soak her burning butt in a nice cool bath. Virginia could do nothing right and with tears in her eyes; she fiercely rocked all day long. "She rocked so hard on the rocking chair that she wore a hole right through my carpet," Grandma Nelle said to Mom when they came for the girls.

Attending 9:00 a.m. Sunday Mass at St. Joseph's Church was mandatory, and no excuse was good enough. Mom made sure that the children were dressed in their "Sunday best." Occasionally Mom and Dad would be able to attend Mass with them and would occupy the two front pews. Whenever they could not attend Mass with the children, Mom expected a detailed verbal report on Father Ring's sermon. She would send the children off with money to take the bus to St. Joseph's. On their way out, the children would huddle together for a unanimous decision to either take the bus or walk to church and save the money to buy candy at the store after Mass. The group of them looked like a school class on a field trip. When people drove by they sounded their horn as they passed the Olivo children. When the children did ride on the bus, they would hear comments.

"Those are Olivos. They are either sexy Protestants or good Catholics."

A new school year began, and Mom held Christine's hand as they walked into the classroom for her first year in kindergarten. There were now six Olivo children in school and four at home. Mom managed to sanely get through school mornings, with the children scrambling to make their beds, brush their teeth, get dressed, eat breakfast, stand in line to have their hair done, kiss Mom on the cheek goodbye, grab their lunches, and fly out the door. The children would leave a mess of dirty laundry, sticky floors, and dirty dishes for her to clean up.

She took time in the mornings for a cup of black coffee and a piece of burnt toast before tackling the housework.

About the time Mom had the house spotless and was finishing up by mopping the floors with Hexol, it was three o'clock in the afternoon. The children would start coming home from school. The walls and floors of the kitchen, bedroom, and bathrooms were cleaned daily. On occasion when the house was not clean, the children knew it meant Mom was sick, which was seldom, or she was going to the hospital for another baby, which was almost an annual event.

Nancy Joyce was born on October 28, 1949, at 11:07 p.m. Mom was thankful that Fanny was still around to help with the young ones during school hours. Tootie, Jeanie, Patty, Sonny, and Virginia were old enough to take over watching the young ones after school.

Virginia wanted to help Mom with everything and soon the notes on the refrigerator were for her only. She prepared the school lunches in the evenings. Assembling two loaves of Langendorf bread across the kitchen table, she would slap peanut butter and jam on sixteen slices of bread and top them with another slice, and that is what they ate—two to three sandwiches each. There was nothing else to put in the lunches, the bananas and cookies did not last long enough.

Sister Lucity at St. Joseph's would collect uneaten lunches from the other children at school, and at the end of the day, give a sack of sandwiches and snacks to the Olivo children to take home and share with the rest of the family.

Babies and dolls were not interesting to Christine until Nancy was born. She stared at her waiting for her eyes to open. "A watched pot never boils" and it took two weeks at home before Nancy opened her eyes. Mom felt blessed with another quiet baby.

Parents are teachers by divine right; therefore, the home is the primary school. Parents are to sustain the teaching authority at home and must not attempt to relinquish their parental authority to the school.

Fathers and mothers today often bewail the fact that they can no longer get their children to obey them. Remember that parents are bound by the fourth commandment of God. For it is in carrying out their duties and obligations that they show love and reverence, and deserve honor and obedience.

—*Jacqueline Rose Olivo*

Chapter Thirteen

Lucky Thirteen

Jeanie *(Courtesy Rose Olivo)*

In the month of May, 1950, St. Joseph's School held a celebration in honor of the Blessed Mother, Queen of May. It was a huge event at the school, and each student was encouraged to make a shrine to the Blessed Mother. There was a first prize award for the most unique. Mom, with her artistic flair, could not resist helping her girls design beautifully crafted shrines. Watching one of her girls run from the bus stop into the house holding the first prize award, was one of the many excitements that she shared with her daughters.

That year, the school chose Jeanie as the May Queen. For the May 1st celebration at school, she wore a white dress with a floral wreath on her head, held a basket of flowers, and scattered them in the schoolyard as she led the procession to the Blessed Mother statue. The other children were dressed in colorful clothing, and they wore flowers in their hair. The classmates held the long, brightly-colored ribbons as they danced around the Maypoles, the boys and girls alternately weaving in and out to perform the Maypole Dance.

In September 1950 there were seven Olivo children attending St. Joseph's School. Mom accompanied William on his first day of kindergarten.

She thought she was gaining free moments to spare for herself with four children at home, when the recognizable signs of pregnancy once again appeared. This time it was not only Mom expecting. Marie was pregnant with her fourth child, and her due date was a bit sooner than Mom's. Sandy Ann Bueno was born on April 23, 1951, Marie's second beautiful baby girl.

In the midst of raising and caring for the children, Mom proficiently prepared Dad's tax forms. This year when it came time to file taxes, she claimed eleven exemptions. On the day before the final filing date, she received a phone call from a representative of the tax office in San Jose. He had received their tax forms and told Mom, "Because you are claiming so many exemptions, we would like for you and your entire family to come into the office for a picture with the Tax Collector. We don't usually see large families like yours."

Early the next morning, Mom, Dad, and the children were waiting at the glass door entrance to the Tax Collector's office. The Tax Collector had called the San Jose Mercury News. A reporter and photographer were there to interview and take photograph of the family.

"How can you possibly manage a household of such a large family? How do you stay sane? People wonder, how do you do it?" inquired the reporter.

"It's simple—we all help each other," Mom composedly answered.

Helping each other is exactly what the Olivo family did, especially when one member got sick. Nancy had come down with a serious cold. She was eighteen months old and not talking yet. Mom was up all night, Nancy lay restlessly pulling at her ears. She had a severe bacterial ear infection that had spread to the mastoid bone around the middle ear, threatening to rupture her eardrum. The doctor prescribed an antibiotic that Mom administered as instructed. She prayed that the infection would subside and not cause further complications.

To Mom and Dad, time seemed to fly by in a blink of an eye, and it felt like yesterday that Tootie was a baby. When she left for the hospital, Sonny, William, and Richard began rooting for a boy, hoping to even the score with the girls and not be as outnumbered. Nancy was beginning to talk when Harold Joseph was born on May 30, 1951, at 12:39 a.m.

A whirlwind of baptismal ceremonies, confirmations, recitals, up-coming graduations, and holidays gatherings filled the household. With the many children and other events, the family did not celebrate birthdays with parties.

Look at it this way, your birthday is just another year in your life. It's what you make of your life that's important.

—Jacqueline Rose Olivo

On his next visit, Pa Pa's mind-set was to take his daughters to the movies. Mom and Marie had cleverly planned their great escape to meet at the Montgomery Hotel and go to The Victory Theatre. They did not want a recurrence of Dad's jealous actions and conduct. It was not flattering that he regarded Mom as a coveted possession rather than a loving, caring, virtuous woman. The deep, strong convictions of her faith gave her the patience of a saint and an unconditional love for her family. She had the endurance to accept patiently Dad's imperfections and center on the loving meeting point the two had the day they married. She did not condone or take responsibility for his actions—still she loved him all the same.

Fanny and Big Sonny were visiting when Marie arrived to pick up Mom. They had previously arranged for Fanny and Big Sonny to baby-sit and to stall Dad from leaving the house. That idea fizzled as they left. He was right on their heels. They could hear his truck tires squealing in a spin, leaving the smell of burnt rubber in the air. The second part of their plan worked better when they finally dodged his attempt to follow them. They drove through several alleyways to arrive at the Montgomery Hotel, where Pa Pa was staying. They waited awhile, until they were sure Dad was nowhere in sight and happily left on their way to the movies.

There was no way for Mom to avoid Dad's jealousness. Whenever she was out in public, the few times that she went out, men would toot their car horns or whistle as they drove past. Her foxy and sexy figure was obviously eye-catching and men would stop in their tracks to take a second look. It is no wonder that Dad became possessive of her. She was a beautiful, lovely woman. She did not have many clothes, what she did have, was the latest-fashion. Mom would wear either her navy blue or light blue designer A-line suit from Blum's Dress Shop.

Marialice (Tootie) *(Courtesy Rose Olivo)*

Tootie, now a teenager, paved the way for the rest of the Olivo children. Everything began with her and then cascaded on down the line. She was charming at the age of fourteen and even though dating was not yet an option she found ways to sneak out. Tootie's cousin Beverly, Aunt Josephine's eldest daughter, was seventeen and set Tootie up with a blind date to go dancing with her and her boyfriend at the fairgrounds. When Mom got whiff of the date, Dad was sent out to the fairgrounds to get her.

"How did he like me? Did he really like me?" Tootie kept asking Beverly the next day.

"Sure he likes you, but I don't think he will ask you out again, not after how your father came and got you."

Tootie's witty comments and trendy fads came and went with the wind. She would be the first of the Olivo children to graduate from St. Joseph's School. She then entered Notre Dame High School, an all-girls Catholic school. Fortunately, Mom's tuition agreement with Notre Dame had an annual cost of one hundred dollars, no matter how many girls attended in a year.

Notre Dame's uniform was a black jumper, white short-sleeve blouse, black sweater, white bobby socks, and black and white Oxford shoes. The girls laughed at how they looked like a family of little penguins. Tootie was well liked and maintained her status as an untouchable "Big Wheel" in high school. Her classmates were thrilled if she said "Hi" or engaged them in conversation.

She was adamant that her family and friends call her Marialice now that she was in high school, and she would cringe when someone referred to her as Tootie. It was a hard request for family and friends who were used to calling her Tootie, and her nickname stuck for some time.

Marialice did well in her first year at Notre Dame, setting a speed record of one-hundred words per minute on an old manual Royal typewriter. Sister Reginald, the business teacher, expected the same speed from each of the Olivo girls thereafter. Becoming an accomplished pianist was among her impressive and incredible, dazzling, talents. She worked two days a week at St. Joseph's Church Rectory, and played the organ for the Sunday services and weddings. For fun, she imitated Al Jolson, the famous white person who, for a while, performed blackface. Marialice's personality was as completely exhilarating and electrifying as his.

Marialice *(Courtesy Rose Olivo)*

Three days a week after school, she boarded a train to San Francisco to attend ballet classes with the San Francisco Ballet Company. She performed in the "Nutcracker," a Christmas presentation that the San Francisco Ballet Company staged each year at the Opera House. She also had performances in San Jose and surrounding towns throughout her high school years. Mom sat proudly in the audience for every one of her performances and she would beam for days. On these special occasions, Marie would come to the house and help baby-sit, eagerly waiting for the two to come home and tell her of the performance. Marialice was fulfilling the hopes and dreams that Mom had thought of for herself.

Jeanie became the leader of the pack at St. Joseph's School and it became a big deal for each Olivo child to attain that position. Even though Marialice had graduated from there, seven Olivo children were still enrolled at the school. Richie had been escorted to St. Joseph's earlier that year by Mom and was attending kindergarten. With one in high school, seven in grammar school, and four still at home, Mom was expecting again. Monitoring who was doing what, when, where, and how was no easy task. Two large calendars hung side-by-side in the kitchen on which the children jotted down their schedules and events so that Mom or a baby-sitter could keep track. Even when the boys were on a job with Dad, she had them write it on the calendar.

Once, Mom asked Beverly to baby-sit seven of the children while she and Dad took Marialice to a ballet performance. The most important request of her was not to fall asleep while baby-sitting, as if there was a chance—not with all the liveliness and joie de vivre the children exuded.

Dad and Sonny had a strange evening on October 26, 1951. After school Sonny went on a job with Dad at the Signal Oil Company, on South First Street. The oil company had boarded up the station several years earlier and was now in the midst of repairing it in preparation of a grand opening. Dad discovered loot, several thousand dollars in checks, an empty change sack, and two portfolio folders containing car ownership slips, contracts, bankbooks, bail bonds, and insurance policies. The loot was wedged behind a washbasin in the rest room, the result of a nine-year-old daylight burglary that emptied an office safe in 1942. The loot literally fell on Dad's head as he wrenched the washbasin away from the wall, trying to free a rusty pipe. He took it outside and sat in his truck examining the discovery before he and Sonny turned in the findings. The district manager of the oil company acknowledged the contents, speculating that the burglar became alarmed, and hid the booty.

A reporter from the San Jose Mercury News and the San Jose News wrote a couple of articles in the newspaper the next day:

"1942 Burglary Loot Found by Plumber, and Wrench Starts Check Shower 9 Years Late."

There was no reward. Dad and Sonny talked about it for weeks. Sonny especially enjoyed the recognition and attention he got at school.

Virginia, Jeanie, and Patty at St. Joseph's School Carnival *(Courtesy Rose Olivo)*

The school year presented many exciting events. Jeanie played Mary in the Christmas play and Harold, almost five months old, landed an acting job as the Baby Jesus. It was the first time the school allowed a live baby to play the part. The performance touched everyone's hearts. Harold was such a good baby in his role that a photographer's studio used his photo in advertisements.

The Olivo girls were ready and willing to perform and dress up in costumes. St. Joseph's School carnivals were a big event, they usually were held in the evenings in the school's gym and designed to raise money for charitable organizations. The children were a topic of conversations amongst the faculty and parents. Whenever they performed in a carnival, entered kindergarten or graduated, you could hear the faculty and parents comments: "That's an Olivo," "Here comes another Olivo." "There goes another Olivo." The Olivo children looked alike, yet they fought to establish their own individuality, which made Mom proud of each one of them. Although they did not dominate the school, those that knew who they were followed their progress from sibling to sibling. Mom concentrated on instilling faith, love, integrity, leadership, and a passion to live life.

Rose at 708 Miller Street *(Courtesy Rose Olivo)*

The children's back-to-back activities took managerial skills in scheduling. It meant that at times Mom could not even change out of her housedress, let alone leave the residence. During summer vacation, the older children began to help with expenses by taking temporary jobs to pay for some of their own clothing and entertainment.

"What you earn, you are allowed to use as you please," Mom told them.

During apricot season, Jeanie, Virginia, Patty, and Sonny went to the local orchards to pick or cut apricots. The girls had a lot of fun and enjoyed earning the money to buy a new outfit or two. Sonny, however, was not too keen on picking and cutting apricots. He found a way to get himself fired.

In the wee hours of the mornings Sonny, William, and Richie had paper routes delivering the San Jose Mercury Herald. In the afternoon, they sold the San Jose Mercury News on the corner of First and Santa Clara Streets, in the shadow of the Bank of America building chanting.

"Paper, Paper! Get your San Jose News hot off the press!"

In between selling and delivering newspapers, Sonny preferred to go on jobs with Dad in hope of finding more loot. William and Richie spent time hanging out at Ryland Park with Christine, Jerilyn, and Cathy. A whole new generation of the Olivo family laid claim to the park that summer. Knowing her children were either well-entertained or working made it easier for Mom at home with the little ones.

Mom called Doris, Mary, and Big Sonny to baby-sit the children as she went in to deliver baby number thirteen. Other than Nello and a few of the older children, no one else in the family suspected she was expecting.

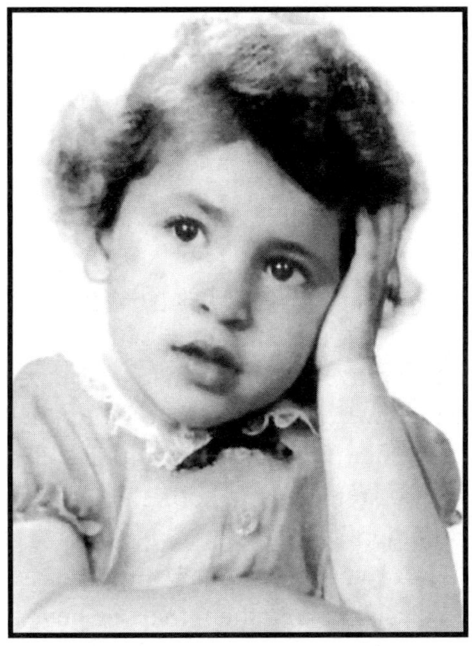

Barbara, "Barbie Doll" *(Courtesy Barbara Olivo Cagle)*

From the Basque Country comes a song and sheet music entitled "Santa Barbara," written for Saint Barbara, the patron saint of miners. The Basque people celebrate the annual festival of Santa Barbara on December 4th. Mom's lineal family members made a living working in the mines. In tribute, she named her baby, Barbara. Barbara Susan was born on June 23, 1952, at 4:07 a.m., "Lucky Thirteen."

Her newest arrival, soon to be nicknamed "Barbie Doll," did not lack for attention. She sang to her softly, "You are my sunshine, my only sunshine, you make me happy…," and "Que sera sera, whatever will be will be…" Mom sang to all her babies.

Jeanie loved to buy pretty dresses for her little sister. Patty was interested in sewing, and she sewed clothes for Barbie Doll. Virginia started sleeping on the sleeper couch in the living room near Mom's bedroom and would lie awake at night, waiting for the sound of the baby's first cry. She would warm up a bottle for her and feed her before Mom awoke. The crib was in the bedroom; Mom did not expect or insist that her older daughters take care of the babies. For that reason, it was from the heart when they did.

Mom was plagued with insomnia. Throughout the day, she would take Catnaps as time permitted.

There were too many names to remember now and Dad sometimes got confused or at least acted confused. It got to the point where he patted them on their heads and asked them, "Who are you?" There were times of frustration when Mom would catch herself going through the names before she got it right, starting off with Marialice, Jeanie, Patty, Virginia, Christine, Jerilyn, on down the line. As downright comical as it was, by the time she got to the right name, her point of frustration had vanished.

Dick and Anne Richardson informed Mom that they were moving. She was sad to see them go. They did keep in touch from time-to-time, especially during Christmas and when she asked them to be Barbie Doll's godparents.

John and Virginia Smothers turned out to be delightful neighbors. John drove a Langendorf Bread delivery truck. The Smothers noticed how the Olivo children were so well-behaved and how Sonny would run to help Dad whenever he called for him, "Sonny, get over here, I need some help."

"How do you manage with so many children?" the Smothers asked Mom in complete wonderment.

"Well, there are a lot of mouths to feed. You have to have a system with as many children as I have," she answered.

Patty with Marsha and Martha Smothers
(Courtesy Rose Olivo)

The Smothers had a set of twins, Marsha and Martha. Virginia Smothers and Mom dressed their girls as cute as could be for Sunday Mass. Patty liked playing dress-up and dolls with them. Christine played with the twins the most since they were so close in age. Marialice and Jeanie were their baby-sitters, and for an extra ten cents an hour, they ironed the Smothers' clothes.

The twins had such big hearts. When Christine told them that she never, ever had a birthday party, Marsha and Martha went around the neighborhood taking orders for homemade chocolate chip cookies to make money to give Christine a birthday bash. Mrs. Smothers had to send the girls back out to every home. They had not collected enough money the first time around to pay for the ingredients to bake the cookies. Everyone on the block pitched in, except for Mr. and Mrs. Raviso "The Grouches."

The Smothers gave an awesome party for Christine. As a special treat, they had sparklers left over from the Fourth of July and lit them for the girls. Mr. Smothers felt terrible when a spark caught fire on Christine's new dress and he panicked while trying to put out the flames. The Smothers had bought that dress for her; it was white and gray, with a whale print on the front of the skirt.

There seemed to be something going on in the neighborhood all of the time, whether big or small. The Smothers' cat, "Snowball," who liked basking in the sun in the Olivo's driveway, was missing. Christine knocked at the Smothers' door to play with the twins; Mrs. Smothers answered the door and asked her,

"Have you seen our white cat?" Christine replied with concern, "No, but there's a dead white cat in our driveway. My dad drove over it."

A good friend of the Smothers, Stanley Harris, stopped by and left his black Model "A" Ford parked at the curb with the keys still in the ignition. It created an irresistible temptation for Marsha and Christine. Marsha said to Christine, "Come on, let's go!" It happened quickly. Marsha got behind the wheel and started the car. Christine jumped in the passenger seat and reached for the door as Marsha put it in reverse. Christine was still holding onto the door and looking down at the asphalt. It felt like they were moving a hundred miles an hour and she screamed, "Stop!"

Marsha stretched her legs as far as she could trying to reach the brake pedal. They went up over the curb and ZAM! BAM! KABOOM! They went through Mr. and Mrs. Raviso's front yard and ended up on the cement patio, chipping off part of the cement steps along the way. It was like the kiss of death to upset these neighbors and the girls knew it. The shocked and bug-eyed look on the Raviso's faces, as they sat on the couch staring out of their living room window, remains mentally etched in the girls' minds.

They ran as fast as they could through the house into the girls' bedroom, closing the door, and hid under a bed. Mom asked, "What happened?" Then she went out to the front yard to see what had caused a commotion. Meanwhile, Christine and Marsha ran out the back door and across the backyard to the Smothers' house and hid underneath Marsha's bed. Mom saw that there was no real damage to speak of, and praise God the girls did not crash into the busy traffic on Taylor Street. The Ravisos wanted compensation from the Olivos and the Smothers for damages and called the police. When the police officer arrived, he listened to the Raviso's story. Then he went to speak with Rose and the Smothers, telling them what he had told the Ravisos, "You don't have a case if you don't have a driver." They went looking for the girls and did not have to go too far. They could see little legs sticking out from underneath the bed, and could hear heavy breathing. To give the girls more of a scare, and while looking at Mom and the Smothers, the police grinned and said, "Well, when we find them we will have to take them in."

If that did not worry Mom enough, the whole Stanley Harris leaving his keys in the ignition incident happened again that same summer. This time Patty was the mastermind and the one behind the wheel. She had been playing with Marsha in the front yard when they noticed that not only was the key in the ignition; the car was running. Patty asked Marsha, "Do you want to go for a ride?" Marsha was game and Patty put the car in reverse and SCREEEEECH! SCRATCH! SMASH! She went over the curb through the Raviso's yard and slammed into the cement steps! It gave the Raviso's one more incident to gripe and grumble about to the neighbors. This time they did not call the police.

Prior to the school year, Jeanie and Patty went to visit their grandparents for a week to learn how to prepare Grandma Nelle's favorite dishes. No one made fried chicken with mashed potatoes, and biscuits and gravy as well as she did. You would have to raise, slaughter, dress your own chicken, and cook it on an old wood-burning stove to have it turn out like hers. She made the yummiest pineapple upside-down cake and her lemon meringue pie was "To die for." There was one other cake she baked one time and one time only. Pa Pa bragged about it for years.

"The cake was good-da. Take a lo-ng time to make. I took a piece to the mine, and Rolly Cruickshank says, 'Where'd you get this cake?' I said, 'My wife make it.' He says, 'Jesus Christ, I never eat a cake like this.' So I told her that Rolly says he never eat cake like this, and she say, 'No wonder,' because this cake—the recipe of this cake win the prize for $25,000. The cake that Nelle make, she make by the recipe worth $25,000 made by some lady in Redwood City, and Nelle, she make the recipe—the same kind of cake. Got all kind of things in it. Got orange, got—different kind of nuts. I never see anything—the richest cake you ever see. I told her to make that cake again; Gad-da dam I can't get her to make. She says it take too much work, and refused to make it, so she didn't make it no more!"

Pa Pa raved about this cake because it won the $25,000 Grand Prize in the 1950 Pillsbury Grand National Bake-Off. Well, Jeanie and Patty did not learn to bake that cake, yet they did have a lot of fun on their visit with Pa Pa and Grandma Nelle.

That September Jeanie joined Marialice at Notre Dame High School. Marialice was more involved with ballet and Jeanie took her job at the church rectory. Patty was in charge of the Olivo clan at St. Joseph's School, with Mom accompanying Jerilyn, no longer called Lolli, on her first day as the newest Olivo in kindergarten.

There were four little ones at home. Mom did not have a moment to think of when her load would lighten. It was as if she was parenting several families at one time: a family of teenagers, a family of preadolescents, and a family of toddlers and infants. How could she love so many at the same time? The thought came across each child's mind at one time or another. The answer was the same—she just did.

Mom had God's gift of love, and she made each child feel that he or she was the most important. She saw the good in her children and did not look at the bad. That is not to say the bad did not happen. There were "Mischievous Behaviors" that went either noticed or unnoticed. If you asked Mom, she would say it did not happen, she did not know about it, or she could not remember.

Marialice and Jeanie took up smoking for a short time in high school along with other young teens. They fell into the trap of smoking in the bathroom with their friends during breaks. The teens would be standing on the toilets, smoking and talking with their heads popped up over the walls of the stalls. It was a hysterical, comical sight to see. They would stoop on the toilets if they heard noise from the swinging door, quickly smashing the cigarettes into smoky buds, thinking they could fan away the smoke with their hands. Their friends were smoking and for a while it seemed like a good idea.

Jeanie was not as lucky as Marialice when one of the other students snitched on her and her friends. A nun flew through the swinging door of the bathroom in a fury. "Click," "Click," "Click," her clicker went as she pushed open each stall. This was her first offense and Sister Mary, her Study Hall teacher told her to stay after school. The other girls had to write a five-hundred-word essay and left, while Jeanie sat, and sat, and sat waiting and wondering what her punishment would be.

"What is my punishment?" she finally asked Sister Mary.

"Well, that's what your punishment is—wondering what it's going to be!"

One time while at home, Marialice goaded Virginia, who was a sixth grader at the time, into smoking her first cigarette. Mom had company that evening and told the children to stay in their rooms. Of course, she did not know Marialice and Jeanie had already tried smoking, or that Sister Mary caught Jeanie smoking in the bathroom at school.

"Virginia, come here and I will show you something." Marialice brought her into the bathroom where the tub was and ran some water, while lighting a cigarette. "You want to try?" Virginia did not want to at first. Marialice said, "It's so easy. You just have to stick it in your mouth and inhale, and then exhale."

"Sure," Virginia replied.

"Well, this is how you inhale," and she held in her breath. "Now you do it." Marialice put the cigarette to Virginia's mouth and told her, "Now don't let it out, kind of breathe in."

Virginia inhaled and sucked the smoke down into her lungs. She started choking and could hardly breathe. The smell of cigarette smoke filled the kitchen and wafted down the hallway to the living room where Mom and her guests could hear her choking and coughing. Marialice quickly stuck the cigarette into Virginia's hand. Mom got up in a hurry, heading down the hall. As she came into the bathroom, Marialice ran out, leaving Virginia looking guilty as sin, holding the cigarette in her hand. This was the second time she got pepper across her tongue. She stood over the bathtub, rinsing it out welcoming the flow of fresh air back into her lungs. Mom quietly returned to her guests as though nothing had happened. This is how she dealt with the children—she would handle a situation and not dignify it with further discussion.

Virginia, Christine, and Jerilyn got into some amusing situations when they offered to help Mom change Nancy and Harold's diapers. Holding them down long enough to pin on a clean diaper was a challenge, and the toddlers would time and again get away and run through the house in their birthday suits. This sometimes occurred during those rare occasions while Mom was entertaining guests. The three girls would giggle and argue as to whom was to chase the toddlers down; none of them wanted to be the one to disappoint Mom. Their arguments went something like this:

"You go!"

"No, you go!"

"I'm the oldest, so you go!"

"I'm not going out there!"

"Well, neither am I!"

"It's your fault!"

"Uh, huh!"

"You better, or I'll tell Mom on you!"

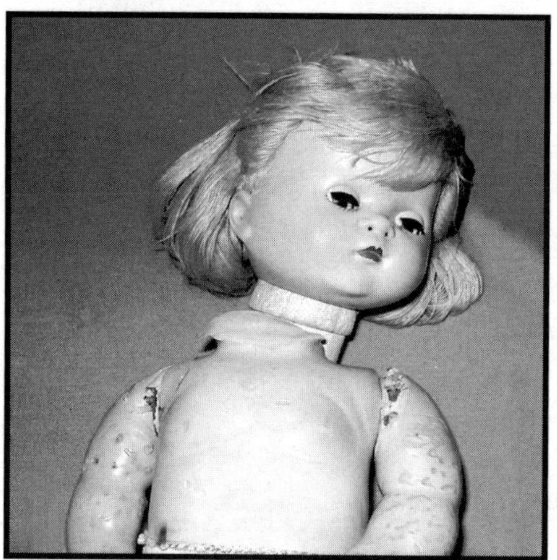

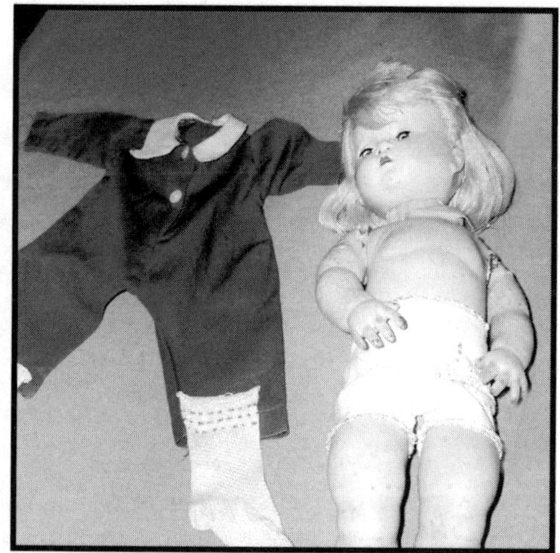

Sparkle Plenty Doll *(Courtesy Rodger and Helene Nunez)*

Rodger and Helene would take Jerilyn home on weekends for sleep-overs with Louise. The girls amused themselves with dolls, especially the expensive Sparkle Plenty Doll characterized in the popular Dick Tracy comic strip. The doll's skin was made of a life-like soft rubber material, and the hair was long, silky, yellow embroidery yarn. The doll was about fifteen inches tall, with moveable eyelids, and dressed in a dark blue jumpsuit.

Helene even made extra outfits for the girls to re-dress the doll. Jerilyn and Louise used their imaginations during playtime; one of them was the doctor and the other the nurse. They gave the doll a physical examination and decided that her health was indeed failing, she needed immediate care. Out came the scissors, and chop, chop, chop, they cut the dolls hair. Then they grabbed some ink pens and pencils and began poking holes into its arms and legs.

"What are you two doing?" Helene asked.

"The doll got sick and needed shots" the girls answered. They had the doll's arms, legs and head removed, it was totally disfigured.

Both Jerilyn and Louise had the habit of chewing their fingernails down to their cuticles. Nothing Mom could do would stop Jerilyn. Helene had heard that putting cayenne pepper on the nails would help to break the habit. That did not work for Louise, she liked to lick the stuff off just to feel her tongue burn. She chewed on Sparkle Plenty's fingernails so that the doll's nails could look like hers.

Nello Sr. *(Courtesy Rose Olivo)*

Dad occasionally left the house before the children left for school. Christine, William, and Richie would run outside to play the moment they were dressed and had finished breakfast. As Dad backed out of the driveway in his metallic green 1941 Lincoln Zephyr, he would check both side mirrors to make sure none of the children were in his view before shifting gears.

The car had wide running boards on both sides with just enough room for Christine, William, and Richie to sit. The three children liked to sit on the running boards for a short ride down the driveway before jumping off. Mom and Dad were unaware that the children considered it play. On this particular morning, Mom was outside at the front door and waved goodbye to Dad. Suddenly, she saw the three children sitting on the running board of the passenger side of the car and yelled for him to stop.

"What? What?" Dad shouted back as he rolled down the window.

At that moment, William and Richie jumped off, and Christine stumbled and got side swiped as she tried to jump. She was not moving, scared stiff and in shock. Mom felt as if her heart had dropped to her feet as she ran for her. After a quick exam, she was greatly relieved to see that Christine was not seriously hurt. She kept her home from school that day and gave her the royal treatment. Enjoying the attention, Christine pretended to be sick the next day. Mom caught on to her play-acting and told her:

"You're not sick; you are going straight on to school today!"

There was nothing wrong with her except for a couple of scrapes and bruises. If you were to hear Christine tell the story today, she had tire marks all over her body.

William loved tinkering around with Dad out in the garage. Dad gave him his own set of tools and nails to pound away on scraps of two-by-fours and other pieces of lumber. That satisfied him for a little while until he had a better idea. He snatched a couple dozen four-inch long nails from Dad's supply and went out to the front of the house to build a fort on the one-hundred-year-old bay tree. He used the fort to spy on the neighborhood boys, up and down the street. When he was not out in the street playing, or with. Dad in the shop, you would find him in his fort. He amused himself tying to pound those four-inch long nails into the tree without bending them. The evidence remains in the tree to this day.

One-hundred-year-old bay tree *(Courtesy Barbara Olivo Cagle)*

Mom recognized Christine's insurgent attitude and realized she had a rebel on her hands. She turned out to be more of a tomboy than Jeanie. She would be up in the nut trees or with William in "his" bay tree. She liked to play ball with him, Richie, and the neighborhood boys out in the street. Mom told her many times not to go outside without shoes. She liked running around barefoot and was outside shoeless more often than she was with shoes. It darned near served her right when she stepped barefoot on a nail protruding out of a two-by-four William left in the back yard. To her way of thinking, it was a huge nail in a huge board. With no tears, and sheer determination, she wobbled, dragging her foot and the board up to the back door steps. Uncle Jimmy picked her up, brought her into the house, and sat her on the counter. He held the board as Dad removed the nail from her foot.

Removing a nail from Christine's foot was small stuff compared to her involvement with the wringer-type washing machine that Mom used. She had nothing better to do on the day the nail was removed and was back outside in no time. Suddenly, she got curious about Mom's washing machine. Before she knew it, her fingers were caught in the roller. She panicked. She visualized being pulled bodily through the wringer and coming out flat as a pancake on the other side. Richie finally noticed her predicament and told Mom. Mom came running out and popped the wringer. As Christine relates, "That wringer had taken in my whole arm. I kid you not! That wringer went all the way up to my shoulder. It wasn't funny at the time. My word, I was so scared, I thought my head was going to go through that wringer!"

Nancy was three years old and standing on a chair next to Mom while she was washing red beans in the sink to soak overnight. With her little fingers, she would pick up a bean and stare at it for the longest time. Like most mothers, Mom was amazed as to what goes on in little minds and how quickly they can act. Nancy had put a bean in her left ear, the same ear that she had an infection in a few months earlier. The bean was there to stay. Mom could not retrieve it and had to take her to the doctor. He was amused at how far into her ear the bean went.

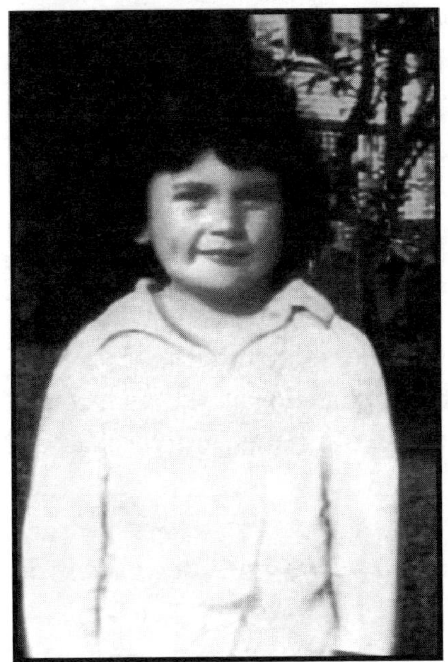

Nancy *(Courtesy Rose Olivo)*

There was much to be thankful for on Thanksgiving Day, 1952. Rodger, Helene, and Marie came to the house with their children. Mom cooked and baked for a week before the event and bought the biggest turkey she could find. Helene was famous for her cream puffs and the children looked forward to them at every big event.

When Rodger and Helene arrived on Thanksgiving Day, They noticed Nancy shyly hid behind the front door as Mom and Dad greeted them.

"Don't worry, when I come home from work, she does that to me, too," Dad said while patting Nancy on her head.

Jerilyn grabbed Louise's hand and off they went. After dinner, with their tummies full, they escaped to lie down on Mom's bed and tell stories. William and Richard played with Raymond and David, and Cathy played with Karen. The other children helped watch the toddlers.

Later in the evening, Dad brought out the accordion for entertainment. It was then that a mouse appeared! The poor thing was more scared than anyone else. The girls jumped up and down on their beds, screaming, while the boys went running through the house trying to trap it. Finally, Helene came to the rescue with a flashlight and checked underneath the beds until she was eye to eye with the mouse.

"Quick, get me some peanut butter and a trap."

Within moments, the mouse took the bait. No matter how clean Mom kept the house, it was very old and mice would occasionally appear.

Richie, Jerilyn, Cathy, and Nancy were in the Christmas spirit and could not wait to decorate the house. They thought they would surprise Mom with a gingerbread house. Jerilyn brought down a ten-pound bag of sugar from the pantry, and Cathy brought down a ten-pound bag of flour. Richie took a quart of milk from the refrigerator, and Nancy brought out spatulas from the utensil drawer. The four children sat on the kitchen floor and poured out the bag of sugar, the flour, and the milk, mixing everything with their hands and the spatulas. When the powdery flour dust settled, the four of them had more ingredients on them than was on the floor. They had created a squushed mixture one-half inch thick on the kitchen floor when Mom walked in on them. She stood there and stared for the longest time. The children could tell by her silence she was not happy and scrambled up and made a beeline for the back door.

Jerilyn was cute as a button with long banana curls and cuter when she got a short haircut. She looked different and Christine could not stop staring at her. Jerilyn finally complained to Mom, "Mommmm, if you don't tell her to stop looking at me, I'm going to…!" Christine could have scratched her eyes out.

A few days later, Jerilyn got back at Christine. She found something that belonged to Christine and asked, "Mom, if you find something, is it yours?" Mom was busy and answered, "Yes." She then realized that she had gotten herself in the middle of a taunting between the two girls as Jerilyn chanted, "Finders keepers, losers weepers!"

If you must—say 'hush-up' not 'shut-up.' Dwell on the good, because if you do, then there will be no room for the negatives.

—Jacqueline Rose Olivo

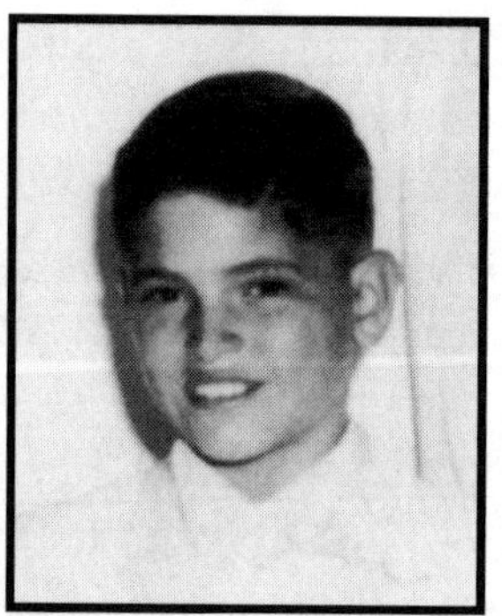

William and Richie *(Courtesy Barbara Olivo Cagle)*

William and Richie were close. Playing baseball out in the street with the neighborhood boys was their favorite pastime. Mom bought them different sports uniforms and they would form their own teams.

William was the one who got away with everything. All he had to do was bat his big, hazel eyes, with those long eyelashes, and he got his way. The only time he got in real trouble with Mom was when she heard him swear at Junior Miller, the boy across the street. Screaming and shaking with fear, he got his first teaspoon of pepper, and in his mind, it might as well have been a shovel full. Richie stood there bug-eyed watching him bent over the tub, lapping up the cold water from the faucet. He promised Mom that he would never, ever swear or use off-color language again.

"That was one thing Mom did not forgive when she felt we were deserving. She couldn't let those things slide," declared William.

She did not swear and would not allow her children to either. The worst you would ever hear her say was "Doggone it!" She needed to set an example for the rest of the children to keep them in line.

I don't believe it accomplishes anything by swearing except to lower yourself.

—Jacqueline Rose Olivo

Nello, Richie, Sonny, and William
(Courtesy Rose Olivo)

William made sure to go to confession on Saturday and on Sunday. He and Richie served as altar boys. Dad had fun with the boys and saw that they were exposed to his favorite baseball and football teams, the San Francisco Giants and the San Francisco Forty-Niners.

The city's minor league baseball team, the San Jose Giants that played at Municipal Stadium and the San Jose State Football Team that played at Sparta Stadium were also favorites. Dad took them to the Giants and 49er's games in San Francisco at Seals Stadium and at Kezar Stadium. Sonny did not go with them. He was a little older now and was more interested in finding ways to make money. Soon, his younger brothers followed suit on a smaller scale.

William was no dummy. He knew how to make money in the days when movie tickets were ten cents. In addition to his paper route income, he learned from his older brother to save the bus money. He walked to school and church. Then he would go to the store or to the bank with nine pennies and ask to exchange them for a dime. Most merchants and bank clerks would feel bad that he was short a penny, and give him a dime for nine pennies. The Olivo boys knew how to make money stretch, as did their father.

Dad took advantage of the fact that he had a large family. He had no problem telling people how many children he had, repeatedly using the story to get the full mileage while eating out or purchasing groceries. As a part of his daily routine, he met with Uncle Georgie and Uncle Jimmy for coffee and doughnuts in the morning. He would mention to the owner of the shop how many children he had, and the owner would send him off with a flour sack full of day-old doughnuts. He would come home with a flour sack time and again. When one shop was out of day-old doughnuts, he would make the rounds to different doughnut shops. Mom would warm up the doughnuts and the children thought they were "yum-yum" fresh!

Make the mistakes you need to in order to grow
Allow love to purposely show
May your leadership be ever strong
Practice what's right and know what is wrong
Set an example for others to follow

—Jacqueline Rose Olivo

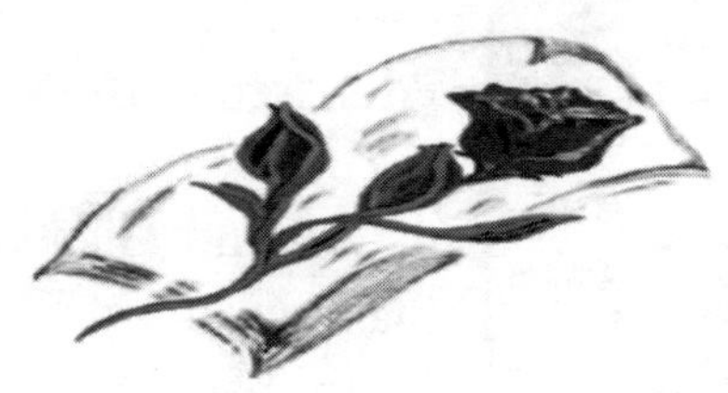

Chapter Fourteen

Next Go-'Round

Cathy

Patty *(Courtesy Rose Olivo)*

On the first day of school in 1953, Mom was with Cathy in the proverbial kindergarten first-day routine. For Cathy, she was excited. For Mom, it was her tenth go-'round.

Patty entered Notre Dame High School, with her two older sisters. Sonny and Virginia were in seventh grade and leading the Olivo line of seven attending St. Joseph's School and three were at home.

Richie took over counting the lunch bags. He passed them out to each child as he or she stood in line to go into Dad's bedroom to ask for milk money. Dad now started his workdays in the mid-mornings and would hand out the milk money and small change to the children before they left for school. Mom made sure he would come home every evening with plenty of change in his pockets. Still in bed and not fully awake, he would hem and haw a few times before saying, "Go ahead, get in my pocket; there's plenty of change." The children would take the money on their honor.

Mom was busy fixing the girls' hair. Once the children were out the door, she wanted to get to the housecleaning. In the mornings she would have to beg and plead with Dad to get moving.

"Will you please get up? Will you please get up?"

Mom was a gravida XVIII, which included four miscarriages. You heard right! Rose was in the family way again. Her days were filled with nurturing the children and praying to God for strength, endurance, and the ability to keep her family healthy, happy, fed, clean, and well-educated.

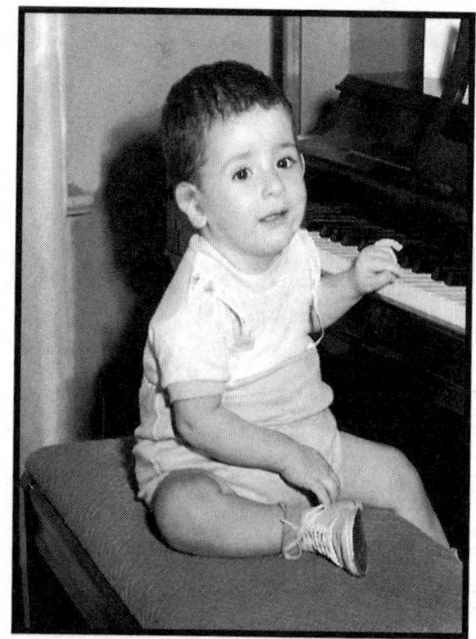

Kenny *(Courtesy Ken Olivo)*

The neighbor twins took notice that Mom many times sat by the kitchen window, facing the side yard to watch the children play. When they did not see her, they asked the children, "Where is your mother?"

"She's gone to get a baby," they answered.

Kenneth Paul "Kenny" was born on March 6, 1954, at 6:35 a.m. with a healthy set of lungs. The boys were happy to have another brother.

Sonny kept up with his tomfoolery when he played practical jokes on April Fools' Day. This year, he walked in the door and left it open behind him. With his arms across his chest, he whimpered, "Ah, oh, Mom, I'm having a heart attack!" and fell flat on his face, motionless. Those at home saw him and became scared, thinking he was seriously out. Mom stood there, shocked and gasped a cry of pain, "AAAARRGGHHH!" She reached for his shoulder to turn him over and he quickly stood up laughing and shouting, "April Fools!" He then went into the kitchen and drank a quart of milk in one shot.

Rose, Nello, and their fourteen children at St. Joseph's Church, April 17, 1954
(Courtesy San Jose Mercury and Barbara Olivo Cagle)

The San Jose Mercury Newspaper wrote:

"San Jose's Largest Family? Well—In the Running!"

Mom had the children dressed in Easter finery, including bonnets for each girl, when the family attended services at St. Joseph's Church. The church expected women and girls to wear some sort of head covering when attending Mass. In the left photo, sitting in the front pew left to right were Barbie Doll, Harold, Nancy, and Cathy. In the second pew were Jerilyn, Richie, William, Christine, and Mom holding Kenny. In the third pew were Patty, Jeanie, Marialice, Virginia, Dad and Sonny. In the right photo the silver-haired, The

Reverend Harold E. Ring, "Father Ring" acknowledged Mom and Dad's large family and took it upon himself to get to know the Olivos. He often came to the house with Holy Water to bless the family.

"Now you be a good boy!" Father Ring said patting Sonny's head.

The Olivos participated in the church choir, organ playing, altar preparations, and rectory office assistance. The large church had quarters for the priests on the above floors. The Olivo teens and school friends would hang around after Mass or choir practice to try and earn bragging rights. To satisfy their curiosity and add a little suspense, they would snoop through the church's long, poorly-lit hallways and steep, winding, pitch-dark staircases to the upper floors. They did not dare turn on a light for fear a priest would catch them. Their purely innocent motives were to get away with it and live to tell the others at school.

Nello's truck and advertising sticker *(Courtesy Rose Olivo)*

Dad was a Journeyman Plumber fourteen years before he obtained his Master Plumber License. He opened his own business, Nello J. Olivo Plumbing & Heating, at 183 Bush Street, his father's home. He stored most of his tools and pipes in the dirt basement at home on Miller Street from where he actually managed the business. Mom did the bookkeeping to save money, as if her life was not full of enough responsibilities. They wanted to save as much as possible, hoping the business would show a profit. The children joined in praying and saying the rosary with Mom nightly to overcome financial obstacles.

Dad brought in used plumbing fixtures and toilets for Mom to clean up and make look like new. When Christine noticed her up in the wee hours of the morning cleaning the unspeakable filth, she sat down next to her and began scrubbing using old toothbrushes to get to the tough areas. When they finished one set, Dad would bring in another, Mom and daughter cleaned every one of them to a sparkle, as well as the entire kitchen afterward.

Olivo Little League Team; Richie standing on left and William kneeling on right
(Courtesy Rich Olivo)

Once Dad's business got underway, he sponsored a little league baseball team and William and Richie played on the team. Richie was the star pitcher with a darned good throwing arm. Dad provided the uniforms for the team, with Olivo Plumbing & Heating embroidered on the baseball patch on the front of the uniforms.

Both boys were eager to help Dad on the job whenever he needed them, even though Mom was not too pleased when it interfered with homework. The boys did not mind, especially when it led to going out with Dad to the Cow Palace in San Francisco to watch the 49ers play basketball against the Globetrotters during off-seasons.

William was quite different from Sonny. He actually enjoyed going with Mom to Marialice's dance lessons. He became interested and thought it was neat to watch the dancers. Mom let him dress up in a marching costume to parade with Virginia at the Eagle's Lodge events, which she and Dad attended. He wore a black top hat, red shirt with black suspenders, and black pants. Virginia wore a red satin dress and held a baton.

The younger ones had older sisters' and brothers' constant doting attention. As Kenny grew older, much like some of the others, there was no need for him to talk. His older brothers and sisters did the talking for him. They knew the moment he curled his little hands into fists, raised his brows and clenched his teeth that he wanted something. All Mom could say before he went to a higher level of communication was, "Whatever he wants, give it to him!"

Collecting walnuts that had fallen from the tree was Kenny's personal conquest, and he carried around a lunch bag full as if it was a security blanket.

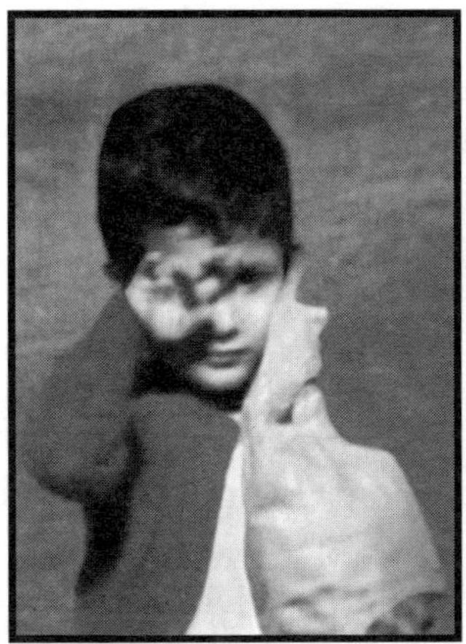

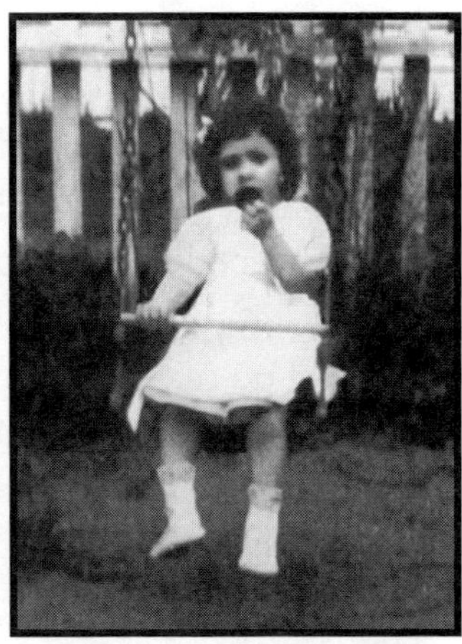

Kenny with his bag of walnuts and Barbie Doll *(Courtesy Barbara Olivo Cagle)*

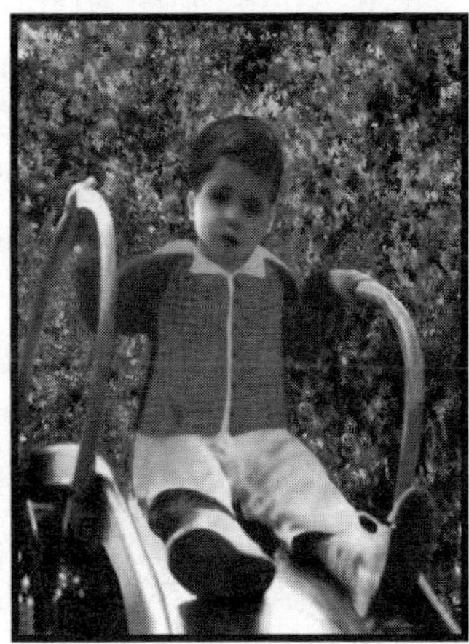

Harold and Barbie Doll *(Courtesy Rose Olivo)*

In 1954, Mom and Dad invested in a super-eight movie camera, screen and projector. Watching the children gambol on the screen and replaying the film time after time created a memorable and visual reality of Mom's life with her children. A movie night was a big deal. She prepared plenty of popcorn for everyone. Sonny, wanting to take charge as the oldest son, started up the projector and the little ones in their pajamas found a comfortable sibling lap. Those movie nights with hilarious laughter were unforgettable for the children.

In September, Nancy was ready and more than willing to make her debut in kindergarten. Smiling with her banana curls bouncing, Mom let go of her hand and she was no longer a shy little girl, she made friends quickly. There were three attending Notre Dame High School, eight Olivo children attending St. Joseph's School and three at home. Dealing with the children's escapades throughout the school year gave Mom little time to relax.

Graduations came in June 1955: Marialice graduated from Notre Dame, and Sonny and Virginia graduated from St. Joseph's. Mom did her best to carry on with their needs and wishes.

Keeping up with Sonny and trying to lead him on the straight and narrow path was not easy. He was a controlling type of kid and used to getting his way. There was no stopping him when his willful, wayward, one-track mind spun youthful antics in many directions. He would sneak out at night and take off in Dad's old metallic green Lincoln Zephyr. He did not have a driver's license and no sooner got into town than the police would stop him and bring him home. He would go out many nights trying different routes. He tried the back streets to no avail; the police would catch him. One Friday, he drove off with the car early in the afternoon. He took several of his friends to a drag race up and down First and Second Streets. At 6:00 p.m. Mom and Dad reported to the police that someone had stolen the car. The police found Sonny with the car at 9:00 p.m. and took him to Juvenile Hall. He kept trying to tell the police that he was Nello Senior. Mom received the phone call that the police had him in custody.

"Okay, my husband and I will be down to pick him up. That's our son, we won't press charges."

"Once we pick up kids and they come through the door, you can't pick up the kid until they appear before the Juvenile Court," the police officer responded.

Good or bad, it happened on a Friday and a judge would not be available until Monday. Sonny spent the weekend in Juvenile Hall. Mom and Dad arrived Monday morning. He stood there looking down with his hands crossed and explained to the judge what had happened, that he had taken his parents' car.

"Are you going to press charges?" the judge asked.

"Of course not, he's our son" said Mom.

In Juvenile Hall, the court allocates each child a counselor. The children then were assigned cleaning and cooking chores when they were kept overnight. As they were walking out of the courtroom, the counselor queried, without expecting an answer, "Why do you let your son hang out with kids like that?"

Mom asked Sonny, "Well, did you learn anything from this experience?"

Sonny, with hands in his pockets and kicking the ground as he walked, slyly chuckled, "Yah, I learned how to crack two-hundred eggs in two minutes, two days in a row."

The children tried to tittle-tattle. No one in the family had been in that kind of trouble before and they told each other whatever one knew potentially and speculatively. Mom had an incredible gift of stopping chitchat that was nothing more than gossip, which if repeated, could cause misunderstandings later. She established trust and confidentiality with each of her children. She taught her children that if they wanted to be treated with respect, they should respect others and not be too quick to judge. Give the benefit of the doubt to the other person, unless you know for sure.

Sonny may have put Mom to the test one too many times. He wanted to find a set of wheels and think of ways he and his friends could celebrate. Dad brought a couple of broken-down cars home for him to take apart and get running again. That kept him busy through the summer between working on his paper route and making tortillas at the Tortilla Factory until two in the morning. He quit his paper route when Uncle George, who ran the American Can Company, pulled some rank and offered him work there even though the age requirement was eighteen.

Whenever Sonny did have free time, he would visit his Uncle Joe who recently had a stroke. Uncle Joe used to live in a ramshackle barn on the west side of First Street. It was beautiful with red carpeting, chandeliers, and antique vintage furniture. Not many got inside, other than siblings, for fear of vandalism. Not even Sonny, until the day Uncle Joe moved into a new Victorian home on Thirteenth Street and needed help.

When he could not drive anymore, Sonny would bang on the door and shout, "Come on Uncle Joe, I will drive you out into the country."

His offer to drive was merely a motive to get out and spin his Uncle's wheels wild in the countryside. He liked to drive fast and tried scaring the hell out of him. Uncle Joe would yell, "Okay! Okay! Slow down you crazy kid! I want to smoke my cigar." He chewed on the tobacco some before lighting it up and then sat dumbfounded that he spit into a closed window.

Mom and Dad were shocked when they heard Uncle Joe's beautiful Victorian home burnt down soon after he bought it; what a shame and disaster. He was at work that day and could not figure out what caused the fire. The fire department suspected arson; no proof was found. Uncle Joe closed down the laundry business and spent the next couple of weeks in deep deliberation about his future. The ordeal of the fire, and a previous stroke, prompted him to leave town with Dorothy and resettle in Stockton, California. That was the last the Olivo family saw of him.

Time flew by quickly. A new school year began with three girls attending Notre Dame. Sonny was at Bellarmine College Preparatory High School, an all-boys school under the Jesuit Order. Six younger ones were at St. Joseph's School and three children at home. Mom's concerns for Sonny had just begun. The school's Dean, Father Corvi, was forever calling her with something or other concerning Sonny.

One day he took off with Dad's Lincoln Zephyr again, this time driving it around the campus of Bellarmine onto the pedestrian walks to show off. A faculty member sent him to the Dean's office. Father Corvi reprimanded him with a memorization assignment from Shakespeare's Hamlet in a prose and poetry book. In order for him to return to classes, he had to recite perfectly the assigned pages. For each class he missed, he received an "F" for the day. It took him three school days in the Dean's office to memorize the assignment. Father Corvi was inexorable, and had Sonny memorizing the index of the prose and poetry book backwards and forwards, and cross-referencing the dots between the titles and page numbers. It was a grueling experience for him. For example, Father Corvi asked him what page had x-number of dots after the title, what title had x-number of dots after it, what page went with what title, and so on.

Sonny went to the Dean's office three times a week. Father Ring, St. Joseph's pastor, tried to keep him at Bellarmine. His frequent visits to the Dean's office were too much and he was happy to be released from the school. The Jesuits asked that he not return.

Patty, Jerilyn, and Barbie Doll "Suzy-Q" *(Courtesy Patty Ray)*

Patty remained interested in sewing and fashions during high school; coincidentally, her sewing teacher, Sister Monica Julie, had been her kindergarten teacher at St. Joseph's School. With the hard-earned money she made from her after-school jobs, Patty bought enough material to sew matching outfits for herself and her siblings. Jerilyn, Barbie Doll and Harold showed off the outfits at the Notre Dame Fashion Show. Barbie Doll was nicknamed "Suzy-Q" for her modeling career.

Jeanie was a member of the American Scholarship Federation and the varsity athletic manager for volleyball. She and Virginia were close in high school—the two girls were like the "Bobbsey Twins." Virginia gained instant popularity by association with her sisters.

Patty, Virginia, and Jeanie at a mutual friend's wedding *(Courtesy Patty Ray)*

After Jeanie graduated and summer vacation began, she and Virginia would meet friends at John's Drive-In and follow each other in cars to Santa Cruz. They would camp out there on the beach Friday and Saturday nights. It was hard to tell the two apart. They had the same haircut, same black eyebrows, same makeup and dark, shiny tans contrasted by identical white bathing suits. The two introduced themselves as twins, "The bitter half or the better half." They enjoyed the nightlife dancing at the piano bars, and repeatedly begged Patty to come join them out on the town; she finally did.

The three sisters had the best evening of their lives. They pretended to be drunk and sang together song lyrics backwards or mixed them up. "Show me the home to go away, I'm bed and I want to go to tired, I had a little hour about a drink ago, and it head right to my went."

They looked sharp in straight skirts and Cashmere sweaters. Patty had one steady beau, Bob Ray, while Jeanie and Virginia played the dating game. Sometimes they had more than one date a day or swapped dates.

Jeanie would say to Virginia, "You need to go out with my date tonight. He will be here at six to pick me up and it will be you he picks up." She pleaded with Virginia, "Will you please go out with him? I can't go out with him. I'm going out with somebody else that I really like. She did not have to beg Virginia for too long before she gave in and said, "Alright!"

One or the other would answer the door and say, "Hi, I'm your date for tonight." That is the way it was for some time, each girl pretending to be the other whenever it suited them. Mom waited up for them, knowing that she would have to lend a comforting ear to all of the boy woe stories well into the wee hours of the morning.

Mom loved sitting with her girls in the evening over friendly laughter, questions and answers, discussions and most importantly, the closeness. When they became adolescents, and went to a dance, came home, and complained that a boy did not ask them to dance as often as they would have liked—those were the times that Mom tried to make enjoyable at home. The smell of cookies baking in the oven, or the girls trying to talk and help at the same time, that was the distraction needed and soon they forgot about the dances, parties or whatever was bothering them.

Mom believed the best way to communicate an idea with a child was to tell them a story:

> From the time you were born, you were like a garden of flowers, nourished and growing until blossomed. There are a variety of flowers: roses, lilies, daises in various colors and sizes, fresh and beautiful.
>
> One day Prince Charming entered the garden and the big question was, 'Which will he pick, will it be me,' asked a rose. 'Look, here I am. See my beauty. Inhale deeply of my lovely fragrance, touch my petals and feel the soft velvety smoothness.'
>
> Prince Charming loved the flowers. They pleased his senses, and he was grateful to these beautiful flowers for the pleasure they so willingly gave him. However, he soon tired and went away. When he returned, there were so many flowers to choose from, that he went further into the garden. He felt this one and played with another. He would not actually pick one to take out of the garden with him. Then one day he came looking for the one to pick and take with him. The one he wanted to keep with him always. He looked at some that had been touched. Their petals were no longer fresh, he moved slowly past those first in the garden to those last in the garden. There he picked a lovely little daisy, fresh and every bit as beautiful as those who were standing boldly out in front, and who had always been the first to greet him when he came to visit. Now he had chosen the one he would carry out of the garden to love and cherish.

Bob Ray and Patty *(Courtesy Patty Ray)*

Bob Ray was getting to know the family. He was impressed on how vivacious, beautiful, and slender Mom appeared. She looked as young as Patty and more like her sister. When "Me N Eds," the very first pizza parlor in Sunnyvale opened, Bob took Patty there to eat this wonderful thing called pizza. Both thought that the pizza was the tastiest, most exotic dish either of them had ever tried.

"I think my mother would like this."

At the cost of a dollar-fifty, they decided to bring a large pizza home to her. She did not know and had not heard about pizza. She was pleasantly surprised by the smell of melted cheese, tomato sauce, sausage, pepperoni, mushrooms and olives, and took her first bite.

"Wow, where did you get this?"

Mom was grateful to have Bob around. He was likable and helpful in giving her rides whenever she and the children needed to go somewhere. She still had not learned to drive and depended on Dad most of the time to take her and the children places. He would make them wait, standing for hours before he would pick them up. Mom suffered immensely from varicose veins that were the result of many pregnancies, and her legs would hurt when she stood for long periods of time. With Bob dating Patty, and his willingness to help, it created a little more freedom for her.

Tom Rose and Marialice *(Courtesy Rose Olivo)*

The New York City Ballet offered Marialice a prestigious opportunity to dance on stage. It was an offer she could not refuse and fully intended to accept. She also received an impressive and once-in-a-lifetime invitation to perform with the dancers on the Jackie Gleason show. Going to New York would have taken her away from her family and those she knew and loved.

Tom Rose was Marialice's high school beau. He came to the house to ask Dad for Marialice's hand in marriage. Out came the engagement ring, and on bent knee, Tom asked her to marry him. He had enlisted in the United States Navy in 1952, when Marialice was a sophomore in high school. In 1955, the Navy selected Tom for Naval Cadet Training and sent him to Pensacola, Florida. In 1956, he was commissioned as a Naval Aviator. The planning of Marialice's wedding soon replaced the fleeting thought of her dance career in New York and wedding bells rang in September. Mom invested in a beautiful wedding gown, one that would last through the years and her daughters would be able to use for future weddings.

Sleeping arrangements shifted at the Olivo household. Marialice no longer had a bed to herself. She counted the days to her wedding, especially after Barbie Doll wet the bed while sleeping with her. Christine, Jerilyn, Cathy and Nancy bundled up in the roll-down bed. Patty tucked in with Jeanie. Virginia "nosed" her way to the living room sleeper couch, while Sonny, William, Richie, Harold, and Kenny slept on bunk beds. Unbeknownst to the rest of the family, a crib in Mom and Dad's bedroom was ready and waiting for the next little bolt from the pink.

They had to plan for a wedding, a baby, and to arrange for a funeral. On the evening of March 22, 1956, at the age of eighty-three, Grandpa Enrico died of heart failure. Dad checked on him daily—that day he had not seen him. His father had been rough on him growing up, yet, they were close and he regretted not being there for him during his last moments. He laid his father to rest in the same vault as his mother, on the family plot at Santa Clara Mission Cemetery.

Sonny and Lorene *(Courtesy Barbara Olivo Cagle)*

Lorene Denise was born on June 29, 1956, at 2:48 a.m. Tom Rose and Marialice were godparents. Mom and Dad now had fifteen children. The young ones nicknamed Lorene, "Rinky-Dink." She was the cutest baby. Her older sisters showered her with attention, buying her dresses and wanting to take her places as if she was their own. Playing "patty cakes" was a much-loved playtime for Patty and Rinky Dink. Patty could not wait to get home from school just to rock her in the rocking chair until she fell asleep. Jeanie and Nancy would come up with various gibberish nursery rhymes like—"Inky-Dinky-Doo" to sing to Rinky-Dink.

Richie was quick to notice any jingle or quote that was catchy and sang "Inka Dinka Doo" to Rinky-Dink while mimicking Jimmy Durante's famous nose-twitch. Everyone liked to listen to Jimmy's radio shows, with his unusual and secretive sign-off, "Good night, Mrs. Calabash, wherever you are."

Chapter Fifteen

Out of the Nest

Tom and Marialice Rose *(Courtesy Rose Olivo)*

Marialice's wedding day was September 8, 1956. Mom was a great wedding planner. Father Ring officiated at St. Joseph's Church. Mom arranged for a reception at the San Jose Women's Club, where over one-hundred and fifty relatives and friends joined in the festivities. Marialice did not ask any of her sisters to be bridesmaids. She would have hurt too many feelings, selecting some of her sisters, and not others and decided to ask her friends. Cathy was the flower girl, and Richie was the ring bearer. A band played at the reception. Marialice and Tom had the first dance. Then Mom and Dad proudly took a whirling twirl on the dance-floor, knowing it was the beginning of many more weddings to follow.

The merriment at the reception went without a hitch until Jeanie had indulged in more champagne than she could handle. Marialice walked in the powder room and saw her sitting on the divan, looking ridiculous with two lit cigarettes stuffed backwards in her mouth. She was showing off to some of the guests her ability to put fire in her mouth. Mom was furious when she learned of what Jeanie was doing. She quickly and quietly handled her, discreetly sending her home in a taxicab. Sitting at her kitchen table that night and recalling the joyous, festive events of the day, Mom became amused, breaking into laughter over the comical scene of Jeanie's condition.

Marialice and Tom left for a honeymoon on Catalina Island, a popular resort getaway located twenty-six miles off the cost of Santa Barbara, California. After the wedding and honeymoon, they settled at the Naval Air Station, Whidbey Island, Washington.

Pa Pa and Grandma Nelle stayed at Rodger and Helene's for a few days after the wedding. The whole family got together at the house so Pa Pa and Grandma Nelle could visit with the grandchildren.

September meant school time, the Olivos were back to seven attending St. Joseph's. Harold waved goodbye to Mom to explore independence as the newest Olivo in kindergarten. Christine proudly took charge of the group as an eighth-grader. Patty and Virginia were "paving the way" at Notre Dame for the younger sisters and working at St. Joseph's Church Rectory. After his shenanigans at Bellarmine College Preparatory High School, Sonny transferred to Abraham Lincoln High School, referred to as "Lincoln High School." With the older children in school, Mom had more time to spend with Barbie Doll, Kenny, and Rinky Dink.

Mom missed not having Marialice at home, and looked forward to her daughter's weekly, evening calls. She told the children to listen for the ring tone before answering the phone, because they had a party line with the Smothers. Marialice excitedly spoke with Mom and shared the news of her and Tom expecting their first child. After giving her support and comfort with her pregnancy, Mom was uneasy telling her that she also was expecting in July. She was careful not to spoil any joy Marialice felt in having her first baby, and kept that special bond a mother has with her daughter when her daughter has a child on the way.

Harold enjoyed kindergarten and liked coming home from school early to play with Barbie Doll. Of Mom's sons, Harold was the one most interested in little critters, bugs, and butterflies. She bought him a butterfly net and bug box for his collection. Barbie Doll would follow Harold around while he hunted for insects among the bushes and fruit trees along the fence between the Olivo and the Smothers properties. One day he encountered something much larger than an insect moving quickly through the bushes. He held the butterfly net near the ground, and a rodent ran up the handle and bit him on the right index finger. Holding onto his finger tightly, he ran through the front door with Barbie Doll on his heels.

She was crying and Harold was screaming, "Mommm! A big mouse bit me!"

Barbie Doll went back out with Sonny to show him where they saw this "big mouse," and with a shovel, whacked the rodent dead. Mom was concerned that the "big mouse" might be rabid or have rat-bite fever. She called Doctor Campisi for advice. After describing to the Doctor what the rodent looked like, Mom learned that it was a roof rat, common in the area and likely disease-free. Roof rats feed on citrus and other fruit such as pomegranates and figs, and this rat, although nocturnal, decided to take its chances out in the daylight. As a precaution, the doctor suggested she bring Harold in to the office.

Mom was thankful when Bob Ray, who was visiting, offered to take Harold to the doctor for a tetanus shot and blood test. When the blood test came back negative, it turned out to be nothing more than another adventurous day in the Olivo yard.

Immaculate Conception Catholic Church Camanche, California *(Courtesy Patt Pereira)*

Rodger's family trip to see Pa Pa and Grandma Nelle for the weekend was humorous. Mom and the children looked forward to hearing from him about how Pa Pa was doing. On Sundays he and Helene would go to church at the Immaculate Conception, a Catholic church in the small town of Camanche, next to Campo Seco. Pa Pa was Catholic and Grandma Nelle was not. Rodger would ask him, "Would you like to go to church with us?"

"Noa! Them priest, they just wanna money in the pota,"

He proceeded to tell a story of him growing up in Spain and how a priest could not find anyone to assist or serve for a big wedding that was scheduled. The priest told Pa Pa he would pay him from the money in the pota, so he agreed. After the wedding was over, the priest told him that he had not collected enough money in the pota, and could not pay him.

"He gave me no—thing. That was it. I no go no more!" exclaimed Pa Pa.

The Immaculate Conception Church was old. The floors creaked with every movement, even tiptoeing. Rodger and Helene's children, Louise and Raymond, covered their mouths and tried to contain the laughter when they saw a mouse run across the organ keys while the organist was playing. Spider webs and dirt covered the windows, which no one could see through. Louise raised her eyebrows and gulped when Raymond pointed to the pile of mice droppings on the windowsill next to where she was sitting. He kept track of the mice droppings from visit to visit, in order to see if the droppings were still there on the next visit, and sure enough, there would be more each time.

Needless to say, the church was in need of repair and a good cleaning. The talk in 1963 was that the town of Camanche would be completely under water when Calaveras County created a dam there and no one wanted to spend money on the church.

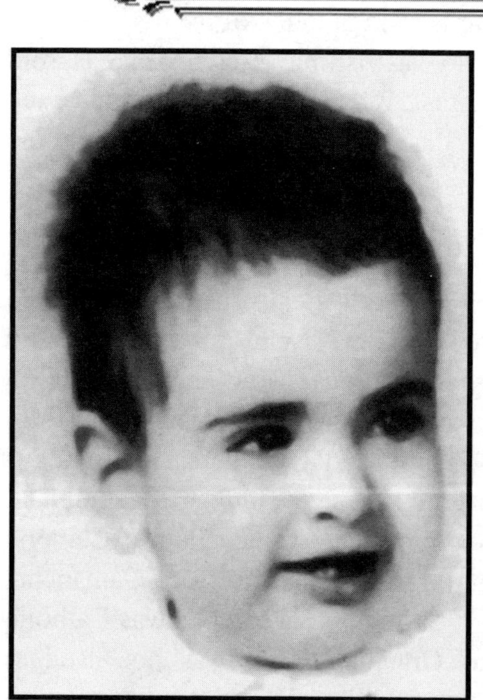

Stevie *(Courtesy Rose Olivo)*

As summer time approached the Olivo children anxiously awaited the end of the school year. Patty's graduation from Notre Dame High School was the only celebration that year. Jeanie continued to work while attending San Francisco College for Women—Lone Mountain and then later at San Jose State College.

Marialice and Mom were both expecting in July. Mom and Dad's first grandchild, Thomas Gerald Rose Jr., was born on July 8, 1957. Nine days later, Steven Edward Olivo was born on July 17, 1957, at 12:06 p.m.

Sixteen children had blessed Mom and Dad's life, ten girls, six boys. If God made the day a little longer, Mom could have still used a few more hours.

Steven was nicknamed "Stevie," Mom's little "Teddy Bear." He was cuddly and had an abundance of hair. Everyone wanted to be his favorite sister or brother and fought for his attention. Whenever he cried, Richie would imitate one of two old-time comedians, Laurel or Hardy. He would flutter his fingers or scratch his head and scrunch his eyes. William would go into his whole take on Abbott and Costello, "Who's on first?" Both of them were like clowns and the cheese of the house. Jeanie went out and bought Stevie a baseball outfit that was big enough to last a while. Virginia liked to clean and bathe him, and Patty enjoyed taking him with Rinky Dink to the Rose Garden.

When Sonny was home, he would pick up Stevie, swing him between his legs, throw him up in the air and then catch him. Mom could not stand to watch. Stevie did not mind; the two were buddies. Sonny became his godfather when Mom had him baptized.

Sleeping arrangements changed once again. Patty took over Marialice's bed hoping to be alone. An uproar would continue through the night when one of the younger ones wet the bed. William would sleep walk in the middle of the night and cause a ruckus. Jeanie would pull the sheets and covers away from whoever was sleeping with her at the time and they would tussle and wrestle with her disturbing everyone's sleep. It was a losing battle to sleep with her.

Mom had a good sense of duty in keeping the children up-to-date on routine immunizations; however, one of the children contracted whooping cough, and she feared exposure to the others. Infants had the greatest risk of dying from the disease, and Mom became seriously concerned when Stevie and Lorene caught a mild case of the disease. She placed foil bags by the beds, once one child heaved, another was soon to follow. She instructed everyone to cover their mouth and nose when coughing or sneezing, and to wash their hands frequently. It was horrifying for several nights.

Mom and Dad sat at the kitchen table one night praying, and Dad, who had been busy working long hours, mentioned, "Geez, I can't remember ever having a real conversation with some of our girls."

By the grace of God, the children got well, and whooping cough passed. After that experience, and from then on, Jeanie let whoever would sleep with her win the battle over the sheets and covers.

When Marie's children, Karen and Sandy came to the house, they would head straight for the playground equipment. When she told the girls that it was time to go, the younger Olivo sisters wanted them to stay and would hide Karen and Sandy in the house.

Marie sometimes offered to take Cathy, Nancy, and Barbie Doll for a day or a weekend. Nancy and Sandy would have screaming contests to see who could scream the loudest. Well, that got on Marie's nerves, and she would line

Karen, Nancy, and Sandy in 1957 warming up after a fun day at Santa Cruz
(Courtesy Marie Bueno)

up the girls for punishment, which usually was a soft pat on the behind for the older girls and the pretense of a pat for Barbie Doll. She would send Barbie Doll off, winking her eye and saying, "I knew you weren't a part of that."

Nancy spent more time with Aunt Marie, Karen, and Sandy than her sisters. Marie loved going to Santa Cruz and would stop by Mom's to pick up Nancy to go along with them. She would pack sandwiches and all sorts of snacks. The girls would be hungry after playing in the water, chasing the waves, and collecting seashells. Marie enjoyed those times lying on the sand and tanning, walking on the boardwalk, and watching the girls have fun on the kiddy rides.

St. Joseph's School Emblem *(Courtesy Barbara Olivo Cagle)*

Ding! Ding! Ding! The St. Joseph's School bell sounded over the PA system. Mom came in holding Barbara's hand, no longer called Barbie Doll, or Suzy Q, and carrying the rug for her mid-morning nap in kindergarten. Barbara was thrilled to come home with new songs and rhymes and could not get *Bend and Stretch* out of her mind. William, in seventh grade, was the oldest of the seven Olivo students at St. Joseph's, and Christine was tickled to be in high school with Virginia, at Notre Dame. Sonny was working his way through Lincoln High School and making new friends. Patty was working and dating Bob Ray. Jeanie was working and going to college. Mom had three little one's at home.

She would let Barbara play after school with a new friend that lived around the block. The playmate had a big playhouse supplied with toys, dolls, and doll clothes. One day, she was having so much fun playing with the dolls when it was time to leave. She stuffed as many dolls and doll clothes into the two jumbo-sized pockets of her pants that they would hold. It seemed logical to her that she could borrow them to play with for a couple of days. Her friend stood there and watched with no objection. Her friend's mother on the other hand had been watching from a second story bedroom window and with resentment in her voice, yelled out, "Hey! What do you have in your pockets?"

Barbara stood in shame as she lowered her head, stuck out her hands and emptied her pockets, crying uncontrollably, "I only wanted to borrow them for a couple of days. I would have returned them." She ran home, and with tears in her eyes told Mom what had happened.

Another time, Barbara walked out of a local store with a candy bar and a six-pack of orange soda. No one caught her—or at least not exactly. She was happily sitting on the ground under a cherry tree in the backyard, enjoying every bite of the candy bar, and ready to take the last bite of it, when she noticed wiggling—little—white—worms trying to escape their fate.

It is a good lesson to feel ashamed. You must not take what is not yours, even if you planned to return it. You should get permission to borrow it in the first place.

—Jacqueline Rose Olivo

The Reverend Father Joseph L. Dondero, Society of Jesus "Father Joe" *(Courtesy Rose Olivo)*

Father Joseph Dondero, referred to as "Father Joe," was a Jesuit priest who returned in 1958 to serve at St. Joseph's Church after being away for eight years. He had met Mom previously in 1948, the year that he began serving as an associate pastor at St. Joseph's Church and had officiated at the baptism of Rodger and Helene's son, Raymond. Mom was Raymond's proxy-godmother.

Father Joe took over Father Ring's visits to the Olivo household. The first time he visited was in the evening, Mom cracked open the door and held it firmly. She was reluctant about letting him in. She had much work to do and the children were doing homework or playing. Father Joe was a big man, six-foot-five and stuck his foot in the door. He assured her his visit would be short and after the initial introductions, made his way into the Olivo home.

He was a pianist, and a good one. He went right to the piano and started playing. Soon the older children gathered around him. Father Joe was a hit and the children enjoyed him. He was amazing and became a godsend to the entire Olivo family. On subsequent visits, he would wrestle with the boys and get on the floor to let the little ones climb all over him. He took pleasure in the lengthy debates he had with Jeanie and Nancy, the topic did not matter, and told Nancy she would make a good attorney. He used to be an attorney before he entered the Jesuits.

Father Joe looked at Mom and realized she had a full-time task raising a family—it was a whole load of work. He began visiting once or twice a week for an hour or two. Many of the children were pre-adolescents and teenagers. He knew that there may be tougher times ahead. Nello worked much of the time, so whenever the children had little problems, he would talk to them quietly.

He told Rose, "My job is to help the people. I will talk to the kids and help them and entertain them. I will give them, you know, little instructions and counseling." Mom put her faith in him and when she had problems, she would say to the children, "Well, you'll have to talk it over with Father Joe." It was a big job. One day, chuckling, he said to her, "What you need is a chaplain for the Olivo family to take care of the problems, just one guy—assigned to the family." He was forever saying, "I don't know how you do it, all the washing, sewing, cleaning, and taking care of the health of the kids. I don't see how. It is a heroic thing you are doing, up all night, constantly, unbelievable! For a large family in modern times; there's a kind of tendency to break up the family. The greatest example your family has set is that it has all held together. You all love each other. You all bind together. You help each other. The whole thing is really marvelous. Without the grace of God and the ideal family, it would not have happened. It takes a huge effort and no one is willing to make that kind of effort now-a-days to do it."

Sometimes Jeanie did not want to talk with Father Joe, preferring to study. She was attending San Jose State College and as in the past, she wanted to get "A"s. When Father Joe came to visit the family, she would hide in the girls' closet, holding a flashlight over a book in order to study.

"Where's Jeanie?" Father Joe would ask.

She had instructed the others to tell him she was not home. On his next visit, Jeanie headed for the closet with Cathy and Nancy following right behind her, and three girls hid in the closet.

"Where are the girls?" he asked.

Beckoning him to follow her to the girls' bedroom Mom opened the door, saying, "Geez, I don't know where they are." Father Joe went into the bedroom and opened the closet door to find the girls hiding.

Some of Sonny's friends had ridiculous nicknames such as, Goofy and Pon Pon. One day he and his friends decided to play hooky from school. Those were the days when, for some reason, many kids played hooky, and Sonny was no exception. He and five of his friends decided to drive up to Mount Hamilton, the highest peak overlooking the city of San Jose. It is located in the Diablo Range, and the Lick Observatory sits at the highest point. Alum Rock Park is located on the western flank, adjacent to Mt. Hamilton Road leading to the top. There was snow on the mountain, and they wanted to fool around in it. The road was extremely steep and dangerously winding. There were many hairpin turns, no guardrails, and pavement only wide enough for one car with turnouts for yielding to descending traffic.

Sonny drove Dad's Lincoln Zephyr, and of course, still did not have a driver's license. After spending the afternoon in the snow, the boys drove back and halfway down the hill the brakes went out. As the car picked up speed, he steered into a ditch along the hillside in order to gain control. Banging up the front fender, he drove the narrow road next to the hill to avoid the steep drop-off on the hairpin turns. It scared the holy daylight out of the boys, and one of them in the back seat was literally bawling his eyes out. The boy just wanted to make it home. As they neared the bottom of the hill, the car slowed down. He and the boys opened the doors and dragged their feet on the pavement and dirt, in order to stop the car. With shoes scraped and muddied, they recovered some composure. The boy in the back seat could not wait to get out, and hiked his way home. Sonny drove the car carefully in low gear the rest of the way home, and tried to synchronize the lights. That was a little tricky. More importantly, he made it home all right. It was a good thing there was another Lincoln Zephyr in his back yard that was not working. He had to take the fenders off that one, prime them, and replace the ones on Dad's car.

Sonny had his share of altercations. Mr. Henry, Lincoln High School's football coach was walking down the corridor and saw him taking on one of his star wrestlers. Johnson was his name, a big guy, and Sonny was holding him out a window. Henry asked him to join the football and wrestling team. Sonny told him he was too busy working. He was not too busy working though, to get into fights or steal some booze, which landed him again in Juvenile Court. This time when he came walking out of the court, he heard the counselor say to another mother, "Why do you let your son hang around with a bad guy like that." The counselor was pointing at him. Just then, something magical happened to Sonny. He reflected on the words of wisdom Mom and Father Joe had given him over the years. He went too far in a juvenile prank and it became a criminal offense. That is when he decided to turn his life around and set a better example by guiding his younger brothers and sisters.

In one of Father Joe's counseling sessions he said, "Evil is overcome by good and is endured by patience. It is the lesson Christ came to teach us by word and example. Love one another, do good where there is evil, do not become bitter, revengeful, angry, hateful, and sucked in by the black hole of evil. Take away the plank from your own eyes before you try to remove the speck of dust from your neighbor's eye. Accept your portion of suffering and transform it into something good. Ask God to bless you with the gift of grace to be what he wants you to be and to do what he wants you to do."

Hebrews 12:11 "At the time it is administered, all discipline seems a cause for grief and not for joy, but later it brings forth the fruit of peace and justice to those who are trained in its school."

Chapter Sixteen

Moments in Time

Nancy, Cathy, Barbara, Louise, Pa Pa, Raymond

Richie, Christine, Virginia, Sonny, Patty, Jeanie, and William

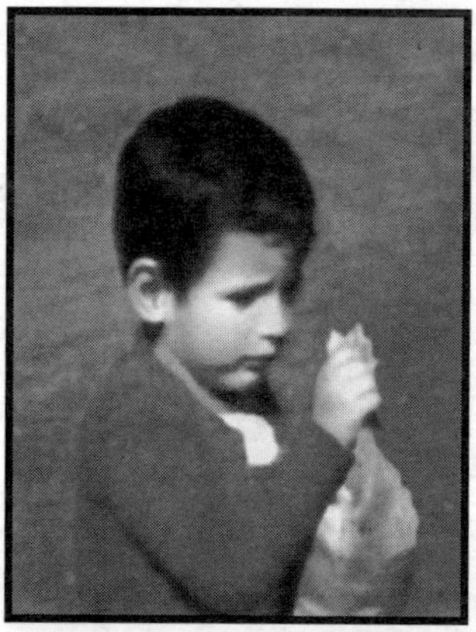

Kenny with bag of walnuts

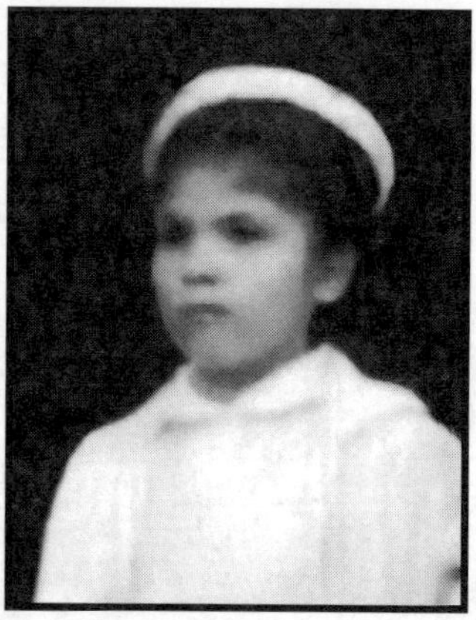

Nancy

Rose

Sonny

Eight Olivo children

Marialice, Mom, and Jeanie

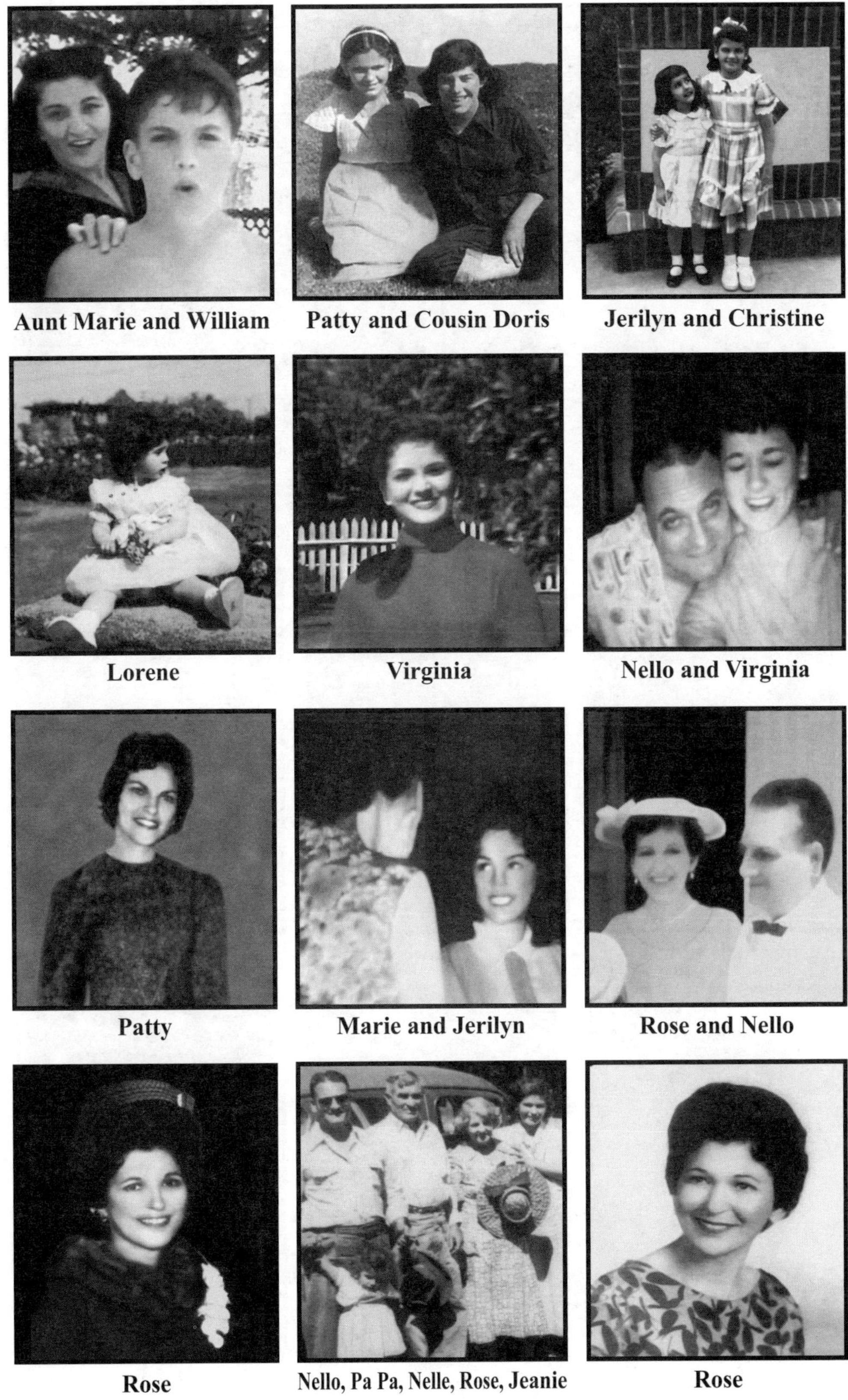

Aunt Marie and William

Patty and Cousin Doris

Jerilyn and Christine

Lorene

Virginia

Nello and Virginia

Patty

Marie and Jerilyn

Rose and Nello

Rose

Nello, Pa Pa, Nelle, Rose, Jeanie

Rose

Jerilyn

Jeanie, Dad, and Marialice

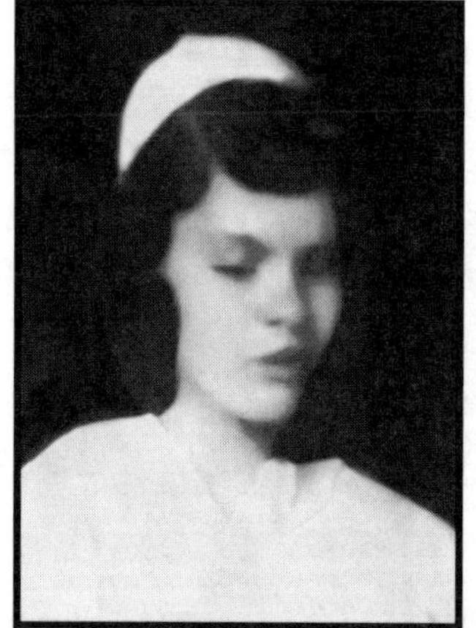

Christine

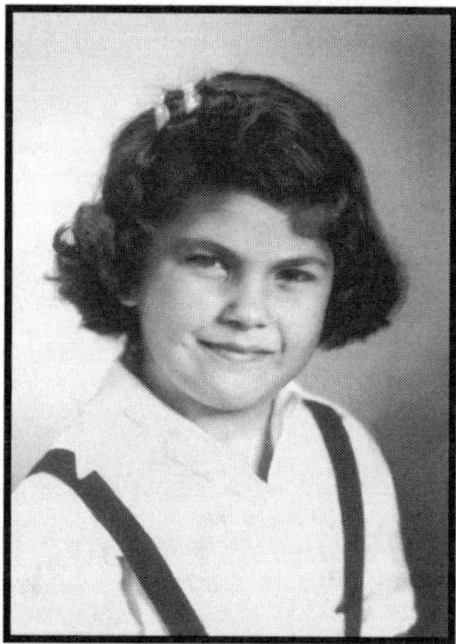

Nancy

William

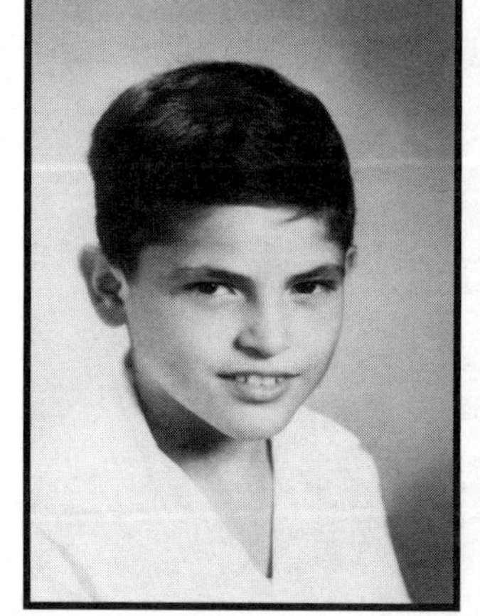

Richie

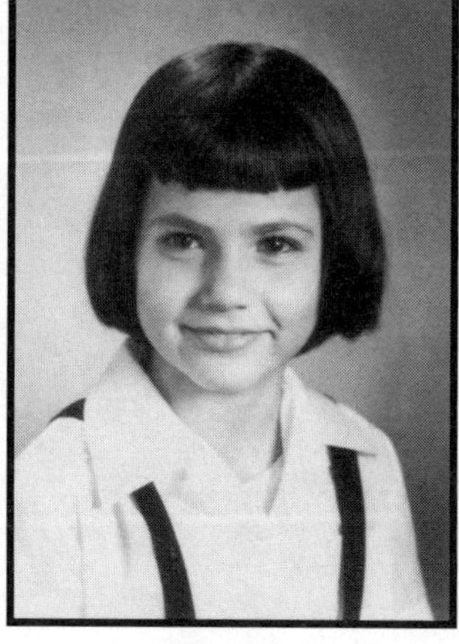

Cathy

Jerilyn

Cathy

Virginia (back), Cathy, Jerilyn

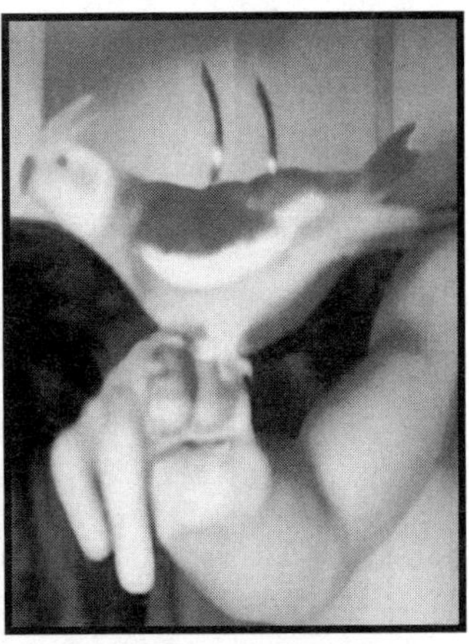
Corky, Family Bird

Jerilyn, Harold, Cathy, Nancy, Barbara and Corky

Harold, Jerilyn, Nancy, Cathy, Barbara, and Corky

Backyard at Miller Street house

Patty, Jerilyn, and Barbara

Nello, Doris, and Stanley with children

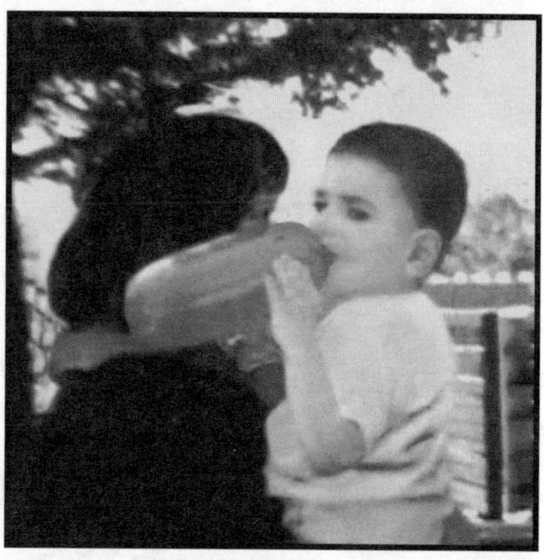
Marie and Stevie

Rose and Barbara

Marialice

Pa Pa, Rose, Marie, and Rodger

Patty

Virginia and Patty

Barbara

Father Joe

Jeanie

Nello and Jeanie

Nancy and Kenny

Kenny and Christine

Harold

Lorene

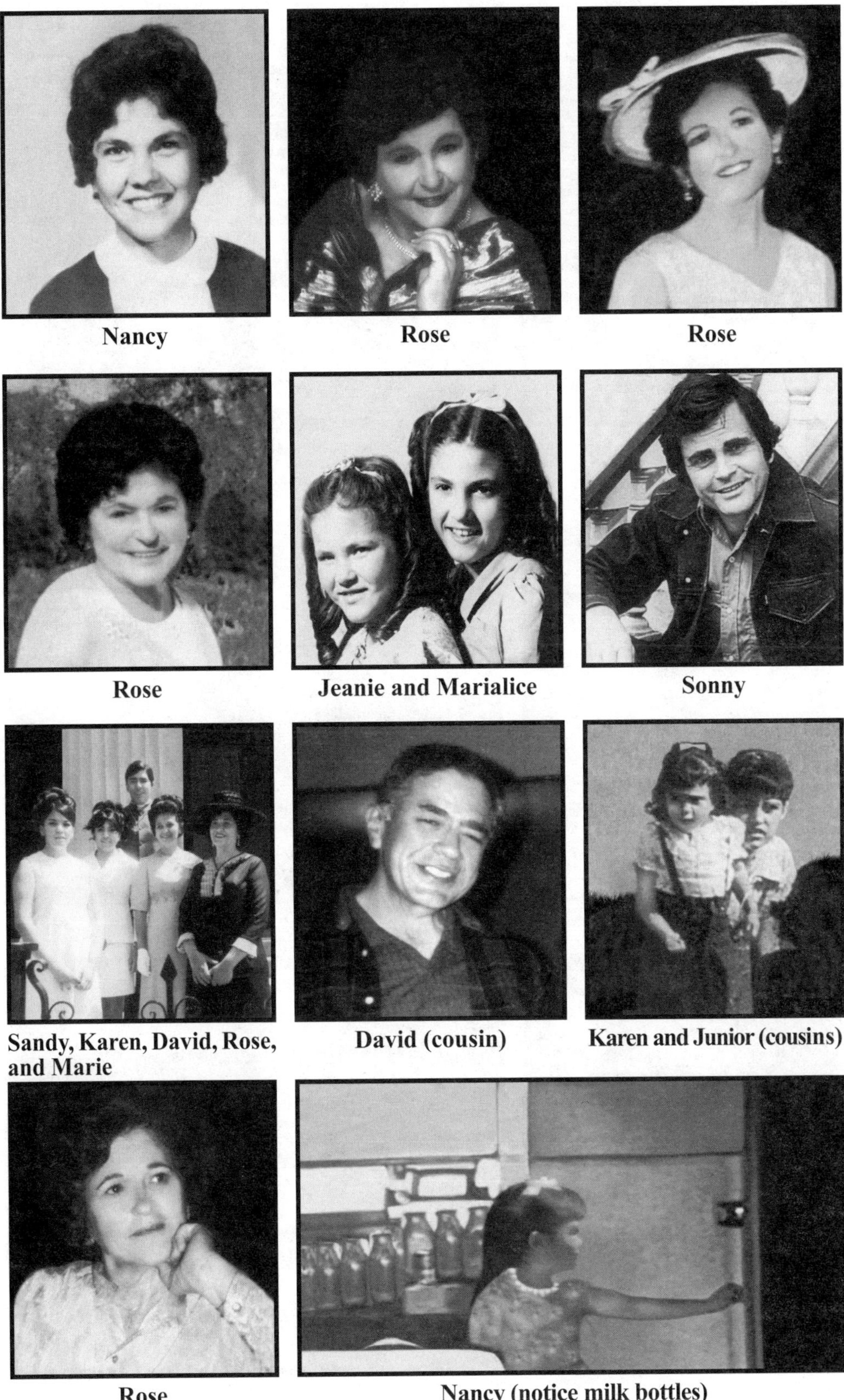

Nancy

Rose

Rose

Rose

Jeanie and Marialice

Sonny

Sandy, Karen, David, Rose, and Marie

David (cousin)

Karen and Junior (cousins)

Rose

Nancy (notice milk bottles)

Stevie

Rich

Nello and Lorene

Lorene

Stevie

Stevie

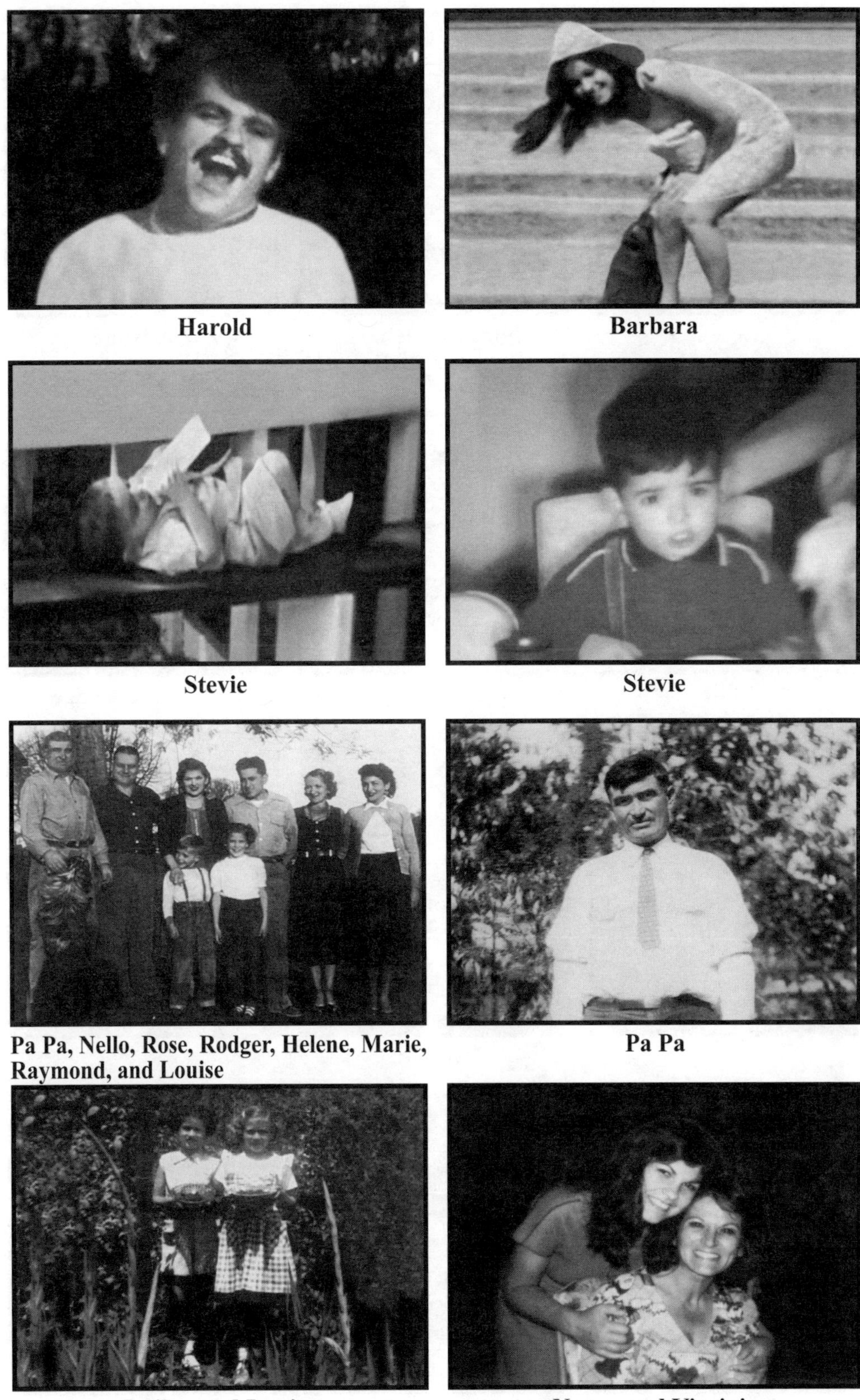

Harold

Barbara

Stevie

Stevie

Pa Pa, Nello, Rose, Rodger, Helene, Marie, Raymond, and Louise

Pa Pa

Jerilyn and Louise

Nancy and Virginia

Lorene

Bill and Barbara

Christine

Bill

Raymond , Louise (cousins)

Helene and Rodger

Harold

Barbara and Harold

Marialice and Jeanie

Bill, Barbara, and Ken

Rose

Nello

Rich

Rose and Nello

Ken and Mom (left) and Cathy who founded and commissioned the Perpetual Kelley Cup Award for the Bay Area Women's Soccer League (BAWSL).

Nancy

Cathy

Sonny

Group gathering at Pa Pa's

Nello

Pa Pa

Jerilyn

Jerilyn and Lorene

Barbara: Rose's rose bushes

Barbara tap dancing

Marialice Jeanie Patty

Sonny Virginia Christine

William Richard Jerilyn

Cathy Nancy Harold

Barbara Ken Lorene

Steve Rose and Nello

First OLIVO FAMILY ReUnion

maybe the only one
SO BE THERE!!!!!!
that's an order!

DAD
the
master plumber

Camping with all the comforts
But no room service
(shucks)

MOM
grand duchess of the clan

MARIALICE
fashion lady

STEVE
the guitar 49er

JEANIE
traveling C.P.A.

LORENE
navy wife

Date.........July 11, 12 and 13th 1986
Place........Walden West,Center- map and description attached
Check-in time.....Friday, July 11th, any time after 4:30 p.m.
Check-out time..Sunday,July 13th, 12:00 noon.

Cost..........$36.00 per adult, $26.00 per child under twelve
.........Babies-two & under-free.

Included in cost 5 meals, 3 days-2nights. Free run of retreat grounds. Lots of activities and entertainment and special guests. Indoor beds with firm mattresses. Just bring yourselves, sleeping bags, pillows, towels and casual- clothes. Plenty of *HOT SHOWERS* and clean bathrooms available.

Establishment requires pre-payment (non-refundable)
Please send your check or money order made out to
BILL OLIVO in the enclosed pre-addressed stamped envelope
by April 10th, 1986. For more information, contact BILL
(415: 826-8157) or BARBARA.

P.S. Even *RICH IS INVITED!*

PATTY
the
model

KEN
the realtor

NELLO
singing architect

BARBARA
executive organizer

VIRGINIA
the pianist

HAROLD
the saxaphonist

CHRIS
the jeweler

BILL
from the hill

L.A. RICH
the guitarist

JERI
the lab nurse

CATHY
the vocalist

NANCY
the congresswoman

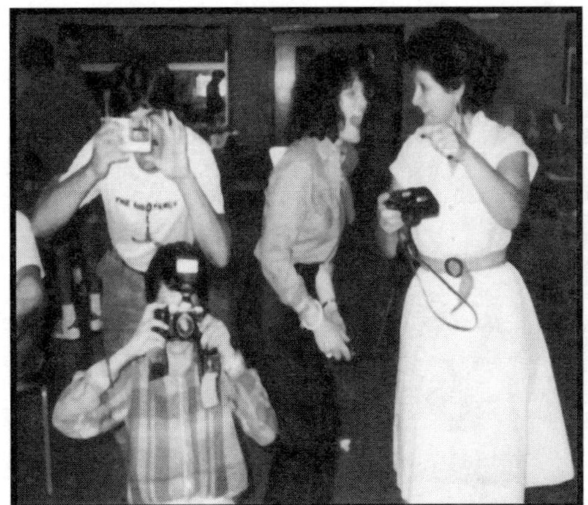

William, Christine, and Virginia

Rose, Raymond, and Louise

Rich, Sonny, Ken, Bill, and Harold

Rodger and Helene

Virginia, Catherine, Christine, Nancy, Barbara, Marialice, and Patty

1986 Olivo Family Reunion; Rose with her daughters

1986 Olivo Family Reunion; Nello with his sons

2006 Olivo Family Reunion

Olivo Family Reunion 1986

Mini reunion in May of 2005, left to right: Barbara, Jeanie, Patty, Marialice, Rose, Ken, Vrginia, Christine, Harold, and Rich, kneeling are William and Sonny

Olivo Family Reunion 2006

Chapter Seventeen

Vignettes

Mom enjoyed the silly stages the children went through as they grew older. Christine, ahead of her time, was hooked on impersonating Elvis Presley's voice and mannerisms. She would grab a broomstick and pretend to be playing a guitar. She liked singing Buddy Holly's *That'll be the Day.*

She came in the kitchen and sat down at the table with Mom and Jeanie giggling, "Hee-Hee-Hee-Hee" and started singing in a low voice. Mom glanced at Jeanie, and Jeanie said, "Oh boy, another one. Here we go again." Little did they know that Christine was practicing to perform in front of her class.

Christine and Virginia were taking a drama class together at Notre Dame, and the students were required to perform. When she got up in front of the class and began singing *Shake Rattle and Roll,* as provocatively as Elvis with his bumpy, bouncy pelvis swing and lip, Virginia got up and walked out of the classroom teary-eyed in embarrassment. Christine could have been the Ms. Elvis Presley of her time! Although the drama teacher did not like Elvis, she gave her an "A," her imitation of Elvis was that good. She nearly shocked the entire faculty when she gave a surprise performance at one of the monthly student body meetings held in the school's gym.

William was younger than Christine and she would drag him to dances and various events. They made space in the living room at home and practiced dance a great deal. The *Record Hop* was a live daily show on *KNTV* which resembled *American Bandstand. Brother and Sister Night* was on Wednesdays. The girls went wild over William. The two won a few dance contests and received a year's subscription to *TV Guide*, which had recently come out. Mom and the children at home would sit around the new black and white TV to watch them. They danced the Jitterbug and the Swing.

Whenever Christine could not get William to go with her, she would take Jerilyn or Cathy. Mom went on the show one time and danced with William. He was something else. He also mimicked Elvis Presley, and the girls from different schools in San Jose knew of him.

Richard was also popular with the girls. He was comical and joked around. When he picked up his guitar, he became serious. Nothing bugged him more than when girls found out he was William's brother, approached him screaming, "AHHH, let me touch you," and ran their hands all over him.

On occasion Jeanie would take Jerilyn, Barbara, and Harold to the San Jose Drive-In Theatre. In order to hear the movie, Jerilyn had to roll down the passenger-side window to hang a speaker on it. There would be a continuous ruckus going on in the back seat between Barbara and Harold grappling over pillows and blankets. For Jeanie and Jerilyn, this was a constant interruption. To make matters worse, if it was not Barbara, it was Harold wanting to get out and go to the snack bar, which was a big treat for them. Halfway through the movie, the two would be fast asleep in the back seat.

One time, Jeanie took Jerilyn to the movie and when the movie was over, she asked her, "Is the speaker out?"

"Yes," Jerilyn answered.

She backed up and watched the whole window fly out of her beautiful, 1958 red and white Plymouth four-door sedan.

Jeanie helped Mom fix some meals. She wanted to learn how to cook. Whenever she was on her own cooking up a storm without Mom's help, Kenny would walk up to her standing at the stove and say, "We have to eat thaaat?"

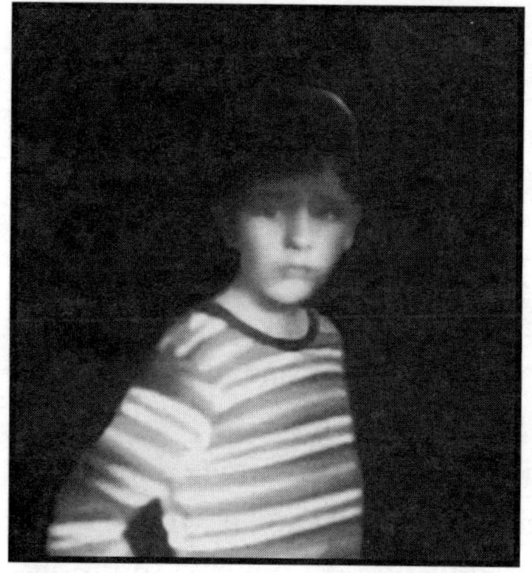

Kenny *(Courtesy Barbara Olivo Cagle)*

Kenny was full of questions. Sometimes when least expected he would run to the door to check out Jeanie's dates. He would look up and ask, "Is that your mannn?"

In the winter of 1958 Jeanie moved in with Aunt Marie. Finally, she had a room and a closet to herself and there was no returning home except to visit. It made more elbow room for the girls at home.

Dad was working on a big job for Robert E. Lee. His home was located on a steep hill on Alum Rock Road. Since Sonny was busy with his own jobs, Dad took William and Richie with him. He parked the truck downhill and put rocks in front of the tires to hold it in place. The two boys did not understand that and when Dad went in the house to talk to Robert, they removed the rocks. Before they knew it, the truck started rolling down the hill.

William yelled at Richie, "STOP THE TRUCK!"

Richie grabbed a hold of the tailgate as if that would stop a fully equipped three thousand pound 1941 GMC truck gaining momentum by the inch. As the truck picked up speed, he held on for dear life. The truck kept dragging him like a dog on a leash. William stared in amazement. Dad and Robert stepped out of the house and saw the truck—they were too far away to do anything. For a moment, everything looked like it was in slow motion. William started running, caught up to the truck, reached for the door, swung it open, jumped in and slammed on the brakes. The truck came to a halt teetering on the edge of an embankment. There was a house below the embankment full of people. They knew because it was dark outside and they could see the lights on in the house. Miraculously the truck was saved and no one was hurt.

Nello's 1957 Ford Plumbing Truck *(Courtesy Rose Olivo)*

Dad was elated the day he came home with a new, custom-built, one-ton, steel baby blue, 1957 Ford plumbing truck. It had a three-and-a-half-foot high fully equipped utility bed, and 110-volt electric outlets supplied by a generator. The trim, removable parts, and controls were chrome, and the turn signal blinkers were red lights. The whole truck was lit up like a Christmas tree. Dad had bought it for advertising his business, Nello J. Olivo Plumbing & Heating. The local Ford dealer and Jimmy Davenport, an infielder for the San Francisco Giants and employee of the Ford dealership during the off-season, helped customize the truck. Jimmy stopped by the house on several occasions to go over the blueprints with Dad. The extras included steel tool bins atop both sides of the truck, a chrome rack extending from the top of the bed to hold pipes and ladders, an electric hydraulic tailgate lift, and a roll-top roof for the bed, which when rolled back would lock to form a shelf against the cab.

Unaccustomed to anything brand-new, the children skipped and danced around the new truck, it was a grand Olivo possession. When Dad parked the truck in the driveway, he lowered the lift on the back for Nancy, Barbara, Harold, and Kenny to leap on. He ran the lift up and down a few times for fun as he showed them how the lift worked.

He promised the children they could ride in his new plumbing truck to see their grandpa and celebrate his seventieth birthday in February of 1958. Of course, not everyone in the family went. Virginia stayed home to baby-sit Nancy, Barbara, Kenny, and Rinky Dink, who were sick with colds. A neighbor,

Roselyn Lawrence, cared for Stevie. William removed a heavy, red toolbox against Dad's wishes, from the cab floor where he usually kept it. With the toolbox removed there was more room for Mom, William, and Harold to sit comfortably in front with him.

Although they could have stood straight up in the enclosed bed of the truck, Richard, Jerilyn, and Cathy chose to lie on their stomachs, facing the cab. It was pitch-black in the bed and Dad rolled open the roof a couple of inches for fresh air. Jerilyn turned on her new transistor radio for entertainment during the long three-hour drive. VROOOSH! The truck ran smoothly as if it was airborne. The children were quiet, said nothing, and after a while, fell asleep.

At 10:30 a.m. there was little traffic on Highway 26 near Jack Tone Road, an hour outside of Campo Seco. The old road stretches from Stockton up to Valley Springs. In a bend of the road, there is a little town called Waterloo.

The feel and sound of the old bumpy road abruptly awakened Richard, Jerilyn and Cathy. The truck was tipping over. It happened quickly and the children felt as if they were moving in slow motion.

"I saw an owner chasing after a medium-sized mongrel dog that ran in front of the truck. I swerved to avoid hitting the dog and the man. I went to the left and hit the shoulder. I turned the steering wheel to the right, and the tires slid on the gravel on the shoulder of the road. I over corrected and steered to the left again and then we rolled over twice," recalled Dad.

When the truck was rolling over, it flung Cathy through the roof opening onto the shoulder of the road. The truck stopped in an upright position, swayed again, and threatened to roll over on the right side. Just then, Mom saw Cathy sitting on the shoulder of the highway, looked up, and shouted, "Oh no!" With adrenalin pumping, Mom pushed everyone in the front seat to the left, in anticipation of stopping the roll to the right. The truck jerked and finally settled perpendicular to Cathy. As Mom climbed out of the cab, she witnessed a miracle when she saw Cathy sitting on the edge of the road without a scratch. The top rack that protected the rest of the family would have crushed Cathy if the truck had rolled to the right. Jerilyn and Richard were silent until they looked at Cathy and asked, "Are you okay?"

Everyone was stunned! Mom examined the other children, and with the exception of William, she found them uninjured, no scrapes, bruises, or sore muscles. There was a gash on William's head from hitting the steering wheel, and she knew he needed stitches. As for herself, she ignored the painful bruise and gash on her right leg, wiped it, and remained calm. She had to for everyone's sake. William's removal of the red toolbox prevented serious injuries. God's angels were watching over the Olivo family that day.

Dad was terribly shaken up and bewildered as he began to mull around and assess the damage to his new truck; the truck had only four-thousand miles on it. The dog was fine and its owners came up to apologize and offer assistance. Mom went inside their country home to call Rodger, who was at Pa Pa's with his family.

"Rodger, the phone is for you." Grandma Nelle said.

"You come alone and don't say anything to anybody,"

"Yeah?"

"If you can come, we were in an accident."

He hung up the phone and everyone was looking at him. "That was Rose. They have a problem with the truck."

"Helene, I want you to come with me." He did not tell her about the accident until they were in the car, at which time he proceeded to tell her, "Well, no, they don't have trouble with the truck, they were in a wreck. The truck rolled over. I want you to come along because of the kids."

When they arrived at the scene of the accident in their 1956 black and yellow Chevy BelAir, they saw Jerilyn and Cathy sitting together in a grassy area alongside the ditch on the side of the road. Jerilyn was looking in a mirror, combing her hair, and laughing with Cathy, who was digging through her cosmetic bag. Dad was still in a state of shock, lingering around the truck, repeating over and over, "Oh, my poor truck. Oh my poor truck."

After looking at William and Mom, and noticing their wounds, Helene said, "We better go to the emergency center."

Everyone gathered his or her belongings out of the truck and put them in the Chevy. All nine of them packed into the car like sardines, when Helene saw a dish of lasagna right-side-up on the white center line of the road. It was too funny and they bellowed in laughter. The Pyrex dish of lasagna, tightly wrapped in foil, had remained intact. Helene picked up the dish, and together with Mom, they inspected it and saw that there were no cracks. "Amazing!" both thought. All that damage to the truck, and the lasagna was saved for a meal at Pa Pa's.

Rodger had to back track to the town of Stockton for the nearest emergency center and William received three stitches. They then headed back to Pa Pa's. Grandma Nelle quickly readied a dinner and included the lasagna that had survived the accident. They celebrated Pa Pa's birthday and God's miracle of keeping Mom's family from serious harm.

From Pa Pa's house, Mom called Sonny to have him rendezvous with them at the site after dinner.

Returning to the site was a frightful reality-check. The rack had caved in, and the entire windshield was gone. Sonny tested the drivability of the truck and decided that he could drive it home. He and Dad placed a hard, clear, piece of plastic inside the frame of the windshield. Once they started moving, the wind blew the plastic into the cab, and Mom had to hold it in place on a very cold February evening.

Marie and her girls spent the night at Pa Pa's. Rodger's car was the only ride available for the three-hour trip home. Rodger, Helene, Dad and the children totaled ten bodies crammed into the Chevy.

Once the Ford body shop looked at the truck, they estimated the repairs as too costly and the damage too great. Dad did not drive that truck again. He did not do anything with it; he did not sell it, and he did not fix it. The truck just sat there in the back yard, parked in the carport with "Tin Lizzy," his 1924 jalopy. The backyard was where he kept his antiques and other useless items he accumulated. It was years later before he sold the truck for junk.

After the accident, Dad was depressed. It was sometimes difficult for Mom and the children to live with his idiosyncrasies, oddities, and embarrassments. He slowly developed an excessive enthusiasm for saving antiques and junk. Mom and the family could have benefited from knowing more of his condition had he been medically treated.

If I had panicked at each fall, nose bleed, every emergency or sordid detail, I would not be here. So I entered a calm mode.

—Jacqueline Rose Olivo

Harold

Perfect Attendance Award
(Photos courtesy Barbara Olivo Cagle)

Harold loved bringing home straggly stray cats. He would hold them up to his face and caress them. Mom would not allow cats in the house and told him not to play with them. That did not stop him. One day he contracted ringworm from one of the wandering cats and lost his hair. Mom kept putting a purple medicine on his head. He was out of school for several months and she had no choice other than to have him repeat first grade. It took an entire year before his hair grew back.

Every June at the end of the school year, the students would line up in the auditorium at St. Joseph's School to receive report cards and awards: Honor Roll Certificates, Citizenship Certificates, and Attendance Certificate Awards. The Olivo children came home with one or another. It was astounding that several of the children came home with Perfect Attendance Awards, kindergarten through eighth grade.

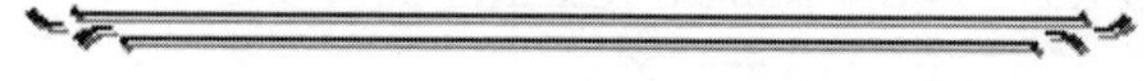

Alpine Park parish picnic June 1958 *(Photos courtesy Barbara Olivo Cagle)*

In 1958, St. Joseph's Church and school held their annual carnival and barbecue at Alpine Park, a small private family park south of San Jose in the Almaden area. It was a festivity the children and adults looked forward to each year. Balloon, dart, bingo, spin-the-wheel, ring-toss, and cakewalk booths, horseshoe games, hoola-hoops, ping-pong, volleyball, baseball, and swimming were part of the fun. Prizes were donations from various stores and businesses. The entire Olivo family and relatives would attend.

For this event, Mom had dressed her family in matching outfits. She purchased them from the Merry Mart in every size available and at a good price. The pants were solid red, and the tops were red and gray, with a diamond design for the girls and stripes for the boys. Mom had no problem keeping an eye on the children amongst the crowd.

Dad divvied out a pocket full of change for the children to spend at the carnival booths. Just about every Olivo won a cake to bring home.

Although Barbara knew how to swim, the pool was only open to children age ten and older. She took her dime and worked her way through the crowd to a booth that displayed a doll which mesmerized her. She laid her dime down on lucky number thirteen and stared at the wheel spinning and spinning.

"Thirteen, thirteen, come on thirteen!"

The wheel stopped on number thirteen and Barbara won the doll. She was proud of her prize and ran quickly to show Mom.

Inspired by the clothes Patty had made, Barbara became interested in making clothes, too; she started with her doll. Patty, had moved in with Jeanie at Aunt Marie's home, which left Barbara short on ideas. Undeterred, she went looking through the drawers of Mom's sewing machine cabinet and found a needle, thread, scissors, and a few scrap pieces of material. With that, she made her doll a dress, skirt, and blouse without patterns or instructions on how to sew or use a needle.

"Let me see what you have made. How did you do that?" asked Mom.

Barbara explained how she hand-stitched the doll clothes. To Mom's astonishment, she realized that her daughter had a natural ability. Up to that time, Mom did not allow any of the girls to use her sewing machine; even Patty did not use it and did her sewing for the fashion shows at school. Of the ten girls, Barbara was the one taught and allowed by Mom to use the sewing machine whenever she pleased. At the young age of six, she was sewing clothes for herself, for her dolls, mending clothes for her older sisters, and aspiring to be a clothes designer some day.

Patty and Jeanie enjoyed living at Aunt Marie's. It took a while for Patty to notice how Marie ran the house. Whenever something was amiss, one of the girls would blame it on the other. Aunt Marie would question them about who had left an empty glass of milk in the kitchen sink without rinsing it. That sort of thing bothered her—it was hard to clean the dried film of milk left at the bottom of the glass.

"Well, I didn't do it. That must have been Jeanie" Patty would answer.

The summer of 1958 meant days of frolicking at Ryland Park for the Olivo children. Cathy, Nancy, Harold, and Barbara were taking swimming lessons and every summer the park would hold a beauty contest where the girls had to parade around the swimming pool in bathing suits. There were different contests for different age groups. Cathy arrived wearing one of her older sister's hand-me-down swimsuits, with a couple of holes in the side seams; it had seen better days. She was in the ten-year-old group and felt embarrassed in her worn-out swimsuit. She figured she would not be noticed once she was in the pool. She wanted to swim and did not realize it was the day of the beauty contest. The lifeguards blew whistles, which meant for everyone to get out of the pool. She got out as told and started to walk away when one of the lifeguards asked her to remain for the contest.

"I can't."

"Why?" the lifeguard bent down and asked in a whisper.

"I can't because I have some holes in my suit."

"Nonsense," the lifeguard said, and insisted she parade around the pool.

The contestants were to stretch their arms out in front of them. Cathy tucked her elbows into her waist without completely stretching her arms out and went around the swimming pool that way. To her surprise, she won the beauty contest. She chucked the swimsuit the moment the children got home.

At Ryland Park, an unsavory incident involving Barbara was heartrending for Mom. She and Harold were playing together with their best friends, Suey and Joey, who lived around the block. Cathy and Nancy tried to keep track of where the two were most of the time. The park was large enough to lose sight of them and on occasion, that would happen. Especially when some boys were flirting with Cathy, or when Nancy was playing with her friends.

Barbara was happily swimming that day when an artist, sitting on the lawn took notice of her. He sent a couple of girls who were hanging around watching him sketch to go get her from the pool. The girls thought he was cool and told her that this artist specifically wanted to sketch a picture of her.

"Me? Really? Are you sure?" She was only six-years-old. Impressed by the offer, she went to see the artist, feeling as if she was "The Chosen One." She left

Harold, Suey, and Joey at the pool. She sat down on the lush, green lawn in her wet swimsuit with her legs off to one side.

"Please cross your legs" the artist requested.

Barbara complied. In front of the boys and girls who were watching, the artist reached to touch her privates and slipped down the strap of her swimsuit. She was shocked and sat frozen in repulsion at the nasty action. For a moment as he got her attention, she found herself staring into his eyes. She will never forget his face. His eyes were dark and sunken; his eyebrows bushy, and his face rough with stubble. He held a charcoal pencil in his right hand. She noticed his yellowed and dirty fingernails. He reeked of cigarette smoke. The other children saw what he was sketching and ran off, leaving her alone. Wanting to see the drawing, and yet frightened by the disappearing act of the other children, she quickly jumped up and escaped back to the pool area, where her brother and sisters were looking for her.

She kept silent, not willing to say anything to her sisters, and trailed behind them as they left the park to go home. She was startled when she saw the artist sitting in a car under one of the shady trees at the entrance to the park. He had been keeping an eye on her, and when he saw her, he beckoned her to the car. He rolled down the window and pushed open the passenger door. He had a bag of peanuts on the front seat and asked if she would like to have some and go for a ride. Fear rushed through her body as she ran off like the wind to catch up to her brother and sisters. Still, she said nothing until they got home.

Mom asked the children how the day at the park went and found it odd when Barbara told her that there had been an artist sketching a picture of her. She took her into the master bedroom for a private talk, looking her over for any signs of abuse. She immediately reported it to the police, and they found the perpetrator back at the park, sketching another child. They arrested him and confiscated his drawings of naked children. Charges were pressed and a court date was set. The thought of such a squalid and vile man was nauseating. It was painful for her to watch her daughter sitting on the witness stand, testifying how and where the perpetrator had touched her, and then identifying him. A mother and a daughter should not have to go through such an ordeal. She did what she thought was right to protect the children, and realized she had to pull the reins tighter concerning the children's adventures at the park.

The older children teamed up with the younger ones to help Mom keep a closer watch on them when they were away from home. She assigned Nancy to Barbara. Nancy was nearly three years older. They had fun playing the card game, "War," which sometimes lasted a couple of hours. For a while, Nancy took Barbara to her favorite spot in the backyard where she liked to pray. It was between the barn and alongside the "Grouch's" fence, where she had been nurturing a grotto of roses and a variety of flowers.

"Come on, let's go and pray," she said, taking Barbara by the hand.

Nancy would tell her to kneel down with her, close her eyes, make the sign of the cross, and put her hands together to pray and say the rosary. Barbara would peek with an eye open to look up at her sister, and proudly thought of her as a holy person that someday may become a nun.

First grade at St. Joseph's School in 1958 had new procedures and more school hours than Kindergarten. Harold's previous bout with ringworm set him back and he was in the same class as Barbara. They lined up in the front schoolyard with the rest of their older sisters and brothers, William, Richard, Jerilyn, Cathy, and Nancy, and the entire student body.

Reciting the *Pledge of Allegiance* daily was traditional for the student body. Occasionally they would sing *The Star Spangled Banner, America the Beautiful, or My Country 'Tis of Thee.* They waited patiently as one of the nuns reached deep into the pockets of her habit for an old round pitch pipe. The nun would then blow a few pitches to find the right octave to begin the songs. She directed the tempo by moving her bent hand up and down as though she were going through the scale.

The boys and girls stood single file in alphabetical order in the yard according to grade, beginning with the first and ending with the eighth. The teachers would inspect the students for cleanliness and compliance with the school's uniform code. They inspected their teeth and hands, the length of their hair, the length of the girls' slips and skirts, the boys' T-shirts, and looked for pressed uniforms and polished shoes. The inspections went quickly as the teachers walked down each aisle, at the same time taking roll call. It was rare when the principal would have to send a child home for not passing inspection. The student body then marched into the classrooms to the tune of *Stars and Stripes Forever.*

Once or twice a week, Father Joe would be present at St. Joseph's inspections, and would make his rounds to each classroom. Cathy got in trouble one time when a couple of classmates heard her say, "There's Father Dough Dough," and tattled on her. She had to report to the principal for punishment. At the chalkboard in front of the whole class she wrote "The Very Most Reverend Father Joseph L. Dondero, Society of Jesus," one-hundred times.

"I had to stick with the nuns," Father Joe whispered to her with a sly grin.

Cathy was normally a good girl. She would ignore Rich and not get angry when he would pinch or poke at her. She was not trying to be a "goody-goody," she was just a good girl who did not get into much trouble or need scolding. When she came home from school that day, Mom was surprised to hear what happened and had a talk with her. That same day Christine saw the opportunity to stick it to her. She told Mom that she had heard Cathy swear. Boy, did she get a kick out of getting her sister into trouble. Mom's forms of discipline had become laissez-faire and different from that of the older group. She had not poured pepper on tongues for quite some time. She did not swear and expected the same from her children, to which end, Cathy got the pepper. The children at home watched sadly with lumps in their throats. Cathy did not put up a fight and stoically took her punishment, later saying nothing about it to Christine, who felt ashamed afterwards.

In his senior year at Lincoln High School, Sonny had many girls' hearts aflutter. He went from the meanest to the nicest boy in school that year and had girls screaming over him. He would walk around wearing a white T-shirt with the sleeve rolled up and a pack of cigarettes tucked inside, for looks; he did not smoke. He was one of the hottest boys in school. He finally had a driver's license and drove a 1953 candy-apple-red Oldsmobile convertible. He had spent the year fixing the car up from a crash he had shortly after he bought it. The paint shop finished touch ups two weeks before the senior prom. William had recently become interested in cars and spotted the keys in the ignition. He started it, up and put it in reverse, and backed up into the bay tree. KRARASH! He jumped out of the car and hid in the bushes as Sonny came out of the house and saw the car. He then sneaked into the house via the back door and asked Mom to protect him from his "Big, Bad Brother." As Sonny came in looking for him, he scurried to hide under her bed. Mom took Sonny back outside. She literally turned the hose on him to cool him off. To this day, William does not know why his brother did not give him a thrashing.

William was not done joyriding. One day, while Jeanie was sleeping, he took the keys to her 1957 black Corvette with a removable hardtop and dual quad carburetors; best car Jeanie ever had. He was lucky this time driving it up and down the sidewalk in front of the house and was not caught.

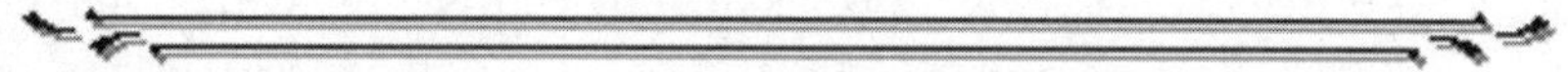

There were not enough days in the week for the boys who wanted a date with Virginia in her senior year. She, too, had many hearts aflutter. Tiny, a petite blonde girl was her new best friend at school. They were a matched pair in cuteness. The two of them did things together with Jeanie, including double dating. "Cruising" that is, driving aimlessly up and down First Street, was still a favorite pastime, even for the girls. Virginia looked older than her age, and since ninth grade, boys asked her out to the senior prom and other formal school dances. Mom made her gowns until she started working at St. Joseph's Church Rectory and was able to buy her own. The favorite part of getting dressed for the dances was wearing the mink stole and long white evening gloves that belonged to Mom.

She wanted happiness for her girls and asked how their love life was going. Along with the dates, there were tears. When her daughters cried over this boy or that boy, she would remind them that there were other fish in the sea, and not to give up on any of their dreams or aspirations. She would say to them, "There is room at the top for everyone."

In April of 1959, during Easter vacation, Mom and Dad went on a weekend excursion together to Reno, Nevada with Rodger and his family. They visited the sites in the area and took a tour through the old town of Virginia City. On the way home, they stopped at the Gerlach Hot Springs, just north of Reno. They actually saw the boiling water coming up through the ground and Dad insisted on getting out of the car to take a closer look.

During a detour through Truckee, they had a short visit with his Uncle John Ciardella, Sr., who owned and operated a bar in town. It was a surprise visit and the first time Mom met him.

Rose and Nello's trip in Nevada 1959 to Gerlach Hot Springs, Black Rock Desert, and King Lear Peak *(Courtesy of Rodger and Helene Nunez)*

I believe that a lot of people forget to be patient
With others and themselves
They are afraid of giving something away
There are a lot of selfish people like that
Those are the people that flip you off on the freeways
Why live a life of "Road Rage?"
Live a life where you let the other guy in the lane in front of you
You may lose a moment of time,
Yet, you are really putting another moment onto your life
Not getting all stressed out, getting angry, raising your blood pressure and
Eventually ruining your whole day

—Jacqueline Rose Olivo

Chapter Eighteen

No Bed of Rose's

Robert and Patricia Ray *(Courtesy Rose Olivo)*

Harry Pann "Big Sonny" *(Courtesy Pasquale Greco)*

There were three graduations in June, those of Sonny from Lincoln High School, Virginia from Notre Dame High School, and William from St. Joseph's. Mom focused on helping Patty with her wedding plans for August 8, 1959. She had Marialice's wedding gown altered adding a Sabrina neckline and additional pearls. She asked Jeanie and Virginia to be two of her five bridesmaids, and Harold was the ring bearer. She looked stunning on the day of her wedding as Dad walked her down the aisle. Father Joe performed the ceremony at St. Joseph's Church. Bob and Patty Ray greeted more than one-hundred-fifty guests during their reception at the San Jose Women's Club.

"Big Sonny" was a singer with a voice like Billy Eckstein. They asked him to sing the *Hawaiian Wedding Song* at their reception, and he sang it oh, so beautifully. The whole room quieted and everyone listened attentively, moved to the point of goose bumps.

After their reception, Patty and Bob honeymooned on Catalina Island, the same resort as Marialice and Tom.

With Patty married, a room became available for Virginia at Marie's home. She moved in and worked at a nearby bank. It was nice for her and easier for Mom with a little more room at home. Marie enjoyed her vibrant, bubbly personality and usually had dinner ready for her when she got home from work.

September 1959 brought on a new school year. There were seven Olivo children attending St. Joseph's School as she walked Kenny to the kindergarten classroom. Richard, now called "Rich," was in eighth grade and took charge over the rest of the Olivo clan at school. William entered his first year at Bellarmine College Preparatory High School. The two continued to hang out with each other. They both liked music and going to dances, which prompted them to begin playing an electric bass guitar. Rich became good at it and created some of his own music. He kept them in his head rather than write the scores down. The more he played, the better he got and began to get attention from the girls. Mom did not mind him practicing in the house, it kept the younger children quiet for hours listening to him play.

Mom was eager to get through the Christmas season. She was anxious to make plans for her first vacation and wanted to see snow. In February 1960, she took off for two weeks with Rodger and his family. The plan was to go to Lake Tahoe, Klamath Falls, Mt. Shasta, and Whidbey Island to visit Marialice and Tom. Virginia offered to watch the children and the house. The neighbor, Roselyn Lawrence took Stevie. Once on the road, the sights were fascinating. Mom was having a wonderful time, except it was hard for her not to think about Dad, Virginia and the children. "I should be home" she said to Rodger and Helene.

Louise and Raymond enjoyed the quality time with Mom. They played games with her in the back seat during the long drives. One of the games was, "I'm thinking of something." The two would have to guess what the other was thinking. She and Louise would sing *Anything you can do I can do better, I can do anything better than you!*

Virginia wanted her to have a good time. When Mom made her nightly calls, she told her everything was fine. Well, the children were OK, except Dad was not fine. He could not handle being without her. He started throwing fits and tore up the bathroom walls, insisting that he was going to remodel. He made a mess of the house. Virginia realized how difficult he could be. It was as if he went mad.

After a couple of days, Mom, Rodger and his family arrived at Marialice and Tom's home on Whidbey Island. The visit turned out to be fun for everyone. The trip home seemed to go by quickly. When Mom got home, instead of receiving a joyous welcome, there was an argument that no one could hear. She and Dad kept that private and behind closed doors, the "Silent Treatment" was the result.

You take the wind out of the sails by not responding to anything said!

—Jacqueline Rose Olivo

Barbara and Harold's First Communion, May 1, 1960 *(Courtesy Barbara Olivo Cagle)*

The second grade teacher was preparing Barbara, Harold and the rest of the class for first communion. The two recited for hours with each other memorizing the Lord's Prayer and learning the requirements taught in the catechism. The beautiful white outfits and the big processions in church made them feel special.

Barbara and Kenny played at Janet and Robert's home after school. They were brother and sister and close friends. On days when Janet went to her dance class, Barbara would go along to watch. She learned some of the tap dance routines and they practiced together. The two danced at school functions and Barbara dreamed of taking dance lessons, too.

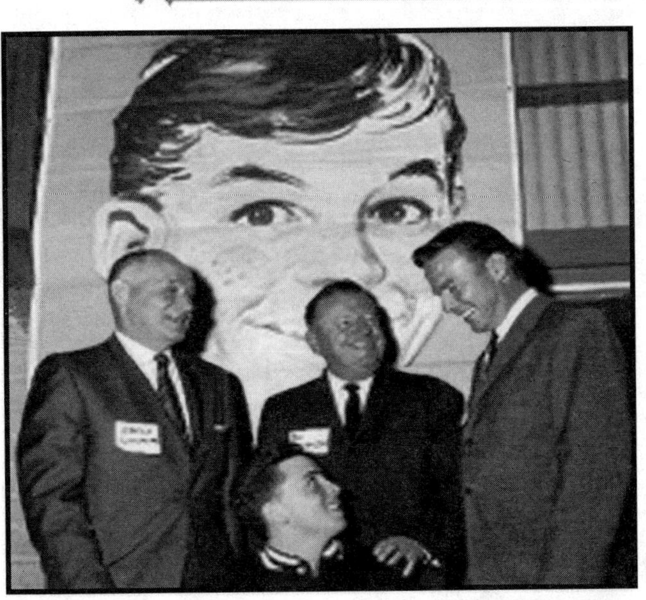

Harry E. Slonaker at the Boys City Boys' Club (left)
(Courtesy Ray Mc Casland)

Rich looked forward to graduating from St. Joseph's School. He spent many of his summer days entertained at the local Boys City Boys' Club (BCBC) of Santa Clara County, Inc. It was a non-profit youth development organization, founded by Harry Slonaker in 1944, for boys age eight to seventeen. BCBC was close to home on the corner of Jackson and Fourth Streets. The club offered programs promoting and enhancing the development of boys. Its purpose was to instill a sense of competence, usefulness, belonging, and influence through education, recreation, health, career exploration, leadership development, and game events, thus giving it the double title BCBC. The boys called the man who founded it, "Uncle Harry." Uncle Harry was like a father to the boys and treated them like his own. He believed in the motto "It's better to build boys than mend men." Directing the boys toward positive accomplishments made him proud and the boys enjoyed him. The center had pool tables, ping-pong tables, chess and checkers tables, an area for horseshoes, and ball fields.

Rich won the championship in the chess competition, and he was good at checkers, too. He had earned the honor of carrying the torch around the ball field for the opening of the BCBC 1960 Olympic Games. It was an awesome year for him. He introduced Harold to the club and many new friendships developed.

Harold at BCBC *(Courtesy Ray Mc Casland)*

Harold at Ryland Park *(Courtesy Rose Olivo)*

Ryland Park was still a favorite place for the Olivo children to hang out and frolic on summer days, and Kenny was now going there to learn to swim. At one of park's recreational events, Harold won first-place in a wagon wheel-decorating contest. A snapshot was taken of his big smile to show Mom.

For "The Summer Park Festival," the park chose a King and Queen. One of the park instructors, a tall blonde lady, wanted Nancy to enter the contest. The only problem was that she did not have a special talent needed to enter. The lady took her aside and said, "I'm going to teach you a few tap-dance steps. Now brush brush tap, brush brush tap, brush tap, brush tap, tap tap tap!" Nancy continued to practice the shuffle until she could perform it perfectly. She wanted to do well and win; many of the other girls had taken dance lessons or had a different talent. When it was her time to perform, she went through the routine without a hitch and won Queen of Ryland Park.

Cathy and Nancy were good swimmers and competed well in their age group. A scout for the U.S. Olympic Swimming team watched the two girls compete and approached Mom with an offer to put both of them on a Junior Olympic team. The girls wanted to do it. The involvement and time away from home was too much and Mom said no.

The new school year had six children attending St. Joseph's School and two at home. Jerilyn was in eighth grade, a cheerleader and head of the Olivo children at St. Joseph's. William, now referred to as "Bill," transferred to Lincoln High School, and Rich attended Peter Burnett Junior High School, the same junior high school Mom had attended.

In June of 1961, Mom proudly attended the graduation of two of her children, Christine and Jerilyn happily accepted their diplomas. Christine went to live with Marie when Virginia married, and soon after, she too, left to get married.

The San Jose Mercury News wrote on Father's Day, June 11, 1961:

Father of 16 likes 'Togetherness'

Mr. Olivo, who likes to ponder life's problems, declared there's "no problem" in bringing up 16 youngsters.

"I don't like doing things by myself. I just don't feel up to par alone. A big family keeps you going, alive and bouncing around."

Nello confessed, "I don't know how I could keep up with the repair bills if I had to hire someone to do them." He said about Rose, "I don't think you'd find anyone else that would do what my wife's done. I've been in many homes in my business where the wife seems to be having a terrible time, with maybe just two kids."

The article featured photographs of the family and was a wonderful tribute to Mom and Dad. It soon became hard to get the whole family together. There were eleven children at home and the older children were establishing their own futures.

Youth changes with each challenge and trial of life
With each success, a new mold takes place
And makes a future filled with hope
Faith is eternity and the new mold is made of love

—Jacqueline Rose Olivo

Nello | Rose | Marialice

Jeanette | Patricia | Nello Jr.

Virginia | Christine | William

Richard **Jerilyn** **Catherine**

Nancy **Harold** **Barbara**

Kenneth **Lorene** **Steven**

Most of the above are the original photos of the Olivo family featured in the San Jose Mercury News June 11, 1961. *(Photos courtesy Rose Olivo)*

OWNER	Olivo #1659	TEL	CY5-2251	L.R.	large	EXT.	rustic
RENTER	owner	TEL	same	FIREPL	none	STORY	one
KEY AT	there	POSS	30COE	D.R.	yes	ROOF	comp/shgle
1ST LN	clear AT no % INT	T/FUND	none	FURNSH	none	GARAGE	2/d
BY	none	MO PAY	none	BKF RM	in kit	PATIO	no
2ND LN	none AT no % INT	DUE DATE	none	SHOWER	no	FENCE	yes
BY	none	MO PAY	none	FLOORS	pine	SEWER	yes
LN COMT	none	VET EX	none	FURNACE	floor	G. SCH	Burnett
ASSMT	none	TAXES	$400	BASEMT	small	HI SCH	Lincoln
L.O.	CYPRESS REALTY	TEL	CY2-6000	FNDATN	cc	BUS	1 blk
S/MAN	Pearson & Westersund	TEL	AN9-1572 DR9-2008	EXPIRES	7/25/61	COND	poor

REMARKS: Value in land, R-3 zoning now, possible professional or commercial zoning. Don't disburb property owners, as value is not in the residence.

CROSS STREET	GEO. AREA	MAP KEY	LOT SIZE	ZONING	SQ. FT.	DN. PAYMT
Taylor Street	NSJ	25-C-2	78x150.25	R-3	1000	C or C/L

ADDRESS	CITY	ML NO.	RMS.	BDRMS.	BATH	AGE	PRICE
708 Miller Street	SJ	1659	6	3	1	old	$66,000

INFORMATION DEEMED RELIABLE BUT NOT GUARANTEED TO BE CORRECT— SAN JOSE REAL ESTATE BOARD

708 Miller Street Listing *(Courtesy Rose Olivo)*

Mom and Dad put the house up for sale with Pearson & Westersund. No one knew—there was no sign out front. The real value was in the land. The county had re-zoned the property to R-3, for use as professional or commercial. The listing price was sixty-six thousand dollars, which would give them enough money to buy a larger home. The house was on the market for a few months and the listing was about to expire. The real estate agent came to the house to renew the listing. Dad was in a hurry and was talking while he signed the papers. Mom sat down to read the documents carefully. When she got to the last page, she jumped up and said, "This is our deed to the house, I won't sign it over to you!"

She was angry and appalled at the agent's gumption, trying to get them to sign over the deed, and considered taking the agent to court for fraud. When she learned the real estate agency had a court date set for the same fraudulent action with another client, she waited. He was convicted and that was satisfaction enough for Mom. She was glad she did not have to waste her time taking him to court. The broker assigned another real estate agent to renew the listing. The family was impressed with Mom's determination and ability to stand up for herself. Dad had already signed the deed. If Mom would not have caught it, the family could have lost everything.

Rich made a name for himself when he transferred to Lincoln High School in his sophomore year. He formed a band called the "Rich Olivo's Band." It consisted of a drummer, pianist, guitarist, saxophonist, and himself on the electric bass guitar. The school asked the band to play for the Sadie Hawkins Day dance and other school dances and festivities. He also played the drums and fiddle. He was extremely talented and could have played any musical instrument he desired.

Mom and Dad became accustomed to all the cacophony from the music jamming sessions, accordion, piano, drums, clarinet, electric guitars, cheer leading routines, dancing, singing, and a blaring TV with a sports event. Each of the children found some sort of talent niche that interested them and Mom encouraged them with no complaints of the noise.

Six children attended St. Joseph's School in September 1961. Cathy was the eighth-grader and student body vice-president. Mom accompanied Lorene on her first day of school in kindergarten. As a freshman, Jerilyn was the only Olivo girl at Notre Dame High School.

Stevie was the last child at home. Kenny worried about his younger brother home alone with no one to play with. He would stare at Stevie sleeping in the bunk bed. It was the funniest thing when Mom walked into the bedroom and saw Kenny there perched over Stevie as he was sound asleep. He had his right forefinger in Stevie's ear and another finger holding his eyelid open, wanting to wake him up to say goodbye before he left for school.

The house had not sold and Mom and Dad decided to cut back on expenses. Most of the children were older and could withstand some luxury downsizing.

One of the items they discussed was how milk cost too much money having it delivered to the house. Mom started buying it from Kelly's Grocery Store and when she was not looking, Dad would water it down to make it last longer. They figured to cancel the contract with Peers Dairy anyway, once they moved. Oh, how the milkman felt bad when Mom gave him the news. The Olivos were his biggest account for the longest time and the milkman was sorry that they did not need him any longer.

Mom and Dad received an offer on the house from a company that wanted to use the property as a parking lot. They agreed on the fair value of the land at a sales price of fifty-five thousand dollars.

The Olivo Home on Martin Avenue *(Courtesy Barbara Olivo Cagle)*

They had been looking at many homes and there was a big house on Martin Avenue that Mom liked. They put in an offer, contingent upon the sale of the home and on Miller Street. Full-grown palm trees lined both sides of Martin Avenue and an array of beautiful homes reflected pride of ownership. The house had a two-car garage with a workshop, fenced yard, covered patio, and playhouse. Dad wanted a different house, an old dilapidated house that was ten times bigger than the current home. Mom was upset and had Virginia talk to Dad. He would listen to her advice to a certain extent.

A wealthy couple had owned the house on Martin Avenue and had moved to New York. It was a big house and had not received much interest from buyers. On the other hand, it was perfect for Mom and the family. The asking price was thirty-two thousand dollars. Dad offered twenty-five thousand dollars. The sellers rejected the offer. After a few months and several counter offers, the sellers came down in price to twenty-eight thousand dollars. They re-offered again at a price of twenty-five thousand. The sellers countered to twenty-six thousand-five-hundred dollars and not a penny less. With additional coaxing and pleading from Mom and the children, Dad finally signed the papers.

"Too bad it took so long to get a bigger house," said Virginia Smothers, her neighbor.

"It just wasn't meant to be, I guess." Mom paused in thought and then said of the Miller Street house, "It was good in the sense that it was small. I knew I could keep an eye on everyone."

On October 31, 1961, the Olivos became proud owners of the home on Martin Avenue. It was positively, one of the happiest moments for Mom—at last, her wish came true and she was in her dream home. Dad estranged himself from the whole deal after signing the papers. Mom got her way, yet he made it difficult for her and the children. It should have been a happy time for the entire family.

Dad left the main moving process to Mom and the older children. There was plenty of help and it took one week to move. Mom had all the young ones picked up after school one day and brought to the new house. "Wow!" thought Barbara, "We own a mansion!" The younger ones ran through the house on the beautiful hardwood floors. It was bare and had plenty of room to wrestle on.

Jeanie moved back home, and she and Sonny were the first ones settled in the new house. They were not asked to pay rent, although Dad was insistent that they pay their share of utility costs. There were two bathrooms and six bedrooms, with a bed for every child. There was one room big enough for a single bed, which Dad used. Without a room for herself, Mom would climb into bed with one of the girls.

Dad made life impossible for Mom. He would bunch up the clean wash and throw it in with the dirty laundry, resulting in her having to stay up at night to do more wash. He brought dirty, broken antiques, and work tools into the house that she would have to take out the back door to the garage. In the morning, when everyone got up, there would be smaller antiques that he found, paid for, or took from a family member laid out across the kitchen counter and breakfast table.

Marie knew that Dad had sticky fingers and told him, "You come into my house and take something in my home, I'll chop off your hands!"

Even though there was a silent squabble between them, Dad continued to express his undying love for Mom.

"I love you."

"Oh, come on, you don't know the meaning of the word 'love.'"

"What do you mean I don't love you? Well, I love you, that's what it means. It means that I love you!"

With the extra money from the sale of the old house, the two invested in a small rental home on Naglee Avenue, near the Rosicrucian Museum. Dad stored most of his junk and antiques there.

The Olivos felt comfortable in the new home and neighborhood. St. Leo's Church was within a stones' throw from the house, which allowed Mom and those who were up early enough, to walk to church daily for the 6:00 a.m. Mass. It was a blessing to live close to a church.

Every night Mom and the children would gather together in prayer, kneel and say the rosary in the living room. Many thanks were given to God for providing for the family. Stevie was young and not interested in praying. He would stay in the living room and entertain himself with toys until he got tired of that and went looking for something else to do. One evening, he found a bobby pin and wondered what would happen if he stuck it into an electrical outlet. A spark emitted with a current that bolted him across the living room. His right thumb and forefinger were scorched and sore where the bobby pin branded its mark and the lights went out.

"Quick, get some ice!" Mom lovingly held Stevie in her arms, trying to quiet him from the shock. It was a scary thing to happen to him, and a painful lesson learned.

Sonny *(Courtesy of Rose Olivo)*

Sonny thought the whole Olivo world would come crashing down when he left home to get married. He worried about Mom and his younger siblings. He told her and his brothers and sisters to call him day or night if they needed him, which they did quite often. He would be there in a flash.

Before Sonny got married he helped Mom, Bill, and Rich decorate for the first Christmas at the new house. They began after Thanksgiving by setting up a manger scene at the front living room window with colored strobe lights. A few days later, they hung several cords of blue Christmas lights on the exterior, outlining the house and windows. Mom beamed with happiness at the first sight of the decorations and people drove by slowly to see the beautiful display. It was a wonderful holiday for the children to remember. The older brothers and sisters bought gifts for everyone and the floor around the Christmas tree was covered with presents.

Mom grew up with an appreciation of Mother Nature's beautiful and amazing world of flowers. She hoped some day for a home with rose trees and bushes. Patty, Sonny, Virginia, Christine, and their families would stop by the house on weekends and bring a new plant for landscaping or a decoration for the house. The children were thrilled to bring Mom gifts, enough so that she could fragrance her home daily with fresh cut flowers.

Jeanie worked hard working three jobs. Mom was concerned with the long hours she worked.

Try to slow down. Take it a little easier and enjoy life while you're young. There's time enough to work like an idiot when you get to be my age.

—Jacqueline Rose Olivo

There were many baby showers, with one daughter expecting after another. The family seemed to grow yearly with grandchildren. Marialice was expecting her third child when tragedy struck.

Thomas Gerald Rose, Sr. *(Courtesy of Marialice Olivo)*

On December 4, 1961, Marialice called Mom. Tom died in an aircraft accident and was lost at sea. He was a Lieutenant, stationed at Point Mugu, California. He and Marialice lived in Port Hueneme. He had been practicing touch and go landings on San Nicolas Island. Point Mugu dispatched two helicopters and a crash boat to the scene immediately after the accident at 1:45 p.m. The search was continued throughout the day with additional recovery attempts from naval divers and two minesweepers. Navy officials believed he was strapped in the F9F jet fighter under one-hundred-and-twenty feet to one-hundred-and-eighty feet of water. Marialice was devastated.

Mom traveled with Tom's parents to Port Hueneme to bring Marialice and the children back to San Jose. Before leaving for San Jose, she left Marialice at the beach to walk the shoreline and say her good-byes to Tom. She was seven months pregnant and grateful that he had chosen a name for their son. There was a memorial service for him at St. Joseph's Church, San Jose.

Arrangements were difficult, with two families living under the same roof. Mom consistently displayed compassion and respect for Marialice's ways. The two took turns preparing dinner, with the children eating in shifts. Harold, Barbara, Kenny, Lorene and Stevie would sit with Marialice's children.

She expected her brothers and sisters to eat everything on their plates before leaving the table, setting a good example for her children. One night she sent Barbara to bed early. She had prepared lasagna and Barbara could not eat it, she threw it up after a mouthful. Careful not to offend or interfere with Marialice's ways of discipline, Mom waited until after dinner to sneak upstairs with a glass of milk and a piece of French bread For Barbara. She could not bear for any one of her children to go to bed without something in their tummy. Marialice lived at home for several months before she bought a house in Saratoga.

Bill's 1954 Oldsmobile *(Courtesy William Olivo)*

Before Bill and Rich received driver's licenses, they were looking over the few old cars and trucks Dad brought home. They drove around at first in his green, beat-up, four-wheel drive, 1953 Willys Jeep pickup truck. Later on Bill picked out an old, ugly green 53 Nash Rambler and drove it until he found a second car, a 54 Oldsmobile. He took the Olds apart, put in four carburetors, and chromed every possible nut and bolt. He installed a 45 RCA record player with its own shock absorbers, and painted the exterior a meadow-flake green.

Mom noticed his efforts and encouraged him to turn the car into a show car; he did and won many trophies. He even bought a 57 Triumph motorcycle to match the car. He enjoyed taking his sisters for rides on the hot bike.

Rich's 38 Chevy *(Courtesy Rich Olivo)*

Rich sold a black and white electric guitar to buy a car, a 38 Chevy, four-door sedan with suicide back doors. His brother-in-law, Bob Ray sold it to him for peanuts. Bob knew Rich needed a car, and it was an extra vehicle he had parked in his driveway. He gave him a good deal. Rich was proud and spiffed it up with a metallic gold paint job. He was generous with his time and helped Mom by giving the younger ones a ride when needed.

Bouffant hairdos were in and Cathy was ready to try the new style at School. The problem was, the nuns did not like the fad, and sent Cathy to the principal's office to comb out the ratting. To add to her embarrassment, an announcement was made over the PA system that there was to be no more ratted hair at school!

Thank goodness, graduation was around the corner. Cathy would miss going to school with Nancy, they were close. On the other hand, she could not wait to get her foot in the door at Notre Dame High School.

In the summer of 1962, Grandma Nelle called Mom, Marie, and Rodger asking for assistance with Pa Pa after he had a minor prostate operation. They made time for him. There were enough older children at home now to keep watch over the household, while Mom spent a week in Campo Seco with Pa Pa. Grandma Nelle's patience had run out with his cantankerous attitude and she wanted to spend a few days with her son. Mom was left on her own with Pa Pa.

At first he did nothing more than complain. She served him half of a cantaloupe with a scoop of vanilla ice cream in the middle for a refreshing dessert and he looked at her and grumbled.

"What kind of SHEET you serving me?"

Well, as the saying goes, "The SHEET hit the fan." Pa Pa then realized he was in a powerless position as Mom snapped back.

"It's not SHEET! It's GOOD for you!

He ate it and that was the end of fussing. As for the response, it was the first time Mom used that kind of language. After speaking up to Pa Pa, she began to enjoy him, and he likewise enjoyed her.

When it came to Marie's turn with him, she brought Sandy. On one of the mornings after Grandma Nelle returned home, and Pa Pa was regaining his strength, Marie, Sandy and she took a drive to Stockton. Grandma Nelle wanted to go shopping and did not want to take the bus. They went to Montgomery Ward where she wanted to buy two nine-by-twelve rugs, one for the living room and one for the bedroom. By the time they got home, Pa Pa was extremely cranky and crabby, and he asked, "What you buy?" She told him, and he hit the roof. He was angry for three days and took it out on Marie. He voiced how she did nothing right. He made sure to let her know that Rodger, Helene and their children were wonderful. Then he started criticizing how she looked in a pretty, flowered dress she was wearing.

"Where you get that dress? You get that from the Indians?"

Pa Pa literally walked over Sandy who was lying on the floor reading a comic book. She was eleven years old then, and that was all it took for him to ruffle Marie's feathers.

"I work for my money. I paid for my own dress, and I didn't ask you for a single penny!"

Marie was not one to be shy and Pa Pa loved a good fight. He would stomp his feet to intimidate her. She was not going to let him get away with it, not at all, she packed up and left.

"Where'd Marie? What's she gonna do? She's gonna go home?" Pa Pa looked at Grandma Nelle for an answer.

"Well, Joe, what do you expect?"

It took a few months for Marie to get over it. She told Mom, Rodger and Helene, "I will not go see that old man again! I wasn't going to let him get mean with me. He said nasty things."

On Pa Pa's next visit to town he went over to Rodger's and asked him to call Marie and smooth things out between them. Rodger phoned her and said "Dad and Grandma Nelle are visiting me. Would you like to talk to him?" Marie hesitant to say anything, talked small talk, and later she agreed to see him.

Pa Pa and Grandma Nelle did not always stop by Mom's when they stayed with Rodger. Instead, they would invite her over, and she would bring a couple of the children. Pa Pa and Grandma Nelle enjoyed the younger ones. They offered the children, "A dollar for a kiss?" That went over well with Stevie and Lorene, who wished that they could see more of them.

Jeanie came home with a big surprise after work one day and announced she wanted to take Cathy, Barbara, Lorene, and Stevie on a fun-filled trip to Disneyland. She heard about the eighty-five acre theme park with an endless array of rides and wanted to treat her younger sisters and brother. It did not take long for the children to pack and climb into her blue 1959 Ford Galaxie Fairlane 500 for thc vacation of their lives. Mom hugged each one goodbye and waved as Jeanie drove down Martin Avenue and turned around the corner. She made the trip educational for the children by stopping at state and national historical markers and other points of interest along the way. At Disneyland, they stayed in one of the theme park hotels, anxiously awaiting the discovery of magic. They were wide-eyed over the enormous sights, rides, and detailed cartoon characters' costumes. Cathy and Barbara bought colorful form-fitting shift dresses and feathered hats to bop around in through the park, feeling like Eliza in *My Fair Lady.*

On the way home, they stopped at Knott's Berry Farm, a western theme park with over one-hundred-fifty acres of high-speed thrill rides. They continued their adventure through the Movieland Wax Museum, where they walked within inches of famous Hollywood movie stars' waxed images. It was a full week of excitement, they could not wait to get home and have the movie films they took of the trip developed to show Mom their escapades.

September 1962 brought another school year. Cathy was the Freshman Class President at Notre Dame High School and a class cheerleader. Nancy was the oldest of the Olivos at St. Joseph's School. Mom walked her youngest child, Stevie, now referred to as "Steve," to kindergarten. With the children in school, she had a few hours to herself for the first time in twenty-five years. She established an account with a taxi service, Yellow Cab, to take her places, and for the children to use on rainy days. The school bus stop was two long blocks from home and she did not want them walking in the rain.

The children would see Mom at school talking to the principal, or going to one of the Mother's Guild meetings. One time she came to school and knocked on Barbara's classroom door to bring the lunch that she had forgotten at home.

Barbara was proud when her classmates oohed and aahed, and said, "Is that your mother? She is beautiful!"

Mom had also come to school to hand in the money that Barbara had collected from selling over six-hundred school raffle tickets in a fund raiser to benefit the school. She had her mind set on selling the most raffle tickets and won the first place prize; a Waltham 14 Karat gold watch, the first watch she owned.

Nancy as an eighth grader took the ultimate honor as May Queen. Mom made a beautiful white satin dress for her, with a fitted bodice and the skirt fully gathered at the waist. A ribbon of embroidered red roses and green leaves accented the dress.

Bill and Nancy were the next two Olivo children to graduate in June 1963, Bill from Lincoln High School and Nancy from St. Joseph's. The pomp and circumstance was a proud experience for Mom and she enjoyed her children's accomplishments immensely.

The summer of 1963 was eventful. The children no longer played at Ryland Park. It was too far from the house to walk. Steve went there to learn how to swim the summer before moving. His legs cramped on the first day of lessons, he got scared, and did not return. He was the only Olivo who missed taking swimming lessons at the park.

The older children's new stomping grounds were at Herbert Hoover Junior High School and Lincoln High School. The schools were within walking distance and both had swimming pools. In the evenings, they danced and hung out at the Record Hop or the Wuzit.

Barbara was going through that awkward growing-up stage and the thought that Mom had adopted her crossed her mind. Distraught and in tears, she approached her mother and vented on the subject. "How can you love so many children? We can't possibly be all yours. I don't ever have birthday parties like my friends do."

Hearing and feeling her daughter's emotions hurt Mom. With bridal and baby showers, weddings, graduations, confirmations, the birth of grandchildren, more baptisms and first communions, it was one celebration after another. She tried to help her children understand that it was nearly impossible to celebrate everyone's birthday. That did not mean she loved them any less. With that said, she arranged a surprise birthday party for Barbara. The girls from her class were invited and she was completely caught off-guard. She cherished how Mom made the surprise such a special event.

The Alameda Roller Rink was two blocks from home and that became the big hangout for Barbara. Harold and Kenny remained involved with the Boy Scouts and took the bus to the BCBC. Lorene and Steve kept busy with the new neighborhood friends they had made.

And as you grow older, the road may grow harder
Little hope may prevail when these times come
Look to your heart, there is where God dwells amongst
The dreams of your childhood, placed in your life
Like road maps through this future toward God

—Jacqueline Rose Olivo

Considering the previous years, the count was down at St. Joseph's for the school year of 1964 with Harold, Barbara, Kenny, Lorene, and Steve in attendance. Mom's presence at school activities and the Mother's Guild became frequent. Jerilyn, Cathy, and Nancy were adding their own trail of accomplishments at Notre Dame High School and the popularity of Rich's band soared at Lincoln High School.

Rich was a very thoughtful older brother. When he noticed that Kenny was interested in the guitar, he bought him a blue Fender Jaguar Guitar and taught him how to play it.

When he graduated from Lincoln High School, he bought a motorcycle to ride around with Bill and his friends who belonged to a motorcycle club called, "Disciples." Rich did enjoy going on many adventures with them even though he did not join the club.

Jerilyn was interested in business classes and hung out at the Wuzit on weekends. She had a steady beau, Al. After a first date with her, Dad gave him a ride home in his black Ford truck. Al had a great sense of humor and so did Dad. After starting the truck, he laid his false teeth on the dashboard and questioned Al, with a raised eyebrow, "So, are you Italian?" Al glanced at the false teeth and looked back at him with hesitation, "No, I'm Sicilian."

When Al visited the Olivo household he blended in like a piece of furniture. On almost any given day, the children would see him sitting on the living room couch waiting for Jerilyn. Lorene and Steve thought it was their cue to jump around and play. They would kick him in the shins and try to get him to wrestle with them. "I will go away if you give me a quarter," Steve tested him. When he had about enough, he grabbed Steve by the back of the collar and whacked his behind good. Steve ran crying to Mom that Al spanked him. Mom turned to

Al all poised. "Well Al, if he does that again, let him have it!"

Cathy had a beautiful soprano voice and received solo parts in many school musicals. She was also the class mascot. Bellarmine Preparatory High School held plays at Notre Dame High School and bused boys there for rehearsals with the girls. This, of course, took place under the watchful eyes of the nuns. It was Mom's habit to ensure she attended the first showings of the productions.

Like her sisters, Cathy worked at the office at St. Joseph's Church Rectory after school. In the evening at home, she and a girl across the street would flash upstairs hallway lights as a signal. When the coast was clear, she would sneak over to her house to talk, bake cookies, and play games into the wee hours of the morning. Cathy was interested in the girl's brother and he would sometimes join in the fun. It was not long before Mom and the other mother caught wind of their impishness and put an end to it.

Nancy was Freshman Class Vice-president at Notre Dame. She was good at debating and enjoyed political topics. Pa Pa loved a good argument and conversing with her often led to a debate. When he realized he was not going to get anywhere with her, he would end it with, "Ah, you don't know what you talk about."

Harold started going on jobs with Dad in the summer. He taught him the plumbing trade, or rather how to wheedle himself out of any confrontation concerning money, or how to handle a situation when not showing up for a scheduled job. As Harold remembers it, Dad exclaimed, "I was chased down, sworn at, double-crossed, cheated, spat at, and sat upon while doing jobs."

Dad's list of excuses were never ending. He would tell people how many children he had to look after, or say they were in the hospital, how he had a broken back, broken legs, broken hands, and was sick. He chanted a new story every week, and the story changed from house to house.

Barbara baby-sat Marialice's children on the weekends. She took the money she earned and bought a brand new blue Schwinn three-speed bicycle. Dad took her to pick it out and helped her get a good deal. Once she had her own wheels, there was no more holding her down.

When she had friends over, they would sit and listen to Rich play the electric guitar or hang around Bill while he worked on his car. It was especially awesome when she and Mom went to the car shows and watched Bill receive a first place trophy.

While Beatlemania was raging throughout America, Barbara and her friends dressed up like the Beatles and performed at several school and guild functions, imitating the group and lip-syncing. They would practice for hours and sing the Beatles' songs repeatedly. Mom understood and enjoyed watching her go through the different teenage phases, with the humorous and ridiculous fads that went along with them.

Another dimension of music boomed through the house as Kenny and three of his friends formed a band. There were calls from the neighbors whenever the jam sessions extended into the late evenings. Sometimes the neighbors even called the police to cool down the noise. Kenny also played sports. He was the captain of the basketball, baseball, and football teams at school. He was tall and handsome. The girls were after him and he was not interested. He was more interested in showing how strong he was by asking Barbara to pinch him as hard as she could and then stand there looking poker faced at her.

Kenny and Harold were hard workers and kept busy with early morning separate paperboy routes. On Sundays they were altar boys for Mass just as Bill and Rich had been. After the service, the boys would go into the sacristy to change. They would get into the unconsecrated hosts to eat and have a taste of wine, the best part of the job. It was their secret, as with many other young altar boys, and they were lucky that the priests did not catch them in the act.

Lorene's First Communion *(Courtesy Barbara Olivo Cagle)*

Lorene was elated to receive her first communion. It was her day to shine all dressed in white.

She and her best friend Suzy, spent many a day playing in the Olivo's backyard playhouse. She was shy and observant of her siblings' every move, keeping clear of any trouble.

Steve made friends with homeless cats, as Harold used to do. Since there were fewer children living at home now, Mom gave into his insistence on keeping this one orange stray cat, which he named Mouse. He and Dad were the only ones who liked Mouse. The girls especially did not like the blasted cat, it clawed at their nylons every time they came in the house.

On the Fourth of July, Harold and Kenny were lighting firecrackers in the back yard. Steve watched how his brothers lit them off and stuck a firecracker in an old coke bottle. When the firecracker did not go off, he looked into the bottle thinking it was a dud. Suddenly, it went off in his face.

"I can't see! I can't see!" Steve screamed. The force of the explosion cut the ridge of his nose and caused temporary blindness. The injury could have been more serious and certainly was a big scare for both Mom and the rest of the family.

Steve's best friend lived across the street. The two were interested in collecting butterflies and bugs. They rummaged through Mom's kitchen cabinets

Steve and Lorene with Father Dondero *(Courtesy Barbara Olivo Cagle)*

to find containers to put the insects in for safekeeping. By the time she realized what happened, it was too late. Steve and his friend showed her the collection of insects, caterpillars, and worms. They had bored holes in the bowls and lids of her best Tupperware to allow the little creepy-crawlers to breathe. The two boys then sat to watch a TV program. After it was over, the friend went home to get a bike and go to the store. Mom wished he had stayed longer. He was fatally hit by a vehicle while in a crosswalk. She spent a good part of the remainder of the day comforting the boy's mother and Steve.

A new school year arrived bringing more free time for Mom as her children matured. In 1965 Barbara and Harold were in seventh grade, Kenny in fifth, Lorene in third, and Steve in second. Jerilyn was a senior, Cathy a junior, and Nancy the Sophomore Class Treasurer at Notre Dame High School. Cathy and Nancy worked at St. Joseph's Rectory on alternate days, and Mom was there to help, too, when the girls' school activities conflicted with work.

There were strict rules against hair-coloring or the wearing of any make-up at school, as well as at home. With so many older sisters, it was easy for the younger girls to catch on quickly. One day, Barbara was spending an unusually long time in the bathroom, and Jerilyn began begging to get in. When she unlocked the door, Jerilyn could smell hair-coloring solution lingering in the air. Barbara had wanted to experiment with a couple of shades lighter than her natural color, to obtain glimmering highlights. Jerilyn brought it to Mom's attention. With a disappointed hesitation she said, "Well, it's not too noticeable."

The mere fact that the younger children were sliding by with behavior that the older ones could not have gotten away with was annoying to them.

Harold and Barbara *(Courtesy Barbara Olivo Cagle)*

Barbara was a school cheerleader in seventh grade. She and Harold had fun at school and after school. They hung out together at school parties and particularly at the neighborhood roller rink, where they made many of the same friends, Faye, Kaloaha, Danny, Darryl, Red, George, Mike, and Joe.

Requesting songs or trying to win a prize from a radio station was one of Barbara's favorite pastimes. On the home telephone while trying to dial a station, she noticed there were conversations going on between the busy signals, like a party line. It went something like: buzz-"Hi"-buzz-"I'm"-buzz-"Barbara" buzz-"Who"-buzz-"Are"-buzz-"You?" This would go on for hours. Through this form of communication she secretly arranged a blind date with a boy three years older than her, at the movie theatre. Mom did not know about the "buzz-buzz" blind date which ended quickly when the boy expected to meet an older blonde-haired girl.

Barbara met her steady beau, Randy, at the roller rink. Sometimes they would meet at the Spartan Stadium on Tenth and Alma Streets. During the San Jose Bee's games Randy sold popcorn and peanuts. Harold, Kenny, Lorene, and Steve went to watch the games, while Barbara watched Randy.

The "surfing" craze was big in California. Teenage girls wanted a surfer girl look with long, beautiful straight hair. Mom was beside herself when she saw Nancy and Barbara ironing the curls and waves out of each other's hair. Now that was a sight for a parent to see, and the thought of their hair sizzling up into nothing or spiked-split ends was unnerving.

Mom got nervous and started rolling napkins up one at a time when her teenage daughters were out with friends. She rolled a twenty-dollar bill in one once and lost it when it landed in the garbage can. Barbara found it, told Nancy, and they bought a few pizzas and invited some skating friends over for a party on the patio.

Dad had a business phone in the house that was locked up to keep the children from using it. Steve was good at figuring out how to maneuver the dial past the lock and to make calls. No one else could do it, he had the magic touch and when the other phone was in use, Steve was the one everyone asked to dial out on the phone.

Toward the end of every school year, St. Joseph's School allowed the seventh and eighth graders a full week of free dress. Barbara sewed most of her clothes and free-dress week was a great time to show them off. Dress code inspection in the front of St. Joseph's School was in full force even during free-dress week. She went to school dressed in a nice light-blue denim shift she had made. It was such a hot day, that she decided not to wear nylons and rubbed oil on her legs. Sure enough, during inspection the principal went right up to her and felt her legs. She pulled her out in front of the entire student body and announced this was not the way for Catholic girls to dress. The principal insisted she leave and not return without nylons. Instead of calling Mom, or taking a taxi or city bus, she grabbed her books and ran the one-mile distance home in tears. She stormed in the house bawling.

"I will never go back to that school again! Never, ever, ever again!"

Mom was surprised yet understanding, she knew returning to school that day was not an option. As an alternative, the two talked and planted flowers in the back yard.

The state of society in the next generation depends on the manner in which the young people of today are instructed and trained toward leadership. With the wonderful training and love you receive at home, and the best possible schooling your father and I have provided, you can become a leader of leaders. In which ever direction your endeavors take you, always strive to be the best of whatever you are.

—Jacqueline Rose Olivo

Jerilyn strived to be a good typist in her business class with Sister Reginald "Sr. Regie." A variety of San Jose offices would call Notre Dame High School near graduation time to ask for one of "Sr. Regie's girls" to work for them. Most businesses knew she trained her girls well in office procedures. They were responsible, honest, industrious, professional, avoided chewing gum, and knew how to dress properly. Jerilyn was one of her best.

She also was a history buff, and like Mom she read many books.

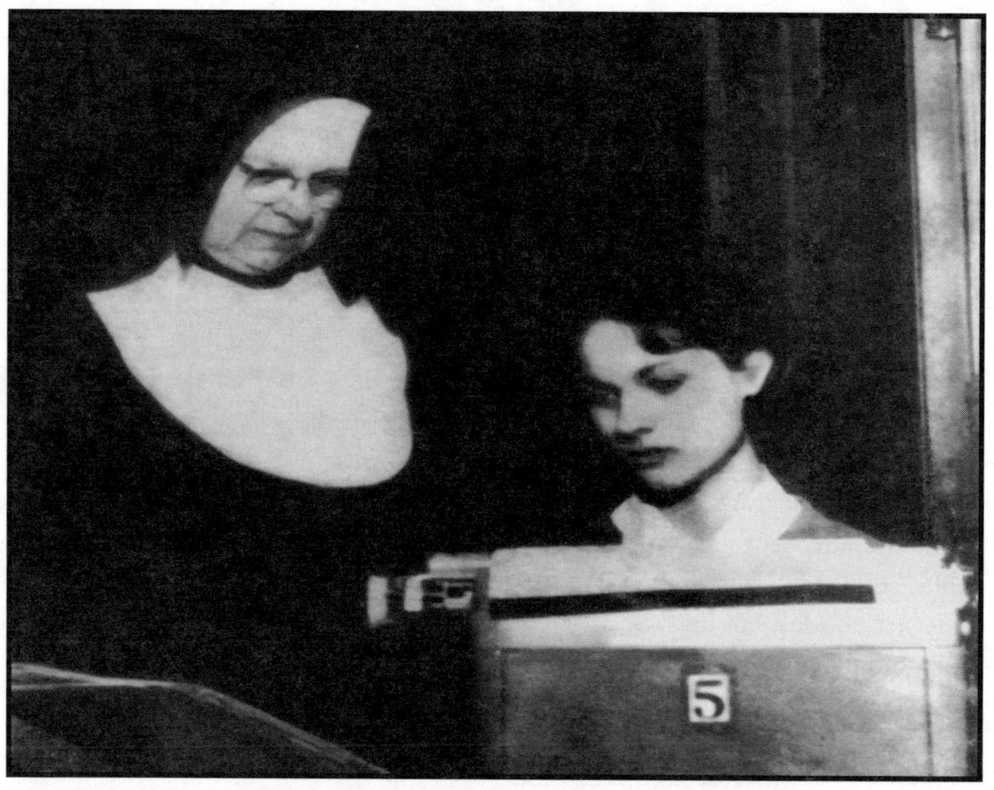

Jerilyn and Sr. Regie *(Courtesy Rose Olivo)*

Mom's symbols of strength were an inspiration to all of her children. She did not let anything, including Dad's odd ways and jealousness, get her down. She drew from a profound spiritual sense of strength from God to overcome obstacles.

—Barbara Olivo Cagle

Chapter Nineteen

The Mob and the Job

Harold and Barbara 1965 *(Courtesy Barbara Olivo Cagle)*

The 1966 school year was fulfilling for Mom. The mothers of her children's school friends called upon her to accept the presidency of the Mother's Guild. After much prayerful thought, she accepted the position. The children were proud of her and she was doing something she thoroughly enjoyed.

Harold and Barbara held the reigns for the Olivo family at St. Joseph's School that year. Kenny, now called "Ken," by his classmates was in sixth grade, Lorene in fourth, and Steve in third. At Notre Dame High School, Cathy was a senior and performed in the school play, *The Sound of Music.* Nancy was Junior Class Treasurer.

The school year was busy with more than the usual activities. Mom held a few home socials at the residence to raise funds for St. Joseph's School. The fashion shows were gala events with over two hundred people circulating through the home at one time.

Marialice asked Barbara to baby-sit her children during one of the home socials. She grudgingly went to baby-sit, knowing that she would miss the excitement of a big party. She was under the impression there would only be adults attending. Not so! The following day at school she learned her classmates had come along with their parents to the house, and they had a separate party in her bedroom! Talk about missing out on the fun!

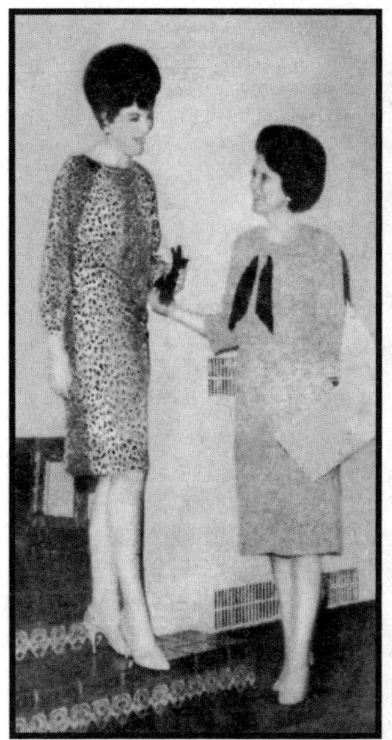

Rose models for "Encore" in Lou's Village *(Courtesy Rose Olivo)*

"Encore" was the theme of the 16th annual St. Joseph's Mother's Guild Fashion Show Luncheon. The fashion show was solely a fund-raising event for the benefit of St. Joseph's School, and The Reverend Joseph L. Dondero was the moderator. Mom was Guild President, and a member of the San Jose Community's Parent Teachers Guild (PTG) and the Archdiocesan Council of Catholic Women (ACCW). She also was involved in the Confraternity Christian Doctrine (CCD) Program, and at one time, taught fourth grade under the program. This gave the children a sense of importance. Mom's involvement with the school and community affairs made them proud of her. She had been spiritual chairperson for the guild before her presidency and was inspired to compose a journal of her speeches, quotes, and poems.

She was prolific in her thoughts and reflections on the church and motherhood. "I should have written a book and entitled it, *The Book of Mother's Sermon's*. I love to sermonize. I do it without realizing I'm doing it. I just start and there is no stopping it. I remember many times when asked a simple question by one of my children, my answer would run into a whole afternoon or evening of friendly laughter, discussions, and most importantly closeness, especially with my teenage daughters. I sometimes said I must have missed my calling."

Oh Why? Oh Why?

Oh why? Oh why? The aching heart! Breaking heart!
The while we hold ourselves apart
Long from accepting, far from rejecting
Love me well, withhold condemning
Life's trap, unrelenting
And we chose an eternity!

Oh why? Oh why? The aching heart! Breaking heart!
Heavy with things to which we give no voice
We chose a lifetime ago the road we were to travel
Unmindful then having been allowed a choice
We wove a web too incredible to warrant unravel
And we chose an eternity

Enduring the turmoil, securing the covenant, unending
Oh, where am I going and what am I knowing, rendering
Smiling through a vale of tears, surrendering
I must go, Society will not know
The aching heart! Breaking heart! Eternally!

Dream Dreams

Take courage, my child, and reach for your dream
It may seem as far as a star
A dream a mystery for you to unfold
It is not tangible therefore, if you must hold
It will never be too late
As you think of your yesterdays
To take to the road that leads to completion

Dream dreams and believe, dream goals and achieve
The years fly by—it's never too late
There is a new song to sing
A new friend still to be made
A tragedy yet to face
Nothing can ever take the place
It's never too late

—Jacqueline Rose Olivo

Mom modeled in many of the fashion shows. One which was special for her had two of the children modeling with her. The theme was *When I Was a Little Girl Growing Up Through Each Stage in Life.* Lorene modeled in her school uniform and allowed a young boy to carry her books. She walked down the runway, turning to the audience to giggle. Later Mom and Marialice walked the runway. It was quite an impressive performance and talked about for days.

As the school year ended, there were three graduations: Cathy from Notre Dame High School, and Harold and Barbara from St. Joseph's. Mom knew how to prepare for large events and told Harold and Barbara they could hold a graduation party for the whole class. Everyone came, even some of the mothers. Mom allowed the children to paint, hang up posters, and arrange musical instruments in the basement. Classmates coupled up and danced to the latest tunes. It was an awesome time and just what the two needed for their self-esteem, especially Barbara since she and her skating beau, Randy, broke up.

The older siblings sometimes referred to the younger ones as spoiled. The younger ones received more than the older ones ever did, or so they thought. There is considerable give-and-take in a large family. On one hand, the younger ones did not get the opportunities to know their grandparents; on the other hand the older ones did not fully experience the difficulties Dad had with depression. Mom was the stronghold of the family. She taught her children through the good times and the bad; the adversities of time change, the lessons learned stand the test of time.

Pa Pa's health was failing and he no longer traveled. He was home bound with prostate problems and wore a catheter. Grandma Nelle did her best to take care of him, calling upon a neighbor to help lift him in and out of bed when needed. At times Mom, Marie, Rodger, and Helene would go for short visits. The older children visited occasionally and kept in touch through letters.

Rose 1966 *(Courtesy Rose Olivo)*

After Mom's 1967 Presidency of the St. Joseph's Mother's Guild, an opportunity arose for work at St. Joseph's Rectory. The priests had lost the services of a cook and were desperately looking for someone new. The resident rectory was on the upper floor of the church, which was located halfway between St. Joseph's School and Notre Dame. There was an old elevator to the upper level. When it was not working, Mom would have to climb the dark, long and narrow stairwell to the upper floor. She often walked the mile to work even though she suffered from varicose veins. With Dad planning to retire, the job was great for her and the children.

While at the rectory, Mom also took on the job of sewing the nun's habits. That turned out to be a big project and she needed Patty's help with finishing the job.

There was plenty of food at home. Mom did not leave the house without placing a meal in a slow cooker and Dad did not give up his ways of picking up leftovers from restaurants and donut shops.

Bobbie Freshman Cheerleader 1966
(Courtesy Barbara Olivo Cagle)

Barbara was a freshman at Notre Dame High School creating a name for herself as Class Viking Cheerleader. Her best friend Bernie nicknamed her "Bobbie," and that is now what she is called. She wanted to be involved in as many activities as possible at Notre Dame. She was in choir, a cheer leader, in the Pep Club, in the St. Clare Teen Club, and went to the basketball and volleyball games after school. In the evenings, she would go to Notre Dame School dances or mixers held at other schools and churches. She did less skating and went to the St. Clare Teen Club to hang out and dance. She was too funny when she went looking through the kitchen medicine cabinet for some aspirin before going to a dance with blasting music. Mom observed her.

"What's the matter? Do you have a headache?"

"No, I want to take a couple aspirins now in case I get one later."

Bobbie would laugh like crazy while telling a story or joke, and then with a straight face blurt out, "Now that was NOT funny!" The finale would cause her listeners to laugh more at that than at the humor in her original story or joke.

Nancy was a senior and showed Bobbie around school, they became closer. Nancy was studious and smart like Jeanie. She would open a book, close it, and knew it. The nuns were expecting some of that from Bobbie. She had other ideas and was somewhat flighty. Writing notes to her friends in the classroom and extracurricular activities were more entertaining than trying to fill the shoes of her "brainy" sisters. One thing she was good at was keeping mementos like awards, certificates, letters, news articles, and photos of her and her family.

Harold attended Herbert Hoover Junior High School and took saxophone lessons. Ken was in seventh grade at St. Joseph's and involved in sports. Mom, and sometimes the children at home, attended his games. Lorene was in fifth grade and Steve in fourth.

Bobbie, Lorene, and Steve would go to the church rectory after school activities to be with Mom. The priests did not seem to mind. Not many other students went inside the priest's quarters. Steve liked to eat the cookies that were in place at the table and would sit down with the priests at dinner time.

"Have you ever read anything in the Bible?" Steve asked Mom one time.

"Yes I have. It took me ten years to do it little by little."

"Why?"

"I needed something to make it through sixteen children, the crying, the bills, and with your father hardly ever home."

Mom felt that reading and believing what she read, if only a few verses at a time, would help her make it. She told Steve how she and Dad met.

"Many girls chased after him, he was so handsome, and the girls went wild over him. I considered myself lucky to be with him. His friends used to call him 'James Cagney'."

Steve believed the James Cagney theme, because he heard Dad answer the phone, "James Cagney, Jr." on several occasions.

Nancy worked at the church rectory office, and Bobbie would go to be with her and Mom. The girls would go upstairs at times, to help prepare the food or serve the priests. It was a special time for both Mom and the girls.

At the end of the school year, Notre Dame held tryouts for the school's cheerleaders, song girls, and varsity basketball and volleyball teams. Bobbie wanted to try out for the Gremlins' Song Girls. Nancy sat in the living room for hours coaching her and watching her practice routines. Bobbie returned the favor by drilling Nancy on Latin memorizations. The hard work paid off when she was selected as a Gremlin Song Girl. To be selected was unusual for a freshman and she was excited. Her summer was suddenly filled with practices and sewing song girl outfits.

Nancy, too, was a winner, academically. She graduated with honors and a commendation for four years of straight "A's." She was involved in the Language, Choral and Spirit Club, Forensic League, Reporter's Board, and Yearbook. After graduation, she realized her dream of joining the convent. She experienced her goal for a few months and decided later that year to leave the religious order.

When the new school year arrived, Bobbie was eager and ready for Song Girl performances at Notre Dame. The bus trips, searches, folk masses, and dances filled her life with new adventures.

Harold attended Lincoln High School and played in the school band. He did not have a driver license, yet he was out driving that old, green, beat up, four-wheel drive, 53 Willys Jeep pick up truck. Ken was in the graduating class at St. Joseph's School and became the May King. Lorene was in sixth grade and Steve in fifth.

Bobbie as Notre Dame Song Girl 1967-68 and Bobbie acting in Notre Dame's Drama Festival *(Courtesy Barbara Olivo Cagle)*

The Drama Festival was the highlight of Bobbie's sophomore year. She played Mercutio in Shakespeare's *Romeo and Juliet. © 2006 Sparknotes LLC, http://www.sparknotes.com/Shakespeare/romeojuliet All Rights Reserved.*

An excerpt from Act III, Scene I: A public place.

Enter Mercutio, Benvolio, and servants:

Mercutio: "I'm hurt! A plague o'both your houses! I am sped. Is he gone, and hath nothing?"

Benvolio: "What, art thou hurt?"

Mercutio: "Ay, ay, a scratch, a scratch; marry, 'tis enough. Where is my page? Go, villain, fetch a surgeon."

Romeo: "Courage, man; the hurt cannot be much."

Mercutio: "No, 'tis not so deep as a well, nor so wide as a church-door; but 'tis enough, 'twill serve: Ask for me to-morrow, and you shall find me a grave man. I am peppered, I warrant, for this world. A plague o' both your houses! 'Zounds, a dog, a rat, a mouse, a cat, to scratch a man to death! A braggart, a rogue, a villain, that fights by the book of arithmetic! Why the devil came you between us? I was hurt under your arm."

Romeo: "I thought all for the best."

Mercutio: "Help me into some house, Benvolio, or I shall faint. A plague o'both your houses! They have made worms' meat of me. I have it! And soundly too: your houses."

Bobbie exited through the darkened stage searching for the doorknob to the bathroom. Suddenly, she grabbed a hold of a fire alarm handle. Instantaneously, the alarm went off! Knowing what she had done, she froze as the entire student body, teachers, and guests excitedly exited single-file out of the auditorium.

One of her classmates, Leslie, turned to her, and with the cutest big puppy eyes, said, "I wish I was the one who pulled it."

Stopping one of the nuns, Bobbie explained how the alarm was pulled. The nun yanked her into the line and told her to assemble out in the yard with everyone else as expected for any fire drill. Mom was outside and Bobbie ran up to her the moment she saw her, "I'm sorry Mom. I'm the one who pulled the alarm. I didn't mean to do it, please protect me. I'm in a lot of trouble."

In her profound wisdom, Mom convinced the principal that this was a good thing; to be drilled when least expected. As reported in the yearbook referring to the Shakespearean Festival, "Perhaps the most exciting event, which stirred laughter in many hearts, fear in others, and even brought tears to a few eyes, was the accidental, totally unexpected fire drill."

That summer Mom was waiting for Sonny to come to take her to lunch. He drove a white 1963 Buick Riviera. He told her when he picked her up that he was thinking about buying himself a new car, then said: "If you get behind the wheel of this car and drive, I will give it to you."

Mom went out with Sonny a few more times and he taught her how to handle the car. She then took driving lessons at the California Driving School and obtained her driver's license. She was fifty years old and finally able to drive herself; it was like a new lease on life. There was no more wanting or waiting for rides and the children were elated with Mom's newfound freedom.

Bobbie Notre Dame Song Girl 1967-68 *(Courtesy Barbara Olivo Cagle)*

For the 1969 school year, Bobbie was a Notre Dame Song Girl and Harold mastered playing the saxophone at Lincoln High School. He was a good actor and landed a role as the uncle of the princess in the school play, *The Mouse that Roared.* Ken attended the Archbishop Mitty High School for boys; Lorene was in seventh grade and Steve in sixth at St. Joseph's School.

It's never too late to use a talent
Dug up from its secret hiding place
Nurtured into a saving grace
Maybe all it needed was a little lace

—Jacqueline Rose Olivo

Sundays became an adventure for Mom and the children at home. Those who attended an early mass with her went out for breakfast. After breakfast she would occasionally take a long drive to see new sights of interest. Dad generally did not get up early enough to go out with them. Once he heard that they were going to drive to Hearst Castle and offered to pay for the gas. It meant the travelers could not leave without him and had to wait while he went through his two-hour morning routine of getting ready.

Dad was fun on these trips to castles and mansions. Antiques were his hobby and he knew a great deal about them and their worth. It was an inspiring trip to Hearst Castle and worth the long drive. Bobbie had been taking driving lessons at summer school and drove the group home.

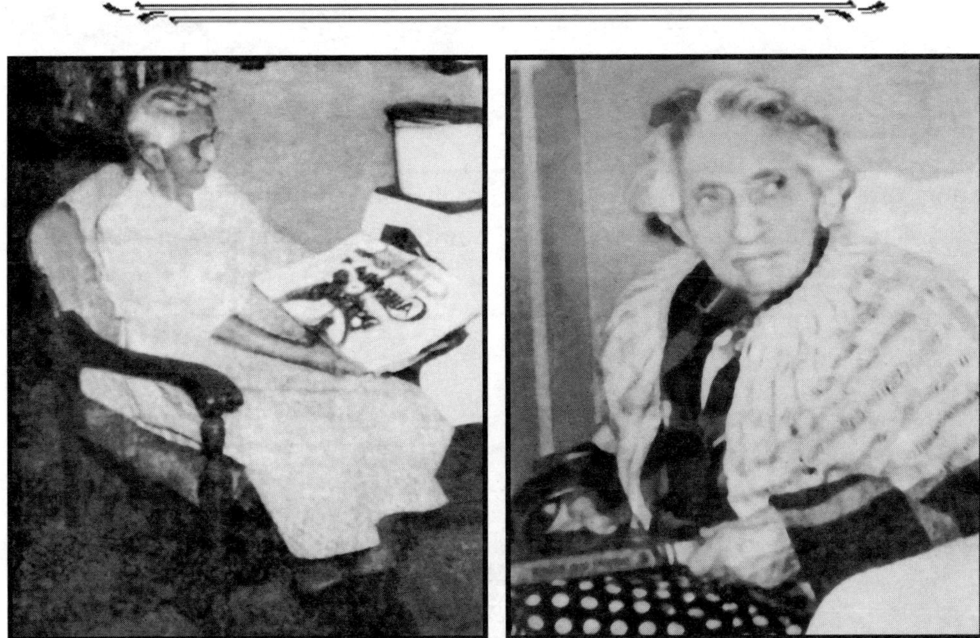

Rose Ablos Robie, Rose's namesake *(Courtesy Ronald Robie)*

Josephine, Lawrence, and Jimmy the siblings of Mom's mother, stayed in touch with her. They and some of their grown children often made a presence at Olivo gatherings. Josephine wrote to the older relatives in Campo Seco and kept Mom informed of anything noteworthy.

Rose Ablos Robie, Mom's aunt and namesake was one-hundred-and-one years old when she died January 11, 1968. She lived in Campo Seco for most of her life and was officially recognized as Calaveras County's oldest resident. She was featured several times in various Calaveras County newspapers and became a highly respected pioneer resident. "I raised my family the best way I could. What else was there to do?" A reporter quoted her saying and tracked her life more closely in her octogenarian years. She was excited to have her picture taken and enjoyed going for walks. For pictures she would remove her apron, fix her hair, and rub a little rouge onto her cheeks. Even though her hearing was poor, she remained alert. She and Kate, her sister, served many years assisting at the Campo Seco precinct during political elections.

Aunt Rose Robie and Aunt Kate were invited to ride in the back seat of an uncovered wagon during the towns' one hundred year centennial celebration in 1950. *(Courtesy Patt Pereira)*

The remains of an old Campo Seco hotel and precinct *(Courtesy Shirley Capps)*

Chapter Twenty

On the Move

Rose in Kauai, Hawaii 1968, in Oahu, Hawaii, April 1969, and her "license plate"
(Courtesy Rose Olivo)

Mom began traveling once Jeanie moved to Hawaii. After Christmas, she took Lorene to visit in Kauai for two weeks. Kauai is the oldest and fourth largest of the Hawaiian Islands, and known as the "Garden Isle." She wanted to see what Jeanie was doing and found her sharing a home with five college girls. Jeanie joined them as they visited the different islands. The trip was remarkable. Mom took enough photos to fill several albums.

On Mom's fifty-first birthday, March 1, 1969, the whole family gathered and showered her with gifts. The children agreed that it was about time she enjoy herself and they started to give of themselves sixteen times over. They sent her on a second trip. This time she stayed on Oahu, Hawaii's main island.

For her birthday, Sonny bought her a set of license plates personalized with 16 X MOM.

Most of the children were now married and the number of grandchildren grew yearly. The wonderful thing with grandchildren was Mom could enjoy them and then send them home to their parents. She had a knack of making each one of them feel as if he or she were the most important to her, a knack she also had with her own children, her daughter-in-laws and son-in-laws.

Dad had retired and handed the plumbing business down to his boys. He had more time to spend with the grandchildren, too. The kids liked their grandpa. He would take them out back to the garage/shop. The children called it the "BLACK HOLE" where they spent good times together. One of the tasks they enjoyed was walking on his back. It was great because he paid them more than he ever paid his own kids to do the same.

Mom wrote long letters to Jeanie. She used the typewriter at work while waiting for the food to bake or would write longhand in the wee hours. In May of 1969, she told her,

> You can't imagine the things that keep me on the run. Bobbie was in a serious car accident on May 10, the Saturday night before Mother's Day.
>
> Bobbie was on her way with Phil, a friend of hers, to pick up another friend in Campbell. They were coming off the freeway onto Camden Avenue when a car with four people in it ran a red light. They plowed right into her friend's car. She rode to O'Connor Hospital in an ambulance, with siren screaming and the red lights flashing, which added to the excitement.
>
> Before that happened, I had reccived a call from the hospital in Mariposa where Pa Pa and Grandma Nelle have been. The Doctor said he did not expect Pa Pa would live through the night, and if we wanted to see him, we should go right away.
>
> At a quarter to seven in the evening, Marie and I started out for Mariposa. We went in her car and she had a little trouble with it; so we stopped at a gas station and it took two hours to fix. Anyway, we arrived at the hospital at midnight. Rodger and Helene were already there and we went in to see Pa Pa. They were right; it sure didn't look like he could make it through the night. He was in an oxygen tent because he had pneumonia and the nurse said his temperature was over 104. He had emphysema, which is a filling of the lungs with fluid. He had a kidney infection and was passing blood, and he couldn't eat. He had lapsed into a coma before we arrived, he did not know that we were there. The Doctor said we could only wait.
>
> About three o'clock in the morning, Pa Pa came out of it and looked at each one of us. He mentioned our names and then fell back to sleep. The nurse said that we should try to get some rest ourselves. We went to a motel and slept about four hours, then we went back to the hospital and in the meantime, a priest had given him last rites. He had his last rites four times already. It seemed like every time he was in the hospital he got religious and would ask for last rites.

"By mid afternoon, we decided to return home. There was little sense in us staying on as the Doctor said he could go on indefinitely. I had to work that evening which was Tuesday. We came home knowing that we might have to turn around and go back. That was a full week ago, and Rodger called each evening to tell me 'No change.' So you see Jeanie, what I mean when I say I have been busy. We will probably go to visit him this weekend, if we don't hear anything before that. I will let you know how he is doing.

Marialice sent me a beautiful Mother of Pearls ring for Mother's Day. It has one large pearl in the center with six pearls around it for the boys and ten pearls around the outside for the girls. I had been hearing about those mother rings that have the birthstones of each child in the setting and I had thought how nice it would be to have one made someday. Then I get this one from Marialice and I thought how much more appropriate with pearls. As you know, I think of my children as being precious pearls. It is so beautiful. I wear it all the time.

PS Bobbie received a little sum of money from the insurance company and with that she for sure will be able to go to Hawaii. I thought at first that she should save it for education, etc. On second thought maybe I should let her do whatever she wants, as she was the one who suffered. Then, too, I would have to go with her, wouldn't I? Well, we will just have to wait and see. As it turned out, family circumstances prevailed and Mom and Bobbie did not take the trip to Hawaii.

On May 24, 1969, the hospital transferred Pa Pa to the Hy-Lond Convalescent Hospital in Merced, California. Grandma Nelle moved from their Campo Seco home to be closer to him and to live with her son. Mom and Marie went to visit him. It was a nice cheerful hospital. He figured he was not going to go home again and humored himself by charming the nurses and pretty ladies in front of his daughters. He said to them with emphasis, "It's MY plea-sure to meet you. Look good! Look sharp! Be sharp!"

Mom, Rodger and his family went to visit Pa Pa on Father's Day, June 14. He was wide-awake sitting up in bed.

"Take-a me outside. I wanna get outta here!" he said to them as clear as could be. Of course, that was not possible. Mom, trying to divert his attention, noticed that there were apricots on his dish.

"Take a bite now; it's your favorite fruit" Rose said while serving him. He loved his apricots and appeared to be feeling good. He was in no pain and it came as a surprise that night when Mom received a call at 11:05 p.m. that Pa Pa had passed away from congestive heart failure. His burial was on June 17, in Lakewood Memorial Park where Grandma Nelle gave him a quiet memorial. Mom stood solemn, as did Marie, Rodger, and Helene. Pa Pa had a will, he left his liquid assets to Grandma Nelle, the house to Rodger, and his bonds to Mom and Marie.

To glow from obscurity,
To envision this note
To envelope then release
Emotions revealing lasting purity

—Jacqueline Rose Olivo

Every one of Mom's children were active during the school year 1970. Harold transferred to Pioneer High School for his senior year to stay with Virginia who lived nearby. He was involved with the band and drama class. Ken transferred to Lincoln High School where he played football and became a member of the Young Republican Men's Club. Lorene was in eighth grade at St. Joseph's School and Steve in seventh.

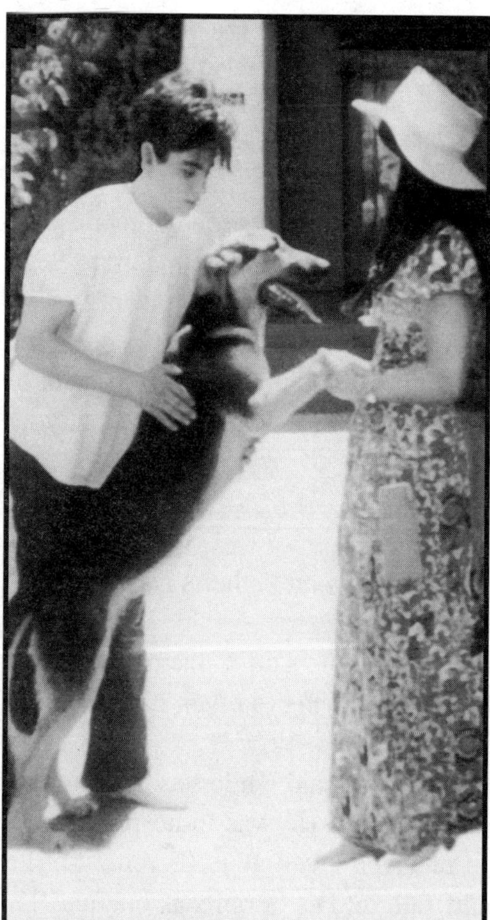

Steve, Lorene, and Peno *(Courtesy Barbara Olivo Cagle)*

Peno was Rich's dog until he left the area and Steve took over caring for the dog. It did not take long for Peno to become a member of the household.

Lorene was at the perfect age to baby-sit her nieces and nephews. Her older sisters and brothers would invite her along on their vacations to help with the children. She went on many travels, sightseeing trips, and camp-outs and loved to tell Mom of her adventures.

Bill and Rich were into dance. Rich joined the Fred Astaire Dance Studio and took ballroom dancing. He told Bill and he joined, too. The two were greasy and wearing leather shags one day with the motorcycle gang, and the next day in a tuxedo and ballroom dancing. They attended the Western Region Dance Olympics, in Las Vegas, the weekend of February 13-15. They took first and second place in the Cha Cha, Swing, Waltz, and Tango—Theater Arts.

Bobbie, Head Song Girl 1969-1970 *(Photos courtesy Bobbie Olivo)*

Senior year for Bobbie proved to be her most memorable. She served as Notre Dame's Head Song Girl. She and Harold took tap-dance lessons together and performed several sister-brother routines. Archbishop Mitty High School chose her as the 1st runner-up Homecoming Princess.

On February 13, 1970, Notre Dame sponsored a senior ski trip to Squaw Valley, California, located about six miles from the North Shore of Lake Tahoe and eight miles from the mountain town of Truckee. Bobbie did not have snow gear and borrowed a nice furry jacket, hat, scarf, and gloves from her sister, Jeanie, without permission. Jeanie was in Hawaii and had no use for them at the time so it seemed like a good idea.

Early in the morning, on the 14th of February, Bobbie and some of her classmates found a perfect place to toboggan where a group of boys had paved a way in the snow for a smooth ride. At 9:15 a.m. it was snowing heavily. She and her classmate Lucy wanted to be the first daring souls among the girls to take the toboggan ride down the slope. Wrapping the rope around her arms and with Lucy behind her, she asked the boys to give them a push. The slope was steeper than she realized, and the toboggan picked up speed rapidly. With the wind and snow blinding her, she could not control the toboggan. For a split-second the snow cleared and she saw a huge pine tree in front of her. That was to be the longest split-second of her life. At that very instant, she had an out-of-body experience. It was as though she was flying. She looked down at her physical body lying on a table. Spiritual beings were busily working on her in a very bright room. She saw the faces of people she knew in her life moving around the table talking. What Bobbie heard was a discussion of her fate. Unable to visualize with whom she was having a conversation, she responded, "I understand that I may die, and if I live, I accept the fact that I may be paralyzed."

At that instant she relaxed, and the ropes untangled from around her arms. Her whole body felt numb. She heard and felt the impact as her legs wrapped around a tree and her head whiplashed forward. Her pelvis took the brunt of the force and eased the blow to her head. The toboggan bounced back several feet from the tree, and both girls were conscious. A couple of classmates ran for help while the others gathered around the two girls. Blood was gushing out of Bobbie's forehead and her classmates were concerned. "I'm not worried about my head; it's the rest of my body" she said. She knew she was badly hurt and tried not to move.

Lucy fractured her toes. They lay packed in the snow, talking to classmates and waiting for help to arrive.

Emergency medical technicians showed up within fifteen minutes and a half hour later, wheeled Bobbie on a gurney into the emergency room of the Tahoe Forest Hospital near the ski resort. The doctors cut through her clothing and noticed she had covered her feet and legs up to her knees with plastic held in place by rubber bands. Her face had swollen from her forehead to the bottom of her nose. She was thinking of her sister and how angry she was going to be if that jacket was not put back together in one piece.

The x-rays showed that her pelvis was fractured in each corner and she had one massive hematoma forming on her forehead. The school coordinator notified Mom that Bobbie was in an accident and spoke to one of the attending doctors.

"What kind of accident and how badly is she hurt?"

"A toboggan accident, she hit a tree; however, she is conscious."

"Well, that sounds like she is very hurt. What's the extent of her injuries? Does she have any broken legs? Can she walk?"

"No, her pelvis was fractured and she will need hospitalization. Do you want us to take her to a hospital closer to you?"

"Yes, O'Connor Hospital in San Jose, if it doesn't hurt her to ride. Can she make that trip?"

"I think so. We will call you back with the estimated time of arrival."

Mom informed the rest of the family and anxiously waited for her safe return home.

Jack with the Donner Ambulance Service drove Bobbie and another injured teen the grueling two-hundred and twenty-one miles back to San Jose. The other teen had a broken leg and screamed and moaned the whole trip. Bobbie had a strong dose of morphine. Still, she remained conscious and wished the other teen would quiet down. That evening, at 8:15 p.m. the ambulance pulled into the entrance of O'Connor Hospital and rushed her into the emergency room. Mom, Dad, and Harold saw her briefly; she was banged-up and unrecognizable.

Harold was deeply disturbed by the state of her condition and went off to inform family members and her friends. Mom and Dad completed the admission papers and had a consultation with Dr. Dedinsky. The doctor thought that Bobbie would not walk again, and if she did, it would be with crutches.

Mom was back early the next morning and remained seated by her bedside well past hospital visiting hours. She brought books to read, and wrote letters, occasionally dozing off in a chair.

Bobbie nearly slipped into a coma the second day. She could not move, blink an eye, speak, or hear. She snapped out of it when the nurse on duty slapped her.

After a few days, Bobbie started to recover and was allowed visitors. Family and friends poured in and provided Mom with the opportunity to take breaks. Bobbie made an occasion of it and had her visitors sign a guest book. She was surprised one day when a friend from dance class came to visit and fainted at the sight of her. After coming to, the friend proceeded to do what she came to do; shave Bobbie's legs, wash and style her hair, and brought a mirror. She looked at herself for the first time since the accident.

Prayers and the positive energy from family, friends, and classmates were the best healing. On March 4, after three weeks of hospitalization, the doctor released her for recovery at home. She had to lay flat on her back with limited movement of her head and arms. Mom became a full-time nurse. Rich and Ken were helpful and offered to do the bedpan service when needed.

Jeanie returned home from Hawaii. She and Mom would play Scrabble or other games with her. Jeanie would prepare a special tray of cheese, crackers, grapes, and wine. There were a few comments from her siblings that Mom was spoiling Bobbie. If so, to Bobbie, she was just being Mom. She gave to whomever was in need most.

After two weeks at home she tried to move. She concentrated on her right leg, raised it up off the bed, and pointed her toes to the ceiling. She yelled for Mom to come and Mom immediately called Dr. Dedinsky. He came over to the house and said it was miraculous. He started in-house physical therapy and within a week, Bobbie was able to move her legs. Although recovery would take some time; there would be a recovery.

Mom called the school to arrange for the teachers to provide homework for Bobbie to graduate with her class. She made her first appearance at an athletic award presentation in the auditorium. She was unsteady as she held onto Mom's arm. When the student body saw her, they stood up and applauded her astounding recovery. She received the Notre Dame Athletic Block and membership into the Block Notre Dame (ND) Society. Eight weeks after her accident, she was back in school and resumed school activities, including Song Girl performances with leg kicks, and cart wheels. Socially, Harold bought her professional roller skates and they were out skating with the gang again.

Mom proudly attended three graduation ceremonies that year: Harold from Pioneer High School, Bobbie from Notre Dame High School, and Lorene from St. Joseph's.

Harold bought himself a 1970 blue Ford Maverick. He and Bobbie spent a few weeks following Sonny while he undertook producing an educational film called, *You've Got What?* The two acted in the film and had the time of their life.

Bobbie in *A Little Bit of Broadway*
(Courtesy Barbara Olivo Cagle)

That summer Bobbie played in *A Little Bit of Broadway* and *Fiddler on the Roof* at the Montgomery Civic Theatre in San Jose.

In August, Rich asked Harold to come along with him to sign up for the Army. Leaving the recruiting office, it was Harold, not Rich, who was interested in the Army. At the end of August, he left for Fort Lewis, Washington, for eight weeks of boot camp. Bobbie thought it was great; she took over the payments and ownership of his car.

Harold *(Courtesy Harold Olivo)*

Take advantage of opportunities, try to not ask many questions or place too many obstacles in the way or read too many words between the lines. Let your intelligence and maturity tell you who you can accept at face value, and then meet them with equal directness.

—Jacqueline Rose Olivo

Lorene was the last of the ten Olivo girls to enter Notre Dame High School in 1970. Steve was in eighth grade and the last Olivo to attend St. Joseph's School.

The Olivo boys loved to dance and Steve was no exception. He began to spend time at the Wuzit where many of his older siblings spent a good deal of time and he came home with the latest dance steps to share with the rest of the family. He was strumming and picking the guitar, and making up his own music.

Steve *(Courtesy Rose Olivo)*

At the Wuzit he met Diane Zuniga and the two became an item. They were either together or talking for hours on the telephone. Mom made it a point to get to know her children's friends, and she especially liked Diane. She took the two of them out to many baseball games. Steve was into baseball and a huge San Francisco Giants fan. Watching the games with him was a special time for Diane. Although they liked each other, they eventually went their separate ways.

Bill and Rose *(Courtesy Barbara Olivo Cagle)*

Rose, front left, and relatives in La Arboleda, Spain, May 1971 *(Courtesy Rodger and Helene Nunez)*

In October, Mom took her first long trip with Dad and attended Harold's graduation from basic training. They wanted to get there quickly and took the shortest route to Fort Lewis, Washington. They were proud of him on the day he graduated. He was the only son who served in the military. He was allowed one day to spend with his parents before he left for Fort Bliss, Texas. He was trained as a "Military Occupation Specialist" 24F20 HAWK Fire Control Mechanic. After seeing Harold off, Mom and Dad drove on to Seattle and visited with friends. Returning home they took the coastal scenic route.

Bill and Rich continued with their ballroom dancing and on occasions took Mom to the Fred Astaire Studio to dance the Tango and Cha Cha. At the next National Olympic Ballroom Competition, Bill won the Champion of Champions award in the Theatre Arts Division and was awarded an expense paid vacation to the Bahamas.

On May 21, 1971, Mom, Marie, Rodger and his family rendezvoused with Jeanie in Europe for three weeks. Dad had commitments and could not go. Mom finally got to go to places she had found interesting in her readings.

The trip was amazing. She had the opportunity to meet Pa Pa's sister, Engracia, and her family in La Arboleda, Spain in the Basque Country.

Rose with Nello's Italian relatives, May of 1971, Massa Martana, Italy, Province of Perugia *(Courtesy Rose Olivo)*

Rose and Marie at Trevi Fountain Rome, Italy in May of 1971 *(Courtesy Marie Bueno)*

In Pouzauges, France, the group met Pa Pa's brother Manuel and his family. His resemblance to Pa Pa brought tears to their eyes. The next day, Rodger and his family remained in France, while Mom, Marie, and Jeanie went on to Massa Martana, Italy to meet Dad's relatives.

Legend has it that if you toss a coin over your shoulder into the Trevi Fountain that one day you will return to the eternal city.

One regret Mom had for an otherwise wonderful vacation was missing Steve's graduation from St. Joseph's. He was the last of the long line of Olivo children to attend the school. Arrangements were made for the older children to attend his graduation and the ceremony went well, yet Mom felt she owed St. Joseph's School a great deal of gratitude for helping her raise her family. The Olivo children received one hundred-and-twenty-eight years of education at the school.

For the school year of 1971, Steve attended Herbert Hoover Junior High School and liked the new stomping grounds.

Lorene was lonely and shy at Notre Dame High School and talked Mom into attending Lincoln High School to be with her friends. Ken was a senior at Lincoln High School. Bobbie taught Lorene pom-pom and cheer-leading routines for tryouts at the school and she became a Lion's Cheerleader.

Ken 1972, in his senior year at Lincoln High School *(Courtesy Ken Olivo)*

The numbers 50 and 78 distinguished Ken from his teammates on the school's varsity basketball and football teams. In basketball, he was a forward, and in football he played offensive tackle and defensive end.

"Go Ken, Go!" cheered Mom and the Olivo fans from the stands.

Ken was a star athlete in every sport he played and achieved "All League" honors his senior year in the Santa Teresa Football League.

After his graduation, Dad took him to Santa Cruz to buy a car, a 1972 240Z silver Datsun. When they got home, Ken decided to wash the car and drove into the backyard. He found a five-gallon can filled with what appeared to be dirt. He emptied it behind the playhouse, washed out the can and refilled it with soapy water. Wow, the car shined with sparkles! He did not know the dirt in the five-gallon can was actually real gold dust. Dad had painstakingly panned it when Pa Pa had taken him to a mine in Livermore. That was the time when Pa Pa told him to look out for the quick silver, "You take in the lungs, it's gonna kill you," he said.

Ken was washing the car and Dad was tinkering in the back of the garage/shop in his "BLACK HOLE." He moseyed around as he usually did, dragging either his right or left leg, depending on which day of the week it was, and oohing and aahing over mysterious aches and pains. His eyes went in the direction of the five-gallon can and his face took on a look of horror. He could move fast when he wanted to, and barreled his way through the junk pile toward Ken. He was angry, very angry! He was not noted as a big disciplinarian; however, when one of the children got into his junk, or in this case his gold, he got after them. He soon had Ken down on the ground helping him to recover the gold dust. Later, it became one of Dad's favorite tales told to family and friends.

Harold in South Korea, May 1, 1971-June 2, 1972 *(Courtesy Harold Olivo)*

Mom was devoted to writing to Harold and Jeanie who were both living in far-away countries. Jeanie was living in England and Harold was assigned to Camp Red Cloud, Uijeongbu Enclave, South Korea. He had a weird experience while on a special detail-traveling mission to check on the radar equipment in the surrounding camps. He met up with a soldier with the same first name, Harold. They looked identical and the other soldiers asked if they were twins. The two were amazed with the look-a-like coincidence and name.

Bobbie in Germany, and in Greece. Jeanie, Bobbie, and Nancy in Austria *(Courtesy Barbara Olivo Cagle)*

In her writings to Jeanie, Mom suggested Nancy and Bobbie tour Europe while she was living in England. A few months later, flight arrangements were made with TWA. Jeanie sent a list of exactly what to pack for light traveling. With backpacks, the girls had one change of clothes. They departed from San Francisco Airport on July 8, 1972. It was the first time either of them flew on an airplane. Mom saw them off and said, "Be sure to write every chance you get and send your film home. I will have them developed by the time you return."

Jeanie met Nancy and Bobbie at the airport in Rome, Italy. With International Student Identity Cards, they were able to stay in youth hostels. They spent six weeks hitchhiking, or riding on mopeds. They visited historical sights of Italy, Sicily, Germany, France, Yugoslavia, Greece, and Austria. Touring Europe the way they did exposed them to a variety of adventures. The bathrooms were an experience with trying to aim for a hole in the floor, and then pay the equivalent of a nickel for a square of toilet paper.

One night a youth hostel was not open and a farmer let them stay in his fruit barn sleeping on crates. Showers and water were a luxury, to the point where spit-bathing became an art. With one change of clothes, laundry was a daily requirement. Trucks were the best form of transportation for long distances and a ride with one allowed them to hang their clothes out the windows to dry.

Hitchhiking was acceptable and a common means of transportation among Europeans and international students. The girls had safety rules such as do not accept a ride with more than one man in the vehicle. One time, they became desperate when it started to rain. They had rejected several rides and decided to accept the next ride even though there were two men in the vehicle. The driver got happy and unzipped his pants to show the girls what he had. Jeanie, seated next to him, started laughing hysterically. Her eyes widened and looked as if they were going to bulge out of her eye sockets. She looked back at Nancy and Bobbie who were fighting off the other guy's roaming hands and pointed at the driver, yelping.

"We've got a problemmm! Grab your backpacks! We're jumping out!"

On the way to Massa Martana, Italy, the girls asked a truck driver to drop them off a mile from their relative's home. They wanted to change clothes and freshen up. They were walking into a field when a couple of young boys spotted them. Jeanie, speaking in broken Italian, pointed to a piece of paper with the relative's address, and asked them if they knew of this home. The boys spoke excitedly with their hands flying in all directions and ran down the road. The girls did not understand a single word. Minutes later, the boys returned in a car with their older brother who spoke English.

"So, you are the Olivo girls. We have been expecting you."

Arriving in Pouzauges, France was another great occasion. A truck driver dropped the girls off on the road short of Pa Pa's brother Manuel's home. They had to hike up a steep hill to the house. As they approached, they saw a man outside working in the garden picking string beans. They rushed up and showered him with hugs and kisses. He looked just like Pa Pa and there was no mistaking him for their uncle.

Both the French and Italian relatives were gracious and looked after the girls with attention, food, and wine.

Rose in Oahu, Hawaii, January of 1973 *(Courtesy Rose Olivo)*

Harold, August 30, 1973 *(Courtesy Harold Olivo)*

Mom had two children left to see through the high school years. Lorene was a junior and Steve a sophomore. Both attended Lincoln High School. During the school year of 1973, Mom made two trips to Oahu, Hawaii, one in January and then again in July, both with Marie. The two were obviously having fun. They would get in an elevator and gab for twenty minutes before they realized that neither one of them pressed a button. They came home singing *Tiny Bubbles* after seeing a Don Ho performance while boat dining along Oahu's tranquil shores of paradise. It was a good trip. After returning home Mom had major surgery on the varicose veins in both her legs, and was laid up for a few weeks. Upon her release from the hospital, she spent a week recovering at Rodger and Helene's.

Mom focused on getting back on her feet to meet Harold at the airport on August 30, 1973 and welcome him home. She was elated and proud to see him in his Army dress uniform. The family met at Virginia's house for his welcome home party and Father Joe joined in the celebration. During his three years of service in the military he was promoted to Specialist 5th Class and he received three medals: The National Defense Service Medal, Armed Forces Expeditionary Medal, and Good Conduct Medal.

Lorene, Cheerleader—Head Song Girl 1973-1974 Lincoln High School *(Courtesy Lorene Linnehan)*

The 1974 school year flew by quickly. Lorene was Head Song Girl at Lincoln High School and geared up for graduation. Steve was playing baseball, strumming the guitar, and having fun with his friends.

Warrant Officer Donald J. and Barbara Cagle, April 21, 1974 *(Courtesy Barbara Olivo Cagle)*

A few months before Lorene's graduation, Bobbie gave Mom short notice that she was getting married. Her fiancé was scheduled for a long Pacific deployment and they wanted to get married before he left. Mom coordinated the details in three weeks and the wedding ceremony was held at the Chapel on Moffett Naval Air Station, California on April 21, 1974, with a reception at the Officers' Club.

A carpet of lavender daisies growing in the garden made for a beautiful spring day. Bobbie's favorite color was lavender and she chose those daisies for her wedding bouquet. She wore the family heirloom full-length laced wedding gown. The Sabrina neckline drew attention to her long neck, and sprinkled sequins illuminated the lace bodice of the gown down the full-length fitted sleeves to a fingertip raindrop pearl. Rose-point lace insets accentuated the bouffant nylon skirt, which flowed into a cathedral train. A veil of illusion fell from her flowered crown of seeded pearls and sequins. After the ceremony and reception were over, Bobbie and Don had an additional reception at Mom's home which lasted into the wee hours.

Lorene, and a sister who remains unnamed, decided there was not enough excitement at the home reception. They grabbed a couple of paper bags, stripped down to their underwear, streaked through the house, and ran out onto Martin Ave to a get-a-way car. Later they made a quiet re-entry into the house.

Bobbie and Don honeymooned in Lake Tahoe. His mother had traveled to California from Wisconsin and planned to join them. When Bobbie learned of the plans, she asked Mom to come along, too.

"Mom, please come. If Don's mother is coming, so are you."

Mom had a suitcase packed at all times, ready to take off at a moment's notice for any emergency or a trip just like this one. Whoever heard of a honeymoon with both mothers-in-law tagging along? You guessed it. The unimaginable thing did happen. Don's mom walked in on the two of them while they were in bed on their first honeymoon night! Where was the lock on the door?

Later that year Mom visited the newlyweds at Hamilton Air Force Base, in Novato, California, North of San Francisco. She was standing in the kitchen with Don when she asked him a peculiar question.

"Geez, Don, could I have a beer?" Don knew Mom did not drink beer and asked, "Would you rather have a glass of wine?"

"No, beer is fine." It was her way of making him feel comfortable.

"Are you two thinking about having children?" Mom asked. It caught Don totally off guard and his mind went blank for a second. He had no idea what to say and hesitated before he answered.

"Well, Mom, I'm putting everything I've got into it." She looked him in the eyes, took a small sip of the beer, and smiled with a titter.

"Oh!"

Sweetly and humbly, she turned and walked into the living room. She sat the beer down and went to visit Bobbie in the bedroom. You should have seen the expression on her face. It was priceless! Unbeknownst to them, Bobbie was already pregnant.

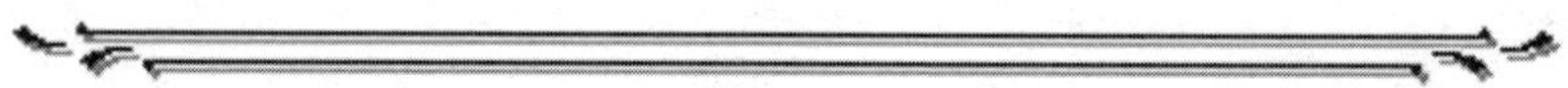

Mom saw her youngest son and child, Steve, graduate from Lincoln High School in 1975. He remembered well the Christmas of 1974 and the unforgettable surprise for Mom and wished he could watch it over again. She needed a new car and the children pitched in to buy her a car for Christmas:

Steve and Pooper, 1975 *(Courtesy Barbara Olivo Cagle)*

They got this big box, a huge box full of crunched-up newspapers, crepe papers, scrap papers, and old Christmas wrappings. In it, was a wrapped box, inside of another wrapped box, inside of another wrapped box. Mom got way down in the box and got excited. She was tearing everything out. Everybody had fun watching her open it, she had no idea what was in the box. She did not find a thing. She rummaged through the papers and boxes again and asked in uncontrollable laughter, 'What is this? Where's the present?' Finally, she noticed deep down in the bottom corner of the last box a set of keys. She wasn't sure what they belonged to. Sonny opened the front door, and there outside, parked in the driveway was a 1975 yellow Ford Mustang, wrapped up in crepe papers, ribbons and bows. I believe that's one moment, everybody who was there would love to relive.

Mom cared about other people's desires for material things and not her own. All she wanted was one or two special little items, and she was happy. She had her little rocking chair that she loved, and a radio-TV. She could have had more than that. All she had to do was ask, and the family would find some way to get nice things for her for entertainment or something. When we were kids, she would get us what we wanted, or at least tried. Everybody has things they want, to fulfill their desires, I want a guitar and amplifier.

Last but not least, I think one of the main things that kept our family together, because Dad was hardly ever home, was the fact that she in some way kept God in each of our lives. She would say something that had to do with God, or what God would do, and you knew He was in control of the situation. I think that's what helped me. Shoot! That's not the least of everything it's probably the most.

My favorite quality about Mom that stands out is when she sees somebody enjoying something and they share it with her; she seems to have as much fun at that very moment sharing the exact amount of joy as they are having.

Doggone it! The others in the family must have been from a different time zone. Cuz Mom has not cooked anything bad! I don't remember pea soup or lumpy oatmeal. She cooked the best spaghetti, the best enchiladas, and tuna on toast. Oh, man was that good!

Father Joe said it best:

> What an accomplishment for Rose and Nello, supporting and guiding sixteen children through all those years in parochial and public schools. It was a big job. I realized that the work of Rose, and of course Nello, who had to supply the money to keep the family going, was not easy, and it took a great effort on their part to do it, and with the help of God and the church, they did it. For Rose, she was not only a symbol of motherhood; she was also a beloved matriarch of the Olivo family.

The first thing Dad wanted to do after Steve's graduation was to visit family relatives. He said to Mom, "Let's go visit my cousin, Humbert Joseph Ciardella, Jr. in Carson City, Nevada. We will stay overnight in a hotel." They had been out of touch with the Ciardella family for a very long time and recently had heard that his Uncle Johnny had passed. Mom could not go, Bobbie was expecting a baby any day, and she had made plans to help while Don was out to sea.

Dad arrived at his cousin's house unexpectedly one late afternoon in July and rang the doorbell. Humbert Jr.'s daughter, Sherry, opened the door, stared at him and exclaimed "Oh, my God!" Then she closed the door on him. He had spooked her at how identical to her grandfather he looked. She reopened the door right away and said, "Hi!"

He introduced himself and when Humbert Jr. and his wife, Mary Jane, arrived home from work they visited for a couple of hours and went out to dinner. "Do you have any children?" Humbert Jr. asked. Dad hemmed and hawed and finally dug into his pocket. He pulled out a string of photos that fell to the floor and they stood amazed.

"I have sixteen children," Dad chuckled.

Bobbie with Jocilyn Roselle Cagle
(Courtesy Barbara Olivo Cagle)

As promised, Mom went to help Bobbie with her baby. Jocilyn Roselle was born on July 14, 1975 and weighed 7 pounds 14.75 ounces, her birth date. The delivery experience was recorded and photographs taken by her friend, Judy, to share with Mom and of course Don, via mail. Later, at Jocilyn's baptismal reception, it tickled her to tell the family of her visit with Bobbie. The two had looked at Jocilyn's birthing photographs while recapping and listening to the entire recording of her delivery. "After having sixteen children of my own, it sort of lost its luster," laughed Mom.

Rose in Oahu, Hawaii, September 1976, and with Nello in Verona, Italy, July 1975
(Courtesy Rodger and Helene Nunez, and Rose Olivo)

Rose at Oslo, Norway, July 1977, and fishing the Fjords in Bergen *(Courtesy Barbara Olivo Cagle)*

Rose's first time having Poi and on Moorea Lagoon, Tahiti September 1977 *(Courtesy Rodger and Helene Nunez)*

St. Joseph's School Dad's Club and Mother's Guild made the arrangements for a group trip to Europe. Mom and Dad had seen the children through high school and decided to take the trip, Marie joined them.

Toward the end of the vacation, Marie left with the rest of the tour group. Mom and Dad stayed on a few more days in Italy to visit his relatives. They ate at an outdoor café in Verona, Italy, named "Olivo." Verona is known for the most famous lovers in history: Romeo and Juliet. The visit was fascinating and provided Dad with plenty to talk about for some time. There was several years between Mom's travels to Europe and her next trip.

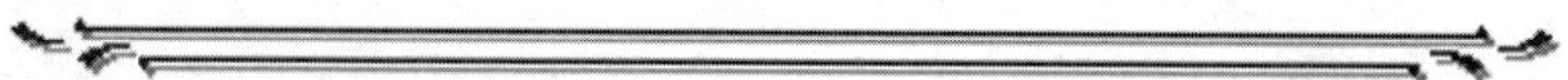

Dad needed surgery on his back in the spring of 1980. He had two vertebral discs fused together and lost six inches in height. Mom tended to him around the clock. Once Dad was able to move about, his former Miller Street neighbor, Stanley Lawrence, came to visit with him. They were like two peas in a pod tinkering around the house fixing this and jury-rigging that, wires everywhere. It was an electrician's nightmare. One of their favorite concoctions was wiring the front doorknob with a low-voltage buzzer that when turned on would zap anyone who touched the door knob with a shock. He got a kick out of turning it on. The children, in-laws, and even Mom feared touching the front door knob after experiencing the zap and became testy with Dad's fuzzy sense of humor.

Mom knew how to handle the challenges Dad or the children presented. She turned to God for strength. He did not fail her. She was overjoyed whenever she saw a twinkle of passion in her children as they grew in renewing and expressing their faith. Praying together before meals and get-togethers remains a tradition in the Olivo family. One could expect to hear a few humorous interjections of singing "AAAAAMEN" to close the prayer. Whether they were traditional Catholic Christians or new Born Again Christians, some of her children had a proselytizing zeal to spread the word of Jesus. "I tell you the truth, no one can see the kingdom of God unless he is born again," John 3: 3.

I firmly believe that everyone, no matter how self-sufficient they think they are, needs this very private conversation with God, especially when the going gets rough.

—Jacqueline Rose Olivo

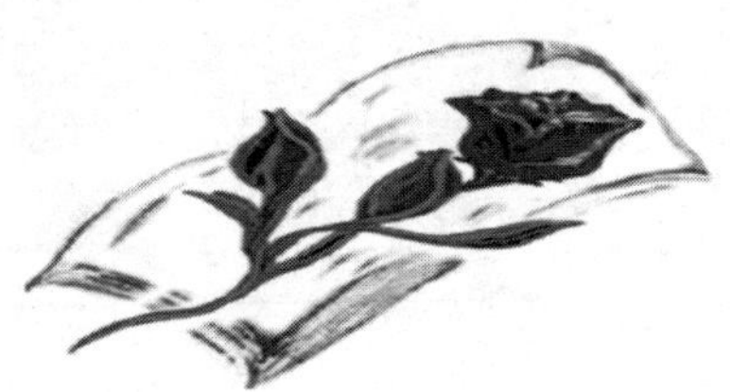

Chapter Twenty-One

Good and Not so Good

Ballroom dancing competition for Bill and Rich was in the past and their love for cars heated up, especially Bill's. One of his prized vehicles was a 1969 Hurst/Olds with a 455 cubic inch engine, packaged in fire-frost gold stripes with a white color scheme. It was a limited production purebred muscle car, one of nine-hundred and fourteen made that year. As one of the hottest cars in town, it flew like the wind and whistled to its own music. The car was valued at ten-thousand dollars.

Car shows were a big event for Bill. He won so many trophies that he had nowhere to put them. He owned several cars, a different one for each day of the week. He had both right side and left side steering wheel vehicles and loved to show them off to his dates.

"I like to drive a certain one depending on what type of girl I'm dating," Bill would say.

Ken worked for Bill at the time and had him believing that he wanted his '69 Hurst/Olds; however, Steve had his eye on it, too. Since Ken already had a car, Bill went ahead and struck a deal with Steve.

It was close to Christmas when he took the car for a test drive. He was unmindful that he had not made any payment yet, or kept up the insurance for the car. He ran into a curb and hit a tree at the corner of Twelfth and Julian Streets. His body curled up underneath the dashboard with his head wedged beneath the bent steering wheel. His body was not visible. The force of the impact pushed the hood through the windshield and sliced over the driver's side to the back seat like a sharp blade.

Unbelievable as it was, Steve survived the crash without a scratch. What a lucky guy that day. Clearly, God was looking out for him.

Mom knew the car meant a great deal to Bill and Steve. She was sick when she learned the insurance had lapsed.

"Mom, Steve's alive, without a scratch! He could easily have been decapitated," Bill told her, "We're fortunate that he is OK."

Steve wanted to get the car back in working condition and have it look as good as it did before the accident. He did not have a job and Mom used her credit card to buy parts for the repairs. In the evenings, the two brothers worked on the repairs. The costs kept rising and finally, Bill sold the car for fourteen-hundred dollars. He loved the car and still talks about the accident as though it happened yesterday.

Nello in his "BLACK HOLE"

Nello's with his 1924 old 'Tin Lizzy' and junk. The above photos give you an idea of how Rose and the younger children lived. *(Photos courtesy Barbara Olivo Cagle)*

Nello *(Courtesy of Rose Olivo)*

Prior to Dad's retirement in 1981, the Rosicrucian Museum purchased the rental house on Naglee. Dad had one month after closing to move his antiques and junk off the property. Instead of renting a storage unit, he hauled truckloads of supposedly valuable antiques into the beautiful backyard and garden that Mom had tenderly created. It was Dad's house, too, she thought; he had a right to be the way he was and a right to do the things he wanted to do. If he wanted to collect antiques, let him collect. It was his hobby and part-time business.

Bill, Steve, Ken and his newly-wed wife Gail helped Dad with the move. He watched them like a hawk, as if he was taking inventory. It was weird how he knew what he had down to the tiniest nut and bolt.

"Where do I put this or that?" Ken or Gail would ask Dad.

"You put the brass in the brass pile. You put the steel in the steel pile. You put the aluminum in the aluminum pile, and you put the junk in the junk pile," he answered.

There were piles for wood, glass, iron, rocks, etc. After asking him numerous times where to put things, Dad finally threw up his arms and grumbled.

"Oh heck! Brass is brass, steel is steel, and junk is junk!" Then when he got tired of trying to organize the priceless junk, he mumbled.

"Oh, hell! Life is life! Hell is hell!" Life is hell!

Discouraging as it was for Mom to look at the backyard, she had delight in beautifying the front garden.

In 1984, Marie became severely ill after she retired from the General Electric Company. She came down with a cold and earache that turned life threatening. Her granddaughter was living with her and found her unconscious in bed. She called Marie's daughters, Sandy and Karen. By the time they arrived with their husbands, she had regained consciousness, with serious fever, and seemed confused. The sons-in-law were able to put her in the front seat of Sandy's car and she left for O'Connor Hospital. Karen stayed behind, made telephone calls to the family before leaving, and the granddaughter baby-sat the little ones.

On the freeway to the hospital, Marie became delirious and kept trying to open the car door to get out. Sandy was forced to pull off the freeway. She was moved to the backseat and had to be restrained. When they arrived at the hospital, she was put in a full-body straightjacket packed with ice. She had an extremely high temperature and was diagnosed with meningitis.

Mom did not get the initial message from Karen. Later that night after she returned from Bingo at St. Joseph's, she received a second message that she should come to the hospital. A specialist gave Marie a fifty-fifty chance of making it through the night, and another doctor changed that to thirty-seventy. Rodger and Helene were with Marie's children when Mom arrived at 11:30 p.m.

"Auntie Rose, my mother is dying," cried Sandy.

"YOUR MOM IS NOT DYING!" she said with strong conviction as she shook her finger at Sandy. Mom was not ready to say goodbye to her sister. Shortly, before dawn, Marie's temperature broke. Years later she said, "I dodged a big bullet that day."

As Marie came out of it, she noticed an intern standing outside the door to her room. He said "Hi," and did not move.

"Why doesn't he come in?" she asked her nurse.

"He was the one who was holding you down when you first came in and you bit him on his arm," answered the nurse.

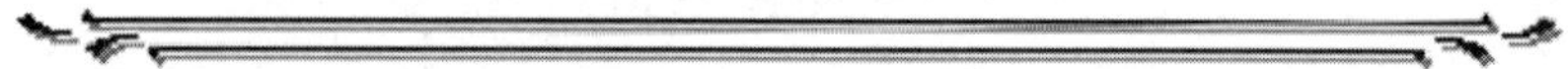

Harvard University Undergraduate Graduation was the reason Mom talked Marie and her friend, Myrtle, into taking a month-long trip driving to Boston. She was going to be present when her daughter, Nancy, received her Bachelor of Arts diploma, magna cum laude. Marie had recuperated from her bout with meningitis and looked forward to the trip.

Mom recalled Nancy's phone call from a few years earlier.

"Guess what Mom? I got accepted into Harvard."

"So, what's that mean?"

"Well, it's one of the best schools in the country." Mom took a moment before she realized what Nancy had said.

"Oh, that Harvard."

It was a great accomplishment for her. She was a 4.0 student at University of California, Irvine and chosen as one of thirty-three transfer students out of the whole country that year, among thousands of applicants. Mom assured Nancy she would be there for her graduation and booked an air flight in advance.

Nancy called Mom prior to graduation.

"Guess what? I got accepted into Harvard Law School." There was silence. Mom hesitated and finally responded.

"Well, what does that mean?"

"Well, it means I get to go to Harvard three more years," she explained.

"Oh Nancy, I bought my plane ticket a year ago. Are you saying I need to wait three more years to go to your graduation?"

"No Mom you get to go to two graduations."

It was then that Mom decided to drive to Nancy's graduation in Boston.

Rose, Marie, and friend Myrtle June 1984,
(Photos courtesy Marie Bueno)

Mom, Marie, and Myrtle were excited with the trip. Within a couple of days the three of them meticulously put together a plan to visit the places and sights along the way. The cross country trip took them through thirty-eight states. With foresight, they packed the car. Heavy suitcases were placed in the back of the trunk and the easy-to-grab overnight cases in the front. They prepared an ice chest with drinks, cheese, sausage, raw vegetables and other finger foods. Marie was the banker. Each one put three hundred dollars into the Bank of America money bag that they used for gas, lodging, and tips. They paid individually for meals. Mom did most of the driving. However, when a swarm of bugs mucked up the windshield she exclaimed, "I don't do windows." Myrtle gladly serviced the car when they stopped at gas stations.

Mom wanted to stop and see Jeanie who was going to college and living in Colorado Springs, Colorado. Independence Pass, east of Aspen, was a spectacular vista. It was the state's highest paved pass at 12,095 feet in elevation. Those three women had a great time and got along famously. Mom and Marie had one small quarrel as they drove through Omaha, Nebraska. Marie saw highway signs leading to Father

Flanagan's Boys Town and wanted to go there.

"Oh no, we're not going there! We don't have to go there!" said Mom. You could hear a pin drop. Marie slid down in the back seat puckered up mad. Myrtle did not say a word. Surprised at her own actions, Mom spoke up after driving a ways and said, "Marie we're here. Look up!"

Marie and Myrtle took a tour of Father Flanagan's Boys Town, while Mom drove around. That was the end of the spat and the only one they had.

They arrived on a Monday and stayed at the Sonesta Hotel on the Cambridge side of the Charles River overlooking the Boston Skyline. Mom and Myrtle went in to confirm the reservations, while Marie stayed with the porter to make sure he put the right baggage on the cart. There were four bags and Marie tipped him four dollars. Mom went right up to the room as soon as she received a key and Myrtle finished up with the registration. The porter stopped by the desk to find out the room number. Myrtle told him and tipped him four dollars. The porter took the luggage to their room and knocked at the door. Mom opened the door for the luggage, accepted it, and tipped the porter four dollars, too. When Marie and Myrtle joined Mom in the room, Mom mentioned to Marie "I need four dollars out of the money bag. I tipped the porter four dollars."

"I tipped him four dollars, too!" Myrtle said.

Astounded, Marie cried out in laughter, nearly choking on her words. "That porter, he made off with a twelve dollar tip, I also tipped him four dollars!"

The trip to Boston was every bit as exciting as the three expected. The graduation was inspiring. King Juan Carlos I of Spain and Ted Koppel gave graduation addresses. Following graduation, they went to dinner and after dinner attended the "Boston Pops" concert.

The next day they went on to New York City and saw a couple of Broadway shows. The car held up through most of the trip until the muffler came loose. Mom pulled into a service station on a Sunday to get it fixed.

"We don't do repairs on Sundays" said the attendant.

"We can't travel around like this!" Mom, puffed in frustration.

"Do you have a wire or something we can use to wire it up?" asked Mrytle.

"We've got a clothes hanger in the car," Mom exclaimed to her.

Myrtle took the clothes hanger and started to scoot under the car. When the attendant saw that these women were serious about fixing the muffler themselves he offered his assistance and they were back on the road.

When Nancy graduated from Harvard Law School and received her Juris Doctorate, Mom took a flight to Boston. Both had cheek-to-cheek smiles. It was a proud day for daughter and mother. Following graduation Nancy returned to Los Angeles for a Ninth Circuit Court of Appeals Clerkship.

Nancy Castenholz June 1987 *(Courtesy Rose Olivo)*

To Mother with her sixteen children: by number eleven.

Forever Moments

Hectic, hasty, chaotic yet sweet,
Those were the days of little feet.
A two-bedroom house with not enough beds,
A big backyard with a playhouse shed.

How did she count and always keep track?
Not for a moment could she dare turn her back.
Her motherly scope-so large and deep,
Groomed, taught, and nurtured us with memories to keep.

No, we were never just mouths to feed;
We were her light beams-each special indeed,
With rainbow resplendence, we played, we cried,
And always, our family torch would brighten the skies.

She fostered joy and strength to harness time's pace,
Rhythmic, sparkling and firm no matter the place.
Our family's shield sports honor and reflection,
It's our Mom's legacy of vast love and affection.

Thanks Mom. We love you beyond love's name;
Your beauty and soul will forever be our life's frame.
From God and beyond, you did arrive,
To elevate life and create an extraordinary tribe!

© —*Nancy Joyce Olivo Castenholz*

Olivo Family Reunion at Walden West Center, July 1986 *(Courtesy Rose Olivo)*

Mom opened the 1986 Olivo Family Reunion in prayer as the Olivos and extended families gathered in two circles, one inside of the other. She gave thanks to Our Lord for everyone's safe arrival, asked for a weekend of fun, and a safe return home. The circles rotated and everyone had an opportunity to greet one another. Bill and Bobbie arranged for the food, entertainment, and activities. A stationary movie camera captured the talent and fun on-stage and off. It proved most of the Olivo families were hams as they danced and waved at the camera.

Everyone had such a wonderful time at Walden West in 1986 that they decided to return the following year for the 1987 Olivo Family Renuion. Laughs were had by all when the big TV screen played the camera shots from the first reunion. The movies inspired "pranks" as the theme for the 1987 reunion with sleep becoming a luxury.

It seems Impossible to measure how much it means,
How deeply it affects us to feel strong abiding sense of family
That anchors and enduringly connects us

—Jacqueline Rose Olivo

"16 Children"

I was raised in a home with 16 children
A two-bedroom home, with an outside stool and a whole lotta lovin'
That was back when a dime would buy a loaf of "Wonder" bread
And Mama put us down two by two in bed

Billy would walk & talk in his sleep at night
And little Richie would wet his bed "n" wear rubber tights
And I never got a wink cuz Harry would make a stink
That there were five in the tub 'n' two bathin' in the kitchen sink

We had a feelin' you couldn't find
A beat, a rhythm, a rhyme
The girls were always in the groove
The boys always on the move
And Father Joe would say a prayer
For the ones who stepped outta line

Daddy would always complain that his body had too much pain
While Mama's in labor with a baby—add another name
And Kenny never gave a care and Jeannie would raise my hair
While Stevie's in the corner just lovin' his teddy bear.

(Refrain) We had a feelin' you couldn't find
A beat, a rhythm, a rhyme
The girls were always in the groove
The boys always on the move
And Father Joe would say a prayer
For the ones who stepped outta line

(Refrain) I was raised in a home with 16 children
A two bedroom home, an outside stool and a whole lotta lovin'
That was back when a dime would buy a loaf of "Wonder" bread
And Mama put us down two by two in bed

Now, when we grew up we left that two bedroom home—took our memories
Mom & Dad gave all they had then they set us free
They gave up their youth
To give us a life to better the one they had
Ohh and we thank you Mom & Dad

(Refrain) We had a feelin' you couldn't find
A beat, a rhythm, a rhyme
The girls were always in the groove
The boys always on the move
And Father Joe would say a prayer
For the ones who stepped outta line

I was raised in a home with 16 children

Olivo Family Reunion, June 1987 *(Photos courtesy Barbara Olivo Cagle)*

"SOME THINGS TO PONDER ABOUT FAMILY REUNIONS"

Mom's Artwork and Letter to Family, August 1987 *(Courtesy Rose Olivo)*

After the 1987 family reunion, it was discussed that the reunions should be scheduled less frequently. Mom wrote everyone:

> Thinking of having a family reunion every two years reminded me of a very dear friend who had not seen her family in Norway for forty years. She was the youngest in her family. She was eighteen years old when she married and came to live in America. She was fifty-eight years old when she returned to Norway for a family reunion. She told me that she was astonished at how they all had changed; they were like strangers to her. Her brothers were now bald, and her sisters, instead of the beautiful blonde-haired women she remembered, were white-haired, had wrinkled skin, and had become so strange in their customs and way of life. She said she could hardly wait for the visit to end.
>
> Thank God, something like that will not happen in our family. Forty years! Wow! No! Two years will not be that bad.
>
> The same thing occurred when a priest at Saint Joseph's Church (some of you may remember The Reverend Kulwiecz) was given a trip to Poland for a family reunion. This was a gift from the parishioners for his fiftieth jubilee in the priesthood. When he returned, he said he wished he had not gone, because he didn't know anyone.
>
> So you see two years for us won't be bad at all. Especially if everyone keeps in touch with each other, sharing pictures, etc.

Then there is another reunion that I know of that takes place regularly every year—never miss—five children with their families and several grandchildren half the size of our family, all gathered at their mom and dad's home. Their agenda consists of eating and arguing. They play and argue. They converse and argue. They sleep and argue. They become angry and argue, and before leaving, they even throw a punch or two. Some leave so angry they vow not to return. Their mom and dad are relieved to see them go and hope they will not return too soon.

Thank God! Nothing like that has taken place at our reunions.

God blessed us with the one great big joyful and magical reunion with almost everyone present. You are all aware of the beautiful time we had. A year later, we had the second one and some thought it was too soon after the first. I tend to agree, because we all know there were about twenty-five family members who did not appear at the second. If we go with a yearly event, I'm sure you will all agree with me that this is what will happen. Some will attend one year and some the next and that is not my idea of a good reunion.

God willing, the elders of the family—namely Dad, Rodger, Helene, Marie and I—will be around for a good long time and they will be looking forward to the next great big one, say, in two or three years.

Small children change and develop so much in a year—how much more so in two or three—making it more exciting to see them after a little time has elapsed. Now this doesn't mean that we would not be seeing them or each other at different times in between.

I, for one, will visit many during the year, perhaps not all in one year, certainly within two. This will give me the opportunity to get to know each little one individually a little bit better to hold, hug and squeeze, to play with, discuss world affairs with, solve a math equation on the computer, and talk with. I don't tire of listening. All my children and grandchildren are a joy to me.

Mini-reunions in between bigger ones are a wonderful idea. Then you know that every time a few gather at someone's home, be it for Thanksgiving, Christmas, birthdays, etc., we have what is called a mini-reunion. I don't think it wise to schedule a reunion as such, because it could turn out to be a maxi, and then we would be right back to square one.

So far, you have read what I like about my family reunions, what I enjoy seeing, hearing, doing, and some may call this downright selfishness on my part. You are correct! I do want all this and more! After all, my family is my pride and joy. I derive my greatest pleasure when I am seeing them perform their thing, recite their poem, sing their song, play their instruments, wear shiny dresses, dance, tell their jokes, and display their talents. I enjoy listening to the spokesman from each family giving a rundown of each person's achievements, activities, etc., since last I saw him or her. If I don't see and hear all of this at reunions, how else would I know about the many talents that my grandchildren and great-grandchildren have?

Now, if what I have written here (and you did leave it up to me to decide) is overruled by the majority and another line of action is taken, just let me know, and I will be there. So will Dad, Rodger, Helene, and Marie.

I have told you exactly how I feel about the reunions we have had. Let's not have them so often that they lose their luster and become a chore to get there and humdrum as the aforementioned reunions I related to you at the beginning of this letter. Not so often that there would be some missing one year because they know there will soon be another. The first and foremost thing is for everyone to be present at the same time.

After I am gone, I would hope my children and their families would regularly continue meeting somewhere as a tradition. At that time, you may cut out the singing, dancing, and entertainment in general or anything else you haven't liked up to now. Until that time comes, whenever we have a reunion (hopefully in 1989), come on guys, indulge your mother. Be prepared to perform, because you know I will love every minute of it and Dad will too! So there!

To My Very
Dearest Loved Ones
I hope you have
enjoyed reading this
as much as I have
enjoyed putting it
together. Love Always
Mom

Rose cruised to China, Japan, and Korea on the "Odyssey"May 1988, and to Alaska on the "Star Princess" July 1989.

Rose cruised to the Caribbean on the "Royal Princess" July 1990, and she extended the tour to include Panama, Puerto Rico, Acapulco, Mexico, Virgin Islands, St. Thomas, Venezuela, and Curacao. Rose in Egypt, May 1992, on her last trip abroad. She toured Israel and the Holy Land. *(Courtesy Rose and Jeanie Olivo)*

Olivo Family Reunion June 1993; six years passed since the last family reunion in 1987. *(Courtesy Rose Olivo)*

Father Dondero was seriously ill in 1993. However, he insisted on attending the Olivo family reunion and opened the weekend with quite an unforgettable speech:

> It is a privilege and an honor for me to be here at the reunion of the Olivo Family. We spent many happy years together at Saint Joseph's, especially when the children attended Saint Joseph's School. I began to feel like I was part of the family. It wasn't easy, some problems, yet it was interesting and exciting.
>
> We see the results of the effort of Rose and Nello right here at the reunion, the love that binds this family together. How did Rose and Nello accomplish all this? It just didn't happen. They worked night and day to give their family a good life. They sent them to Catholic schools where they learned the importance of religion and values that keep all good families under the protection of God.
>
> Without our faith in God, the world has no meaning. We are deaf and blind and fail to realize that the history of men is a tale told by an idiot full of sound and fury signifying nothing.
>
> With faith, we ask God to help us to be what we ought to be. If every one of

us had that faith, the world would be what it ought to be: a world of truth, justice, beauty, love, and peace. We would realize that the only thing that counts when we come to the end of our life is; how do I stand with God?

I don't go out anymore if I can help it; yet I would not miss coming to this reunion, because it is a symbol of what a family really is meant to be. I don't want to sound too heavy. Some things have to be repeated again and again to warn people of coming disaster.

Our civilization is in grave crisis. Why? In the name of progress and liberation, the family is being shattered. They call it the 'me' generation. Nothing matters except 'me': I am first before God, family, neighbors, country.

Families are being torn apart; children are being abandoned, molested, drugged, and destroyed. We are forgetting that the family is the foundation that the Will of God ordained for us, and when we go against the Will of God, watch out for an intervention.

So we have here an important example, model, lesson, of what a family should be, strongly united in the love of God, in the support of each other, in respect for each other.

These reunions are a living expression of all these values. You are truly a great example of what the Will of God set for the family. I am privileged to have been associated with you, and I can't praise you enough for what you have accomplished as a family.

The Reverend Father Joseph L. Dondero, Society of Jesus
November 29, 1909-June 28, 1997

May God continue to bless all of you.

Fr. Joe

I taught love for God, a flower, a tree's splendor
And still an abundance of love remaining for me

—Jacqueline Rose Olivo

A Note from Rose J. Olivo

"To: My Family and Relatives! Mark your 1998 calendar now!!! Friday, February 27th-Sunday, March 1st for a weekend of family reunion and a celebration of my eighty years of the GOOD LIFE! To be held at the beautiful Sheraton Resort Hotel—Saturday night hotel accommodations gratis! This is a gift to my wonderful family. Join in making my eightieth birthday the BEST EVER!"

Family and friends filled Saturday evening with just that. The laughter was like music. Christine did the honors of opening a birthday tribute to Mom:

> To start off with, we have to ask ourselves, what a 'Mother is? She is someone who sings to you with all that's in her heart, *You Are My Sunshine*, and loves you with the love that God poured into her to give, and more. She's there to listen to what you have to say with her wisdom and advice, she guides you in the right direction. She's not only a loving, caring person; she is also a best friend. She comforts and protects you, hurts when you are hurting, suffers when you are suffering, and is there when you need her.
>
> Yes, she denies herself so she can be there for everyone's needs.
>
> She is not only our Mother. She is a very special human being that God has so graciously let us have as our very own. If anyone ever wonders how much she loves every one of us, one needs to look at how much our Mother denied herself all those years. Her greatest concern has been for the comfort and well-being of her family.
>
> I think we must say, 'Mother, what we see here this weekend is an example of your concern for our comfort. You chose this beautiful hotel for us to enjoy our reunion. For this we say, Thank you!'
>
> All the love Mother had in her heart she imparted to us in her teachings. She

taught us to be kind to people no matter how unfeeling they were. I can't count the times Mother told us how to behave.

'If you can't say anything good about others, don't say anything. I don't want to hear it. We must not retaliate or take revenge. Leave that to God.'

We had to be nice; to speak softly and wait our turn to be heard. If by chance we were a little loud, Mother would speak to us in a near-whisper so that we really had to be quiet to hear her. By no means did we use bad language because we knew the pepper would burn on our tongues.

We didn't call any of our elders by their first names. We said Mr. or Mrs., or aunt or uncle. When Mother overheard one of us say, 'Hi, Marie,' on the telephone. She corrected that person by saying, 'Hey, just a minute, what's this business, 'Marie?' She's your aunt!'

Mother taught us to be proud, not jealous, of each other's accomplishments. I remember the straight 'A' students we had in the family along with all those perfect attendance awards. Nancy went four years without missing a day of school, right Nancy? Even more, Bobbie went from kindergarten through eighth grade without missing a single day. Yes, Mother kept her family quite healthy.

After seeing most of her children grow up and leave home, she stepped out and became involved in Saint Joseph's and Notre Dame's Mother's Guilds. In due time, she became spiritual director and then president of the Saint Joseph's Mother's Guild. She also taught Confraternity Christian Doctrine (CCD) classes on Saturday mornings. The National Council of Christian Women asked her to speak at their meetings. When she modeled for fashion shows, we were proud to point and say to our friends, 'That's our Mother!'

With Mother's wise teachings and work ethic influencing our lives, we did our best to make her proud of our varied accomplishments. Even the spouses of her children and grandchildren, she claims them and loves them as her own. She has a 'Brag Book' on everyone in the family.

1st Corinthians, 13: 4-8 says, 'Love is patient; love is kind. Love is not jealous, it does not put on airs, it is not snobbish. It is never rude, it is not self-seeking, it is not prone to anger; neither does it brood over injuries. Love does not rejoice in what is wrong but rejoices with the truth. There is no limit to love's forbearance, to its trust, its hope, its power to endure. Love never fails. Prophecies will cease, tongues will be silent, knowledge will pass away.'

Mother has personified this love. She has said time and time again, 'Should I live so long, God willing, to see all of my children out there in the world raising God-loving families of their own?'

So here we all are tonight, gathered together to say: HAPPY BIRTHDAY, WE LOVE YOU MOTHER!

Commemorations from each of the children followed.

There was little time for planning another family reunion. Dad's health was failing and he could not get around. He fell asleep in the recliner off and on throughout the day. Mom spent most of her time ensuring he was well-fed, taking the medications he needed, and getting him to doctor visits. Jeanie and Steve were living at home and helped. Dad was a big chore. The rest of the children took turns coming home throughout the next few years to visit and help. Whenever Bobbie came to visit and Dad was feeling well, she spent time recording his stories. He loved his children:

Marialice—"You're a good girl. I used to take you to a lot of places, here and there, you remember? I took you to the Eagles Lodge and you used to dance on stage. You made me happy."

Jeanie—"I remember saying 'Testa dura!' to you," Dad knocking his head with his knuckles.

Patty—"You always helped me in the garden. You had your own garden space and planted tulips and ranunculus."

Sonny—"At that time you were just a young kid. I bought you some boxing gloves. They were tiny little things. I don't think you remember that. I had you in the garage always doing something."

Virginia—"You knew how to play my accordion."

Christine—"You keep calling long distance to me to read the Bible. Too costly. Boy, what a bill!"

William—"I remember you wanting to car race. Instead, you got into car shows. I remember stopping by to help you with your garden. You've got to get that special cow manure. Why that's the best manure you can buy if you want to grow crops."

Richard—"You owe me five bucks. I give you number one for the hit parade. The list is too long to mention. You did all that work in my kitchen and the bathroom. That's why I'm not fighting about those things you took from me. I remember sponsoring your baseball team and got you to be the pitcher. I went to pretty near all your games."

Jerilyn—"You took me to the flea markets on Sundays. I looked forward to that. In case of an emergency just go lookin' for me at the Jack in the Box, or at Dunkin' Donuts."

Cathy—"You called me to fix something in your house. I looked forward to your visits when you would take me to breakfast and buy an extra meal to take home for dinner."

Nancy—"You called me 'Daddeo.' You helped me fix my rental house."

Harold—"You are the only one who served in the military. I remember visiting you with your mother in Washington for Army Basic Training Graduation. You left your rifle in the back of your mother's car on the floor—Buick. You were already out of the car, and I noticed it was still there and beckoned you back to get it. It was nice to have one of my sons in the service. Harold, I am proud of you for what you went through. I guess you did all right. All I want to know is why you cut up my three-seater bike?"

Barbara—"Your toboggan accident, I did what I had to do to help. I had fun antique shopping in Spokane with you. Thank you for everything you've done for me and mending my clothes. Very grateful, and thanks for the coat."

Kenny—"I remember visiting you and your family in Colorado Springs for a whole month. I bought a lot of things. The only thing I remember I should have bought—I could kick myself for not, was a music box. An old man had this special box I wanted so dearly, a Stella music box. I was ready to buy it for eighteen-hundred dollars. You never buy anything. You have the looks of more like my father. I enjoyed visiting you."

Lorene—"You smile all the time at me. You move in, move out, move in, and move out. I never know what you're going to do next."

Stevie—"I used to catch you playing in the playhouse all the time. I let you see my three-hundred-year-old watch and my mom's watch. You washed my clothes and my bedding and would wash my car everyday. All the time when you smelled good you did all right. You would go fishing and would bring the fish home with a smile from one side to the other. You would clean the fish, prepare it and fry it up."

"None of you were lazy. You went out and did what you set out to do."

Even though it was hard for Dad to get around, he kept his car keys. The boys built a railing and ramp at the entry of the house and when he was feeling better, he would maneuver his way down the front steps with his cane to get to the car. There was little mileage on the 1986 Chevy El Camino Conquistador, with red velour interior and a sunroof. Dad had the body repainted a light green with a silver top. He was adamant about driving the couple of blocks it took to visit his friend "George" and pick up the daily newspaper. He would go to Jack in the Box and talk to whomever would listen to him. Some days when he did not feel well, he would get in the car and just sit there, then go back in the house.

To get Dad in the car for trips around town was a huge hullabaloo. Mom would read a book or take a nap, as she waited the half-hour or so it took him to do the 'Nello shuffle' out of the house and down the steps. He became a 'Jekyll and Hyde' with his obnoxious temperament and jealousness. It was like unleashing a demon you did not want to meet. The family took it in stride, yet it was hard on Mom and downright embarrassing when he started using foul language. He fell out of bed a few times and yelled for her help. As an older person herself, Mom could hardly muster enough strength to lift him up on her own. How she did it, no one knows. At eighty years old, she had the stamina when needed.

In February 2000, Dad fell, and was wedged between the wall and the bed. He was in considerable pain. It was early morning and Mom did not hear him for a few hours. When she found him, she had to call for help and an ambulance came and took him to O'Connor Hospital. Mom had to make a decision and Dad was transferred to the Skyline Healthcare Center in San Jose. He had suffered a minor stroke and was in a wheel chair. A wonderful cure happened at Skyline. The doctors regulated his intake of vitamins and medications, and he started to behave like a normal man. It was as if he had been brain-locked all those years. His mind cleared and he said words that touched people.

Sonny visited him one day and mentioned a concern.

"Well son, I think you should take it into consideration" Dad responded His comment took Sonny completely by surprise. He had not given him any fatherly advice his whole life. They went on to have an intelligent conversation. Sonny's eyes welled up with tears, and it moves him to this day when he talks about it.

It's never too late to meet life's challenge
To unwind the tangled web
Along the way with endless patter not to deceive
To till the land and make things grow
It's never too late to make a new friend
It's never too late to change the way
It's been far too long and seems to say
It's the only way

—Jacqueline Rose Olivo

Mom asked Dad what she should do with his antiques. He said, "Do what you want, they belong to you now," and he did not talk about the antiques again. The children tried to talk to him about it and he avoided the conversation. He chose to live in the present, not the past. For Mom, it was like a nightmare trying to deal with the stuff. The children were a big help. It took two years to go through it all and decide to either sell or junk it. They had good times looking through each pipe, box, and jar. They were sure that Dad had hidden treasures. They did find some valuables and interesting objects that they brought in to show Mom. Some days they worked dawn to dusk. Bobbie and Christine tried to make it fun. "Look what I found!" "No, look at what I just found!" the two would exclaim in awe. They, as well as the others, visited several times and tried to do their share of cleaning up the mess. Some of the children thought Mom got less than half the value she should have for the antiques. For her, she wanted it to be over and settled for less. It was wonderful when she began to rejuvenate the flower beds and garden.

Patty was a pillar of strength for Mom during Dad's stay at the nursing center. She lived nearby and was able to visit him daily and be with him for doctor appointments. She looked after Dad and kept him fed and healthy.

Jeanie spent hours with him on weekends. He looked forward to her taking him to the church services in the community room. He participated in reciting the prayers and sang the songs. Sometimes he went up to play the drums.

Bill often stopped in after work and brought a few tools for Dad to tinker with and keep his mind active.

When the children from out of town came to visit, Patty and Jeanie would let them know what he liked. They would step aside to let everyone have special 'alone time' with him. Sad and yet amazingly ironic, God had given the children back Dad, and Mom her husband. The past was past, and the family simply enjoyed his love and innocence. He had become a child of God.

All is forgiven
Of that which was forbidden
Created for and possessed by
Unworthiness

—Jacqueline Rose Olivo

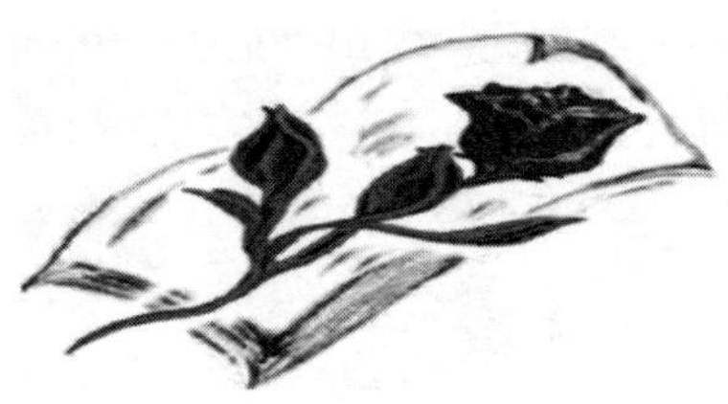

Chapter Twenty-Two

The 16th at 12:06

Steve and Diane's paths crossed again in January of 1993 when they renewed their friendship and became an item. Later that year, Diane was recuperating from a serious bout of the flu and wrote from her heart:

January 1993, Steve with Diane Zuniga
(Courtesy Diane Zuniga)

A wonderful experience happened to me the weekend I became ill. I discovered a man so loving and caring, so gentle and giving. I couldn't have asked for a man more thoughtful to help me with my medication, keep me warm, and hold my hand. No request I made was too big or too small. He did all he could do to help me get well. In the worst of it all: the high fevers came and went. His love and care kept me going even when it seemed I'd never show improvement. We had our little differences when I didn't want to cooperate. Still, his gentle persistence and knowledge helped me to see it his way. He was the best companion on those long and restless nights, when the illness kept me awake. As he strummed his guitar into the wee hours, the music soothed my weary ear. I never dreamt I could be blessed by such a love as Steve. As each day passed in our new-found relationship, different experiences brought us closer together. I truly stand in awe knowing God loves me enough to bring me my helper, my friend and greatest love of all.

The Olivo family embraced Diane with love. She went on to call Rose "Mom," and Mom regarded Diane as one of her own. When Diane was stricken with breast cancer in 1999, Steve was there to help care for her and sat with her during the chemotherapy. She had all the mood swings and lost her hair. He was solid support through it all. They wanted to get married, yet both knew it was not the right time.

In June 2002, Steve had an accident while using a multi-purpose insect spray in Mom's garden. As he reached to turn off the water, the container of insecticide exploded in his face and the attached hose flew out of control.

He hurried into the house, holding the container, and yelled, "Emergency, emergency—help! I can't see—this bottle exploded all over me!"

Bobbie who was at home on a visit quickly dialed the eight-hundred number on the container. The operator referred her to Poison Control and they immediately followed the directions for an antidote. Steve's eyes were swollen, his nose drained, and his stomach burned. He was in pain all night.

Mom was concerned and insisted that Steve see a doctor. Bobbie was returning to Spokane the following day and promised that she would follow-up with the responsible company to take care of any doctor bills. Steve and Bobbie bonded over the next several months, talking to each other by phone on a daily basis. They wanted to get together for a couple of days to go fishing and camping during her next visit in November.

"You don't have to pack the kitchen sink," Mom commented.

"Don't worry Mom, I have to bring an extra suitcase this time for my fishing and camping gear."

Bobbie had the habit of bringing an extra suitcase full of gadgets and electronic equipment. She was much like her father in that respect. She and Mom planned to spend two days in Camarillo visiting Christine and her husband, Bob, who was in the hospital.

Steve called Bobbie the night before she left Spokane.

"Bobbie, what do you think about going fishing first when you get here?"

"I'm sorry, I can't change my plans; however, I'm excited about going with you on Sunday, just you and mc."

"I can't wait, that's going to be too late."

"Why?"

"I don't know—I just want to go now. I will call Jeff or Rangit. I won't see you when you get here. I will be back on Saturday and we can take off on Sunday."

"Sounds like a plan. I love you. Bye."

"I love you, too. Bye."

Jeff and Rangit were two taxicab driver friends Steve used to drive him to the canal where he liked to fish.

Steve discovered a fishing spot along the Highline Canal below a farmer's house in Los Banos, seventy-seven miles southeast of San Jose. He fished it for a couple of years. Alvin and Lena, a farmer and his wife, were in their mid-eighties. They had a farm along the canal not far from his fishing spot. Alvin first saw Steve sitting on an ice chest out in the blazing sun waiting for a taxi ride home. "Well, I've seen you out here a few times and I decided it doesn't look like you're a threat. So you can sit here in the shade with me." That is how the two met. They became friends and enjoyed talking about family and life.

On November 14, 2002, Steve had fished for several hours when suddenly he slid into the canal. Frantic, yet, not willing to let go of the pole, he kept a hold of it with one hand as he reached for a bush with the other. The pole snapped. He dragged himself up the bank, left his fishing gear, and walked to Alvin's house. It was late in the evening and Alvin and Lena were in bed. A light was on in the house, so he knocked on the door. He was muddy and dripping wet. Alvin invited him in and offered him a pair of overalls as he phoned the taxicab driver Rangit at home. He had that kind of relationship with the cab driver. Rangit had already gone to bed and said it would be a while before he could get there. Steve talked with Alvin and recapped the event. Not wanting to keep the old man up, he insisted on waiting outside for the cab driver. Besides, he wanted to retrieve his gear and ice chest from the canal. By the time Rangit arrived, Steve was trembling cold and welcomed the heated cab.

Earlier that same day, at 5:00 p.m. Mom picked Bobbie up at the San Jose Airport. When they got home she noticed a beautiful white angel trumpet tree next to the front porch in full bloom. The blossoms smelled extremely sweet with an intoxicating perfume much like that of jasmine.

"They don't last long when cut," Mom said.

"Can I pick one anyway?"

With a favorable expression, Mom went inside. Bobbie followed soon after and in the kitchen found a paper cup filled with water on the counter. She thought Mom had set it there for her to put the flower in and placed it in the cup. After dinner mother and daughter turned in for the night; they expected to depart early for Camarillo on Friday.

At 1:00 in the morning, Bobbie woke with a start. Someone was tiptoeing across the room.

"Steve?" Bobbie asked.

"Oh gees, go back to sleep. I didn't want to wake you. I didn't know you were sleeping in here. I just wanted to slip into a warm bed. I fell in the canal, got all wet, and had to come on home. I didn't want to go upstairs and wake up Mom or Jeanie," Steve whispered.

"Don't worry. What happened? I want to hear all about it." Bobbie was sitting up now and Steve was keyed up with enthusiasm.

"You should have been there. It was a big one. It snapped my pole in half; I lost my footing and slid into the water. You know I can't swim. I grabbed onto a bush and pulled myself out. I still came home with a thirteen-pound channel cat, and a smaller one. They're in the ice chest outside. I left my medication at the canal so I have to go back, and I want to return Alvin's overalls."

"Maybe we can drop you off on our way to see Christine and Bob."

"Ahhh, I'm not sure I will be awake that early. We will see each other when you get back."

"How'd you get home?"

"I waited for Rangit to come and get me, he gave me a ride."

"Well, I'm glad you're all right. Let me give you a hug in case I don't see you in the morning."

Mom was up and ready at dawn. Bobbie found her in the laundry room folding clothes and told her about Steve's fishing story. "Oh how I worry about him fishing; he could have drowned you know; he didn't take swimming lessons like the rest of you," remarked Mom.

"He loves fishing. What better way to go than doing something you love to do?" commented Bobbie.

"I AM NOT GOING TO DIE DROWNING!" Unbeknownst to them, Steve was in the bathroom next to the laundry room.

For a moment the stillness gave her the creeps, then her brother jaunted through the laundry room to the kitchen where Mom and Bobbie moved to and told Mom of his venturesome fishing excursion. He showed them the fish and told Bobbie he had everything packed for a two-day camping trip. All they needed to buy was a longer landing net.

They discussed how he would get his medication and he said he would call Jeff for transportation. Mom told him to eat the leftovers she brought home the night before. He enjoyed leftovers.

"I love you," his mom and sister said, as they each hugged him and left.

That evening, Mom called home and spoke to Steve and Jeanie. All was well, Jeff had picked him up, and they went to the canal and returned home at 3:00 p.m. After her phone call, Steve felt like talking. He left a message on Diane's answering machine and phoned his cousin David. They talked about the Bible, specifically the saving of souls. Steve wanted to know.

"Where in the Bible is it written, 'When we die, we will see God face to face'?"

Jeanie went to bed at 11:00 p.m. and she noticed the light was still on in Steve's bedroom. It was late the following morning when she knocked hard several times on his door. He did not answer, which was not necessarily unusual. By noon she thought it strange that there was not a sound from him yet. His bedroom was right next to hers and he usually was up and about.

An eerie feeling crept through her body, so she ran downstairs, grabbed a knife, hurried back upstairs, and pried open the door. That is when Jeanie found Steve lying on the floor in a fetal position and called 911. Rigor mortis had already set in. Her next phone call was to Harold. She was overcome with emotion and Harold's wife assisted her with a chain of phone calls to the other brothers and sisters. The siblings who lived within driving distance came as quickly as possible and those out of town made flight arrangements.

Bobbie had her cell phone turned off that morning and no one could reach her or Mom. Christine waited at the hospital door for the two of them. Upon arrival she rushed Mom in to visit Bob, and took Bobbie aside and guided her to a spot where they could talk privately. She put her arm around Bobbie's shoulder and told her the devastating news.

"S-h-h. Don't say anything. Just listen." Christine whispered, her words unsure and jumbled, her face ashen, "Steve died early this morning!"

Bobbie gasped, covered her mouth and glanced in Mom's direction.

"Bobbie, you need to turn around and take Mom back, without letting her know about Steve, yet!"

"Wha-wha-wha-a-t happened?" Bobbie asked, her face twisted in disbelief; her body trembled.

"I don't know. Jeanie found him in his room." When Bobbie sniffled, her sister continued, "Stop it right now! Don't you start crying, now. You've got to be strong and get Mom home right away. Promise me you won't say a word to her about Steve. Everyone is counting on you to get her home. You can do this. The brothers and sisters decided it would be best that she doesn't know until she gets home. It's going to be a long five-and-a half-hour drive, and we don't want her to worry the whole way. I will tell her that something has come up here at the hospital and that it's best for you two to leave."

Breathing heavily and with her heart pounding, Bobbie finally took a deep breath and exhaled.

"Okay, I can do this! I can do this!" She thought, yeah, right. How can you ask me to hold back my tears? God help me! I can't do this! Oh God, give me the strength to bring Mom home safely.

Bobbie had a quick visit with Bob. They said their good-byes. She walked out of the hospital, turned on her cell phone and looked at Mom hesitant to say anything.

"Give me a couple of minutes, I need to check my real estate messages." Sure enough, there were umpteen frantic calls. But not about real estate. They were all confirming Steve's death.

"You're as white as a ghost Bobbie. What on earth is the matter?"

"Oh. Nothing, Mom. I had a couple of deals go sour and I put a lot of work into them." She hoped her mother believed her.

As planned, Mom drove first to get them through the mountains. The cell phone rang every ten minutes with calls from the brothers and sisters. "Who was that? What was that about? Why is everyone calling you?" Mom kept asking "Has something happened to Bob?" The words he said to her before she left the hospital kept lingering in her mind, "I'm sorry Mom. I'm so sorry."

When she saw the signs Bobbie said "Let's stop at the Apple Farm," and Mom pulled off the highway.

"Oh, I really don't want to go in. Why don't you go on ahead? I'll take a nap in the car."

Bobbie went inside, called her friend Joni, and completely fell apart. She decided, then, that she could not continue making up stories and called her sister Virginia. Mom could be stubborn at times. Back in the car, it was Bobbie's turn to drive; Mom did not let her. The cell kept ringing, ringing, and ringing. Mom, apparently knew something was wrong.

"Why are they calling you so much? It must be something serious."

"Okay, Mom, pull off the highway in Buellton and I'll tell you."

"Well, there's Anderson's Pea Soup. I like stopping to have their soup."

Dear God, my heavenly Father, please give me the words to say to Mom, thought Bobbie.

"Did Bob get worse?" Mom sadly asked as she pulled into Anderson's Pea Soup parking lot.

"It's not about Bob, Mom." Bobbie got out of the car, bowed her head and sauntered around to open the door for her mother.

"It isn't? What's all the commotion about, then?" Mom's look demanded an answer.

"It's about Steve." Choking on the words, Bobbie wrapped her arms around her mother.

"What about Stevie? What's wrong with him?"

"Steve died last night, Mom. He died at home in his bedroom. Jeanie found him. He's with God now."

With the daunting words ringing in her ears, Mom gasped for air, and clenched her daughter for comfort and strength.

"How? Where? When? Who did this to him? Not Stevie! No! He's my youngest. I love him." Mom wept.

"Mom, I'm going to drive now. I'm calling Virginia so that she can talk you through this." Bobbie's eyes filled with tears. Driving the next four hours home took every bit of concentration she could muster.

Mom remained on the phone speaking to each one of the children. Then there was Dad to consider. How would she tell him his youngest died?

"I need this time to gather my thoughts so I can be strong for my children, Dad, and especially for Jeanie."

She took a long sigh.

Mom and Bobbie arrived home about 5:30 in the evening. The boys were waiting on the sidewalk. They gathered around the car and opened the door for Mom. Bobbie went into the house and Patty in tears was the first to greet her. Diane was there too. All the siblings had questions.

"Why couldn't you wait until Mom got home? How did you tell her? What did she say? How did she react? We want to know everything."

Grieving, Bobbie repeated the events of the drive home. Everyone was sensitive and trying to deal with his or her own grief. Steve was the youngest and should not have been the first to go. The family felt broken without him.

When Mom entered the house and walked into the kitchen, the first thing she noticed was the white flower next to the kitchen sink.

"I can't believe it's still alive! I have a thing about white flowers. I don't like to have fresh cuttings of them in my house, especially the white roses, because they die so quickly."

"The fish! The fish! Where's the fish?" cried Jerilyn and Bobbie.

Steve had packed it in ice in the cooler. Bobbie went outside clean it, brought it in, and baked it. Everyone including Mom tasted Steve's catch. In addition to the fish there was plenty to eat. The doorbell kept ringing as family, friends, and neighbors brought food.

Bobbie curled up with Mom that night. The two hardly slept. They did not say anything, thinking the other was asleep. The strong aroma of a burning candle permeated the air. Bobbie followed it to Steve's bedroom, reached for the doorknob, and hesitated. She did not enter and in the morning, Mom said she also smelled a candle burning. "He would light a candle at night many times when he could not sleep."

No one knew how ailing he was until Mom and Bobbie visited his doctors. They learned that he had a mass on his pancreas and the physician suspected pancreatic cancer. Steve suffered through a great deal of abdominal pain, sleepless nights, and anxiety.

God left trails of information that comforted Mom and she felt reassured that He embraced Steve and took him home to heaven. Steve died on November 16, 2002. The sixteenth child died on the sixteenth of the month. The police and firemen reported their arrival at the Olivo residence as 12:06 p.m. Mom looked at his birth certificate a couple of days later. He was born on July 17, 1957 at 12:06 p.m. and the coroner recorded his official death at 12:06 a.m. Other than the coroners report, Mom's desires were that no further autopsies be performed or inquiries made about the death. She just wanted her son to rest in peace.

She needed her children with her, including Diane. It seemed like old times as she watched them from the kitchen as they squeezed together around the table in the breakfast room. They reminisced of the days on Miller Street. They talked about the lumpy mush, oatmeal, the rice pudding and the Christmases, Ryland Park, St. Joseph's School and Father Joe—the mischievous things they got away with or did not, and who got the pepper or the soap in their mouths.

Mom handled her grief by walking through each room of her home, touching and smelling everything she could remember that Steve had touched and she talked to him.

Steven Edward Olivo July 17, 1957-November 16, 2002 *(Courtesy Rose Olivo)*

She lived with him for forty-five years. Dad lived with him for almost forty-two years. Mom told Dad of Steve's death in her own way. She felt she had to say it to him even if he did not understand. His health was failing and his mind fuzzy when she said to him, "I don't know how much you understand. We have lost our son, Steve. Do you know what I'm saying? Do you understand?" As she repeated the words she thought he understood and he cried.

November 20, at 3:00 p.m. was the date Mom arranged for Steve's memorial service. He was cremated and buried in the Olivo plot at the Santa Clara Mission Cemetery. Diane gave the eulogy:

God gave us a beautiful day for Steve's memorial; a beautiful day for a beautiful man. Steve was a wonderful human being. When I've spoken to friends about him I would hear words like: 'He's a sweetheart, he's very kind, he has a good heart, he's terrific, good company, smart, nice to be around, and talented.' I'm not going to say it was easy. We had a lot of rough patches in eleven years—that is insignificant now. If I can shed light on the Steve I knew—I feel very privileged to share a little with you today.

He loved his guitar music, fishing, and working in the garden. He loved animals, especially dogs. He told me many cute stories about Pooper, Poopinski. Pooper died shortly after Steve and I met up again, so I became his companion (supposed to be funny but true).

Steve liked bands from the seventies. His favorite was *Credence Clearwater Revival*. Earlier this year we had a lot of fun when we went to see *The Guess Who* at the arena. He liked *Santana* even though he'd criticize Carlos Santana's playing, saying it wasn't always 'clean.' He learned to play *Samba Pa Ti*—it was a special tune for us.

Steve loved sports—the Giants and the 49ers. He taught me a lot about the Giants and I enjoyed watching the games with him. Earlier this year we went to a game at the new stadium. I felt so bad for him when the Giants lost the World Series.

He taught me about fish and I like it now. Sometimes we'd eat sushi and I'd cringe when he'd eat sea urchin. We loved eating together and trying new foods.

We didn't go on fancy trips or do extravagant things together. We enjoyed the simple things in life—walks in his neighborhood and barbecuing in the backyard at my mom's house. We watched a lot of movies. Our favorites were the old black and white sci-fi movies.

Steve loved gardening. He grew some beautiful vegetables at my house and at Mom's and he was proud of the results. He'd run into the house to show her or me his vegetables. I could always count on him to know the name of every flower we saw during our walks.

He was a great companion. He was also very patient and forgiving. He had trouble forgiving himself, yet he easily forgave others.

He loved his family very much even if he didn't want to be around them. He didn't always do well in crowds and he couldn't take all the 'yackety-yak.' I say this with affection as he said it to me. He couldn't hear or stand it when everyone was talking at the same time.

He adored Mom. Thanks to her, the way she raised him, he was respectful and had lovely manners. Mom meant everything to Steve.

Though he was the best-looking man in the world, he wasn't aware of it. He made me feel like the most beautiful and precious woman—even when I gained weight and became bald!

Steve loved the Lord. We attended church together several times over the years. He told me that he felt the Lord calling him when he was in the backyard a few weeks back. I thought it was in a dream; my mind was jumbled when I tried to remember what he said. I believed him, yet didn't know it would be so soon. We think we know God's plan, and that we have it all figured out.

Steve was the love of my life. For some reason God kept having us run into each other over the years. We met as teenagers at 'Wuzit' in Santa Clara. Steve was cute with his derby jacket and slicked-back hair. When we met again during our high school years, I didn't recognize him with long hair, muscles, and hair coming out of his shirt.

I used to think when I went to heaven I'd hang out with my parents; it will be Steve I will be looking for first. When I hold him again, I'll never let go.

Thank you Steve for the warm memories and fun times. Thanks for putting up with my quirks. You were a good sport about the little pranks I played on you. Thank you for loving me unconditionally—the way the Lord wants us to love one another. Thank you, Mom, and the family for allowing me to be a part of everything done for Steve today. I love you all very much.

I can't get over he's gone. Knowing he's in a better place helps.

Lord, thank you for Steve; he was a blessing in my life.

Steve is in heaven—he's free and at peace. No more pain and suffering.

Much Love, Diane

A couple of days later Mom received news of another loved one's death. Christine's husband, Bob was now gone.

On Sunday, Mom, Jeanie, Bill, and Bobbie went to join Dad for church at the nursing home before leaving for Camarillo to be with Christine. During Mass, it was clear that Dad was sad. Bobbie held his hand, and leaned on him. Then the floodgate of tears opened and flowed from her eyes.

Prior to returning to Spokane, Bobbie walked through Steve's garden tucked way in the backyard where the playhouse used to be. She harvested the tomatoes, green peppers, cilantro, and spearmint he had planted. She dried the plants and divided them into two sets of seventeen packets: one for each of his brothers and sisters, Mom, and Diane. She wrote, "Enjoy a pinch of Steve's spice and share in celebration of his new life. He truly loved every one of us."

Three months later the children found themselves gathered at home once more. Dad had passed. The emotions ran deep in everyone's heart. Several of the children, along with Mom, went to an early Mass said in his memory. As the priest spoke to Mom, her heart melted into a million little pieces and her children comforted her. Lorene wrote a commemorative poem:

My younger brother Steve passed away
At forty-five not in the ground he lay
In heaven in the air
He's with our Father, God, somewhere
I'll see him again one day
For I know that's what God does say
For there is another dawn
Though on earth forever gone

One week later my sister's husband went home
Though sad for us, at peace with God and no more to moan
We came to him, to visit and pray
God said he couldn't stay
Now my father had to say goodbye
Life's just too short
He, too, is in God's house and court

To them we say goodbye!
Forever goodbye is just a lie!
We still do cry
Though through difficult places we trod
We still lift up Holy Hands to God

My nephew, Gregory, had to go home, too
He was ten, his years too few
In our hearts we will always know
They're in God's loving arms
And with that, we let them go!

© —*Lorene Linnehan*

Nello at the Plumber's Convention and display of his antique plumbing tools
(Courtesy Rose Olivo)

None of the children were ready for the expected loss of Dad. His love for Mom and his children were recalled by each in their own recollections. He was a genius in the field of plumbing and a true pioneer. His trade provided for his family during a period of time when few men would have been able to accomplish such an undertaking. He passed on to his children the best of his attributes, his humor and a strong work ethic. He loved his accordion and his antiques. He took time with his grandchildren and great grandchildren, and they loved his stories. In his retirement years, he furthered his interest in antiques, especially the broken ones. He eccentrically fixed or put them back together and no one could sneak past him without hearing a story of a recent antique find.

He walked most of his girls down the aisle and taught the boys the intricacies of plumbing, heating, and air-conditioning. To his children's surprise, he was honored by the United Association Local Union 393 for an exhibition of his antique plumbing tools at the union's centennial celebration in 2004, two years after he had passed. The union photographed the exhibit for publication and Mom proudly displays it in her living room. His son's excelled in the trades of plumbing, heating, and air-conditioning he helped them to learn.

His life was celebrated with laughter at the funeral reception. The story-telling began with his oldest daughter, Marialice, and how Dad taught her the value of money. She was the first to earn a nickel to buy candy by raking and picking up leaves from the orange trees that grew in the front yard. His pocket was full of change, yet, she only got a nickel. One of his favorite requests was to pay the children to walk on his back after a hard day's work. He suffered from back aches. As each of the children got up to say how much they were paid to walk on his back, a nickel from earlier days grew to fifteen cents, a quarter, fifty cents, and a dollar for the grandchildren. One grandchild claimed the record of five dollars, plus a dinner. The children roared with laughter and feigning jealousness, shouted, "You've got to give the money back!"

Dad had time for everybody, including the friends of his children and grandchildren. He welcomed them in the Olivo home.

In the end, he left Mom and the children a legacy of special moments. What impressed Mom most was his custom prior to going to sleep every night. He religiously knelt beside the bed to pray and did until the day he was no longer able to kneel. None of the children saw him do that, his mother brought him up that way. On Mom's last visit with Dad, ever so faintly she heard him whisper, "I love you."

Yes, he was quite a character. The outlaws, the sons-in-law, in the family found him interesting. Jerilyn's husband, Al, expressed it best in this letter to Ken's son, Brandon:

Dear Brandon,

I read your letter about your freeway accident and bump on your head. To tell you the truth, it doesn't surprise me about your dad throwing you out of a moving vehicle like that!!! I guess you're stuck with a nutzo! It was nice that he came back to get you (there's still hope).

Your grandpa warned me about your dad. He told me about how your dad skipped town with all his goodies. Grandpa has an old saying that goes something like this, 'He's no good, never was, and never will be!!!' (Grandpa's own words!)

Just remember your grandpa is the best T.I.W! (Tops in Wops) I think it's wonderful how he's taken me into his family. After all, if Pooper (a five-pound mutt) is part of the family, why not Uncle Al?

I think the worst thing that happened to Grandpa is Uncle Al and your DAD! As a matter-of-fact, shortly after I married your Aunt Jerilyn, Grandpa started doing the Nello Shuffle and forgetting his teeth. He's never been the same. Then it is a shock to have a low-class Italian in the family. Grandpa's been through so much. Just keep writing him—it cheers him up!

Love
Uncle Al

Rose at Nello and Steve's grave site, Santa Clara Mission Cemetery *(Photos courtesy Barbara Olivo Cagle)*

Rose at her mother's grave site, Santa Clara Mission Cemetery *(Photos courtesy Barbara Olivo Cagle)*

Dad was cremated and a grave site service held two weeks later. Mom and most of the children gathered to share the sorrow and remembrance of their great loss. She was overwhelmed. In a moment of grief and silence, she embraced Dad in her heart and thanked our Lord for bringing him to her and giving them their last and most precious gift, Steve, to love and nurture until his death.

A few days after Dad's funeral, Mom and Bobbie returned to the cemetery to pay respect to her mother. This was the first time she had been to the grave site since Pa Pa and the children replaced the headstone and the second time since she was four years old.

She now felt and understood the love and pain that Lydia must have experienced when a mother has a child taken away. She fell to her knees, lowered her head, and spread her arms. A transformation took her back to when she lost her mother. A gentle wind whirled around her—radiating love. She laid a red rose gently on the grave. The bittersweet and deeply-rooted emotions that were held captive within her for years let go and she was at peace.

Throughout your life let your love be
A beacon to others for them to see
The important values someday left behind
Of what a mother and a woman should be

—Jacqueline Rose Olivo

Epilogue

Pen in hand, sitting at her antique oak wood secretary desk, Mom wrote with deep reflection of proud moments in her life:

My children's accomplishments during their school years, such as straight 'A' report cards, awards, honors, and various achievements, especially magna and summa cum laude.

When one of my son's or daughter's were chosen for a role in a school play. I especially remember *Fiddler on the Roof* with Bobbie, *The Mouse that Roared* with Harold, *Bye Bye Birdie* with Cathy, *South Pacific* with Nello Jr., *Swan Lake Ballet* with Marialice, and the numerous dance and piano recitals.

When Patty sewed clothes for herself and for her younger sisters and brothers to model in a fashion show.

Watching Jeanie and Virginia play the accordion on a 4th of July parade float.

When Harold was chosen to play the role of Joseph in the school Christmas play. His one spoken line was the whole show.

My children's school achievements were such proud occurrences. To me the pursuit of learning was paramount for my family. That is where the Jesuits and Sisters of Notre Dame entered my sons and daughters' lives. The first communions, confirmations, and graduations, were proud moments for all of us..

I prayed for guidance, and I know I made the right decision in choosing parochial schooling for my children. They have become fine God loving, compassionate, and productive children.

As each of my children were married, I was exceedingly proud of the beautiful bride or handsome groom. I was also proud of their father—so handsome in his tuxedo, as he escorted his daughters to the altar.

The epitome of fond memories is when Harold donned the uniform of the United States Army and served in a faraway land for his country.

It would require volumes to record the many varied talents, accomplishments, and awards of each person in a family of ten girls and six boys.

The advice gave when asked was, strive to be the very best.

I thank God for the privilege of experiencing the miracle of birth sixteen times during the first twenty years of marriage. A marriage that survived for sixty-six years.

Strong faith in God, and love and respect for one another, have sustained the family through trials and adversity, in sickness and in health, and mostly in the very best of times.

When I graduated from grammar school and was chosen to give the 'Address of Welcome,' I memorized one whole page and I had it down pat. The day before graduation, I came down with the flu and was as sick as a dog, yet I was determined to give that speech. I did not let on how sick I was to anyone—not even to Ma. I could hardly stand on my feet. What was supposed to be a nice slow speech of about five minutes, I rattled off perfectly in one minute and was so proud of myself.

Three years later when I graduated from Peter Burnett Junior High School, surprise, surprise! Again, the principal chose me to give the coveted 'Address of Welcome.' This time I made a perfect delivery, and I was oh, so proud of myself. It was right then and there that I decided to pursue a career in public speaking. I followed that dream for a while in high school until my junior year when I changed directions and headed toward a career in business.

The field of commercial art was my ultimate goal. Then I met Nello, and so much for public speaking, commercial art, and a lot of other dreams.

I have realized the most important dream I held dear. The dream of a good, solid, down-to-earth education for each of my children.

The name 'Olivo' has proudly graced the rosters of many colleges around the country, namely: University of San Bernardino, Harvard University and Harvard Law School, San Jose State, University of Hawaii, Sacramento State, University of California, Northridge, University of San Francisco, Lone Mountain, University of California, Irvine and the University of Colorado, Colorado Springs.

In a World

In a world where so much seems to move so quickly
And each day we have to change and readjust
There is a need for something solid to hold on to
For people we depend on and trust

Now that we are getting older we're cherishing more day by day
The warm family ties we've established
And the love time can not take away

—Jacqueline Rose Olivo

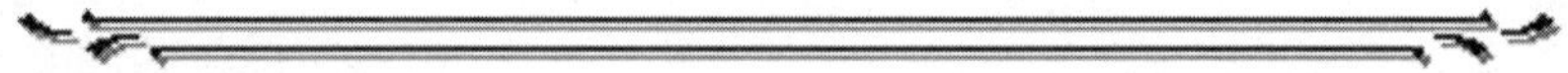

Sixteen Children

Marialice: Real Estate Broker/five children

Jeanie: Ceritfied Public Account/member of California Scholarship Federation/Beta Gamma Sigma, an International Honor Society

Patty: Retired Business Manager Secretary/Cake Decorator/two children

Nello Jr.: Building Developer/Restaurant Owner/Wine Maker/Retired Plumbing Contractor/six children

Virginia: Real Estate Broker/five children

Christine: Independent Business Investment Property Owner/Professional Model/one child

William: Plumber Regional Manager/three children

Richard: Plumber Regional Manager/three children

Jerilyn: Medical Records Secretary/three children

Catherine: Retired Para-legal/Editor/Store Manager/two children

Nancy: Vice-President of Human Resource Director/Juris Doctorate Harvard Law School/one child

Harold: Plumber Office Manager/two children

Barbara: Writer/President of the Spokane Authors & Self-Publishers/ Tap Grandma/Retired Real Estate Broker/two children

Kenneth: Plumbing Estimator & Program Manager/two children

Lorene: Notary/Coordinator for Foreign Exchange Students/School Bus Driver/three children

Steven: Plumber/Journeyed to God on November 16, 2002

About the Author

Barbara (Bobbie) Olivo Cagle

Barbara is the thirteenth of Rose's sixteen children. She was born and reared in San Jose, California. St. Joseph's School was the foundation for her education through eighth grade. In Notre Dame High School, Barbara went by the nickname, "Bobbie." She was involved in numerous school activities, played the drums, was a cheerleader, song girl, sewed, and created various forms of artwork. She aspired to acting and performed in the Notre Dame Shakespearean festival. Rumor has it that she pulled a fire alarm near the end of the festival that created confusion and concern. In her senior year, on February 14, 1970, she was involved in a tragic toboggan accident. Bobbie crashed into a huge pine tree and was confined to a bed for a couple months. The instant before impact, an out-of-body experience flashed before her eyes, and the love of her family and friends left her with a dream to write a story of her mother. During her recovery she collected letters and memorabilia from her family.

In her second year of college she met her wonderful Navy husband, Donald J. Cagle. He was attending college in Palo Alto, California. Prior to their marriage, she traveled Europe with two of her sisters for six weeks. Not long after she returned from Europe, Bobbie and Don were married on April 21, 1974. God blessed them with two beautiful children: Jocilyn Roselle in 1975, and Jason John in 1977.

From 1976 to 1979 Bobbie volunteered her time as a cheerleader and pep club instructor for the Olso American School, in Oslo, Norway. She spent time in North Chicago, Illinois; Monterey, California; and Guam, before residing in Spokane, Washington to rear her children. Bobbie enjoyed an extremely successful career in real estate from 1988 to 2002. She served as President of the Spokane Authors & Self-Publishers from 2005 to 2007. Currently she performs with the "Tap Grandmas" of Spokane.

Letter to Mother

Recording your life has been a deeply moving experience and a dream come true. Praying to our Lord gave me peace of mind to continue the long journey. Reliving your memories with you has been an honor and a treasure of gold branded in my heart. You are truly an amazing woman in every sense of the word, "One of God's Gifts." The readers that relate to their own life experiences and the emotions shared will take pause and reflection. You are an inspiration in the lives of those you have touched.

Thank you Mother.

Love,
Barbara

If you desire to make human beings happy,
give them a task or a cause,
and the harder, the better.
It is when God calls them
that men and women rise to the crest of their power.

—Jacqueline Rose Olivo

Rose and her children at her ninetieth birthday party

Rose's ninetieth birthday bash *(Photos courtesy Christine Wade and Barbara Olivo Cagle)*

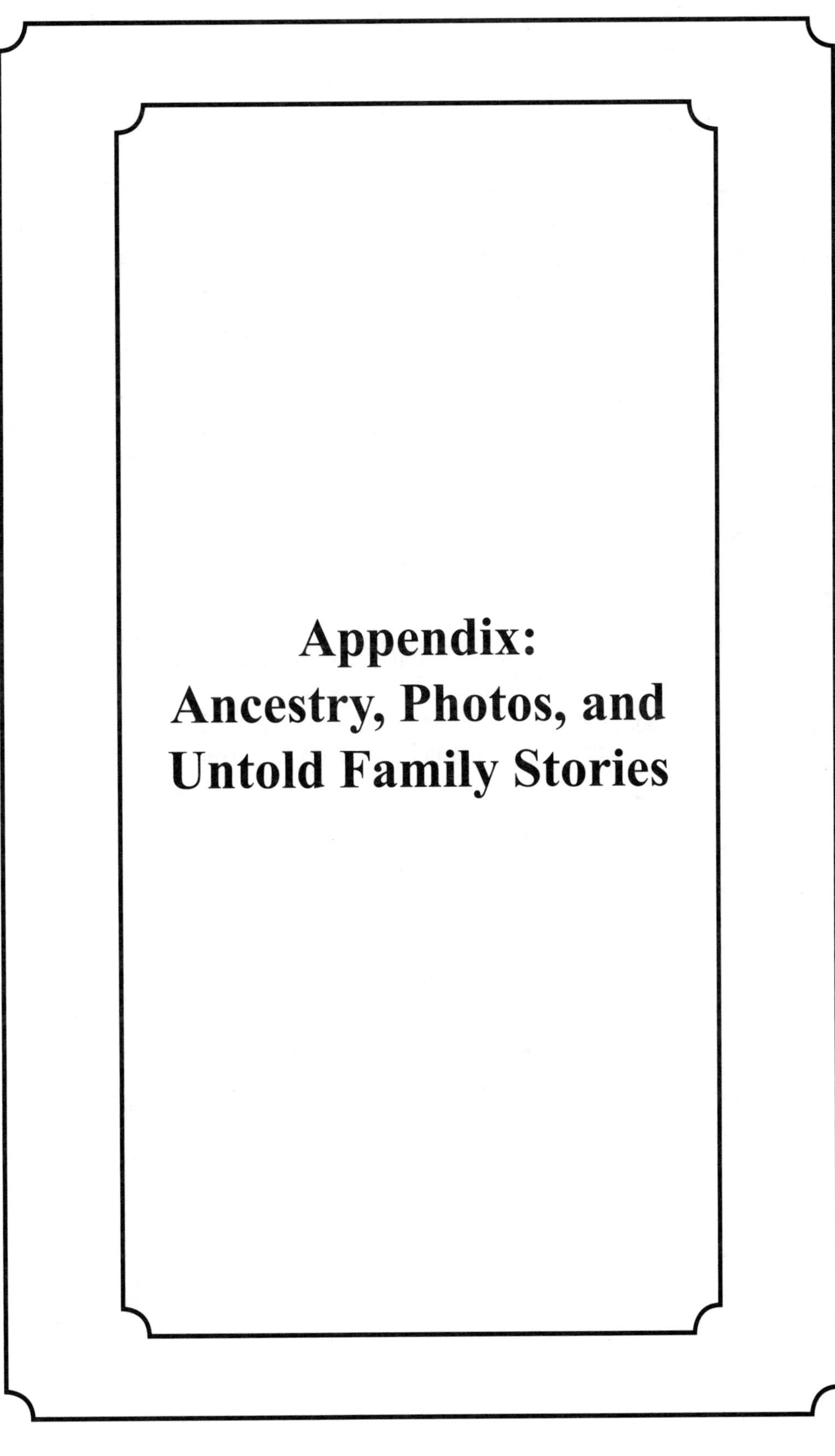

Appendix: Ancestry, Photos, and Untold Family Stories

Rose's Paternal Ancestry
Father: Joseph Nunez (Pa Pa)
Grandfather: Marcial Nunez-Fernandez
Grandmother: Joaquina Abraire
Great Grandfather: Ramon Nunez-Sanchez
Great Grandmother: Maria Fernandez
Great-Great Grandfather: Dionisio Nunez
Great-Great Grandmother: Maria Sanchez

Rose's Maternal Ancestry
Mother: Adelaide Madriago (Lydia)
Grandfather: John G. Madriago, Jr.
Grandmother: Annie Carabajal (Mater)

Rose's Maternal-Paternal Ancestry
Great Grandfather: John G. Madriago, Sr.
Great Grandmother: Secundina Cobarrubia
Great-Great Grandfather: Santiago Cobarrubia
Grcat-Great Grandmother: Manuela Guajardo

Rose's Maternal-Maternal Ancestry
Great Grandfather: Miquel Carabajal
Great Grandmother: Jessie Lopez (Nana)

Nello's Paternal Ancestry
Father: Enrico Olivo
Grandfather: Fillipo Olivo
Grandmother: Ribeca Artemisia

Nello's Maternal Ancestry
Mother: Maria Isola Ciardella (Lena)
Grandfather: Gesualdo Ciardella
Grandmother: Maria Leonini

Rose's Paternal Ancestry

Nunez Coat of Arms

(Courtesy Mike Kennaugh, www.4crests.com)

The Nunez Coat of Arms has a blue shield decorated with three diagonal gold fleurs-de-lis placed diagonally across the background. The surname "Nunez" means "Son of the daring one."

The most well-known ancestor was Vasco Nunez de Balboa, 1475-1517, the explorer who discovered the Pacific Ocean from the west coast of Central America. Born in Spain, he went to Central America in 1500 by boarding an expeditionary boat in secret. Legend has it that he hid himself as a stowaway in an empty barrel, or perhaps wrapped himself in a sail. In 1509, Vasco settled in Darién, at the time considered as the entire Isthmus of Panama. He took on an important role among the expedition's participants, by proclaiming himself governor. Then he, with a few followers, journeyed across the dangerous, jungle-like terrain of the isthmus, leading to his discovery of the Pacific Ocean on September 25, 1513. In many respects, he was responsible for establishing the continental nature of Central America.

Rose's Paternal Ancestry

Abraire Coat of Arms
(Courtesy Mike Kennaugh, www.4crests.com)

The Abraire Coat of Arms displays quarterly; first and fourth or, two wolves passant sable, placed in pale, all with a bordure gules; second and third or, three bars sable. The "or" is the heraldic color gold, and denotes generosity and elevation of the mind granted to a family.

Abraire drives from the place "Abraira" in the provinces of Lugo, Galicia, Oviedo, and Asturias, Spain. The earliest reference to a variant of this name is a record of Casilda Abras. The name dates back to 1771 in the Order of Carlos III as a distinguished person.

Rose's Maternal Ancestry

Rose's grandparents, Marcial Nunez-Fernandez and Joaquina Abraire *(Courtesy Didier Nunez)*

Marcial Nunez-Fernandez was born October 17, 1861 in Vega de Valcarce, Leon Province, Spain. He later married Joaquina Nunez-Abraire born circa 1860 in Villafranca del Bierzo, Leon Province, Spain. The wife's maiden name followed the husband's surname.

The two had five children and they were born as follows: Joseph "Pa Pa"—February 2, 1883; Antonio—circa 1890; Balbino—February 12, 1891; Engracia—December 6, 1893; and Manuel—April 13, 1900.

Rose's great grandparents, Ramon Nunez and Maria Fernandez, had one son Marcial.

Rose's great-great grandparents, Dionsio Nunez and Maria Sanchez had two children, Ramon and Asuncion.

Pa Pa's family, was from the village of Ruitelan, Leon Province, Spain. The village's proximity to Galicia influenced both the family's customs and language. Pa Pa's grandfather, Ramon Nunez's, ancestors were the "Los Postillions" for the village of Galicia. They controlled the post office, the passage of people, and the trade of merchandise on the road through Galicia.

After the birth of Pa Pa's youngest brother, Manuel, in April, 1900, his father, Martial Nunez, moved the family to Galdames, in the Vasco region of the Basque Country to work the mines. The family now was integrated with the customs of Basque. The Basque Country in the Pyrenee's mountain range traverses the area of north central Spain and south west France. The unique language is distinct from other western European languages. Little information was recorded before the sixteenth century with their first book printed in 1545. They have since maintained an uninterrupted literary tradition; the Basque people use this language to preserve their heritage to pass on to their children.

In the latter part of the 18th century Spain experienced economical hardships and political turmoil. Many mines closed down and Queen Maria Christina was appointed Regent for her newborn son, Alfonso XII, the King of Spain. The state of affairs concerned Grandpa Marcial. He was worried that The Spanish-American War, which began in April 1898, would take his son. Grandpa Marcial and Grandma Joaquina wanted to send their sons to America. The conflict between the United States and Spain ended Spanish Colonial Rule in the New World. In the Treaty of Paris signed on December 10, 1898, Spain relinquished claim to Cuba and ceded Guam, Puerto Rico, and the Philippines to the United States. Grandpa Marcial and Grandma Joaquina became concerned when the unexpected defeat, threw Spain into chaos and demoralization. The "Generation of 1898" re-evaluated Spain's position in the world and organized movements to free the Basque areas from Spanish rule. In 1902, Alfonso XII assumed control of the government and political upheaval ensued. In 1903 Grandpa Marcial and Grandma Joaquina sent their son to America. They feared another war and preferred their son leave rather than go into the service.

Pa Pa was the first, then in 1920 Uncle Balbino and Uncle Antonio. His brothers rented a two-bedroom house on Kent Street that had survived the "Great San Francisco Earthquake of 1906." Pa Pa's youngest brother, Uncle Manuel did not immigrate to the United States. He settled in Pouzauges, France, married Pierrette Ruaud, the daughter of a judge. Pa Pa's sister, Aunt Engracia, remained in Spain and married Ambrosio Fuertes Guerra.

Rose's Father, Uncles, Aunt, and Cousins

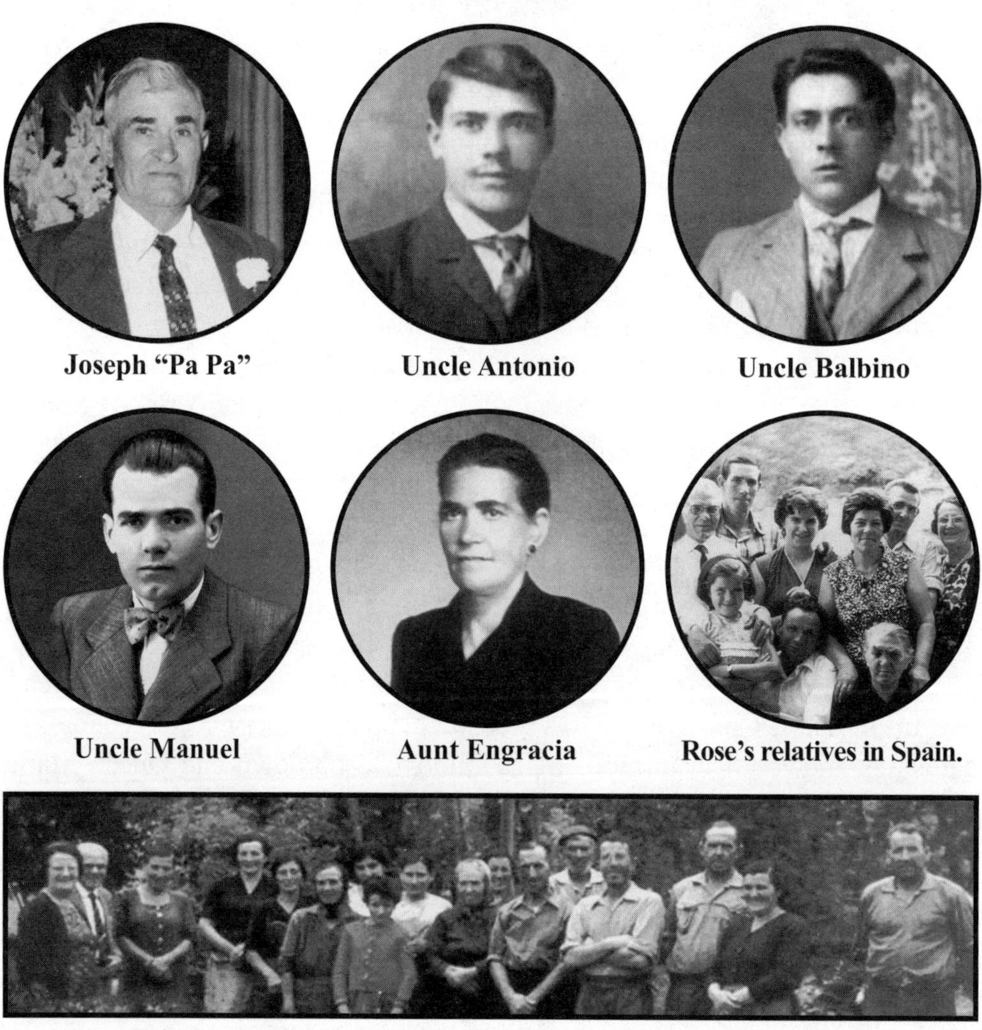

Joseph "Pa Pa" **Uncle Antonio** **Uncle Balbino**

Uncle Manuel **Aunt Engracia** **Rose's relatives in Spain.**

Rose's relatives in Ruitelan, Spain *(Photos courtesy Didier Nunez)*

Rose's Maternal Ancestry

Madariaga Coat of Arms
(Courtesy Mike Kennaugh, www.4crests.com)

The Madariaga Coat of Arms displays honor with five bezants and gules in saltire. In between each bezant are four stars of eight points and a chain of eight azure rings in the trim of the shield. The helmet, crested with three ostrich feathers, represents a strong history of leadership.

The Madriago families carry a distinguished ancestral history. Their homeland spelling and pronunciation is Madariaga (Ma-da-ri-a-ga). The earliest mention of the name dates back to 1664 under the jurisdiction of Vizcaya, in the Basque Country of Spain. The most famous ancestral personage was the Spanish writer and diplomat, Salvador de Madariaga, born 1886 in La Coruna, Spain.

Rose's Maternal Ancestry

Rose's grandparents, John G. Madriago Jr. and Annie Carabajal *(Courtesy Nadine Eck and Marie Bueno)*

Grandpa John wanted to pursue Annie "Mater." His good intentions meant little to her overly protective mother, Jessie, "Nana." Mater and her brother, Rose's Uncle Cooney were raised most of their life by Nana after she divorced her husband. Grandpa John showed his interest in Mater when he built a shanty for her on a parcel of land in Campo Seco, California. With her mother's blessing, the two were married on November 18, 1899. On November 19, 1906, her mother bought the parcel next to them for ten gold coins and Grandpa John built a shanty for her, too.

Mater and Grandpa John had twelve children: Adelaide "Lydia," Rose's mother, Aunt Gertrude, Uncle Lawrence, a set of twins (names unknown), Uncle James, Uncle Frank, Aunt Josephine, four babies (names unknown). Many of the children died in infancy or early childhood. While some of the children played in one room, others were dying from scarlet fever or diphtheria in the next room. The great fires in Campo Seco, 1854, 1859, and 1928 destroyed many of the wooden cross markers that at one time identified graves. When Grandpa John's drinking and hanging out at the saloons became too much for Mater to handle, she booted him out of the house.

Rose's Mother, Aunt and Uncles

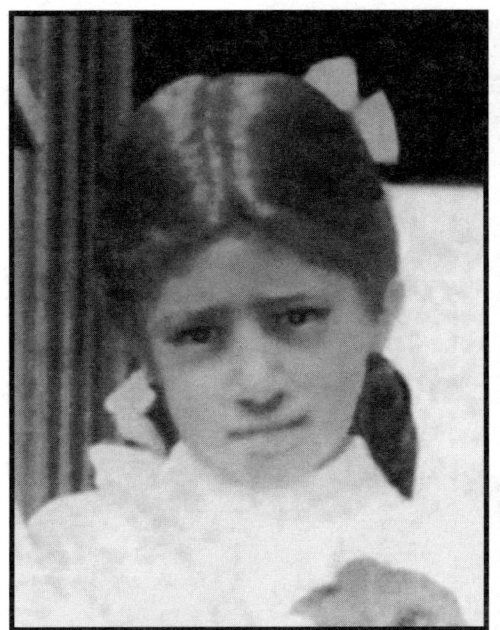

Lydia, and Lydia, Aunt Gertrude, Uncle James, and Uncle Lawrence *(Courtesy Evelyn Simon)*

The earliest photograph taken of Grandpa John and Mater's children was in 1908. Lydia was eight years old, standing on the side porch of her home with her younger sister Gertrude "Gertie," and her younger brothers James and Lawrence. Lydia wore a corsage on her dress and her hair combed into braids. It was Uncle James' baptismal day.

The Campo Seco School House and student body in 1910 *(Courtesy Rodger and Helene Nunez)*

Lydia is seated in the second row center, wearing a white bandana with her hands folded. Uncle James is kneeling in the front row, sixth from the right, and Uncle Lawrence is seated in the second row, second from the right.

Rose's Mother

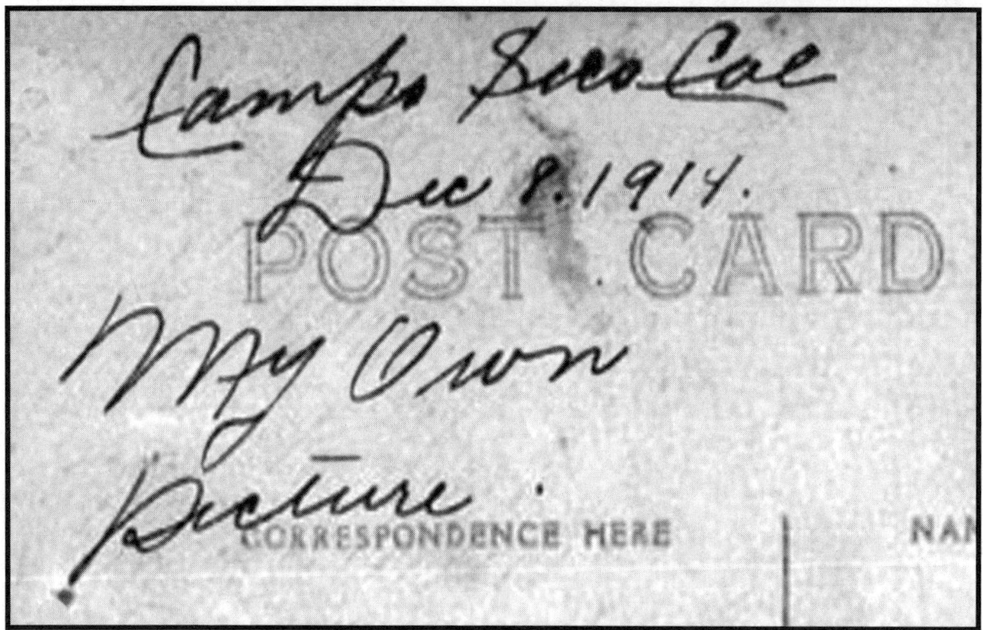

Lydia at fourteen years old *(Photos courtesy Rodger and Helene Nunez)*

Pa Pa had in his possession a postcard with a photograph of Lydia sitting on a hand-carved spindled wooden rocking chair. The mid-length sleeves of her high-necked lace dress emphasized her petite wrists and graceful fingers. A shoulder-to-shoulder black velvet bow fastened the back of her dress. She held a bouquet of roses she had picked from her garden and wore small white flowers interwoven in the braid that topped her long, dark brown hair.

Rose's Maternal-Paternal Ancestry

Rose's great grandparents John G. Madraigo, Sr. and Secundina Madriago Cobarubbia *(Courtesy Nadine Eck)*

Rose's Great Grandfather John Madriago, Sr., was born circa 1826 in Chillán, Chilé, approximately a six-hour drive south of Santiago. He immigrated to the United States during the California Gold Rush and lived in Auburn, California. He worked the mines and married Rose's Great Grandmother Secundina C. Cobarrubia, in March 1871. She had been Bernardo Ablos' widow for two years. It was her second marriage. She brought into the marriage one daughter, Aunt Rose Ablos born on August 22, 1866 in Angels Camp. The great grandparents had four sons and one daughter: Grandpa John Jr., on January 3, 1872 in the mining town of Penryn, north of Virginiatown; Aunt Eliza on January 10, 1874 in Penryn; Uncle Emmet on September 13, 1876 in New Castle; Uncle Phillip on May 1, 1876 in Auburn; and Uncle James on February 9, 1880 in Penryn.

Rose's Great Grandmother, Grandfather, and Great Aunts and Uncles

Rose's Great Grandmother Secundina **Rose's Grandpa John** **Aunt Rose Ablos**

Aunt Eliza **Uncle Emmet** **Uncle Phillip James**

Uncle James Phillip Alias: Harry Stringer **Aunt Kathryn "Kate"** **Uncle Robert "Bob"**

(Photos courtesy Nadine Eck, Shirley Capps, Violet Davis, and Uni Walker)

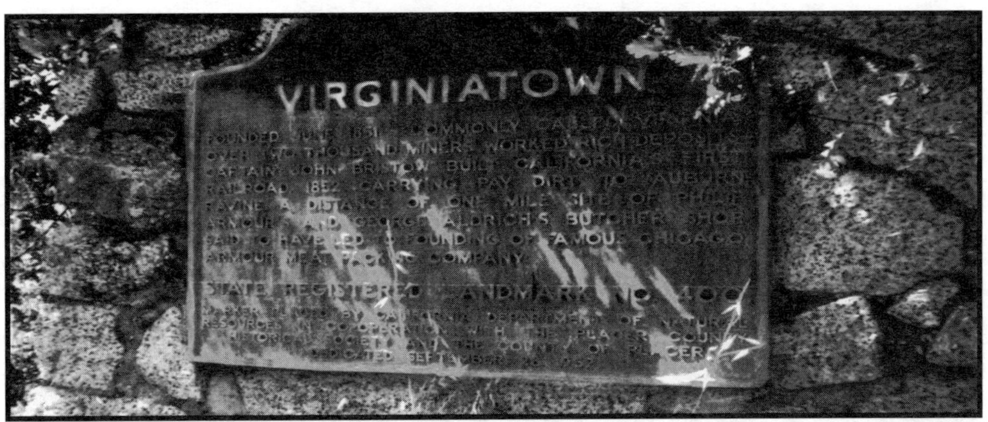

Virginiatown *(Courtesy Barbara Olivo Cagle)*

The Madriago family lived on Virginiatown Road in Virginia, California. A ranch-town in Placer County, located two miles west of Gold Hill and seven miles northwest of Newcastle. At one time, the townspeople split Virginia into Virginia #1 for the original "white" settlement, and Virginia #2 for the Chinese Settlement, which was located west of the present monument. In later years, the townspeople called Virginia, "Virginiatown," to distinguish it from Virginia City in Nevada. The town became one of the safest and surest mining localities in the state. Over the years, more than two thousand miners toiled the ravines in search of gold. It had a prosperous Main Street with hotels, a number of saloons, a livery stable, and various stores. Today it is a ghost town with a monument depicting its past.

Rose's Great Grandparents John Sr. and Secundina were married for ten years when Secundina became a widow for the second time. Her youngest son Uncle James was one-and-a-half years old when Great Grandfather John died on July 31, 1881 of unknown causes. He was buried in Ohpir Cemetery, Placer, California. In 1883, Rose's Great Grandmother Secundina married Francisco C. Riggles and moved the family to Campo Seco. They were married six years when she became a widow for the third time. She had two more children with Francisco, Aunt Kathryn, "Kate" on December 7, 1884; and Uncle Robert, "Bob" on April 7, 1888.

Penn Copper Mine Boarding House
(Courtesy Barbara Hunter)

She christened her children at St. Joseph's Catholic Church in Auburn and at the Immaculate Conception Catholic Church in Camanche. She did not remarry. To support her family, she ran a boarding house by the Penn Mine serving thirty miners. Aunt Kate helped her mother with the boarding house, when it closed down they housed the miners who needed room and board in their home.

Rose's Grandfather and Great Aunts and Uncles

Rose's Great Aunt Rose Ablos *(Courtesy Nadine Eck)*

Rose's Great Aunt Rose Ablos and namesake enjoyed music and loved to dance. She delighted in cooking, crocheting, embroidering, quilting, and gardening. In her late teens, she left Campo Seco to work at Mrs. Green's Hotel in Lockeford. It had a family style dining room, seating four people to a table. The rooms were nice and wallpapered with floral designs. At first, she washed dishes and cleaned vegetables. That did not last long before management asked her to take the position of "Cook." Any social life for Aunt Rose Ablos was nil as she was ready for bed at the close of the work day. She spent her weekends in Campo Seco with her mother and siblings. She was the arc that kept her family together over the years following her mother's move to Sacramento.

Aunt Rose Ablos survived her first husband of six years, Nichanor Vegas. She married Clifford Robie Sr. on August 22, 1900, in San Andreas, California and brought four children into the marriage; Almaeranta, Soila, and twins, Rosie and Nick who died in infancy; together they had three children: Clifford Jr., Frederick, and Bernard, Rose's cousins. They moved from mining town to mining town before finally re-settling back in Campo Seco.

Rose's Great Aunt Eliza Almaranta Madriago Ryno *(Courtesy Shirley Capps)*

Aunt Eliza married George W. Ryno on October 18, 1900, in San Andreas. They had three children William, Phillip, and Alfred, Rose's cousins. She had a green thumb when it came to her garden and kept potted tubs of spices and flowers on the front porch. A huge pepper and umbrella tree shaded the home. Aunt Eliza was kind-hearted and soft-spoken. She had an amblyopic, lazy eye, condition. She was a midwife and generous with her time, aiding the sick and elderly.

Rose's Grandfather John Jr. was not well for the last six years of his life and needed assistance from Aunt Eliza. Daily she crossed the creek hop-stepping on rocks, to check on him. She brought him food, helped him clean himself, and dress him. At the time, she also took on caring for her granddaughter, Alfred's daughter, and Rose's cousin, Shirley. Shirley had lost her mother at an early age.

Aunt Eliza taught Shirley to respect the snakes. Rattlesnakes were dangerous and plentiful in Campo Seco. When Shirley noticed Aunt Eliza enticing king snakes to stay around her property by feeding them and setting out tin cans for them to lay their eggs in, she asked "Why?" Aunt Eliza answered, "They help the environment, and they are our protectors." King snakes have black and white bands, and grow three to five feet long. They eat rodents, birds, and other snakes. They are immune to the venom of the rattlesnake and kill them by constriction.

Shirley saw the grueling hard work Aunt Eliza went through for Rose's Grandpa John during his drunken stupors. Regardless of his inadequacies, she loved her uncle. Her prized possession was a beautiful saddle he had made.

Rose's Great Uncle Emmet Madriago *(Courtesy Shirley Capps)*

Uncle Emmet married Nancy, "Nellie'" on May 8, 1910, in San Andreas and they had one son, Emmet Francis Jr., "Francis," Rose's cousin. A couple years after the marriage, Nellie took her son to live in Tuolumne. Uncle Emmet moved back in with his brothers and continued to work at the Penn Copper Mine Company. It was common to find him in the same gray and white striped overalls, hanging around with Grandpa John, carrying a jug full of wine. They were regulars at the *Cool Café*.

When Francis was older, he went to visit his father often. Uncle Emmet and Grandpa John lived across the creek from Aunt Eliza, in a two-bedroom redwood cabin that she and her husband owned. Both of them suffered from miners' black lung disease and drank to ease the pain. Uncle Emmet died on March 20, 1940. Grandpa John, Aunt Eliza, Nellie and Francis, buried him in the Campo Seco Catholic Cemetery. On April 4, 1941, a year after his death, Francis was in a fatal motorcycle accident. A few months after Uncle Emmet died, Aunt Eliza moved to Sacramento and no longer could care for Grandpa John. On March 9, 1942, he admitted himself into the Calaveras County Hospital. He died there on July 1, 1942, at the age of seventy, from tuberculosis pulmonalis. Aunt Eliza arranged for the burial on July 3, in the Campo Seco Catholic Cemetery alongside his brother Uncle Emmet. Shirley witnessed both her uncles' burials.

Rose's Great Uncle Phillip James Madriago *(Courtesy Nadine Eck)*

Rose's Great Grandmother Secundina and her youngest children, Uncle Bob and Aunt Kate lived in Sacramento when her son Uncle Phillip moved from Campo Seco to join them. The two brothers worked on the streetcars there and Uncle Bob introduced Uncle Phillip to a young Dutch girl, Meta Sprock. On January 31, 1913, Uncle Phillip married Meta in Sacramento. She brought into the marriage one daughter, Lorraine, and with Uncle Phillip, they had eight children: Violet, Leroy, Bernice, Elwood, Leona, Juanita, Gordon, and Robert, Rose's cousins. Uncle Phillip was a quiet and tranquil man; things did not bother him. Meta did all the talking. She was a good cook and firm with the children. They looked forward to the times when Grandpa John came to visit. His surviving nieces and nephews remember that he was good to them. He had little if any contact with his own children and his attention went to Uncle Phillip's family. He treated them with a meal and candy whenever he visited. He would arrive with arms full of groceries and big juicy steaks to barbecue. He would say to Meta, "No, my sister-in-law, I'm doin' the cookin' today." Then he would salt down the top of the old wood-burning cookstove and barbecue the steaks. After the visits, he returned to Campo Seco and went back to the mines and drinking.

Rose's Great Uncle James Phillip Madriago Alias: Harry Stringer *(Courtesy Uni Walker)*

Della, a young girl from Campo Seco, was crazy in love with Uncle James. On the night of April 16, 1904, they were out on the town together, got drunk and ended up married. Twenty-four hours later, Uncle James realized what he had done and left her. He feared she would ruin his reputation and he left Campo Seco. He moved to Port Angeles, Washington and changed his name to Harry James Stringer. His past was behind him and he began a completely new life.

"Uncle Harry" landed his first job as a cowboy, herding cattle. He then was a butcher and later on worked at the Crown Zellerbach Paper Mill until he retired. He married Mae Stiles on June 3, 1922, in Port Angeles, Washington. She brought into the marriage three children: Una, Mae, and Walter who died in infancy; together they had Beulah, Rose's cousins. Uncle Harry lived a good life and became involved and joined the Salvation Army Church. He conducted Salvation Army Church street meetings and became well-known in the community as a Christ-follower. He worked the streets spreading the message of God and provided spiritual and moral regeneration. Aunt Rose Ablos and Aunt Kate wrote Uncle Harry on occasion keeping him apprised of family news. He returned for a visit to Campo Seco in 1952 and no one in the family saw or heard from him thereafter.

Rose's Great Aunt Katherine "Kate" Riggles
(Courtesy Nadine Eck)

Aunt Kate married Ora Edgell On June 9, 1907, in San Andreas. They had two children, Raymond, and Baby Edgell who died in infancy, Rose's cousins. Subsequent to her becoming a widow in 1941, she returned to Campo Seco to live in Aunt Eliza's house. It had been vacant since she moved to Sacramento. Aunt Kate enjoyed the front porch and the colorful sunsets. When her sisters came to visit, they talked for hours on the porch. Since she had lived in the city, she appreciated the nature and songs of the whippoorwills and mockingbirds.

Family gatherings were on the weekends, when the children and grandchildren came for a visit. Aunt Kate loved to cook and it was rare to see her without an apron. The aroma of oregano and garlic permeated through the house. She made the best tortillas. She would have her grandchildren stand around her and watch as she squushed dough with her thumb and index finger into a nice ball, flop it back and forth, and then throw it on the wood stove. As the tortillas puffed up, she would flip them to brown on the other side and say, "Come on, and get your hands full of flour." Beef enchiladas were another favorite. She would use ten pounds of beef to make fifty or more enchiladas. For dessert she made a rum cake that she filled with raisins that had been soaked in rum.

Rose's Great Uncle Robert "Bob" Riggles *(Courtesy Nadine Eck)*

Uncle Bob served in the United States Army. After the Army, he went to work for the Pacific Gas and Electric Company. He also worked on Street Cars in Sacramento and later worked as a mail carrier at the Sacramento Post Office. He had a nice home on Lower Stockton Boulevard and Rose's Great Grandmother Secundina lived with him until she died on April 23, 1927. Uncle Bob let his siblings and family come stay with him whenever they needed a place to live for a while. He made his nieces and nephews chuckle with his funny facial expressions. He smoked a pipe and his house smelled of mint tobacco. A month after his mother passed, he married Myrtle Scrivner on May 23, 1927, in Sacramento. When Myrtle died, he married Kathryn Weiland on March 11, 1962, in Sacramento. Uncle Bob did not have any children with either spouse.

Rose's Aunts, Uncles, and Cousins

Madriago family gatherings *(Photos courtesy Rose Olivo and Shirley Capps)*

Rose's Maternal-Paternal Ancestry

Cobarrubia Coat of Arms

(Courtesy Mike Kennaugh, www.4crests.com)

The Cobarrubia Coat of Arms has a pale argent and azure design with a castle argent, a fleur de lis or, and lion rampant gules. The crest has five plumes azure argent. The surname is a variant of the name Covarrubia and Covarrubias.

The earliest bearers of the name Cobarrubia were in the ancient kingdom of Castile, Province of Burgos, Spain, during the Middle Ages and the Christian Reconquest of Spain. Many of the Cobarrubia family began to relocate in Chilé and other areas, following the period of the conquest.

Rose's Great Grandmother and Great-Great Aunts and Uncles

Great Grandmother Secundina

Uncle Miguel

Uncle William

Aunt Sarah Ramona

Uncle Miguel's Children, Rose's Cousins

Margaret "Maggie"

Frank

Gilbert

Rose's Great-Great Aunt and Cousins

Rose's Great Aunt Sarah Ramona and Uncle Edward Salaun *(Courtesy Nadine Eck)*

Rose's cousins, the Salaun children left to right—Ray, Ralph, Gertrude, Louis, Eliza, Isadore, Ed and Roy *(Courtesy Harold and Louise Saluan)*

Rose's Great Grandmother Secundina and Aunt Sarah were close and planned family gatherings that included aunts, uncles, and cousins.

One of her grandmother's favorite stories involved the legendary and infamous bandit, Joaquin Murietta. He was married to a distant cousin. She claimed that in 1850, Joaquin left Chilé for the California Gold Rush. There was a growing resentment, blatant racism, and discrimination coming from American miners toward South American immigrants. Joaquin claimed to be a Californio from Sonora, Mexico.

Californios were Spanish-speaking and came from Mexico or Spain to settle in California. Many of them received grants for large areas of land. Joaquin established a claim and was working it when the State of California imposed the Foreign Miners Tax. Encouraged by yet another method of harassment toward foreign miners, a group of American miners forced Joaquin off his claim, tied him up, beat him, raped and killed his wife, Rosita, and hanged his brother.

Joaquin wanted revenge; he and his banditos were labeled by the townspeople, "The Five Joaquins." Legend has it that they were responsible for countless cattle rustlings, robberies, and murders, up and down the Mother Lode Country. Since he was a relative, Great Grandmother Secundina and Aunt Sarah provided a hideout for him for a cut of his loot. He frequented neighboring saloons, fandango halls, and gambling joints that operated around-the-clock between Lancha Plana, where his sister lived, and Campo Seco, Placerville, and Sacramento. The exaggerated accounts of his villainous ventures pressured the state to take action.

On May 11, 1853, the California Governor, John Bigler, signed an act creating the "California State Rangers." Their sole purpose was to track down and capture Joaquin, his henchman Manuel Garcia, "Three Fingered-Jack," and all known associates. They consisted of no more than twenty mounted rangers led by Captain Harry Love, a former Texas Ranger. They would be paid one-hundred and fifty dollars a month for three months, and a one thousand dollar reward for any one of the five Joaquins captured or killed. On July 25, 1853, the California State Rangers captured Joaquin and killed Three-Fingered Jack in the Panoche Pass, west of Tulare Lake. They cut off the hand of "Three-Fingered Jack" and locked Joaquin up in the Mariposa jail. Later, the Rangers hanged Joaquin. They were worried that his supporters would storm the jail and release him.

The Rangers beheaded Joaquin after his death, and preserved his head and Three-Fingered Jack's hand in a jar of brandy. The head and hand could be viewed at exhibits in the western states for the price of one dollar. In order to collect the rewards, Captain Harry Love used the viewings as a main attraction to obtain signed affidavits attesting to Joaquin and Manuel's identities. The exhibits were lost in the "Great San Francisco Earthquake 1906."

Rose's Cousins

Saluan family gatherings *(Photos courtesy Mel and Betty Facey)*

Rose's Maternal-Paternal Ancestry

Rose's Great-great Grandmother Manuela Guajardo *(Courtesy Shirley Capps)*

Rose's great-great grandparents, Santiago Cobarrubia and Manuela Guajardo were born circa 1826 and 1829, in the village of Chillán, Chilé. They immigrated to California, and married circa 1850. They had six children: Secundina—July 1, 1852; Miguel—December 23, 1853; Maria—October 25, 1856; Velisario (William)—October 15, 1857; Abelardo—January 14, 1861; and Sarah—August 31, 1862. They spoke English and Chilean-Spanish.

Rose's Maternal-Maternal Ancestry

Carabajal Coat of Arms
(Courtesy Mike Kennaugh www..4crests.com)

The Carabajal Coat of Arms presented in gules, has a bend or charged with the letter F, and five saltires or with three on top and two on bottom. The crest has five ostrich feathers interchanging gules and or.

The Carabajal surname is traced to Castile, an historical Christian Kingdom of medieval Spain, dating back as early as the twelfth century. The name Carabajal connotes a knight or a knight's servant. Carabajals immigrated to Mexico in the early 1500's. Many of the Carabajals and Cobarrubias carry the same heritage from the Iberian tribes of North Africa when the Iberians migrated as early as 3000 BC to the peninsula that is now home to Spain and Portugal.

Rose's great grandfather, Miguel Carabajal, was a Mexican immigrant who came to California and found work as a servant. He chopped wood on a large ranch in New Idria in San Benito County.

Rose's Maternal-Maternal Ancestry

Lopez Coat of Arms
(Courtesy Mike Kennaugh, www.4crests.com)

The Lopez Coat of Arms is predominately or, with a bend sable between two wolves passant of the second, and proudly displays three ostrich feathers.

In Spain, the surname, Lopez, is believed to be derived from a parental first name, such as, son or descendant of Lope, and in Latin, "Lupus" meaning wolf."

Using personal names as surnames has been a Spanish tradition since the ninth century. "Lopez" traces back to Ferrand Lopez, a notable silversmith in 1429. Many Spaniards throughout history immigrated to Mexico and settled as Creole groups looking to become merchants and landowners.

Rose's Great Grandmother Jessie Carabajal-Lopez and sister Marie *(Courtesy Marie Bueno)*

Jessie Maria Lopez, "Nana" was born on December 5, 1866, in Almaden, California. Her parents' emigrated from Mexico. Perhaps she was related to Don Francisco Lopez, the first to discover gold in the Mother Lode Country in 1842, when California belonged to Mexico.

She had an older brother, Uncle Jacinto, who was born in Mexico. He stayed behind with other relatives when their parents immigrated to California. He visited his parents a few times and then they lost contact with him and their other relatives in Mexico.

The family moved to Hollister, California, and there, her younger sister Aunt Michaela was born on December 24, 1872.

Nana was fourteen years old when Miguel Carabajal married her. They had a daughter, Annie "Mater' in New Idria, California, in April 1880. Four years later, she bore a son, Fecundo A. Carabajal, nicknamed "Cooney." Soon after Uncle Cooney's birth on November 2, 1884, Nana left her husband. She took her children and settled in Campo Seco for the next thirty years. Great Grandfather Miguel remained in San Benito County and died there circa 1910.

After Lydia's death, Pa Pa arranged with Nana and Uncle Cooney to raise Marie, Rose's sister.

Nello's Paternal Ancestry

Olivo Coat of Arms

(Courtesy Mike Kennaugh, www.4crests.com)

The Coat of Arms displays five ostrich plumes, argent and vert. Olivo means an olive tree or more significantly a farmer who grows olives or simply an individual who resides in an olive grove. The surname Olivo dates back to the 1380's, to Antonio and Leonardo Oliva, variation of Olivo, who were councilors of Genoa.

Nello's Paternal Ancestry

Nello's father, Enrico Olivo, came to the United States in 1907. Nello's Grandparents Filippo and Artemisia Olivo and his Great Uncle Calistro Scudi and Great Uncle Valerio Valeroni, remained in Italy. Nello's father arrived by boat in New York City and made his way to San Jose, California. In San Jose he worked for the Southern Pacific Railroad Company laying iron railings on the tracks. His fellow workers nicknamed him "Harry," and he answered to either "Harry" or "Enrico." Several years later, he did construction work for Race Paving Company, building roads in San Jose.

Nello's relatives in Masa Martana, Italy *(Photos courtesy Rose Olivo)*

Nello's Maternal Ancestry

Ciardella Coat of Arms
(Courtesy Mike Kennaugh, www.4crests.com)

There is no record of a Coat of Arms having been granted to a Ciardella family. It is believed to have been derived from the personal name Ricciardella. The Sicilian word "ciarda" literally means "blonde." Therefore the surname Ciardella may be interpreted as meaning "son or descendant of the blonde one."

The ancestral Ciardellas were from Sicily. They re-established themselves spreading through Italy in pursuit of religious freedom and better opportunities in politics and estates, i.e. social standings and land property.

Nello's Mother

Lena in her home in Lammari, Italy *(Photos courtesy Rose Olivo)*

Nello's Maternal Ancestry

Leonini Coat of Arms
(Courtesy Mike Kennaugh, www.4crests.com)

The Leonini Coat of Arms displays bravery in azure, a lion or, and overall on a bend of three roses gules. The helmet is crested with a lion issuant or, and in his dexter paw a rose gules.

Leonini is one of the oldest and most distinguished of the Italian surnames. The name comes from the Latin Leo Leonis and literally signifies "Lion-Like." It was recorded as long ago as 1268 when Nicola Leonini, founder of the noble family of that name in Bologna, was a tribune.

Nello's Maternal Ancestry

Nello's Grandmother Maria Leonini *(Courtesy Rose Olivo)*

In 1900, the Ciardella children, Nello's Aunt Asunta, mother Isola "Lena," Uncle Joseph, and Uncle Humberto, "Johnny" left Genoa, Italy by ship. His Grandparents, Gesualdo and Maria, hoped that there were opportunities for the children to succeed and live a more prosperous life in America. They were too old to leave the homeland themselves and believed the streets were "Paved in Gold" in America.

Accompanying the Ciardellas were Aunt Asunta's husband, Peter Masini, and their cousins. Another reason the Ciardellas wanted to come to the United States was the government's political differences with Ethiopia and Eritrea. Italy colonized Eritrea in 1890 to obtain a strategic geopolitical position along the coastline of Ethiopia and the Red Sea. In 1900, Italians encroached on Ethiopian soil and the two governments were in the midst of a crucial Italo-Ethiopian Treaty over the stretch of land.

After registering at Ellis Island, New York City, the Ciardella's boarded a train headed for San Francisco. They stayed in San Francisco until the 1906 earthquake. Many of the Ciardella cousins remained in San Francisco to help rebuild the city. Nello's mother Lena and his Uncle Joseph settled in San Jose; Aunt Asunta, in Gilroy; and Uncle Humberto in Truckee, California.

Nello's relatives in Lammari, Italy and his Grandmother Maria Ciardella Leonini *(Courtesy Rose Olivo)*

Nello's Uncle, Aunt and Cousin

Uncle Johnny, Aunt Julia and Nello's cousin Emma Daley Ciardella

Nello's cousin Emma *(Photos courtesy Humbert Joseph Ciardella, Jr.)*

Uncle Johnny married Julia Daley, a tall Pennsylvania Dutch girl. She brought a daughter Emma into the marriage and they had a son, Humbert.

In 1929, Nello's cousin Emma attended the "California Olympic Tryouts," conducted on Olympic Hill, near Tahoe City, California. The competition determined our National Team for the 1932 Winter Olympics. She was devastated when she could not compete in the finals. The family doctor had diagnosed her with pneumonia. Later, she competed in the women's mushing competitions and in wild saddle bronco and bulldogging competitions at rodeos. Nello's cousin died unexpectedly at the young age of twenty-six from a blood clot, the complication of phlebitis.

Humbert Joseph Ciardella, Jr.

Nello's cousin Humbert Jr. married Mary Jane Garrett, a Truckee schoolteacher, from Scotland. He worked for the Nevada Highway Patrol in the Motor Carrier Division, then became Chief of Registration for Motor Vehicles. Later he retired as Deputy Director of Motor Vehicles.

Aunt Asunta's Family *(Courtesy Pasquale Greco)*

Ciardella family gatherings *(Courtesy Humbert Joseph Ciardella, Jr.)*

Julie, Humbert Jr., Mary Jane, and Sherry Ciardella *(Courtesy of Sara Russel, New Day Photography)*

Roma Sandwich Shop and Capitol Café, Johnny Ciardella and Constable "Butch"
(Courtesy Humbert Joseph Ciardella, Jr.)

Humbert Jr. remembers his father Humberto, "Uncle Johnny" as quite a funny man.

Others saw him differently. "When he was serious, you had better believe him." He was like a self-appointed mayor in the town of Truckee and the townspeople treated him with the utmost respect. Even Constable Butch knew when to take heed. Uncle Johnny did not have a problem pulling out his 38-caliber Smith and Wesson six-inch barrel revolver whenever he did not get his way. One time, when he was busy playing cards with some of his friends, one of the guys brought them sandwiches. He told him to go back and make him a sandwich without mayonnaise. The guy went back, scraped off the mayonnaise, and served it to him. After one bite, he whipped out his revolver, cocked it, and ordered the server. *"Ora mi porti un panino come piace a me!"* ("Now you bring me a sandwich the way I like it!") Joe Galaduci, his bodyguard, stood beside him for backup.

Whenever Aunt Asunta, Peter, and their children came to visit with Uncle Johnny, they arranged to see him at the Capitol Café.

Family Trees

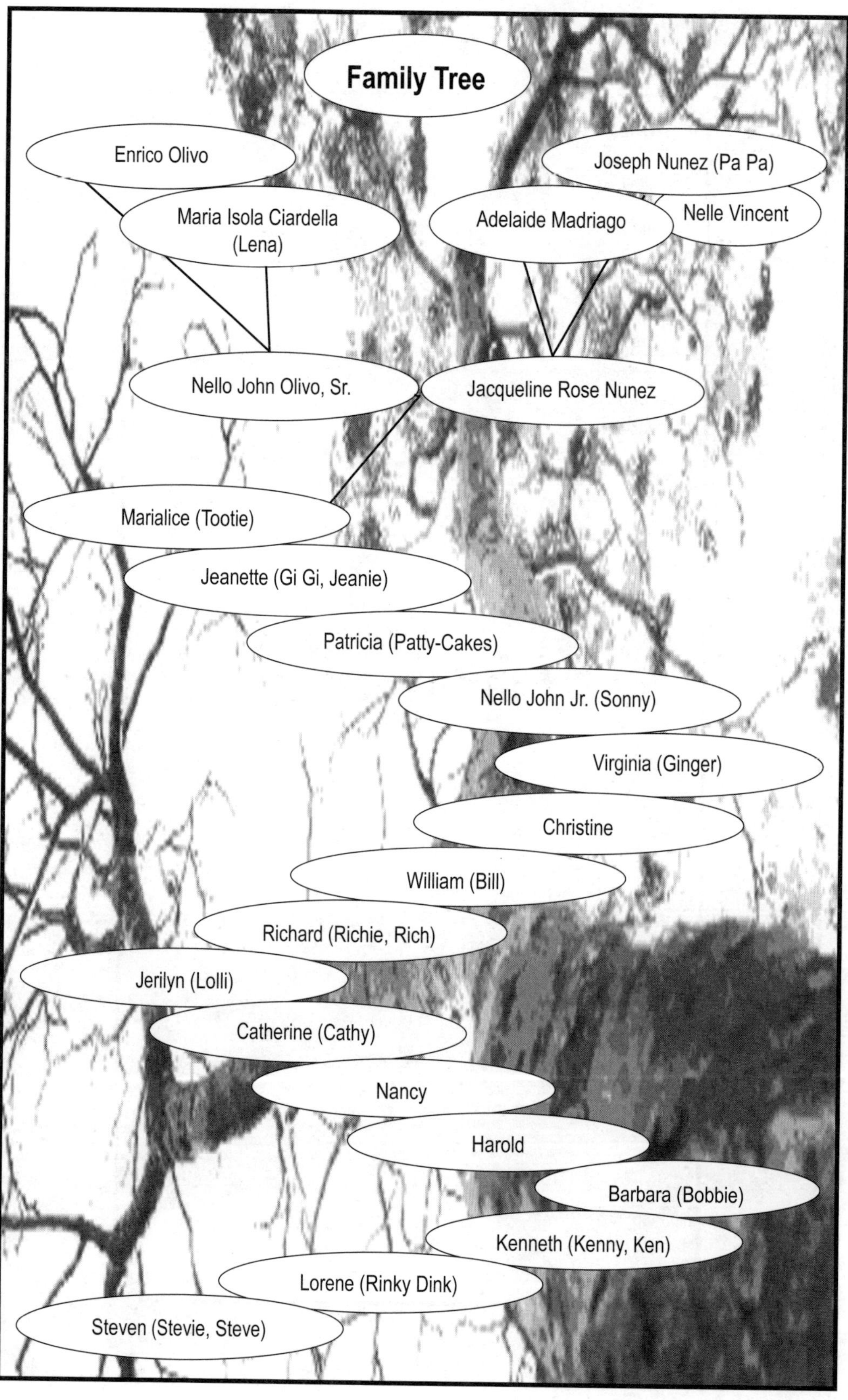

Family Tree
Enrico Olivo
Maria Isola Ciardella (Lena)
Joseph Nunez (Pa Pa)
Adelaide Madriago
Nelle Vincent
Nello John Olivo, Sr.
Jacqueline Rose Nunez
Marialice (Tootie)
Jeanette (Gi Gi, Jeanie)
Patricia (Patty-Cakes)
Nello John Jr. (Sonny)
Virginia (Ginger)
Christine
William (Bill)
Richard (Richie, Rich)
Jerilyn (Lolli)
Catherine (Cathy)
Nancy
Harold
Barbara (Bobbie)
Kenneth (Kenny, Ken)
Lorene (Rinky Dink)
Steven (Stevie, Steve)

Rose's Paternal Ancestry
Nine Generations

Nunez

(Sp.—Spouse) (1-9 represents each generation)

1. Dionisio Nunez, Sp. Maria Sanchez
2. Ramon Sanchez Nunez, Sp. Maria Fernandez
3. Marcial Nunez, Sp. Joaquina Abraire
4. Joseph J. Nunez (Pa Pa), Sp. 1. Adelaide Madriago (Lydia)
5. Rodger Joseph Nunez, Sp. Helene Ferry
6. Louise Antoinette Nunez, Sp. Roger Raimundo
7. Roger John Raimundo, Sp. Rachel Anne
8. Mariana Loudes Raimundo
8. Nathan Raimundo
7. April Raimundo, Sp. Stan Campbell
8. Stan-o Wallace Campbell
8. Helen Olivia Campbell
7. Michael David Raimundo
6. Raymond Rodger Nunez, Sp. Shara Rae
7. Desiree Chanda Bonger
7. Autum Rose Ayres
8. Michael Windom Ayres
8. Krysta Brook Pomin
8. Evan Blake Pomin

5. Jacqueline Rose Nunez, Sp. Nello John Olivo
6. Marialice Veronica Olivo, Sp. 1. Thomas Gerald Rose, Sr.
7. Thomas Gerald Rose, Jr.
7. Kathy Denise Rose, **Sp. 1.** Clayton Shawn Sexton
8. Michaela Marie Sexton, Sp. Matthew Otteman
9. Merrick Matthew Otteman
9. Malachi Thomas Otteman
8. Jessica Dawn Sexton
8. Trevor Sean Sexton
8. Breighley K. Sexton
7. Kathy Rose Sexton, **Sp. 2.** William Pearce Mills
7. David Allen Bennion, Sp. Della Marie Keys
8. Natasha Marie Bennion
8. Troy Allen Bennion
6. Marialice Veronica Olivo (Tootie), Sp. 2. Paul Bennion
7. Kimberly Marie Bennion
8. Brian Michael Ramirez
9. Braedon Ramirez
8. Austin Devin Ramirez
7. Paula Marie Bennion, Sp. Jeff Kevin Bentley
8. Spencer A. Bentley
8. Danielle M. Bentley
6. Jeanette Elaine Olivo (Gi Gi, Jeanie) Sp. 1 Costa Gucci
6. Patricia Clarese Olivo (Patty-Cakes, Patty) Sp. Robert Paul Ray (Bob)
7. Brian Anthony Ray, Sp. Mirtha Amparo
8. Monique Nicole Ray
8. Jiancarlo Alexander Ray
7. Jacqueline Marie Ray, Sp. Paul Winters Jarvis
8. Madison Kingsley Jarvis
6. Nello John Olivo, Jr. (Sonny) Sp. 1. Patsy Mae Baker
7. Denise Ann Olivo, Sp. Karl Elliot Epstein
8. Andy Blake Epstein
8. Amanda Elliot Epstein
8. Joey Joseph B. Epstein
8. Alexie Rose Epstein
6. Nello John Olivo, Jr. Sp. 2. Danica Ann S. d'Hondt
7. Mireille Ellsworth
8. Isebiu Paul Reyes
8. Ilano Juan Reyes
7. Corinne V. Ellsworth Olivo, Sp. Jason Robert Levin
8. Jaredan Maxwell Levin
8. Kanan Meyer Levin
7. Ivan M. Ellsworth Olivo
8. Jesse Alexander Olivo
8. Cody James Olivo
7. America Athene Olivo
7. Austin Jonathan Olivo
6. Virginia Anne Olivo (Ginger) Sp. 1. Warren Edwin Bob
7. Teresa Marie Bob Hynes, **Sp. 1.** William Kelly Hynes
8. Amanda Kelly Hynes, Sp. Sean Paul Coverstone
9. Logan D. Coverstone
8. Heather Lorraine Hynes
8. Sean Gregory Hynes
8. Justine Nicole Hynes
7. John Kenneth Bob, Sp. Kerilyn Tei Leong
8. Kylie Kennedy Bob
8. Katelyn Rose Bob
7. Robert Anthony Bob, Sp. Brent Ronald Bornemeier
7. Gregory Warren Bob
6. Virginia Anne Olivo, Sp. 2. Ray Dowl Redding
7. Beatrice Rose Redding, Sp. Brian Matthew Walczyk
7. Ronald Dean Redding
7. Dale Dean Redding
7. Alan Dean Redding,
6. Virginia Anne Olivo, Sp. 3. Mitch Joe Teeney
7. Randy Joseph Teeney Sp. Kristie Rae Austin
7. Dana Carol Teeney, Sp. Doug Harris
7. Pamela Carol Teeney, Sp. Norm Woodrow Gramush
7. Steve Joseph Teeney Sp. Jill Elaine Turner
6. Christine Ann Olivo, Sp. 1. William Morris Thrash
7. William Michael Thrash, **Sp. 1.** Sylvia Trejo
8. Nichelle EmilyThrash
William Michael Thrash, **Sp. 2.** Patricia
8. William Anthony Thrash
William Michael Thrash **Sp. 3.** Cheryl Lynn
8. Heather Elizabeth Thrash
6. Christine Ann Olivo, Sp. 2. Robert Harrington Wade
6. William Roger Olivo (Bill) Sp. 1. Pamela Jo Lupo
7. Cheramy Ann Olivo
6. William Roger Olivo Sp. 2. Laura Lynn Hodges
7. Chanelle Lynn Olivo, Sp. Ian William Olivo-Read
8. Luciana Lynn Olivo-Read
7. Dominic James Olivo

6. Richard Wayne Olivo (Rich) Sp.1. Bonnie J.Brehm
7. Melissa Ryan Olivo Sp. 1. Rolly Brian Heath Byrd
8. Brian AJ Forrest Byrd
8. Cody Ryan Heath Byrd,
6. Richard Wayne Olivo, Sp. 2. Alice Marie Hare
7. Rodney Glen Bevil
7. Janet Marie Bloom
8. Sharon Marie Bloom
8. Steven Michael Bloom
6. Jerilyn Helene Olivo (Loli) Sp. Alfred E. Doten
7. Kara Maureen Doten, Sp. Joel Craig Hunt
8. Tamara Maureen Hunt
8. Tad Steven Hunt
7. Maureen Katherine Doten, Sp. Steve Leslie Ogren
7. Steve Alfred Doten, Sp. Tomiko Hatanaka
8. Tori Brandon Doten, 8. Kaiden Yamato Doten
6. Catherine Nelle Olivo (Cathy) Sp. 1. Brian Kelley
7. Kevin Michael Kelley, Sp. Aviva
7. Karena Rose Kelley, Sp. Todd Justin Kraemer
8. Tyler Justin Kraemer
8. Avery Marie Kraemer
6. Nancy Joyce Olivo, Sp. 1. David John Castenholz
7. Laurel Frances Castenholz
6. Harold Joseph Olivo, Sp. Young Hea Parks
7. Benjamin Joseph Olivo
7. Joshua Jeremiah Olivo, Sp. Mai Uyen Trinh
6. Barbara Susan Olivo (Bobbie) Sp. Donald J. Cagle
7. Jocilyn Roselle Cagle, Sp. Jonathan Vincent Stevens
7. Jason John Cagle
6. Kenneth Paul Olivo (Ken, Kenny) Sp. Wanda Gail
7. Brandon James Olivo
7. Briana Marie Olivo
6. Lorene Denise Olivo (Rinky Dink) Sp. John Jack Linnehan II
7. Jessica Dawn Linnehan
7. Tiffany Michelle Linnehan
7. John Joseph Linnehan III
6. Steven Edward Olivo (Stevie, Steve) and Diane Zuniga

5. Marie Grace Nunez Bueno, Sp. M. Bueno, Sr.
6. Manuel Bueno, Jr. (Junior)
6. David Allen Bueno
7. David Allen Bueno II, Sp. Kira
7. Zebediah Desoto
8. Hunter Thomas Desoto
8. Isabella Desoto
7. Elias Maximillion Desoto
6. Karen Marie Bueno, Sp. Patrick Michael McMullen, Sr.
7. Alisha Anne McMullen, Sp. Albert Michael Bonk
8. Matthew Michael Bonk
7. Patrick Joseph McMullen, Jr., Sp. Alison Harrriman
8. Cameron Elizabeth McMullen
7. Maureen Michelle McMullen, Sp. Abraham Jacob Silverberg
8. Shawn Avery Clem
8. Gwenevieve Fiona Clem
8. Noah Samuel Silverberg
6. Sandy Ann Bueno, Sp. Salvatore Frank Garofolo
7. David Andrew Garofolo Sp. Linda Calderon
7 Tito Antonio Manuel Guerra

4 Joseph Nunez, Sp. 2. Nelle M. Vincent
5 Eugene Vincent
4. Antonio Nunez
4. Balbino Nunez
4. Engracia Nunez, Sp. Ambrosio Fuertes
5. Amparo Fuertes, **Sp. 1** Benjamin Perez
6. Albia Perez Sp. Jose Luis Palacios
5. Amparo Fuertes, **Sp. 2.** Jose Vasquez
6. Josefina Vazquez Sp. Andres Lopez
6. Jose Luis Vazquez Sp. Genoveva Villar
5. Josepha Fuertes
5. Joaquina Fuertes, Sp. Julian Artazcoz
6. Begoña Artazcoz
5. Modesta Fuertes, Sp. Francisco Rubio
6. Francisco Javier Rubio
5. Amor Fuertes, Sp. Angel Mula, Sr.
6. Angel Mula, Jr.
5. Teodoro Fuertes
5. Antonio Fuertes
5. Elena Fuertes, Sp. Florentino Villalonga
6. Javier Villalonga
6. Maria Villalonga
5. Manuel Fuertes, Sp. Isabel Villacorta
6. Maria Isabel Fuertes
6. Maria Christina Fuertes
4. Manuel Nunez, Sp. Pierrette Ruaud
5. Didier Nunez
5. Charlette Nunez, Sp. Gerard Dugue
6. Karine Dugue
5. Catherine Nunez
2. Asuncion Nunez, Sp. Lolo
3. Aurora Lolo, Sp. Jose Alvarez
4. Jaime Alvarez
4. Ines Alvarez
4. Milagros Alvarez
4. Jose Maria Alvarez
4. Jose Ramon Alvarez
3. Jose Lolo, Sp. Ester Eguren
4. Ana Maria Lolo
4. Jose A. Lolo
4. Esther Lolo
3. Gaspar Lolo, Sp. Miguela Yario
4. Begona Lolo
4. Amelia Lolo
4. Jose A. Lolo
4. Maria Lolo
4. Matilde Lolo
3. Sofia Lolo, Sp. Lucas Azcunaga
4. Victor Azunaga
4. Julio Azunaga
4. Rosario Azunaga
4. Pedro Azunaga
4. Carmen Azunaga

Rose's Maternal Ancestry

Cobarrubia/Madriago

1. Santiago Cobarrubia, Sp. Manuella Guajardo
2. Secundina C. Cobarrubia, Sp.1. Bernardo Ablos
3. Rose Ablos, **Sp. 1.** Nichanor Vegas
4. Almaranta Vegas, **Sp. 1.** F loyd C Scrivner
4. Almaranta Vegas, **Sp. 2.** Luis S Avila
4. Soila Vegas, Sp. Pearson C. Randall
4. Rosie Vegas
4. Nick Vegas
3. Rose Ablos, **Sp. 2.** Clifford Henry Robie, Sr.
4. Clifford Henry Robie, Jr., Sp. Laurie Louise Boring
5. James Clifford Robie
4. Frederick Edwin Robie, Sp. Bernice Lorraine Belrose
4. Bernard Myron Robie, **Sp. 1.** Mary Charlotte Boyd
5. Ronald Robie, Sp. Edith Allyn DeForest
6. Todd Ronald Robie
6. Melissa Lynn Robie
5. Kent Bernard Robie, **Sp. 1.** Sharon Mae Edwards
6. Kent Raymond Robie
6. Karen Jeanne Robie
6. Susan Lynn Robie,
5. Kent Bernard Robie, **Sp. 2.** Dee Anna Hurd Robie
4. Bernard Myron Robie, **Sp. 2.** Laura B. Bettencourt

2. Secundina Cobarrubia, **Sp. 2. John G. Madriago, Sr.**
3. John G. Madriago, Jr., Sp. Annie (Mater) Carabajal
4. Adelaide Madriago, Sp. Joseph Nunez
5. Jacqueline Rose Nunez (Refer to Nunez' ancestry)
5. Rodger J. Nunez
5. Marie Grace Nunez
4. Gertrude Madriago
4. Lawrence Leroy Madriago, Sp. Mamie Rita Caselli
5. Evelyn Elaine Madriago, Sp. Domingo T. Simon
6. Evon Marie Simon
6. David Lawrence Simon
6. David L. Simon
6. Paul M. Simon
5. Loraine Ann Madriago, Sp. Charles E. Grissom
6. Keith A. Grissom
6. Erik Grant Grissom
4. James Louis Madriago, Sp. Grace Pacheco
5. Barbara Ann Madriago, Sp. Tony Raulin Arnedo
6. Carol Ann Arnedo
6. Susan Marie Arnedo
5. Andrea Kristine Madriago, **Sp. 1** Ralph V. Getsla
6. Christopher W. Getsla
5. Andrea Kristine Madriago **Sp. 2** Burt Fincham
6. Mikaela Jeanette Fincham
4. John Samuel Madriago
4. Frank John Madriago
4. Josephine Madriago, **Sp.1** Antonio Caselli
5. Beverly June Caselli, Sp. William E. Lowe
6. Sharon June Lowe
6. Gail A. Lowe
6. Mark E. Lowe
5. Shirley Mae Caselli
5. Dalores Caselli, Sp. Danny Ruiz
6. Michelle Ruiz
6. Denise Ruiz
5. Janice A. Caselli, Sp. Anthony Andrew Padrazzi
6. Cindi A. Padrazzi
6. Corrie J. Padrazzi
6. Lorrie J. Padrazzi
6. Jill C. Padrazzi
5. James Caselli
4. Josephine Madriago, **Sp. 2.** Frank M. Manriquez
4. Jessie Lasada
3. Eliza Almaranta Madriago, Sp. George Washington Ryno
4. William Harrison Ryno, Sp. Mildred Chappell Hobson
5. Stanley Phillip Ryno, Sp. Barbara Jean Richardson
6. Ronnie Leigh Ryno
6. Roger Neil Ryno
5. Gaylon Eugene Ryno, **Sp. 1.** Sharon Lynne Packer
6. Vickie Lynne Ryno
6. Linda Lynne Ryno
5. Gaylon Eugene Ryno, **Sp. 2.** Olga Vivian Goulet
5. Russell Orlando Ryno, Sp. Ljubica Alice Whitcomb
6. Perry David Ryno
6. Sandra Lynn Ryno
4. Phillip James Ryno, **Sp.1.** Hazel Elizabeth Simms
5. Barbara Jean Ryno, Sp. Donald A. Young
5. Donna Marie Ryno, Sp. Albert Le Roy Yarrington
6. Gail Korrine Yarrington
6. Jeffrey Scott Yarrington
5. Phyllis Lee Ryno, Sp. Billy Dean Stewart, Sr.
6. Billy Dean Stewart, Jr.
6. Steven Wayne Stewart
6. Joy E. Stewart
4. Phillip James Ryno, **Sp. 2.** Elsa Marie Fischer
4. Alfred Madison Ryno, **Sp. 1.** Mabel Evelyn Westphal
5. Shirley Elaine Ryno, Sp. Richard Edward Capps
6. Terry Lee Capps
6. Steven Allen Capps
4. Alfred Madison Ryno, **Sp. 2.** Golda H. Knight
4. Baby Ryno
3. Emmet Madriago, Sp. Nancy S. Allen
4. Emmet Francis Madriago
3. Philip James Madriago, Sp. Meta Martha Sprock
4. Violet Amelia Madriago, Sp. Harry William Davis
5. Dolores Wilma Davis, Sp. Albert A. Silva
6. Teresa Marie Silva
4. Leroy Phillip Madriago, Sp. Ethel Mae Wheeler
5. Darlene May Madriago
4. Elwood James Madriago
4. Bernice Ramona Madriago, Sp. Thomas Toby Fenbury
5. Carol Jean Fenbury, Sp. William Rocket Hodges
5. Robert James Fenbury, Sp. Sandra Lane
6. Ashley Ann Fenbury
5. Lynda Marie Fenbury, **Sp. 1.** William Eric Blumhardt
5. Lynda Marie Fenbury, **Sp. 2.** Gonzalo Leuba Perez

6. Allison Elizabeth Perez
4. Leona Meta Madriago, Sp. Irvin Herman Miller
5. Patricia Ann Miller, Sp. John Lawrence Twardy
4. Juanita Lorraine Madriago, **Sp. 1.** Peter Paul Marinovich
5. Peter Phillip Marinovich, Sp. LaRae Jo McKay
6. Nicole M. Marinovich
6. Charles D. Marinovich
6. Samuel P. Marinovich
5. Pauline Marinovich, Sp. Donald L. Pril
6. Melissa Pril,
4. Juanita Lorraine Madriago,**Sp. 2.** David D. Doran
5. Kathleen Patricia Doran
5. Julie Rose Doran
5. Colleen Donna Doran
4. Phillip Gordon Madriago
4. Robert Norman Madriago, Sr., Sp. Margaret Jean Briggs
5. Barbara Lynne Madriago, Sp. Larry Richard Hancock
5. Robert Norman Madriago, Jr.
5. James Martin Madriago, Sp. Paige Janelle Ingoglia
6. James Drake Madriago
5. John Phillip Madriago, Sp. Evelyn T. Caridad
6. Alicia Gabrielle Madriago
6. Kailen Reid Madriago
3. James Phillip Madriago, aka Harry Stringer, **Sp. 1.** Dela J. Edalgo
3. James Phillip Madriago, aka Harry Stringer, **Sp. 2.** Mae Stiles
4. Beulah Eliza Stringer, Sp. Edward Ivan Black
5. Rosaleta Mae Black
5. Una Jean Black, Sp. Delbert Dean Walker
6. Gary Warren Walker
6. Gerald Wesley Walker
5. James Ivan Black, Sp. Merrie Blackwell
5. Leslie Edward Black, Sp. Geneva Hass Black
5. Beulah Mae Black, **Sp. 1.** Glen William Stovall
6. William Edward Stovall
6. Kristina Mae Stovall
5. Beulah Mae Black, **Sp. 2.** Nathanial B. Stratford
6. Edward Stratford
6. Amanda Jean Stratford,

2. Secundina Cobarrubia, Sp. 3. Francisco C. Riggles
3. Kathryn Riggles, **Sp. 1.** Ora Abraham Edgell
4. Raymond Vermont Edgell, Sp. Esther Belle Burnett
5. Nadine Hilda Edgell, Sp. Gerald George Eck
6. Darrell Kimberly Eck
6. Ramona Marie Eck
6. Gary Bernard Eck
6. Roger Glenn Eck
5. Thelma Raye Edgell, Sp. Joseph M. Ralston
6. Jennie Lynn Ralston
6. Jolene Gay Ralston
5. Michael Burnett Edgell, **Sp. 1.** Helen A. McClure
6. Nelson Jay Edgell
6. Donna Jean Fine Edgell
6. James Ray Fine Edgell
6. Ricy John Fine Edgell
5. Michael Burnett Edgell **Sp. 2.** Janet Mae Treese
6. Kathy Marie Edgell
6. David Burnett Edgell
6. Steven Michael Edgell
6. Carrie Diane Edgell
5. Diana May Edgell, Sp. James Edmund Thompson
6. Vicki Lynn Thompson
6. Phillip James Thompson
4. Baby Edgell
3. Kathryn Riggles, **Sp. 2.** Carl L. Heglov (ComLaw)
3. Robert Francis Riggles, **Sp. 1.** Myrtle Corbin Scrivner
3. Robert Francis Riggles, **Sp. 2.** Kathryn Weiland
2. Miquel Cobarrubia, Sp. Virginia Rosales
3. Margaret T. (Maggie) Cobarrubia, Sp. Fred Robie
4. Clarence Robie, Sp. Frances Guay (Knablock)
5. Paul Frederick Robie
4. Louise Pearl Robie, Sp. Chris Geerts
5. Betty Jane Geerts
5. Merrie Margaret Geerts, Sp. Harvey MacDonald
6. Diana Rachel MacDonald
6. Thomas H. MacDonald
6. Mark L. MacDonald
6. Corrine MacDonald
6. Christopher MacDonald
6. Craig MacDonald
5. Gordon Wayne Geerts, Sp. Rosa Marie Gibau
6. Cynthia Elizabeth Geerts
6. Michael Derek Geerts
3. Frank L.Cobarrubia, Sp. Mae O. Watts
4. Lucille Anna Cobarrubia
3. Gilbert Cobarrubia
2. Maria Daria Cobarrubia, Sp. Hilario Vallaria
2. Velasario Cobarrubia
2. Abelardo Cobarrubia
2. Mercedes Ramona Cobarrubia (Sarah) Sp. Edward Louis Salaun, Sr.
3. Isador Delmar Salaun. **Sp. 1.** Susan Cecilla Markey
4. Isador Salaun (Baby)
4. Isador Delmar Salaun, Sp. Martha Alice Leno
5. Llewelyn Marvin Salaun, Sr., **Sp. 1.** Lorene Fay Beauchamp
6. Marvin Salaun,
5. Llewelyn Marvin Salaun, Sr., **Sp. 2.** Joanne Maurer
6. Llewellyn Marvin Salaun, Jr.
5. James Delmar Salaun
3. Isador Delmar Salaun Sr., **Sp. 2** Melba L. Markey
3. Eliza Mabel Salaun, Sp. Samuel Lloyd Markey, Jr.
4. Lloyd Samuel Markey, Sp. Martha Helen Davles Markey
5. Dena Mae Markey, **Sp. 1.** George Scott
6. Keith Scott
6. Mike Scott
6. Kathy Scott
5. Dena Mae Markey, **Sp. 2.** Robert Wagner
6. Robert D. Wagner
5. Stanley Lee Markey, Sp. Lucille Reiswig
6. Terry Markey
6. Eddie Markey

3. Edward Louis Salaun, Jr., **Sp. 1.** Lenora Ethel Markey
4. Betty J.Salaun, Sp. Paul Melvin Facey
3. Edward Louis Salaun, Jr., **Sp. 2.** Elsie L. Sisson
3. Ralph Salaun, Sp. Edith Lorena Carter
4. Edith May Salaun, **Sp. 1.** Danny Hotchinson
4. Edith May Salaun, **Sp. 2**. Albert Daly
4. Iola Ramona Salaun, Sp. John Elmer Raetz, Sr.
5. John Elmer Raetz, Jr., **Sp. 1.**Jerolyn Louise Heist
5. John Elmer Raetz, Jr., **Sp. 2.** Kevin Suzanne Culy
6. Paige Raetz
6. Jessica Erin Raetz
5. John Elmer Raetz, Jr., **Sp. 3**. Debbie
5. Ralph Martin Raetz, Sr., **Sp. 1.** Claudia Peck
6. Ralph Martin Raetz, Jr.
6. Gregory S. Raetz
5. Ralph Martin Raetz, Sr.,**Sp. 2.** Patricia Ann Fennel
5. Ralph Martin Raetz, Sr.,**Sp. 3.** Barbara Ann Phifer
6. Brian M. Raetz
4. Imogene Salaun, Sp. Ronald L. Brown
5. Ben R. Brown
3. Roy Philip Salaun, Sp. Toby
3. Ray Victor Salaun, Sp. Esther Marion Clark
4. Lydia Marion Salaun, Sp. Leo Rosario Jobin
4. Robert Edward Salaun, Sp. Wanda Louise Beck
5. Lavon Daniel Salaun, Sp. Erica
6. Debbie Salaun
6. Cindy Salaun
6. Tracy Salaun
5. Linda Kay Salaun, Sp. Larry Dixon
6. Denise Dixon
6. Daniel Dixon
5. Terry Lee Salaun, Sp. Raymond Marshall, Sr.
6. Raymond Marshall, Jr.
4. Richard Ray Salaun, Sp. Darlene Louise Caldwell
5. Ricky Dell Salaun, Sp. Margaret
6. Christopher Darrell Salaun
6. Keith Salaun, Sp. Debbie Salaun
5. Carol Jean Salaun, **Sp. 1.** James Capurro
6. Jennifer Elaine Capurro
6. Skipper Capurro
5. Carol Jean Salaun, **Sp. 2.** Larry Medlin
5. Jerry Ray Salaun, **Sp. 1.** Cathy
6. Valerie Salaun
5. Jerry Ray Salaun, **Sp. 2.** Judy
5. Dustin E. Salaun
5. Richard Lee Salaun
6. Dustin Salaun
4. Harold Clark Salaun, Sp. Louise Jennie Davis
5. Jeffery Clark Salaun
6. Shaun Jeffery Salaun, Sp. Cindy Fey
5. Lisa Anne Salaun, Sp. Jeff Reiswig
3. Gertrude Grace Salaun, Sp. Harley Ray Doughty, Sr.
4. Harley Ray Doughty, Jr., Sp. Josephine Jimenez
5. Elaine Kay Doughty, **Sp. 1.** Walter Lee Dobbs
6. Christen M. Dobbs
6. Jason Michael Dobbs
6. Brian Thomas Dobbs
5. Elaine Kay Doughty, **Sp. 2.** Ralph Caporusso
5. Sandra Rae Doughty
6. Brandon, Sp. Johnny Knight
4. Maxine Delores Doughty, **Sp. 1.** Laurence Larry Nunes
5. William Randall Nunes
5. Cynthia L. Nunes, **Sp.** Ruark
6. Deveron Ruark
4. Maxine Delores Doughty, **Sp. 2.** Jack Russell Heffron
3. Louis Emmett Salaun, **Sp. 1.** Anna Marie Rowe
3. Louis Emmett Salaun, **Sp. 2.** Mary Rolen,
3. Baby Salaun

Sanchez-Lopez/Carabajal Two Generations

1. Jacinto Sanchez-Lopez
1. Jessie Sanchez-Lopez (Nana), Sp. Miquel Carabajal
2. Annie Carabajal (Mater) Sp. John G. Madriago, Jr. **(Refer to Cobarrubia/Madriago Ancestry)**
2. Fecundo A. Carabajal
1. Michaela Sanchez-Lopez, Sp. Jacinto Tehada
2. Louis Tehada

Nello's Paternal Ancestry

Olivo

1. Filippo Olivo, Sp. Ribeca Artemisia
2. Enrico Olivo, Sp. Maria Isola (Lena) Ciardella
3. Nello John Olivo, Sr., Sp. Jacqueline Rose Nunez (Refer to Nunez ancestry for generations)
3. George Olivo, Sp. Margaret Valencia
4. Clement Olivo
4. Virginia Anne Olivo
5. Melissa Pauline Olivo, Sp. Justin Wilson
6. Jacob Mathew Wilson
4. Gerald Joseph Olivo, Sp. Mary Vargas
5. Francesa Alejandra Olivo
4. Pauline Olivo, Sp. Brian
5. Shea Olivo
4. Loretta Olivo
5. Adrien Joshua Gerard Benitez
4. Vinnie Rossitte Olivo
5. Dominic Adrien Rositte Garrett
3. James (Jimmy) Olivo
4. Robert Olivo
3. Gino Olivo
2. Calistro Scudi, Sp. Maria Anullo
3. Angelo Scudi, Sp. Giuseppa Biondini
4. Lisa Scudi, Sp. Alberto Pannuzzi
5. Angelo Pannuzzi, Sp. Luciana Oddi
6. Michele Pannuzzi
6. Alessandro Pannuzzi

5. Daniela Pannuzzi, Sp. Giacomo Liguori
6. Davide Maria Liguori
2. Valerio Valeroni, Sp. Rosa Bassetti
3. Virgilio Valeroni, Sp. Pia Magnaricotte
4. Fortunato Valeroni, Sp. Liliana Benedetti
5. Maria Cristina Valeroni
4. Massimo Valeroni, Sp. Maria Rosa Russo
5. Gaia Valeroni
3. Fortunato Valeroni
3. Vincenzo Valeroni, Sp. Gina Giulivi
4. Anna Rita Valeroni, Sp. Claudio Sordini
5. Maria Celeste Sordini
5. Benedetta Sordini
3. Anna Valeroni, Sp. Angelo Giulivi
4. Gabriella Giulivi, Sp. Parrinello
5. Romina Parrinello
4. Carla Giulivi
5. Simone Giulivi
5. Andrea Giulivi
3. Veronica Valeroni, Sp. Domenico Bordacchini
4. Paolo Bordacchini, Sp. Gina Fioretti
5. Loriana Bordacchini, Sp. Giuliano Persichetti
6. Daniela Persichetti
4. Biagio Bordacchini, Sp. Carloni
5. Fabio Bordacchini
5. Fabrizio Bordacchini
3. Valentina Valeroni, Sp. Germano Ciucci
3. Marina Valeroni, Sp. Angelo Castelli
4. Gioacchino Castelli, Sp. Rina Langeli
5. Rita Castelli
5. Giuseppina Castelli
5. Sabrina Castelli, Sp. Luca Pacifici
6. Gabriele Pacifici
6. Lucia Pacifici
4. Giuseppe Castelli
4. Graziella Castelli, Sp. Natale Lazzari
5. Sonia Lazzari
4. Valerio Castelli, Sp. Giovina
5.Giuseppe Castelli, Sp. Emanuela
6. Leonardo Castelli
5. Daniele Castelli
3. Gina Valeroni

Nello's Maternal Ancestry
Four Generations

Ciardella

1. Gesualdo Ciardella, Sp. Maria Leonini
2. Asunta Ciardella, Sp. Peter Masini
3. Mary Masini, Sp. Joe Greco
4. Pasquale Greco, **Sp. 1.** Joyce Silvera
4. Pasquale Greco, **Sp. 2.** Jacqueline Hoeppner
5. Natalie Greco, Sp. Katsuhisa Takao
5. Anna Greco, Sp. Patrick Dwyer
4. Pasquale Greco, **Sp. 3.** Grace
4. Pasquale Greco, **Sp. 4.** Elena Andersson
4. Allen Greco, Sp. Michaela DeGregory
5. Genessa Greco, Sp. Erin Smith
6. Venessa Smith
6. Michael Smith
3. Francis Masini **Sp.'s** Pann, Raffler, Balch, D'Innocenti, and Johnson
4. Harry Peter Pann
4. Doris **Sp.'s** Salvatore Cirrola, Oscar Porras
5. Judy Ann Porras, Sp. Gary Sunseri
6. Vincent James Sunseri
6. Megan Ashley Sunseri
6. Nicole Marie Sunseri
5. Salvadore (Sam) Cirrola
4. Mary, **Sp. 1.** Arrighi
5. Robert (Bobbie) Grey **Sp. 4.** Darlene
6. Michael Martin Grey
6. Matthew Todd Grey,
5. Gail Whitesell
6. Sonny, Sp. Roy Whitesell
6. Chad Whitesell,
4. Mary, **Sp. 2.** Wilford Converse Grey
5. Sherry Grey, Sp. Don Clanton
6. Mark Clanton
6. Michele Clanton
3. Dominic Masini, Sp. Thelma
4. Larry Masini
3. Joseph Masini, Sp. Helen
4. Susan Masini, Sp. Gary Johnson
5. Laura Johnson
5. Shelly Johnson
4. Karen Masini
2. John Ciardella
2. Maria Isola Ciardella (Lena) Sp. Enrico Olivo (Henry)
3. Nello John Olivo, Sr. (Neela) Sp. Jacqueline Rose Nunez Olivo (Refer to Nunez and Olivo ancestry for generations)
3. George (Georgie) Olivo
3. James (Jimmy) Olivo
2. Joseph (Joe, Beppe) Ciardella, Significant other Dorothy Leighton
2. Humberto Joseph Ciardella, Sr., Sp. Julia Daley
3. Humbert Joseph Ciardella, Jr. Sp. Mary Jane Mathews Garrett
4. Sherlynn Ciardella (Sherry) Sp. Ted Orsua
5. Robert Orsua, **Sp. 1**. Beth
6. Raymond Orsua
6. Benjamin Orsua
6. Michael Orsua,
5. Robert Orsua, **Sp. 2.** Lynn
4. Julianne Ciardella, Sp. Steve Loyd
5. Chris Loyd, Sp. Jennifer
6. Elena Loyd
6. Stephen John Loyd
5. Ariel Loyd
5. Spencer Loyd

Marialice Jeanie Patty

Sonny Virginia Christine

William Richard Jerilyn